THE HISTORICAL STUDY OF
THE MOTHER TONGUE

THE HISTORICAL STUDY OF
THE MOTHER TONGUE

AN INTRODUCTION TO PHILOLOGICAL
METHOD

BY HENRY CECIL WYLD

MERTON PROFESSOR OF THE ENGLISH LANGUAGE IN THE UNIVERSITY OF OXFORD

HASKELL HOUSE PUBLISHERS Ltd.
Publishers of Scarce Scholarly Books
NEW YORK. N. Y. 10012
1968

First Published 1906

HASKELL HOUSE PUBLISHERS Ltd.
Publishers of Scarce Scholarly Books
280 LAFAYETTE STREET
NEW YORK. N. Y. 10012

Library of Congress Catalog Card Number: 68-24929

Haskell House Catalogue Item # 264

Printed in the United States of America

PREFACE

In undertaking the task of writing such a work as the present small volume, I did not disguise from myself the difficulty of what lay before me ; now that I have completed it, I am in no way blind to the imperfections of the achievement. In a sense, the object of the book is a modest one—to give, not the history of our language, but some indications of the point of view from which the history of a language should be studied, and of the principal points of method in such a study. These methods are chiefly determined by the views which are held at the present time concerning the nature of language, and the mode of its development ; and such views, in their turn, are based upon the knowledge of facts, concerning the life-history of many languages, which have been patiently accumulated during the last eighty years. I have hoped, in the following pages, to prepare the way for the beginner, to the study of at least some of the great writers who have been the pioneers of our knowledge of the development of our own tongue, and of its relations to other languages, as well as the chief framers of contemporary philological theory. Thus the present work aims at no more than to serve as an introduction to the more advanced scientific study of linguistic problems in the pages of first-hand authorities.

v

Advanced text-books of the German type are naturally almost unintelligible to the beginner, who has not undergone some preliminary training in philological aim and method. Of the text-books published in this country, which are nearly all of a more popular description, some are—to our shame be it spoken—mere cram-books, which strive only to give such 'tips' as shall enable the reader to pass certain examinations, while several others, by writers of repute and learning, are lacking in any general statement of principles or reference to authorities, in case the student should by chance wish to pursue the subject further than the covers of this or that small if admirable book. Again, a serious defect, as it appears to me, of many of the best elementary books on the History of English, is that the bare facts are stated, dogmatically and categorically, without any suggestion as to the sources of information or the methods of arriving at the results stated. As a practical teacher of English to University students of various stages of knowledge, from beginners onwards, I know that intelligent students are often irritated, on the one hand, by not being told how certain facts concerning past forms of speech are arrived at, and, on the other hand, by finding no reference to authorities who might give them the information which the writer of the manual so often withholds.

The worst feature in the withholding of such information is that the solitary student, who has not access to University classes, after he has read the books and mastered the facts, has yet not received anything in the shape of a training in the actual methods of the science of language; he has acquired a knowledge of a certain number of facts,

but they exist in his mind isolated, and unrelated to anything else, least of all to a principle of wide application.
Thus he acquires no new outlook upon linguistic phenomena,
no method whereby he can pursue the subject for himself.
It is believed that the chapters upon *General Principles*
which follow, may be of use in putting the student upon
right lines of further thought and study.

In dealing with general questions, I have sought as far
as possible to illustrate principles by concrete examples
drawn from the development of English.

In treating the more specific problems connected with
the Aryan and Germanic languages I have sought, not so
much to supplement the knowledge which it is possible to
derive from the usual small work on Comparative Philology,
as to make this clear on those points where I have found
uncertainty to exist in the minds of students as to the
precise bearing of this or that statement, and also to relate
this part of the subject to general principles of the history
of language on one hand, and on the other to the history of
our own language.   I thought it advisable to add a chapter
on *Methods of Reconstruction*, since, although most of the
small text-books teem with references to *Parent Aryan*,
I have never yet found a student who had gathered from
their pages how anyone knew what Parent Aryan was like.
In this section, as throughout the book, I have striven to
keep ever before the mind of the student the fact that we
are dealing with changes in actual *speech sounds*, and not
with *letters*, which is, unfortunately, too often the impression gathered from elementary manuals.   I believed that
a brief statement concerning the phenomena grouped
together under the name *Ablaut* or *Gradation* would be

useful, seeing that any explanation of them is generally omitted in the kind of books referred to—even in the best.

The task of selection, in treating the development of English itself, was very difficult, and I do not claim to have accomplished it with perfect success. Among the books generally accessible to students who are compelled to tackle the subject without the help of an experienced and highly trained teacher, there are several which contain an admirable marshalling of facts. Since I believed it desirable to devote a large portion of so small a book as the present to general questions, space was not available to restate facts which are to be found in most other books corresponding in size to the present volume. I therefore tried to select such points as I have found are generally the least well understood by ordinary students with no special training, but which are, nevertheless, of the greatest importance to a proper understanding of the facts of present-day English. I have tried, amongst other things, to emphasize, rather more than is usually the case in books for beginners, the rise of double forms in Middle English, and to show how often both doublets survive, if not in standard English, then in the modern dialects—one type in this form of present-day English, another in that. It is desirable that students should realize that much that is considered 'vulgar' in English is merely so by convention— for the reason, that is, that the polite dialect has selected another form, but that a very large number of 'vulgarisms' are historically quite as 'correct' as the received form. This knowledge must tend to a saner and a more scientific view of what is 'right' or 'wrong' in speech. My debts to other books of various kinds are, it need hardly be said, innumerable. I trust that I have made some, if not adequate, acknowledgment in the references given hereafter.

I am proud to acknowledge a special debt to Dr. Henry Sweet, one that is far deeper than any I could have contracted by the mere use of his books, great as that is. For many years past, the cordial personal intercourse which I have been privileged to enjoy with Dr. Sweet, has been an unfailing source of stimulus and enlightenment. I regret that this little work is not a worthier tribute to his teaching and influence. If the following pages should contribute at all to a wider adoption of Dr. Sweet's Phonetic and Historical Methods, in Training Colleges and in the upper forms of secondary schools, and among private students, it will help to bring about a sounder mode of study of our own tongue than that which is commonly pursued in the majority of such institutions.

It is a pleasant duty to express my gratitude to Miss Irene F. Williams, M.A., formerly Research Fellow of the University of Liverpool, who most generously undertook the laborious task of compiling the index to the present volume. This contribution, by an expert English philologist, must, I feel sure, materially increase the utility of the book.

HENRY CECIL WYLD.

ALVESCOT, OXON,
July, 1906.

CONTENTS

CHAPTER   PAGE

I. INTRODUCTION ; THE AIMS OF HISTORICAL LINGUISTIC STUDY - - - - - -   1

II. THE SOUNDS OF SPEECH - - - - -   27

III. HOW LANGUAGE IS ACQUIRED AND HANDED ON -   55

IV. SOUND CHANGE - - - - - -   67

V. DIFFERENTIATION OF LANGUAGE : THE RISE OF DIALECTS - - - - - - -   91

VI. LINGUISTIC CONTACT - - - - -   119

VII. ANALOGY - - - - - - -   128

VIII. METHODS OF COMPARISON AND RECONSTRUCTION -   141

IX. THE ARYAN OR INDO-GERMANIC MOTHER-TONGUE, AND THE DERIVED FAMILIES OF LANGUAGES -   165

X. THE GERMANIC FAMILY - - - - -   195

XI. THE HISTORY OF ENGLISH : GENERAL REMARKS ON THE SCOPE AND NATURE OF THE INQUIRY, AND THE MAIN PROBLEMS CONNECTED WITH IT -   205

XII. HISTORY OF ENGLISH : THE OLD ENGLISH PERIOD   216

XIII. THE MIDDLE ENGLISH PERIOD - - - -   250

XIV. CHANGES IN ENGLISH PRONUNCIATION DURING THE MODERN PERIOD — THE DEVELOPMENT OF ENGLISH SOUNDS FROM THE FIFTEENTH CENTURY TO THE PRESENT DAY - - - -   299

XV. THE STUDY OF PRESENT-DAY ENGLISH - -   339

SUBJECT INDEX - - - - - -   382

WORD INDEX - - - - - - -   393

LIST OF AUTHORITIES REFERRED TO - - -   409

CHAPTER I

INTRODUCTION ; THE AIMS OF HISTORICAL
LINGUISTIC STUDY

THE practical study of language, or rather the study of language for practical purposes, is familiar to everyone, and plays, of necessity, a large part in all schemes of education. In infancy and childhood the mother-tongue is gradually, although instinctively, acquired. Later on, the native tongue becomes the subject of more deliberate study, and to this is added, for the most part, that of other languages, both living and dead.

It is convenient to consider as ' practical ' that study of languages which has as its aim the mastery of tongues for the purpose of using them—that is, for the purpose either of speaking or reading them, or both.

From this point of view the schoolboy acquires, with various degrees of success, the pronunciation, the vocabulary, and the general structure of several languages, both ancient and modern. He is instructed in the rules of inflection and of syntax ; he masters many exceptions, which perhaps, in his eyes, hardly serve to prove the rule.

In all this study of Latin and Greek, English, French,

1

and German, which in this country occupies the chief
energies of boyhood and early manhood, the view of
language which is perpetually before the mind of the
student is one and the same—namely, that of language
in a state of suspended animation, stationary, and unchanging. That is to say, that the various languages are
studied merely in the forms in which they exist at a particular period of their development. There is, as a rule,
but little suggestion from the teacher that the language
under consideration has developed from something very
different; still less that, if it is a living tongue, it will
probably change still further—that it is, in fact, in a
constant state of flux. The literary form of language is
that upon which the attention is almost exclusively con-
centrated, and the student naturally learns to regard
language as something fixed and unchanging. He is not
encouraged to ask the reason for the rules which he has to
master, and must be content with the explanation which
comes so readily from the teacher's tongue : that some
apparent exception to the general rule was made—deliberately, for all that he hears to the contrary—'for the
sake of euphony.' It is but rarely suggested that some
puzzling rule of 'letter' change in Latin or Greek is based
upon the speech habits of the Romans or Greeks hundreds
—perhaps thousands—of years before the Classical Period
of those languages, or that the conditions under which the
'exceptional' form occurs differ, in a way that can be
ascertained, from those which produce the 'normal' form.

It is not intended, in the above remarks, to criticise
adversely the methods employed in teaching the Classics
to the very young ; the age at which scientific explanations

of linguistic facts should be given is a question for educationists to decide. All that it is for the moment desired to emphasize is that the practical study of language differs very considerably from the historical study, in point of view and in method.

Every teacher of the history of English or of any other language knows how difficult it is to convey to young students at the University the first inkling of the historical point of view and method as applied to language.

Nor is this surprising when we consider how different is the way in which one trained in historical methods regards human speech, from that which is the natural standpoint of the practical and literary student of language. To take a few points : the schoolboy has been taught, ' We ought to pronounce as we spell ' ; when he begins to study the history of a language he is told, ' Not at all ; we spell in such and such a way, because originally the pronunciation was approximately this or that.' He has hitherto believed that the written, literary form of language was the real language, and that uttered speech was a rather lame attempt to follow the former ; instead of this view receiving confirmation from his new teachers, he is asked to discard it completely, to think of language as something which is primarily *uttered* and *heard*, and to banish, for the time being, from his mind the fact that writing has been invented. Again, whereas the young student has probably gathered that ' rules ' of speech were made by grammarians, and therefore must be obeyed, he now hears that the grammarians have absolutely no authority to prescribe what is ' right ' or ' wrong,' but can merely state what is the actual usage. and that they are

1—2

good or bad grammarians according as they report truth-
fully on this point.

To many people 'exceptions' to grammatical rules are
as the breath of their nostrils, and 'irregularities' in
language are a source of income. It is therefore dis
concerting to a youth, hitherto bred up in an atmosphere
of linguistic chaos, to be told that the entire conception
of 'exceptions' upon which he has been nourished is
fundamentally fallacious, that there is no such thing as
real 'irregularity' in the historical development of speech,
that anomalies are only apparent, that nothing occurs in
language without a reason, and that this reason must be
sought, even though, in many cases, it elude our pursuit.
It is to be hoped that there is nothing unjust in this
adumbration of the contrast between what we may call the
popular or literary, (in this case they are the same thing)
and the philological view of language. The examples
given as exhibiting the point of view of one who has
never approached the problems of the history of a
language are all drawn from the personal experience of
a teacher.

We may now endeavour to state rather more fully the
main considerations upon which the method of historical
linguistic study at the present time is based. The general
method pursued is the outcome of the views now held
concerning the nature of language, and the conditions
under which it lives and grows.

By the history of a language is meant an account of its
development in all its dialects, of all the changes which
these have undergone, from the earliest period at which it
is possible to obtain any knowledge of them, down to the

latest. This investigation demands the formulation, so far as possible, of the laws of change which obtain at any given moment in the language—that is, a statement of each tendency to change as it arises, and an examination of the factors and conditions of each tendency. Now, all knowledge of any period of a language other than the present, must necessarily be obtained from written documents. What we are investigating, however, is the life-history of the *language itself*—that is, of the feelings and ideas of the people, as they have been handed on and modified through the ages, and of one of the most direct and expressive symbols of these, namely, the various sounds formed by the organs of speech. Uttered speech is itself a mere set of symbols of certain states of consciousness ; a mode of expression often less direct than a gesture, a picture, or a statue, since these can represent a passion, a wish, or a memory of an event in such a way that they may be of universal significance. The symbol in these cases is self-interpretative. The symbols of speech, however, are only intelligible to those to whom they have become familiar by custom, and who associate the same groups of ideas with the sounds. Uttered speech, therefore, is an indirect and symbolic mode of conveying impressions from one mind to another; but *written language* is more indirect still, for it is but the symbol of a symbol. Until the written record is interpreted, and converted into the sounds which it symbolizes, it means nothing ; it does not become language.

This process of interpretation has to be carried out, and the veil of symbolism rent asunder, before we can arrive, in dealing with the records of the past, at the

actual subject of our investigation. We must never lose
sight of the true aim of our search—the spoken sound,
which is the outward and audible part of language. It
is clear that the degree of success with which we reconstruct the earlier stages of a language, and therefore the
measure of accuracy in our views of its history, depends
to a very large extent upon our power of interpreting
correctly the written symbols, and of making them live as
sounds.

But, however successful may be our attempts at re-
vivifying the past history of a language, so long as we
confine ourselves to a single tongue the limits of possibility
are reached comparatively soon—the record fails us often
just when we most need it. In tracing back the history of
English, we have a series of documents which stretch back
for more than twelve hundred years. During this period
the language has undergone many changes—in sounds, in
vocabulary, in accidence, and in the structure of the
sentence. The earlier writings, in so far as they are, within
the limits of possibility, a faithful record of what was
actually the condition of English at different stages of
development, enable us to observe the rise and passing
away of various habits of speech and tendencies to change.
Thus, for instance, we can understand why ʻ*breath*ʼ (brɛþ)
has a voiceless final consonant, and ʻ*breathe*ʼ (brīð) a voiced,
since we can show that the latter word had an earlier
form, O.E. *brǣþan* or *brēþan* (inf.), whereas the O.E. form
of the former was *brǣþ* or *brēþ* ; and, further, that voiceless
open consonants were voiced in O.E. medially between
vowels, but remained voiceless when final. The voiced
sound in ʻ*breathe*ʼ is therefore due to a change which took

place hundreds of years ago, when the verbal forms still retained their suffixes, and when þ was followed by a vowel. In the same way we need not go beyond our own language to understand the difference of vowels between the singular ' *child* ' and the plural ' *children*.' In this case, as in the former, there is nothing in the spelling of the two forms to indicate a difference of pronunciation. In O.E. the singular was *čild*, which originally had a short vowel. Before the end of the O.E. period, however (by 1050 probably), short vowels were lengthened before the combination *-ld*. This old long *ī* developed quite regularly into our present diphthong (*ai*). This lengthening, however, did not take place when the combination *-ld-* was followed by a third consonant. The O.E. plural of this word was *čildru*, which in M.E. appears as *childre* side by side with the weak form *children*, both of which forms retained the old short *ĭ* sound. This sound has remained unchanged down to the present time. The differences between singular and plural here, therefore, are due to the presence or absence respectively, of the conditions of vowel-lengthening in O.E.

On the other hand, there is a vast number of phenomena whose explanation cannot be found within the history of English itself, because their causes lie further back than the period of the oldest English records. The substantive ' *doom* ' (dūm) is related to the verb ' *deem*,' the former being normally developed from O.E. *dōm*, the latter from O.E. *dēman*. Here the difference exists already in the oldest form of English of which we have any direct knowledge. We might surmise, perhaps, that the relation of the two vowels (ū) and (ī) in these words was identical with

that between those of the words '*tooth*' (tūþ), plural
'*teeth*' (tīþ), or *goose* (gūs), *geese* (gīs), which in O.E. are
tōþ, tēþ, gōs, gēs, respectively. Since the differences here
are already well established in the earliest form of English
which has come down to us, we are unable to decide from
a consideration of that language by itself whether this
vowel difference is original—whether, that is, from time
immemorial there have always been two distinct forms of
the roots of these words, or whether the differences arose
at a later date.   In the latter case we should assume that,
owing to causes which cannot be traced in the O.E. period
as we know it, one original vowel had been differentiated
into two quite separate sounds.   Is there any way of
getting beyond the written documents of English and
settling this question?   Can we by any means reconstruct
the forms as they existed before they were separated?
Assuming that the differences are not primitive, can we
supply the missing link which O.E. cannot reveal?   The
answer is to be found in the wider survey of other cognate
languages, known as the Science of Comparative Philology.
It has been universally accepted since Franz Bopp founded
scientific philology, that what are known as the Aryan or
Indo-Germanic languages, are a group of speech-families
descended, or developed from a common ancestor.   English,
as is well known, is a member of the Germanic family
of this group.   By a minute comparison of the peculiarities
of all the sister languages of a family, comparative
philology endeavours to gain a knowledge of a form older
than any of them—their common ancestor.   In the case of
English we should first try, by comparing the Germanic
tongues, to reconstruct parent Germanic, and then, by a

similar process of comparison of this with the ancestral forms of other Aryan families—Indian, Greek, Italic, Slavonic, etc.—to reach some conception of the source of all, the Primitive Aryan mother-tongue. The methods of comparison and reconstruction will be discussed later on, and it is sufficient here to point out the close relationship between historical and comparative grammar. The latter is, indeed, only an extension of the former; it carries the study of the history of a single language further back, and seeks to shed more light upon it by investigating the habits and nature of its sisters, cousins, parents, and grandparents. We may consider Aryan speech as one vast and living stream of language, which has flowed into many different branching channels. These, again, fork out into innumerable rivulets.

Languages which have been separate for thousands of years have altered so much from their original form, and have developed on such different lines, that they are often absolutely unrecognisable as relatives; but, nevertheless, we may reflect that English, as it is spoken to-day, has reached its present form by being passed on from mouth to mouth for thousands of years, from a time when it began to vary from a tongue which had in it the potentialities not only of English, but also of Greek, of Slavonic, and Celtic. Every family of languages, each individual of the family, has its peculiar habits and tendencies of development. One language may very early lose a feature which another will preserve for ages. Again, a certain characteristic may disappear from a language, leaving behind it, however, a trace of its existence. In this case we can see the result, but not the cause, nor can we account

for the result until we find that some other language has
preserved the feature in question.   The change of vowels
in O.E. dōm, dēman, etc., can easily be accounted for by a
comparison with the other Germanic languages, which show
that the O.E. noun preserves the original vowel ō, which
has been changed in O.E. from a back to a front vowel
through the influence of a front consonant (j) which
has disappeared in that language, although it is preserved
in Gothic *dōmjan*, Old High German *tuomian*.   This
particular kind of change, known as *i*-mutation, occurs
in hundreds of words in O.E., though, as a rule, the *i* or *j*
which caused the fronting, disappeared before the English
period, leaving only the effects of its original presence,
which can be demonstrated, however, from cognate languages.

In the historical study of a language we are perpetually
brought face to face with problems, the solution of which
requires not only a careful sifting of evidence, but a trained
judgment in drawing conclusions therefrom.   To deal
successfully with historical linguistic problems the critical
faculty needs to be formed and strengthened by contact
with the actualities of living speech, and clarified by a
knowledge of the general conditions which govern the
development of all language.

Of late years some understanding of the general principles of speech development has come to be regarded as
essential to the fruitful study or just conception of the
history of any language.   It is now commonly held that
the best way to form sound general views as to the nature
of speech-life is to study the facts of living language,
especially as they are displayed most familiarly in the

speech habits of ourselves and our contemporaries. These facts, which we can observe directly, are the best key to the understanding of those forces which helped to mould language in the past, since there is no reason for believing that the conditions under which human speech existed and developed in bygone ages were essentially different from those which obtain at the present day. We should endeavour, therefore, to realize what the 'life' of language really is by the practical study and observation of a living tongue, and, further, that tendencies to modify language, such as we may discover in ourselves, have always been in operation; in other words, the process of the evolution of language is always going on, and the factors which direct it are of the same kind in all periods.

The life of language has two aspects—the facts of human consciousness, which are the subject of psychological investigation, and the facts connected with the mode of expression, which in the case of speech are the sounds which result from the movements of the vocal organs. This latter group of facts are the subject of a special branch of physiological inquiry, that of practical Phonetics.

If linguistic study be confined to a purely literary form of language, and especially to the literary forms of the ancient languages, there is a tendency for the student to get into the habit of considering language as something cut and dried, and fixed once for all in a definite mould.

We are apt to forget that all literary languages are, to a certain extent, artificial products. They are deliberate, and bound by tradition, and they lack the spontaneity of unstudied, natural utterance. The development of literary dialects will be discussed hereafter, but it may be pointed out here that this form of language is slowly evolved from the spoken language, and is in all cases behind this in development, in the sense of being more archaic, and generally less flexible and adaptable. Any new departure in the literary language can only come from the spoken form. In the case of languages which are no longer spoken, and which therefore depend entirely upon literary tradition, development is impossible. In the case of Latin, for instance, which is still largely cultivated as a literary vehicle, it is obvious that no innovation can take place, except, indeed, by the incorporation into Latin style of the idiom of the writer's native tongue, which was largely done by mediæval writers, and possibly, quite unconsciously, at the present day also, even by good scholars. Such innovations as this, however, do not change real classical Latin itself, and are rightly regarded as 'corruptions.' There is no possible source of Latin except genuine Latin authors ; all potentialities of normal *development* are at an end, and Latin prose, when written at the present day, can only be a reproduction of well-authenticated modes of expression, for which sanction can be found in the classical writers.

The literary form of a language which is still spoken, however, is forever receiving fresh life from the colloquial speech. As new words or expressions come into use in the spoken language, they are gradually promoted to a place in the language of literature, and they often remain in use here after they have ceased to be employed in the ordinary colloquial speech of everyday life. Thus the written form of a living language does not become fixed, but is forever undergoing regeneration and rejuvenation. But this new life comes primarily from the spoken language.

Another unfortunate view which the exclusive study of the literary language gives rise to, is that which regards speech as something with a life of its own, something which can exist apart from those who speak it. That which is written remains : scratched on parchment or graven upon stone, the symbols of written language may endure for countless ages. This permanence and independence of the symbol has led men to attribute the same character to that for which it stands.

Now, it is an essential element in the conception which scholars at the present day have of language, that it does not exist by itself, and apart from the speakers. This conception brings us back to the importance of spoken language, for this can only be reached through the speakers themselves. The study of speech, as has been indicated, involves, first, that of certain psychological processes, and, secondly, that of the symbol and expression of these—that is, of speech sounds, which are the result of certain series of bodily activities.

The outward and audible part of language, the *symbol* of what is inward and of the mind, can be reached *directly* and immediately; it can be observed in others as well as in ourselves. The psychological side of language can only be studied directly and immediately by the analysis of our own consciousness. From the use of intelligible symbols we are able to infer in other minds the same mental processes and conceptions as those which exist in our own. For these reasons we insist upon the importance of the careful study of spoken language generally, and also

in particular, upon that of our own speech in both
aspects.

Spoken language is the natural expression of the personality of living human beings; from the nature of the case,
this must vary along with the change of their mental and
bodily habits. A nation, a small community, or an individual, is continually gaining new experiences, feeling new
aspirations, discovering fresh needs. All these conditions
find expression in their speech. Speakers form fresh
associations, and gradually come to use old words in
a new way. The history of a single language yields innumerable instances of change in the meanings of words.
Or words fall out of use, because for some reason they are
superfluous. Again, contact with other nations is the means
of introducing foreign words into the native vocabulary,
both for things and ideas which are quite primitive and
familiar, and for those which pass into the national consciousness as knowledge and experience widen. In the
domain of vocabulary there is a perpetual losing, gaining,
and readaptation of material.

Nor does pronunciation stand still in a living language.
Speech sounds are the result of certain bodily movements,
which we may consider as a group of physical habits.
The habitual movements of the vocal organs vary from
generation to generation, and so, therefore, do the sounds
which result from them. Up to a certain point of literary
development, the written form of a language records,
approximately, the changes of pronunciation, though the
record is probably always some way behind the actual
facts, after the first attempts to write the language down
have been made. But after a time a fixed method of

spelling is introduced, with which the pronunciation grows more and more out of harmony as time goes on. In English, the main features of our spelling became fixed in the sixteenth century, so that the far-reaching changes in our pronunciation which took place during the next three centuries are, of course, unrecorded in our orthography.

The principles and possibilities of sound change, which are so vitally important in modern philology, can only be really grasped by those who have investigated, in their own speech, the processes of articulation, and have observed how these tend to vary.

Before leaving, for the moment, the question of change in pronunciation in living speech, we may consider a little more fully the importance of a phonetic training for the student of the history of his own or any other tongue. We have just seen that sound change is a process which is always going on in language, and it has been noted that the interpretation of the written symbols of the past plays a very large part in historical linguistic study ; and, further, in judging of what took place in the past, we need the help of our actual experience of the present. This is especially true of theories of the change of sounds, for unless these changes can be realized in a practical way, our account of the development of speech forms degenerates into a mere algebraic equation, far removed from the real, living facts. Now, if these assertions are true it follows that a general knowledge of the processes upon which speech sounds depend, and some power to discriminate varieties of sound is essential to the scientific study of language. One result of the one-sided view of language which is almost universal in this country is that hardly anybody really knows what his own *speech* is like. Most people think of language in terms of black symbols on white paper, and not in terms of sounds at all.

They even go the length of pretending that they can hear a difference between such pairs as *horse—hoarse*, *Parma—Palmer, kernel—colonel*, and so on. Of course, a difference can easily be made; pronunciation can be 'faked' to any extent. The point is that in ordinary educated English speech in the South, there is no difference between the above pairs.

Phonetics is still regarded by the majority of educated persons as either a fad, or a fraud, possibly a pious one. If it is insisted that more attention should be paid, in the teaching of English, to the '*spoken language*,' there is an outcry to the effect that English literature is one of the noblest of human achievements, that the ordinary speech of children and even of grown-up people is full of vulgarisms, mistakes in grammar, and solecisms of every sort, and that by dwelling upon English as it is spoken, these errors will merely be confirmed. English, it is urged, is seen at its noblest in the works of the great writers; these should form the sole subject of English studies. To suggest a scientific way of investigating the sounds of the language which we speak, rouses antipathy and opposition.

It is, of course, easy to find reasons against that which we cannot or will not understand. Thus when, a few years ago, the Scotch Education Department introduced phonetics into the list of subjects to be studied in the training colleges, arguments of the most conflicting nature were urged against the measure. The present writer has the best reason for knowing that, whereas one party held that it was preposterous for the Department to try and 'improve' Scottish speech by insisting upon the adoption of English models of pronunciation, others objected chiefly because, they said, to dwell upon what actually occurred in Scotch pronunciation, instead of insisting upon what ought to occur, would tend to confirm and perpetuate the vulgarisms.

As both of these objections, or similar ones, are probably urged not only in Scotland, but also in this country, against the study of phonetics, it is, perhaps, worth while to answer them. In the first place, it should be said that by the study of phonetics is not meant the attempt to introduce this or that pronunciation, but simply a study of the actual movements of the vocal organs which result in the various sounds of human speech. A phonetic training involves, then, no more than development of the power of discriminating between different sounds, and a knowledge of how the sounds are made. If we could *hear* all sounds quite accurately, and knew how to reproduce them, we should have no trouble in acquiring the pronunciation of foreign languages. This is perhaps an impossible degree of perfection for most, but a phonetic training will undoubtedly help in the right direction. It may be added that every teacher of languages must needs be to a certain extent a phonetician ; he endeavours to teach his pupils to pronounce certain sounds ; he pronounces the sound himself, and often tries to explain how this is done. All that is here urged is that he should give right instructions, and not, as is too often the case, a perfectly fantastic account of the position of the tongue, jaws, etc. It should be

2

understood that phonetic study does not involve a preference for this or that manner of pronunciation of English.
In fact, the first lesson which the serious student of
phonetics has to learn is to take facts as they are, to
start with, to begin with his own natural pronunciation,
and to attempt to become conscious of the movements
of his tongue and lips in framing those sounds which he
habitually employs in speaking his native language, without discussing the question of whether his pronunciation
is '*good*' or '*bad*.' A street arab who had thoroughly
mastered the principles of his own '*speech basis*'—that is,
of that group of movements and positions of tongue, lips,
jaws, etc., which occurred naturally in his manner of
speech—and who could accurately describe these, would be
a far more competent phonetician than the speaker of a
very 'pure' and refined form of English who was ignorant
of what his own sounds actually were, or of how he made
them. This brings us to a consideration of the fallacy
that the minute study of one's own pronunciation, if it
happens to be faulty or 'vulgar,' will tend to confirm
and make more inveterate those defects which it should
be our constant endeavour to get rid of. This view is
a very common one, and it amounts to saying that if we
have a failing or a vice, which we wish to correct, it is
better to ignore it, or at most only to have a very vague
idea of its precise nature. Whether this principle holds
good or not in conduct, or in intellectual habits, we need
not discuss here, but it is absolutely certain that it is
false in matters of pronunciation. One reason why so
many teachers of foreign languages fail to impart an
accurate pronunciation to their pupils is that they them-

selves are so frequently quite unacquainted with the speech basis of those whom they are teaching. They are unable to say authoritatively, 'Your English sound is so-and-so, and it is made in such and such a way; this foreign sound for which you are substituting your own sound which strikes your ear as something like it, is so-and-so and it is made in such and such a way, entirely different from that set of articulations which produces the English sound.' If we wish to master a foreign sound, instead of being content with substituting a sound of our own language which, *to the untrained ear*, somewhat resembles it, we must thoroughly understand *both* sounds, so as to discriminate between and contrast, both the sounds themselves, and the vocal movements and positions which produce them.

If, then, it be desired to 'correct' the pronunciation of the native language, the same principle holds, for from the moment that the problem is to acquire a new sound, it matters not whether that sound occurs in another form of English or in some remote foreign tongue, the difficulty is of the same kind—namely, to master a new series of movements, or a new combination of movements, of the organs of speech.

Whatever be the case then, in other spheres of thought and conduct, in pronunciation, at any rate, an accurate knowledge of our 'faults' is the beginning of 'improvement': it is, indeed, a necessary first step.

With regard to the expressions so commonly applied to speech, such as 'mistake,' 'vulgarism,' 'corruption,' and the like, it is inevitable that our views of the propriety of such terms should change in proportion as we learn something concerning the path of development which any language has travelled during a few centuries. The reason for this statement will appear more fully in the course of this book; but it may be said here that most of the abusive terms popularly applied to certain forms of speech have, from the scientific point of view, either no meaning at all, or one which differs widely from that which such terms usually bear.

One who is accustomed to observe how a language changes in the course of centuries; how speakers in one age, or in one province, naturally acquire habits of speech which differ widely from those which obtain at other times and in other geographical areas; how a community tends to modify its speech now in one direction, now in another, sometimes owing to social or other conditions which can be traced, sometimes without any discoverable external cause, one who is an unprejudiced student of the development of human culture as it is expressed in spoken language, is unwilling to assert that one line of development is 'good,' while another is 'bad,' or to dogmatize as to what *ought* to be the form which language shall take. If we regard the unfolding of that body of habits which we call 'language' as a natural process, one which is for the most part unconscious and independent of the deliberate intention of the speakers, we are content to chronicle what actually exists, and investigate so far as possible how it arose: we do not attempt to adjudge praise or blame to this or that phenomenon. In a word, as students of the history of language, we are concerned purely with the facts, *all* the facts that we can ascertain, and from them we endeavour to form a clear conception of what *is*, and of how it arose out of what *was*.

Do we then, admit no 'right' or 'wrong' in language from this point of view? Certainly we do; only we should define these terms, as Osthoff pointed out years ago (*Schriftsprache und Volksmundart*, Berlin, 1883, p. 25, etc.), in rather a different way from that popularly accepted. Whatever exists in the natural speech of a community at a given period is *right for the speech of that community at that particular moment*; it is, whether we like it or not, a fact of the speech history of the community. Any manner of speech—whether pronunciation, word, grammatical inflection, or form of sentence—which is foreign to the natural speech habit of a community at a given period is *wrong*, so far as the dialect of the moment in that particular community is concerned.

The failure to grasp this simple principle is responsible for the popular misconception of the terms '*correct*' and '*incorrect*' speech, and the consequent misuse of them.

What usually happens is that the critic of language has in his mind a vague picture of an ideal standard of language, probably based on his own vague notion of the way he speaks himself, and he proceeds to test all other modes of speech by this standard. If other speakers appear to the censor to approximate to his own standard, he approves them as 'good' or 'correct' speakers; if he gathers that they deviate from the model which he has set up, then they are set down as being 'corrupt,' 'incorrect,' or even 'vulgar.' But he does not realize that those who speak differently from himself are not pretending, for the most part, that they are speaking in the same way as he does. They are quite frankly using the natural dialect of another geographical area, another suburb, it may be, or of a different social class. Probably each man who comes under the condemnation of our critic is, as a matter of fact, speaking his own dialect quite ' *correctly* ' from the point of view mentioned above. On the other hand, a mixture of dialects is not infrequently heard. A speaker tries to adopt the speech of what he considers a more refined or more elevated sphere than that which is customary to him, and occasionally reverts to his own natural way of speaking—to his native dialect, in fact. The error in judging of such cases lies in not realizing that every form of speech, whether it be a provincial or a class dialect, has a perfectly good reason for existing and for being as it is ; each has its own history, and has followed its own path of development. According to this view, therefore, each dialect is equally ' *good* ' and equally ' *correct*.' There are, however, two tests by which the relative superiority of different dialects may be gauged— the one real and absolute, the other artificial and a matter of convention.

A language may justifiably be judged, and its merits appreciated, according to its qualities as a medium of expression. The degree of expressiveness which a language possesses is its true claim to respect. If it can be shown that one form of speech is more flexible, more adaptable to the needs of those who speak it, more capable of expressing subtle shades of thought and feeling than another, then we may surely say that it is the finer language of the two.

The other test of superiority, which we have called artificial and conventional, has a very real existence in English—namely, the test of what is received and re-

cognised as the 'correct' form of speech in polite and
cultivated society. From the purely scientific point of
view, as has been already set forth, no difference of
superiority can be recognised between the speech heard
at the bench of a village ale-house and that of the
Bench of Bishops. But according to the actual feelings
of English society, that of the latter is the more distinguished, graceful, and desirable. It is a fact which
nothing can alter, that there is a form of English which
enjoys a prestige, and a place in the general estimation
of which nothing can rob it. This form of English is
essentially a class dialect; it is independent, or largely independent, of locality ; it is the form of English which
obtains, with an astonishing degree of uniformity, among
the upper and upper middle classes of this country, and it
may be heard with the same purity in Durham, York,
Newcastle, or Birmingham, as in London, Oxford, or Cambridge. So greatly is this standard English prized, that
those who have not acquired it from the cradle upwards,
usually take pains to do so in later life, and there can be
no doubt that it is convenient for those who wish to enter
the public services or to take part in distinguished social
gatherings to possess it, or at least a good imitation of it.
Those who have spoken from childhood this colourless form
of English, free from provincial peculiarities, devoid of the
rasping sound of inverted *r* before consonants, with no tendency to shaky initial aspirates in stressed words, or even
in words which have only a secondary stress, no undue
mouthing or over-emphatic utterance, not unnaturally
regard it as the purest, most harmonious, and most refined
form of English speech. This view of a language, how-

INTRODUCTION

ever, is purely a matter of custom; we always admire most what we are accustomed to hear and to use ourselves. Such an estimate has no absolute value, but is entirely relative and subjective. Speakers of Northern English and Scotch speakers often consider standard English as mincing and affected, in some cases even (*e.g.*, the loss of the *r*-sound before consonants) as slipshod and almost vulgar. So much for habit.

The historical position of this polite form of English is that it is a very mixed dialect, which, by a variety of social and political circumstances, has acquired prominence over all other English dialects by becoming the language of Literature (for the written language is largely based upon it), of the Court, of the aristocracy, of the Law, the Church, the Legislature, and the Stage. It is probable that the Metropolis, Oxford, and the East Midlands all contributed to its origin, while the remoter influences of the North and the extreme South have both helped to shape it. We shall have to consider the rise of this dialect more in detail later on. It might probably be maintained with considerable plausibility that, owing to the circumstances of its history, the standard dialect, which of all forms of spoken English approximates most nearly to the written language, has an absolute superiority to any other dialect of our language as a means of expression, excepting always some of the dialects of Scotland At the same time, it may perhaps temper the enthusiasm of some to remind them that standard English is not nearly so uniform in its sounds or in its other characteristics as a superficial observer might imagine, and, further, that the standard varies considerably from generation to generation; for instance, much that was very 'good form' as recently as the end of the eighteenth century would now be considered 'vulgar' or 'provincial' even by speakers who are not over-fastidious. The pronunciations 'sarvant,' 'goold' (gūld), 'chaney tay-pot' (tʃēni tēpot), and the frequent use of the pronoun 'em (əm), may serve as examples of this fact in the meantime.

The upshot of the foregoing remarks is that we may keep our natural preferences for this or that English dialect, but we must not ignore the fact that other dialects exist, and we should admit that it is not wise to abuse them, simply because they differ from the form that we ourselves use.

It is very important for the student to recognise and observe differences in English speech, and to contrast and compare them. The problem of English philology lies within the differences and agreements of the various English dialects, and questions at issue are the origin, history, and mutual relations of these.

Within the limits of such an investigation, questions arise which contain the germ of all comparative philology; the methods pursued in dealing with the history of the English dialects are those which it is also desirable to pursue in considering the relations of the great Aryan families of languages.

The study of the native tongue, beginning with its spoken forms, and proceeding thence to inquire into the why and wherefore of what exists, is therefore the best introduction to the advanced study of Aryan philology in its widest sense. All the principles of linguistic develop-ment, all the factors of evolution, exist ready for our observation in the living speech of our own English dialects; and while, as has been said, the discipline afforded by their study is a preparation for the larger science, it should be borne in mind that this study cannot be profitably pursued unless the same accuracy of method, and the same exactness of observation be applied in both cases, and, above all, unless the same scientific spirit and the same general conception of the life of language animate all our inquiries.

CHAPTER II

THE SOUNDS OF SPEECH*

PHONETICS, or the science of speech sounds, involves a two-fold training—that of the ear to discriminate minute shades of difference in sound, and that of the vocal organs to reproduce these. The former is only gained by the repeated hearing of varieties of sound and a keen and patient observation; the latter by a knowledge of the processes of articulation and a careful cultivation of the power of recognising the muscular sensations associated with the different movements and positions of the vocal organs in speech.

This power of recognition, which is almost lacking in untrained persons, must be based, primarily, upon the observation of one's own speech. To gain the power to analyze and describe the movements of the vocal organs in uttering the most familiar sounds of our own language is to make the first steps in a real knowledge of scientific and practical phonetics.

Anything like a complete treatise on phonetics would be out of place in such a work as this, and no more is here attempted than to give a brief outline of the classification

* The letters placed in brackets in the following pages are the Phonetic Symbols of the sounds referred to.

of speech sounds according to the *Organic Method*, as set forth in the system of Melville Bell, the author of *Visible Speech*, and made more scientific and exact by Mr. Sweet. For a full treatment of the subject the student may refer to Sweet's *Primer of Phonetics* (third edition), *History of English Sounds*, 1888, and to Sievers' *Phonetik* (fourth edition). The student will be well advised to approach the study of phonetics with the help of a teacher, and also to master one system thoroughly before coquetting with others, as the result of reading a series of treatises by different writers is usually to produce confusion of mind, no proper grasp of any system, and no gain in the control of the speech organs.

The classification of speech sounds according to the organic system is based upon a consideration of the position and condition of those organs which produce the sounds. It is an axiom that the same sound can only be uttered in one way—that is, by a given mode of activity of a particular organ. If the position and the mode of activity be altered ever so little, a different sound is the result. The limit of discrimination of minute differences of position and sound is that of delicacy of ear and muscular sensation.

The organs which play a part in the production of the sounds of speech are: The *Lungs*, from which the air-stream passes through the glottis, mouth, and nose ; the *Diaphragm*, the muscle which controls the volume and force of the air-stream ; the *Glottis*; the *Mouth cavity* ; the *Hard and Soft Palates* ; the *Nose*; the *Tongue*; and the *Lips*. The *Jaws* are important, especially the movable lower jaw, since the tongue is raised or lowered in conjunction with it ; and the teeth and gums, since they contribute to the formation of sounds, with the aid of the lips and tongue.

We may consider briefly the activities of those organs of speech which can be moved at will.

The *Glottis* contains the Vocal Chords, which can be either stretched across it so as to close it, or folded back so as to leave it completely open.

In the former case, if the air be driven through, the vocal chords vibrate, as the air-stream forces its way between them.

The sound caused by the air passing through the closed glottis, and setting up vibration in the vocal chords, is technically known as *Voice*. This vibration accompanies most vowels in ordinary '*loud*' speech, and a great number of consonants, such as *z*, *v*, and *th* in ' this' (ð).

When the air-stream passes through the open glottis, and the chords do not vibrate, as in the ordinary sigh, the sound is known as *Breath*, as in *s, f, th* in ' think' (þ).

A third possibility is *Whisper*, in which the glottis is definitely contracted and narrowed, but the vocal chords are not tightened, and do not vibrate.

The *Soft Palate* or *Velum*, from which the uvula depends, serves to open or close the nose passage, and probably also acts in sympathetic relation to certain movements of the tongue.

The *Uvula* in certain sounds, such as the usual French *r*, trills against the back of the tongue, which in this case is raised.

The *Nose Passage* is open in the so-called nasal sounds, such as the consonants *n*, *m*, *ng* (ŋ) in ' sing ' (siŋ), or in the nasalized vowels so frequent in French, as in ' bon' (bõ), ' fin' (fæ̃), ' un' (œ̃), etc. In these cases the air-stream passes through the nose passage. In the nasal vowels the stream passes through mouth and nose at once, in *n*, *m*, only through the latter.

In other than nasal sounds the nose passage is closed by the soft palate.

The *Tongue* is, perhaps, the most important, as it certainly is the most active, of the vocal organs.

The tongue can move chiefly in four ways : inwards and outwards—that is, it can be retracted or advanced ; up and down—that is, it can be raised or lowered.

If the tongue be retracted or drawn back, the back part, or even the root, is brought into play ; if it be advanced or thrust forwards towards the front teeth, the forward part or the tip comes into activity.

In considering the raising or lowering of the tongue, we distinguish different degrees of *Height*, which, as we shall see, are of great significance in determining the sound of vowels.

In addition to the direction of the movements of the tongue, we have also to take account of the particular part or area involved in uttering a given sound.

Beginning from the back of the mouth, we distinguish the *Root* ; the *Back* ; the *Front* or *Middle* of the tongue ; the *Blade*, which is that portion which lies between the middle and the *Point* or tip ; and, lastly, the Point itself.

Each of these areas functions in the production of speech sounds, and their several activities are associated with characteristic sounds.

The *Lips* are the most easily observed of all the movable organs of speech. They may be drawn back from the teeth so as almost to expose these, as in French *i* in 'fini,' or they may be *protruded* or pouted. The lips can function in the formation both of vowels and consonants ; in the former case they always act in conjunction with the tongue, in the latter they may act either in conjunction with the tongue, independently of any other organ, or by a combination of the lower lip and the upper teeth.

Distinction between Vowels and Consonants.

By a *Consonant* we understand a speech sound in which the air-stream is either completely *stopped* for a moment, as (b, d, g) (in '*good*,' etc.), or in the formation of which the passage is so far narrowed that there is a distinct *friction* set up as the air-stream passes out.

In a true *Vowel* the air-passage is never sufficiently narrowed to produce such friction, although in the case of certain vowels, such as (i) or (u), the narrowing of the air-passage is so great that, under certain conditions, as when the air-stream is forced through with great vigour, an appreciable friction results. In this case the sound ceases to be a pure vowel sound, and becomes consonantal. In pronouncing such words as 'sea' many speakers make the final vowel into a weak *Open* consonant, with a distinct '*buzz*,' uttering (sij) instead of (sī).

It is best to begin the study of speech sounds with the consonants, as the positions of the vocal organs in pronouncing these sounds are more easily realized by the student.

The Classification of Consonants.

In considering any given consonant, we have to determine the following points: (A) The organ or organs *with
which the sound is formed*, and, if the tongue be used, also
the *particular area* which functions; (B) the *mode of
activity* ; (C) whether the articulation is or is not accompanied by *Voice*—that is, by vibration of the *Vocal Chords.*

A. The Organs and Area.—From this point of view
we have first of all to determine whether the particular consonant we are considering is formed in the *Throat* (by a
contraction below the Glottis) ; by one of the areas of the
Tongue already described—Back, Front, Blade, etc. ; by
the *Lips;* or by a combination of more than one organ,
such as the Tongue and Lips.

B. The Mode of Activity.—From this point of view we
distinguish the following classes :

(1) **Open Consonants,** in which the mouth passage is
sufficiently narrowed to produce a very distinct friction,
the air-stream, however, continuing to pass so long as the
position is maintained and the air driven from the lungs.
This friction may be made at any part of the passage along
its whole length—below the glottis in the case of throat
consonants, above the glottis by every part of the tongue,
by the lips, or by approximating one of the lips to the
teeth.   Examples of open consonants are—' *ch* ' in Scotch
' loch ' (χ), made between the *Back* of the Tongue and the
Soft Palate (Back-Open); *s* (s) made between the *Blade of
the Tongue* and the *Hard Palate* (Blade-Open) ; *th* (þ) in
'think,' made between the *Point* of the tongue and the
Teeth (Point-Teeth-Open) ; and so on.

(2) **Stops**, or **Stop Consonants**, in which the passage is for a moment completely closed, and then suddenly opened, so that the air bursts forth with a certain puff. These are popularly called *Explosives*. This stopping of the passage may, like the *narrowing* in (1), be made anywhere along the whole length of the passage. A few examples of *stops* are (k), made by *Back of Tongue* and *Hard Palate* (Back-Stop); English (t), made between Point of Tongue and Gums just behind upper teeth (Point-Stop); (p) made by the lips (Lip-Stop).

(3) **Nasal Consonants**, which are formed, as has been already said, by allowing the air-stream to pass through the *nose passage*. In the case of the English nasal consonants the mouth-passage is always closed, so that (n) is really a nasalized (d)—that is, Point - (Stop)-Nasal; but any open consonant may also be nasalized, in which case the air passes through both nose and mouth at the same time. Besides *n*, English has *m*, formed by the lips (Lip-Nasal), and *ng*, as in 'sing' (ŋ, Back-Nasal), formed by the back of the tongue against the soft palate. Thus (m) is merely a nasalized (b), and (ŋ) a nasalized (g).

(4) **Divided or Side Consonants.**—This class is chiefly typified by the *l*-sounds, which are made by the tongue forming a partial stoppage, in such a way as to permit the air-stream to escape on either side of the point of contact. English (l) is usually formed by the tongue in contact with the gums just behind the upper teeth, in exactly the same way as ordinary English (d), except that, whereas in this case the closure is complete, in that of (l) the edges of the tongue on either side of the point of contact are so far removed from the gums as to allow the air-stream to pass all the time in

3

the manner just described. Some speakers, notably the Welsh, form contact with only one side of the tongue, so that the air passes out between the other side of the tongue and the gums or teeth. Hence the name *Side* consonant. This kind of *Divided* articulation can be carried out between any area of the tongue and the palate. Thus we have in some languages, *e.g.*, Russian, a back-divided consonant—that is, an *l* formed with the same part of the tongue as that which forms the back-stop (*g*).

(5) **Trills.**—This name explains itself, and the typical trilled sounds are the r-series. In Scotch *r* it is the *point* of the tongue which trills just behind the teeth ; in French *r* it is the *Uvula* which trills upon the back of the tongue. In Southern English there is normally no trill, no ' rolling ' of the *r*, the sound being usually some variety of weak *point-open* consonant.

C. Voice and Breath.—These terms, which refer respectively to the activity and passivity of the vocal chords, have already been explained. The vibration of the vocal chords, which we call *Voice*, produces a very characteristic sound, sometimes called ' *buzz*,' and the vibration can easily be felt if the fingers are placed upon the ' *Adam's Apple* ' while such sounds as (z, v, or ð) are uttered with a certain loudness. Open consonants are the best for this purpose, because they can be prolonged to any extent—so long, indeed, as the supply of air from the lungs holds out.

Each and every consonant position may be either accompanied by vibration of the vocal chords or the reverse ; that is to say, that every consonant may be either Voiced or un-Voiced. It does not follow that any given language possesses both voiced and voiceless varieties of all its consonants. Thus in English we have no entirely voiceless *l*, although this is common in Welsh, where it is expressed by *ll*, as in *Llandudno*, etc. ; while in German the voiced form of ' sh,' as in *sh*ip (ʃ), does not exist, and causes Germans great trouble, although it is frequent in French, where it is written 'j,' as in '*jamais*' (žamɛ), etc., and occurs also in English in such words as '*pleasure*' (plɛžə).

One of the first exercises which the beginner should practise is that of unvoicing voiced, and voicing unvoiced consonants. This implies such control of the glottis that it can be consciously and deliberately opened and closed at will. When the student has thoroughly mastered this process, he will find that he has added considerably to his range of easily articulated sounds.

In describing a consonantal sound it is usually only necessary to mention the fact when it is Voiced, it being assumed that such is *not* the case if nothing is said about it. Thus (g) is described as the back-stop-voice, while the corresponding *Breath* or Voiceless sound is described simply as back-stop.

In studying the consonants it is convenient to take them in their natural series; thus, if we begin with the back consonants, we have the following table :

	Back (Voiced).	Back (Voiceless).
Open ...	ʒ, as in Gm. sor*g*e	χ, as in Scot. lo*ch*
Stop ...	g, as in *g*ood	k, as in *c*ar, or *k*ing
Nasal...	ŋ, as in sin*g*	ŋ̥, —
Divided	ɫ, as in Russ. (ɫoʃ*ad*), ' horse '	ɫ̥, —
Trill ...	r, as in Fr. *r*end*r*e	r̥, as in Fr. f*r*ançais

The advantage of this method of practice is, that not only is it exhaustive, since it considers all the possible consonants—at least, in type—of the group, but it also impresses upon the student the natural relationship of consonants which are formed in the same part of the mouth, although in different ways; and, further, if the sounds are practised in order, it helps to make him conscious of the processes of articulation.

The beginner starts with the familiar sounds of the series, and gradually learns the unfamiliar ones by acquiring the power to use his organs of speech in new ways. In the back-voice series only two of the series are familiar to most English speakers—(g) and (ŋ)—but, taking these as a starting - point, the student, by closely observing his muscular sensations, so learns to form the Open and the Divided with the same part of the tongue which he uses in forming the Stop and the Nasal. The power of unvoicing depends upon the degree of control which the beginner has over his vocal chords. The back-trill will probably require considerable practice before it can be formed easily and perfectly, and without making faces. The student will find, as a rule, that the utterance of a new sound, the position for which he has only imperfectly mastered, has at first a peculiar ghastliness and hollowness in the effect which it makes upon the ear. This is due to the fact that the organs of speech are in what is to them an unnatural position, which they cannot maintain with ease—in fact, the performance is at first a clumsy one.

It is important that teachers, at any rate, should acquire by practice the power of forming all the sounds with which they deal, clearly, easily, and with precision, as this gives confidence to the learner.

Full tables of the consonants, and minute accounts of each variety, are given in the works by Sweet and Sievers mentioned above.

The Vowels.

There are four main points to be considered in the analysis of vowel sounds. The peculiar acoustic character of a vowel sound depends upon : A. *The height of the tongue ;* B. *the part of the tongue which functions ;* C. *the degree of tenseness of the tongue ;* D. *the position of the lips.* If we know these four points with regard to any particular vowel, and can put them into effect with our own vocal organs, then we can both pronounce the vowel ourselves, and so describe it that there can be no doubt as to the precise sound we mean.

We will briefly consider the points in the above order.

A. The Height of the Tongue.—We have already said that the tongue can be either *raised* or *lowered*. We distinguish three main degrees of *Height*—*High, Mid, Low.* Each of these positions may be taken by the *back*, the *front*, or the *whole* of the tongue. Thus we have a *high-back*, a *mid-back*, and a *low-back* vowel, and similarly with the *front* and *mixed* or *flat* vowels.

B. The Part of the Tongue which Functions.—It has been already said that if the tongue be retracted the *back* part comes into play, and that if it be advanced the *front* is brought into activity. If the tongue be neither retracted nor advanced, but remain approximately *flat* in the mouth, then neither *back* nor *front* predominates, but the tongue is used along its whole length. From this point of view, therefore, we distinguish the possibilities : vowels made by the *Back* of the tongue—*Back-vowels ;* those made with the *Front* of the tongue—*Front-vowels ;* and vowels formed by the *Whole* of the tongue—*Flat* or *Mixed* vowels. A typical *back* vowel in English is the (ā) in ' father ' (fāðə), a *front* is the (ī) in ' see ' (sī), and a *mixed* or *flat* vowel is the vowel in bird (bā̆d). To realize the backward and forward movement of the tongue, the student may pronounce in a whisper, or articulate silently, the sound (ū) (as in ' boot '), and (ī) (as in ' see '), or, better, the French u (y) in ' lune ' alternately, (u-y, u-y, u-y), several times, when he will at once become conscious of the sawing backwards and forwards movements.

The *front-slack* series is the best for the beginner to practise, to realize the *height* of the tongue ; because most Southern English speakers have all three vowels in their normal pronunciation of English.

The following series should be pronounced in order, care being taken to observe the gradual lowering of the front of the tongue, and the gradual sinking of the lower jaw.

		Front.
High ...	...	(*i*) in b*i*t
Mid ...	...	(ɛ) in b*e*t
Low ...	...	(æ) in b*a*t

The *low-front* vowel is a great difficulty to Scotch and North of England speakers, who, as a rule, do not possess it in the sounds of their natural speech, but must acquire it with great trouble and patience. Such speakers substitute a back vowel, a variety, only short, of the first vowel in 'father.' This particular difficulty is one which the uninformed 'imitation' method hardly ever overcomes, and many people are irretrievably branded as 'provincial' speakers in consequence of their failure to acquire the standard English sound. This is not the expression of a supercilious sense of superiority (there is no particular ethical merit about the *low-front* vowel), but merely a statement of a scientific fact concerning the dialects of Modern English.

C. The Degree of Tenseness of the Tongue.—For practical purposes it is sufficient to distinguish a *tense* and a *slack* condition of the tongue. The muscular sensation which characterizes each may be experienced by pronouncing alternately, and contrasting the accompanying sensations, ee (ī) in 'see' and i (*i*) in 'sit,' or French é (e) in 'été' with English e (ε) in 'bet.'

The tongue may be either *tense* or *slack* while occupying any or all of the before-mentioned positions, so that we have a *high-front-tense*, a *high-front-slack ; high-back-tense*, *high-back-slack*, and so on throughout all the vowels of every series, *back*, *front*, and *flat*.

It should be noted that Mr. Sweet generally uses the terms *narrow* = tense, and *wide* = slack, and these terms are probably quite as much used by phoneticians as *tense* and *slack ;* unfortunately, however, some writers, but imperfectly acquainted with the principles and terminology of the Organic System, have been so far misled by 'narrow' and 'wide' as to understand them to refer to the *narrow-*

ing or *widening* of the mouth passage by raising or lowering the tongue.   In other words, they have confused 'narrowness,' which merely means *tenseness* when applied to vowels, with *Height*, and have gathered that the vowel (*i*) in ' bit,' which Mr. Sweet would call the *high-front-wide*, is intermediate in position between (ī) in ' see' and (e) in ' été,' than which nothing is more false.

The important thing for the beginner is thoroughly to understand the terminology which he uses, and to be able to realize by his muscular sensations the processes of which it is descriptive.   On the whole, perhaps, *tense* and *slack* are to be preferred to *narrow* and *wide*, as being more definitely descriptive of the facts.

D. The Position of the Lips.—The action of the lips is obviously quite independent of that of the tongue, so that, no matter how the latter is being employed, the lips may be either passive, whether slightly parted or drawn back so as to leave the air-stream an unhindered exit, or they may be more or less brought forward or pouted so as to muffle, to a greater or less extent, the air-stream after it passes the teeth.

This pouting or bringing together of the lips is technically known as *Rounding*, and a vowel thus formed is called a *Round* or *Rounded* vowel.

When the student has mastered the processes of retracting and advancing, raising and lowering the tongue at pleasure, he should pass with equal assiduity to that of *rounding* and *unrounding;* that is, he should pronounce a vowel sound—for instance, (i) (*high-front-tense*)—endeavour to feel the position of the tongue, and then, while being careful to maintain this unaltered, he should prolong the

vowel, and alternately advance and retract the lips. The
rounding of (i) results in (y) (high-front-tense-round),
which is the sound of French *u* in 'd*u*r,' 'b*u*t,' 'v*u*,' etc.
This sound, which often presents great difficulties to
English people, may often be perfectly acquired in a few
minutes by the above simple experiment. The same
acoustic effect may be produced by forming a small circle
with the finger and thumb, and pronouncing (i) through
this, when the effect, if the aperture be sufficiently small,
will at once be (y), which, perhaps, the student has long
tried in vain to pronounce. It should be noted that the
degree of rounding—that is, of the smallness of the aperture—is normally related to the height of the tongue, so that
in most languages high vowels have the greatest, and low
vowels the least degree of rounding. But languages sometimes develop vowels in which the rounding is abnormal—
high vowels with the slighter rounding generally associated
with mid or low vowels, or low or mid vowels with a
greater amount of rounding than is usual to those degrees
of height. In the former case we speak of *under-rounding*,
in the latter we say that the vowel is *over-rounded*.

Examples of the latter process are found in Swedish
long *o*, mid-back-tense, with over-rounding, which to
foreign ears sounds like (ū), and in the German *ü*, which
is the mid-front-tense, with over-rounding, the acoustic
effect being identical with that of French (y) to untrained
ears. An example of an under-rounded vowel is heard in
the Lancashire sound of the vowel in 'bush,' 'butcher,'
etc. (mid-back-tense, under-rounded).

In describing a vowel, the four points above discussed are
mentioned in the order in which we have dealt with them

If there be no rounding, it is usually unnecessary to mention the action of the lips, it being assumed that these play no part in the particular sound unless the rounding be stated.

Thus (ū) in ' boot ' is the *high-back-tense-round ;* the (*ä*) in ' father ' the *mid-back-slack.*

From the above account it will be seen that there are thirty-six main normal vowels : three back, three front, and three flat or mixed vowels, according to the height of the tongue—that is, nine positions ; the sounds associated with each of these positions are further increased by another nine, giving eighteen, according to whether the tongue be tense or slack ; and, lastly, every tense and every slack vowel may be rounded, bringing the number up to thirty-six.

Shifted Vowels.—Mr. Sweet, in the second edition of his *Primer of Phonetics,* has recently pointed out that it is possible, while using the back of the tongue, to shift the raised part forward, so that the air-passage is narrowed further forward than in the case of the normal vowels, where the narrowing takes places between the tongue and that part of the palate immediately above the area of activity. Similarly, in articulating front vowels, the tongue may be drawn back, so the area of articulation is further back in the palate, although the front of the tongue is still used. The character of these ' shifted ' vowels is, according to Mr. Sweet's view, sufficiently distinct from that of vowels formed in normal manner to justify the former being classified as distinct sounds. This brings the number of well-marked, distinct vowel sounds up to seventy-two. Many of the Modern English dialects contain ' shifted ' vowels, which it is very difficult to locate, unless this possibility be remembered.

Intermediate Varieties of Vowel Sounds.—It must be borne in mind that the above enumeration and tabulating of vowels according to the Organic System only deals with the chief, distinctive types. Thus (i) (high-front) is quite distinct from (e) (mid-front), both to the ear and to the muscular sense, but it is possible to lower the tongue gradually from the high position to one which produces a sound different from the typical vowel associated with that position, but not yet fully a mid vowel. In such a case we should have to determine whether the position was, as a matter of fact, nearer to the high or the mid. In the former case we should classify the vowel as a high vowel *lowered*; in the latter, as a mid vowel *raised*.

These intermediate positions occur in all languages, especially in dialects. In Danish the ordinary (ē) (mid-front) is so far raised towards the high position that the effect it produces upon the ear of a foreigner at the first hearing is almost that of (ī). In many Scotch dialects the high-front-slack vowel is considerably lowered, almost to the position of the mid-front (ε), and the mid-front is also lowered almost to (æ). So alike is the Scotch (i) in 'bit' to the English (ε) in 'bet' that, unless the mid-front were also proportionately lowered, the two sounds would be confused. As a rule, language shrinks from having two distinct vowels so closely alike as (i) lowered, and normal (ε) at one and the same period—if one is lowered the other is lowered too.

In English there is a tendency, at any rate among speakers of standard English, to avoid these lowered vowels altogether, and to pronounce the normal high and mid vowels. This gives to the standard dialect a certain clearness and distinctness which is often lacking in the pronunciation of other dialects.

Glides.—In ordinary speech the vocal organs, especially the tongue, frequently have to assume, in rapid succession, a series of positions which are very different, and comparatively far removed one from the other, as one sound after another is uttered by the speaker. To get from one position to another, the organs move with great rapidity, and these movements are called *glides*. It sometimes happens that the passage of the organs from one position to another results in audible sounds. The sounds are called *glide sounds*, and sometimes also, merely *glides*.

We may distinguish : (1) Glides produced as the organs pass from repose to activity—that is, when beginning to speak ; (2) those due to the organs passing from one mode of activity to another—these occur during the utterance of words or word-series ; (3) the movements of the organs in passing from a state of activity to one of repose—that is, when pausing or ceasing to speak.

Glides are very important to the student of language, for they not only are very characteristic of any actually spoken language, but in the history of a language they often develop into independent sounds.

To illustrate these two points. It makes all the difference to the pronunciation of French whether a foreigner, especially an Englishman, has acquired the proper glides after the voiceless stops, p, t, k. In French, when these sounds are followed by a vowel, the voicing begins *before* the stop is opened, so that the latter part of the consonant is rarely voiced. In English and German, on the other hand, after voiceless stops, the vocal chords are not closed

until the stops have been opened, so that there is a slight
puff of breath *between* the stop and the following vowel. A
glide after a sound is called an *Off-glide*, so that we say that
in French there is a *Voice off-glide* after voiceless stops, but
in English a *Breath off-glide*. To show how important
glides are in the development of language, we may instance
the process known as *Fracture*, or *Brechung*, in O.E. In
primitive O.E. such a form as *æld ('old') became *æuld in
the South, by the development of the glide between the
front vowel *æ* and the following -*ld* into a full vowel. This
primitive *æu* subsequently became *æa*, written *ea*, in *eald*
from *æld, *beald* from *bæld, etc. The other Germanic
languages and some of the English dialects developed
no vowel from the off-glide in these cases, so that at the
present day we have *old* from an Anglian *āld* (late Anglian),
and in High German *alt*.

The whole subject of *glides* demands the special attention of the student, and he must study the phenomena
in his own speech, aided by the special phonetic treatises;
but enough has, perhaps, been said here to make the term
and the ideas connected with it intelligible in subsequent
references in the present work.

Accent.

Under this head are often included two quite distinct
phenomena—*Stress or Emphasis*, and *Intonation*.

Stress depends upon the degree of force with which the
air-stream is expelled from the lungs. An increase of force
in the air-stream causes increased loudness in the case
of vowels and all voiced sounds.

We distinguish three chief degrees of stress—*Strong*,

Medium, Weak. These terms are, of course, purely relative. When a word consists of several syllables, various degrees of stress are exhibited in its pronunciation. Thus in such a word as '*perceptible*,' the strongest stress is on the second syllable, the weakest on the first, the next weakest on the third, and the second strongest on the fourth. The tendency is to alternate strong and weak stress. When we speak of the stressed syllable of a word, we mean the syllable which has the chief, or strongest, stress. When we say that a syllable is unstressed we mean that it has the weakest stress: some force it must have, otherwise it would be inaudible, and would disappear altogether. The disappearance of very weakly stressed syllables is a frequent phenomenon in the history of language. In Modern English certain words are differently stressed, according to the sentence in which they occur. Thus the auxiliary '*have*' occurs in the forms (hæv) with strong stress, (həv) with weaker stress, (v) when completely unstressed. Compare the sentences: (wɛə hǽv ju bīn ? wɛ́ər (h)əv ju bīn ? ai v bīn in landən).

As regards the *distribution* of stress, we can distinguish three varieties—*Increasing, Even,* and *Diminishing* stress. In English the highest point of stress in an emphatic syllable is the beginning, from which point the force in a monosyllabic word is diminished. In the distribution of stress over a word of several syllables, or over a breath-group—that is, the whole series of syllables uttered with one breath—the force is usually varied during the utterance by alternately increasing and diminishing the air-stream.

Even stress implies that the degree of force is maintained

constant throughout the utterance. This never actually
happens in English, since in the single syllable the stress is
decreased so that it gets weaker and weaker, and if, as
happens comparatively rarely, two succeeding syllables
have an equal amount of stress, the second is uttered with
a fresh impulse of the breath, as in *plum cake* (plám kɛik),
John Jones (džón džóunz).

Stress is an important factor in determining syllable
division.

Intonation is a question of pitch. Alterations of pitch
in speech are produced by tightening the vocal chords for
a high tone, loosening or shortening them for a low
tone.

We have *Rising Intonation*, as in the interrogative,
sharply-uttered ' what ?' *Falling Intonation*, as in the
negative reply to a question—'no !' *Fall and Rise* is heard
in the warning or expostulatory ' take care !' uttered
with a certain impatience; *Rise and Fall* in the con-
temptuous or supercilious ' oh !' These combined tones
are of importance in the history of language, but they
cannot easily be studied except with the aid of oral
instruction.

It should be noted that every speaker naturally pitches
his voice on a certain note as his normal pitch; every tone
which he utters above this is a *rise*, every one below it is a
fall. The *degree* of rise and fall which takes place in
speech is different in, and very characteristic of, different
languages or dialects.

Quantity.—This, again, is a relative term ; long vowels
in some languages are shorter than in others. Differences
of quantity exist in consonants also. In English, final

voiced consonants are long compared to those of German. Contrast, for instance, the final *n* of English ' man,' and German ' mann.'

It is important to distinguish between a *long* and a *double* consonant. The latter class are heard in Swedish, Italian, and many other languages. They even occur in English in such compounds as ' book-case.' In a double consonant the position of the vocal organs is maintained for a certain space of time, and a new impulse of breath is given in the middle, whereas in a long consonant there is no fresh impulse of breath during the maintenance of the position. A further possibility is to utter the same consonant twice—that is, with two off-glides. This is occasionally heard from very self-conscious and affected speakers in English, who are trying to ' talk fine.' ' This hill has a flat top ' would normally be pronounced (ðis hil hæz ə flættɔp), with no escape of breath between the *t* of *flat* and that of *top ;* the affected pronunciation referred to would be (flæt tɔp), with an off-glide after each *t*, before the new impulse of breath. It is to be observed that there is no necessary connection between the *quantity* and the *quality* of vowels; that is to say, that any vowel may be pronounced either long or short. In English tense (i) only occurs long, but in French it is usually quite short. Again, the *mid-front-slack* (ε) is always short in English at the present time in the standard language, but many of the dialects have (ē), which is also common in French, as in ' bête ' (bēt), etc.

Syllable Division.—The essential characteristic of a syllable is that there is no sense of break or interruption to destroy its unity. Anything which causes a break in continuity produces a sense of duality, and tends to destroy the unity of the syllable.

The interruption of the unity of a syllable may be caused in various ways:

1. By alternation of strong and weak stress. So long as the stress is even or gradually diminishing, a vowel may be prolonged indefinitely without producing upon the ear the sense of discontinuity. But if we pronounce a very long vowel, such as ($\bar{a}$), and alternately increase and diminish the stress, we at once break it up into as many syllables as there are increases and decreases: ($\acute{a}$-a-$\acute{a}$-a-$\acute{a}$-a), and so on.

2. By alternating greater and lesser sonority. The vowel (a) is more sonorous than (i), because the mouth passage is wider when pronouncing it, and consequently a bigger volume of voice can pass through. If, therefore, we alternate (a-i-a-i-a)—that is, first strong, then weak, then strong sonority—we cannot escape the sense of as many syllables as there are increases after reductions of sonority.

In a true diphthong, such as (ai), as in English ' bite,' we have, it is true, a gradual reduction of sonority and of stress ; but the sense of unity is not lost, because the reduction is so gradual, and because the second vowel loses its syllabicness by virtue of its lack of sonority as compared with the preceding (a), which also bears the stress. A true diphthong may be defined as a combination of two vowels, of which only one is syllabic, the other having neither stress nor sonority in comparison, and being therefore non-syllabic.

3. The interruption of continuity may be produced by the air-stream being either very considerably hindered,

4

through the narrowing of the mouth passage, as by an *Open Consonant*, or altogether checked for a moment, as by a *Stop Consonant*. The presence of a consonant between two vowels, since it breaks the continuity more or less completely, must of necessity produce two syllables.

The Limits of the Syllable.*—A syllable ends when the weakest degree of stress is reached, and the next begins with the fresh increase. Thus in England we pronounce the name of the famous University and golfing city of Fifeshire, *St. Andrews*, as (sənt ǽndrūz), but in Scotland itself the universal pronunciation is (sən tandrūz) ; that is, we continue to diminish the stress until the off-glide of the *t*, whereas the Scotch reach their weakest stress with the *n*.

Phonetic Symbols.

A few remarks upon the use of a phonetic transcription will not be out of place here.

The Organic symbols are, of course, by far the most accurate, since they are not mere arbitrary alphabetic signs, but are intended to express the actual positions of the organs of speech, the presence or absence of breath, of rounding, of nasality, and so on. But it is admitted that they are cumbersome, and for the transcription of words and sentences a simpler notation can be used with advantage. Sweet's *Broad Romic* is a convenient system of symbols which is widely used, and the *International* alphabet is employed by Passy, Lloyd, Vietor, and many other phoneticians.

After all, any alphabet is a mere convention, and provided we know what *sounds* we intend to express, the

* For a clear and admirable treatment of *Quantity, Syllable Division, Stress,* and *Intonation, cf.* Jespersen, *Lehrbuch der Phonetik,* 1904, pp. 173-240.

simpler the method of graphic expression the better. In dealing with a single language, or a limited series of sounds, it is best first to define in the terminology of the organic system the value of the symbols commonly employed in the ordinary spelling of the language in question, and then to adopt some familiar symbol to express the sound whenever it occurs. Thus, if we know that French *u* in ' but,' ' vu,' etc., is the high-front-tense-round, we may use any recognised symbol we choose to express it, provided our employment of the symbol be consistent. Thus ü, y would both serve the purpose. If we have defined ü or y as = *high-front-tense-round* when transcribing French, there is no reason why the same symbol should not be used to express a different sound in our transcription of another language which does not possess *h-f-t-r*. In Russian, for instance, it is often convenient to use *y* for the *high-flat-tense*, since in that language h-f-t-r does not occur.

This economic principle of using the same symbol for different sounds in different languages has the advantage of avoiding the inconvenience of mastering seventy-two perfectly arbitrary symbols for the vowels, many of which we may never need at all. In oral teaching, when demonstrating on the blackboard, and in scientific treatises, Sweet's organic symbols for the vowels are exceedingly convenient, since they are easily mastered and are perfectly definite in significance. It is useful when writing to be able to express with a single symbol such facts as the exact position of the tongue and lips, thus conveying precisely the shade of sound which we are dealing with. Otherwise we must, in exact discussion, use the cumbersome

THE SOUNDS OF SPEECH

'high-front-tense-round,' which we may, however, shorten as above to h-f-t-r, and so on with all the other vowels.

The symbol T, really a pointer indicating direction, is useful in conjunction with alphabetic signs. T means lowering of the tongue, ⊥ raising, ⊢ advancing, and ⊣ retraction. Thus if (ε) be the symbol for the normal mid-front-slack, (ε T) would indicate the lowered Scotch variety.

Tables of Phonetic Symbols for Consonants and Vowels used in this Book.

THE CONSONANTS.

	Back.		Front.		Blade.		Blade-point.		Point.	
	Breath.	Voice.	Breath.	Voice.	Breath.	Voice.	Breath.	Voice.	Breath.	Voice.
Open	h	ʒ	j̥	j	s	z	ʃ	ž	þ	ð
Stop	k	g	ċ	ġ	—	—	—	—	t	d
Nasal	—	ŋ	—	—	—	—	—	—	n̥	n
Divided ...	—	ł	—	—	—	—	—	—	l̥	l

	Lip.		Lip-teeth.		'Lip-back.	
	Breath.	Voice.	Breath.	Voice.	Breath.	Voice.
Open ...	—	—	f	v	w̥	w
Stop ...	p	b	—	—	—	—
Nasal ...	m̥	m	—	—	—	—
Divided ...	—	—	—	—	—	—

Table of Vowel Symbols and their Values.

SLACK VOWELS.
UNROUND.

	Front.	Back.	Flat.
High ...	*i*, Eng. *bit*	—	—
Mid ...	ε, Eng. *head*	a {Gm. *hat* / Eng. *father*}	ə, *father*
Low ...	æ, Eng. *cat*	—	—

ROUND.

	Front.	Back.	Flat.
High ...	—	u, Eng. *put*	—
Mid ...	—	o, Gm. *stock*	—
Low ...	—	ɔ, Eng. *hot*	—

TENSE VOWELS.
UNROUND.

	Front.	Back.	Flat.
H.	i {Fr. *si* (short) / Eng. *see* (long)}	—	ï, Scot. dial, *buik*
M.	e, Fr. *dé*	a, Eng. *but*	—
L.	—	—	ʌ, Eng. *bird*

ROUND.

	Front.	Back.	Flat.
H.	y, Fr. *lune*	u {Eng. *boot* / Gm. *blume*} (long), Scot. *put* (short)	—
M.	—	o {Gm. *lohn* (long) / Fr. *beau* (shorter)}	—
L.	—	ɔ, Eng. *saw*	—

In order not to multiply symbols beyond what is absolutely necessary, (h) will be used initially in phonetic transcription to express the ordinary 'aspirate' of Modern English; medially and finally it indicates a back-open-voiceless consonant. (r) is not included in the above table; English *r* in the South is a weak point-teeth-open consonant, in Scotch it is a point-trill, in French a back-trill. In some of the English dialects of the South and Midlands it is an *inverted* consonant—*i.e.*, an open consonant formed by the point of the tongue turned upwards and backwards.

ċ, ġ are habitually written at the present day in the ordinary spelling of O.E. to indicate fronted sounds; the latter is generally pronounced as a front-open consonant in O.E., as in *ġiefan*, 'give.' When used in the special way indicated above, all symbols are in this book enclosed in brackets; thus *ġiefan* would be (jievan), etc.

Length is marked by a stroke above the letter—*ā*, *λ̄*, etc. A vowel symbol which is not thus marked is intended to express a short sound, and shortness is otherwise not specially indicated as a rule. The symbol ˜ placed over a vowel implies nasalization, as in Fr. (kõtã) *content*.

Forms placed in brackets are intended to express the pronunciation, according to the above table of symbols. The ordinary spelling is either in italics or in inverted commas—*e.g.*, 'hot' (hɔt), 'father' (fäðə).

It will be observed that the *slack* vowels are represented by italic letters, except in the cases of (ε), (ə), and (æ), which are well known, and convenient; the symbols for the *tense* vowels are all romic. Italic letters, therefore, enclosed in brackets always indicate *slack*, and romic always *tense* vowels.

CHAPTER III

HOW LANGUAGE IS ACQUIRED AND HANDED ON

ONE of the most familiar incidents of daily life is that of
a child learning to speak. It is an experience which every
normal human being has undergone in his own person,
although the memory of the first steps is lost long before
the process is nearly complete. The infant slowly learns
to utter a few intelligible sounds in his native tongue
from those who surround him—his parents, his nurse, his
brothers and sisters. He learns by imitation to reproduce,
at first very imperfectly, the sounds which he hears, and
by constant repetition on the part of his first teachers,
accompanied by explanatory gestures, such as pointing to
a person or a thing, or performing an action while uttering its name, he gradually comes to connect the uttered
sound with the person, the object, or the action which
it symbolizes.

Those who in after-life acquire a foreign language in
the country itself, or among native speakers, nurses,
governesses, etc., in their own country, to a certain extent
repeat the process whereby they originally learnt their
own language. This is undoubtedly the most direct and
natural way of mastering a language, and, supplemented
later on by the artificial aids of grammar and dictionary,

it gives a grip of the genius of a foreign tongue, and forms the speech instinct in a way that no other method can accomplish.   It is a remarkable fact, when we reflect upon the difficulties which in later life beset the learning of a new language, especially the new pronunciation, that within a few years the child acquires with perfect exactness, in all normal cases, the pronunciation of those speakers from whom he learns his native language.   Of course, there are cases of inherent defective utterance, in which certain sounds remain difficult or even impossible to pronounce perfectly to the end of the life of the speaker.   It is also true, as we shall see, that no two speakers of the same community or the same family do, in all respects, pronounce exactly alike.   Still, the fact remains that after a few years the child can and does, to all intents and purposes, reproduce the pronunciation of the circle in which he is brought up, with so great a degree of fidelity, that his pronunciation is felt by everyone to be identical with that upon which it is based—the speech of his family and closest intimates.   It would appear that this power of learning by imitation pure and simple is, as a rule, limited to the sounds of the mother-tongue, or at most to one or two other languages which are acquired in early childhood.

To understand the reason of this we must inquire more closely what are the processes which actually come into play in the utterance of speech sounds.

First of all the organs of speech perform certain movements, in order to get into the position necessary for the production of the sound to be uttered.   This series of movements, and this position, which is maintained for a

certain time, gives rise to characteristic muscular sensations. Then the sound is uttered, and this, again, produces
a definite physical sensation upon the auditory nerves.
These muscular sensations and this auditory experience
are the physiological processes involved in each utterance
of a sound. But this is not all; each nervous impression
is recorded in the consciousness, and goes to form what
may be called *memory-pictures*. In the utterance of a
speech sound memory - pictures are formed—(*a*) of the
sound itself, (*b*) of the muscular sensations arising from
the movements of the vocal organs into the required
position, and of a certain characteristic tension required
to maintain the position during the utterance of the sound.
That is to say, that in addition to the memory-picture of
sound, there are also formed memory-pictures of the movement series and of the position. These memory-pictures
of sound, movements, and position, are the psychological
processes which accompany the utterance of every speech
sound. These memory-pictures are formed unconsciously,
but until they are formed it is impossible to reproduce a
speech sound. This is why a child only slowly acquires
the power to reproduce the sounds of his mother-tongue.
The first mental picture formed is that of the sound itself,
as heard from others. Then there is a tentative groping
to reproduce it, but the necessary series of organic movements, and the position, have generally to be learnt, as the
results of many mistaken attempts. Thus, when a child
substitutes a point-stop (t) for a back-stop (k), and says,
for instance, (t*i*s) for (k*i*s), it is probable that he can
discriminate between the two sounds when he hears them ;
but his inability to do so in his own speech is due to the

fact that he has not yet learned to form a stop with the back of his tongue, although he can do so with the point. The movement of retracting the tongue, and the position of the tongue pressed against the soft palate are unfamiliar, and have to be acquired by experiment. When once the unaccustomed movements have been performed, a faint mental picture is recorded, which makes the next utterance easier. With each repeated carrying out of a series of movements the memory-picture becomes clearer and more definite, until at last, the series being faithfully and definitely imprinted upon the memory, it can be reproduced accurately at will. The memory-picture of the sound is often more distinct, because the sound is heard not only from our own pronunciation, in which it gradually becomes associated with those of the movements and position, but also frequently in the pronunciation of others. Whereas, then, the sound-picture is made stronger by hearing other speakers, the movement and position pictures can only be made clearer by our own pronunciation of the sound. The sound-picture sometimes remains clear when the position-picture has become blurred, and faint from lack of habit in uttering the sound, in which case the former helps to correct and reconstruct the latter, because the result of our attempts at pronunciation does not satisfy our recollection of the sound.

It may be noted here that it is important not to allow those who are learning a foreign language to get into the habit of wrong pronunciation; since each repeated utterance of the wrong sound makes the memory-picture of the movements and position clearer and deeper, and therefore increasingly difficult to eradicate. Teachers who

trust to imitation alone in imparting a foreign pronunciation, often repeat the desired sound hundreds of times with
little result, the reason being that while the pupil's correct
sound - picture may indeed be strengthened, the wrong
position-picture remains uncorrected, and becomes clearer
and more imperishable each time the same mistake in
pronunciation is made. Thus a discrepancy often arises
between the memory-picture of the sound and that of
the process of reproducing it. It is this existence of the
memory-pictures of the sounds and positions which occur
in our own language, and which we have strengthened for
years by daily habit, that makes it so difficult to form
fresh memory-pictures in later life. Our speech habit
has become inveterate, and we cannot easily acquire a
different one.

With the young child the case is different. His mental
and bodily habits are of recent formation, his speech
basis is not fixed ; he can easily change it, or form a new
set of memory-pictures, both of sounds and of physical
movements : hence he can more readily acquire the sounds
of a foreign language than the adult.

The complex processes of utterance, even those involved
in producing the sounds of our mother-tongue, are for
the most part quite unrealized by the speaker. The
series of memory-pictures graven upon the consciousness
give rise to the familiar series of movements and positions,
and to the sounds associated with them, and yet we are
unaware both of the psychological and of the physiological
part of the process. A phonetic training involves learning
to realize and recognise both of these aspects of utterance.
We have to bring the mental pictures and the resultant

movements and positions from the plane of unconscious-
ness or subconsciousness to that of full consciousness.
Most people, as soon as they think about the subject, can
realize mentally, the series of movements which are necessary to the pronunciation of many of the familiar consonants, such as *p*, *t*, and even *k*, though this is more
difficult, without (even silently) going through the actual
movements themselves. But most untrained experimenters
will probably find, at first, that they are unable to realize
at all, the series of movements required for the pronunciation of even such familiar *vowel* sounds as (ī), as in
'*bee*' (bī), or (ō), as in '*saw*' (sō). To assist in bringing the
familiar but unrealized processes of pronunciation into the
realms of definite consciousness, the beginner may be
recommended to pronounce some familiar sound aloud
several times, concentrating his attention upon the movements which the vocal organs instinctively perform ; then
to ' whisper' the sound, still closely observing the movements ; then to go through the series of movements silently,
not even uttering the sound in a ' whisper'; and finally to
reproduce the series mentally, without carrying out the
movements at all. It will be seen that such an exercise
can only be carried out with sounds which are perfectly
familiar, and which the vocal organs can produce instinctively through the existence of a clear (although
subconscious) memory - picture. It follows that the
necessary and proper basis for phonetic training is the
careful study of the mother-tongue, and of that particular
form of it which we naturally and habitually use. Thus
it would be an unsound method for a dialect speaker, or
one whose pronunciation was strongly coloured by a ' pro-

vincial accent,' to begin the scientific study or sounds by considering first of all the sounds of some ideal ' *standard* ' of English speech which were quite unfamiliar, and which he would almost certainly not reproduce accurately. This is especially true of Scotch speakers, who, even if they do not speak ' *broad Scotch*,' have in nearly all cases a strongly-marked Scotch speech basis, for which there are, of course, good historical reasons. It cannot be too strongly insisted upon that the student must cultivate a ' *phonetic conscience*,' and study the sounds of his own natural speech *as they are*, without attempting to change them or ' fake ' them in any way. They are the only sounds which he is an absolute master of, which he makes instinctively and without taking thought, and they are therefore the only sounds upon which he can properly begin his observations. When he is able to analyze the mental and physical processes involved in his own natural pro-nunciation, the student can proceed, being now a master of the power of analysis, and having gained some conscious control of his vocal organs, to practise new series of move-ments, and thus to acquire new sounds.

From the above considerations, the reason for our reiterated insistence upon the importance of our own form of speech as the basis of scientific linguistic study will, perhaps, become more apparent. Anyone who has gone through the somewhat difficult mill of systematic linguistic training can but smile at the arguments adduced against beginning with the native dialect by those who are com-pletely innocent of any real knowledge of what is aimed at, or of the methods whereby it alone can be achieved.

The fact that *the processes of speech utterance are*

naturally unconscious is an important one, in view of the bearing which, as we shall see hereafter, it has upon the question of sound change. This fact can readily be ascertained by any beginner who tries to realize mentally, in the manner suggested above, *how* he produces any vowel sound which is familiar to him in his own pronunciation of English. Such an attempt will at once bring the truth of the foregoing statement home to the student in the most convincing manner. It is, however, just one of those essential general principles, an ignorance of which renders unreal and fruitless any discussion of the important question of *sound change,* and of the closely allied conception of *phonetic law.*

It is probably the too exclusive study of the literary form of language which fosters the view, so often taught, or at least implied in the teaching given, that speech is deliberate and conscious, and that the speaker, *even when talking naturally and untrammelled by conventional models,* definitely intends to pronounce in a certain way, which he elects to use rather than another.

In writing, the whole process is fraught with a certain deliberation, which is encouraged by the necessity of paying attention to the formation of the letters and the correct spelling, although even this becomes largely instinctive by long habit. There is in writing, however, a constant attention to literary form, a deliberate selection of words and forms of sentence, which takes place here to a far greater extent than is possible in any but the most studied kind of public discourse, and which is almost entirely absent from familiar and colloquial speech.

At any rate, it is certain that the natural speaker is

quite unconscious even of the precise acoustic effect of the
sounds which he uses, while of the subtle and delicate
adjustments and co-ordinations of the vocal mechanism he
is completely ignorant. He does not attempt, consciously
at least, either to preserve or to modify any sound or
syllable.

The pronunciation of other speakers, which we may call
the 'speech environment,' certainly exercises an influence
upon every individual. From others he learned his pronunciation to start with, and from those with whom he is
brought in contact throughout his life he, in a sense, goes
on learning so long as his sense of hearing lasts:—that is
to say, the speech of the individual tends to approximate
to the average speech of those with whom he is brought
into contact. This influence of one speaker upon another,
which will be discussed more at length in another chapter,
is, however, normally, unperceived by those who undergo it.

The case in which a speaker, from Scotland, let us say,
comes to England, and definitely and deliberately tries to
get rid of his 'Scotch accent,' and adopts the speech of
the South, is nothing against the general principle that
the influence of one form of speech upon another is exerted
unconsciously. In the case cited we have, to start with, a
conventional and artificial preference for Southern rather
than for Northern English, and, further, what takes place
is simply that the speaker chooses to learn another dialect.
This differs only in degree from the case in which a Dutch-
man in Germany elects to acquire and to speak German.

If it be true that the language of every speaker undergoes, throughout his life, a continuous influence from other

speakers with whom he comes in contact, it would seem as though the process of 'acquiring' a language was one which is never complete, and which never ceases while life and intelligence remain. And this is, in a sense, the case ; but it is possible and useful to set a limit in thought to the period during which the native language is being acquired. Certainly, as far as pronunciation is concerned, we may say that, up to a point, the child is still 'learning' to speak. There comes a time, however, when he has mastered all the sounds in use among those with whom he lives. Those with whom he associates most closely during this early period of life, may be considered as his 'speech parents'—those from whom he learns. After this the circle of persons with whom he comes in contact will, in all probability, be greatly widened with advancing years. The unconscious influence of this growing circle of speakers affects his pronunciation ; but less and less so after the early years, for the reason that the individual has already 'learnt' his language, has formed his own speech basis, and has an independent existence as a speaker. Therefore the *unconscious* influence of other speakers upon the pronunciation of an individual acts slowly, and is comparatively slight after this first period. As regards the other sides of language, vocabulary and sentence-structure, these are undoubtedly susceptible of unconscious modification for a very much longer period. These aspects of language are the expression of personal culture and experience, and naturally tend to become richer, more complex and more varied, with the growth of the intellectual and moral man.

The life-history of the speech of the individual is a part

of the history of the language; and so, the problem of the acquirement of his language by the individual, is part of the general problem of the development of language.

For we cannot regard language as something which is handed on in a fixed and definite form from one individual, and acquired in precisely the same form by another. It is changed, however inconsiderably, in the very process of transmission, re-minted at the outset by the crucible of the new mind into which it passes, and the slightly different physical organism, which performs afresh the movements of speech.

Thus we see that the elements of change in language lie in the transmission from one generation to another, and in the essential differences which exist between individuals.

The conception of an absolutely uniform language, existing even during a single generation, and in a single small community, is in reality a mere hypothetical assumption.

We shall now have to consider how far uniformity of speech actually does exist, in what way definite tendencies of change arise in the individual, why and to what extent these are shared by the community at large.

NOTE.—In pursuing the study of the General Principles of the development of language, which are dealt with in this and several subsequent chapters of this book, the student should consult:

SWEET: *Words, Logic, and Grammar*, Trans. Phil. Soc., 1875-1876. *History of Language*, Dent, 1900. *History of English Sounds*, §§ 1-241, Oxford, 1888.
STRONG, LOGEMANN, AND WHEELER: *History of Language*, Longmans, 1891.

PAUL: *Principien der Sprachgeschichte.*

> [An epoch-making book ; has contributed largely to form the modern point of view. Most writers on General Principles at the present day draw their inspiration primarily from it.]

WECHSSLER : *Gibt es Lautgesetze ?* 1900.

OSTHOFF AND BRUGMANN : *Vorwort* to *Morphologische Untersuchungen, Erster Theil,* 1878.

Other works will be referred to in the course of the following pages. My debt to all the above is very great —I acknowledge it here—for the general treatment of the subjects discussed in the next few chapters.

CHAPTER IV

SOUND CHANGE

By the phrase 'sound change' is meant those changes in pronunciation which take place in every language in the course of time. It is easy to convince ourselves that changes of pronunciation have occurred in English, for instance, in the last 200 years. Pope's lines—

> 'And praise the easy vigour of a line,
> Where Denham's strength, and Waller's sweetness join'

—are often quoted to illustrate the fact, borne out by other evidence, that the rhymes in his time were (ləin—džəin). Again, the same poet writes:

> 'Fearing ev'n fools, by flatterers besieged,
> And so obliging, that he ne'er obliged,'

where the last word was undoubtedly pronounced (ōblīdžd). These rhymes at least illustrate the fact that less than 200 years ago two English words were pronounced by a cultivated person like Pope, who frequented the best English society of his day, in a manner which at the present time would strike people of the same standing as strange, if not vulgar.

If we consider the written records of still earlier periods of our language in the light of that method of interpreting the old symbols which we owe primarily to the late

Mr. A. J. Ellis, the differences of pronunciation which we
are able to feel certain existed between the speech of these
periods and that of the present day are so great that,
putting aside the other differences of vocabulary and the
general structure of the language, we cannot doubt that
the English of King Alfred, of Chaucer, and even of
Shakespeare, would be largely unintelligible to us, if we
were able to 'hold an hour's communion with the dead.'

If this remarkable amount of change has taken place in
a few centuries in the pronunciation of several generations
of Englishmen living in England, how much greater will be
the degree of change which the pronunciation of one and
the same language will undergo in the course of several
thousands of years among separate nations living in
widely remote countries! We can form some idea of the
possibilities of the extent of divergence from an original
form under these conditions if we consider the diversity
which the same word exhibits in the various Aryan
families of speech.

It might seem at the first blush improbable or impossible
that Scrt. *dhūmas*, Gk. $\theta\acute{\upsilon}\mu\text{os}$, Lat. *fūmus*, O.Sl. *dўmŭ*, Gothic
dauns, O.E. *dū-st*, from earlier **dunst* (Eng. *dust*), can
have anything in common as regards form, and yet, unless
the modern science of Comparative Philology is entirely
vain and its methods futile, all these words are merely the
various pronunciations, developed in the course of long ages,
of the same original word or 'root' among different branches
of Aryan speech.   In the case of the O.E. word *dŭst* there
is also a difference of suffix; Lat., Gk., Scrt. and O.Sl. agree
in having an original long *ū* compared with a short, but
also original vowel in the other languages ; while the Gothic

dauns has, again, a different, but equally original, form of the vowel; otherwise the above forms are completely cognate.

It is proposed in this chapter to discuss how, and from what cause, the sounds of speech undergo change.

And first let us say that, although the phrase 'sound change' is convenient and in universal use, it is, from the point of view of strict accuracy, erroneous.   For we are to consider that a sound in itself cannot change ; it is uttered and is gone : it has in itself no permanence.   When we say that the *same sound* is repeated, we mean that an identical, or nearly identical, series of movements of the vocal organs is performed, and that the same acoustic effect is produced as upon a former occasion.

The permanent element in uttered speech—that part, therefore, which is capable of a historical development— is the psychological element, those groups of memory-pictures upon which we dwelt in the preceding chapter.

The pronunciation of the same word in the same community is different from one age to another ; we say, speaking loosely, that in this case the sounds of the community have changed.   What has really happened is that the underlying memory-pictures of sound and movements undergo gradual modification, and are different in one age from what they were in a former, and, in all probability, from what they will be later on.

If this is borne in mind, we may continue to speak of '*sound change*,' meaning thereby a change in the aggregate of mental pictures possessed by all the individuals of a community, the result of which is that a series of *substitutions* takes place of one sound for another, until the sounds actually pronounced by a later generation in the same word differ widely from those pronounced by an earlier generation (*cf.* Wechssler, pp. 26, 27).

If the pronunciation of a language changes, it can only be due to the fact that the vocal organs are used by the members of a community in a different way at one period from what they are at another; the series of movements of the vocal organs, the positions which these assume in speaking, and therefore the underlying mental pictures of these, have been modified.

We have said that that group of physical movements and those underlying groups of mental pictures which exist at any moment among the members of a community constitute what is known as the 'speech basis.'

An inquiry into the causes and processes of sound change, then, is actually an inquiry into the conditions under which the speech basis of a community is gradually modified.

It will be convenient to consider the question, in the first instance, as it affects the individual, since the speech of a community is obviously merely the collective utterance of the individuals of which it is composed. The relation of the individual to his community will be discussed in the next chapter.

All bodily movements which are the result of volition can only be carried out by virtue of the subconscious memory - picture which they reproduce each time the action is repeated. Until this memory-picture is formed, the series of movements is uncertain and imperfect. If we take the case of such a highly-specialized series of co-ordinated movements as those necessary to 'cast a fly' in fishing, or of using a billiard cue so as to produce a 'screw,' it is evident that these, like the series of movements of the vocal organs which produce a speech sound, can only be successfully carried out as the result of considerable practice. In all cases the memory-picture must be clear and definite. Now, it is evident that although a practised fisherman can generally throw a fly so as to produce approximately the desired result—in this case, that is to say, to put it modestly, at least in such a way as not to flick the fly off—he nevertheless does not reproduce in each successive cast precisely and absolutely the same series of movements; there are variations in the degree of force, in the direction, in the curves described by the hand as it is raised and brought forward again after the line has been straightened behind the fisherman, and in many other ways too subtle to analyze. Yet each successful cast (successful in the sense indicated above) satisfies the person who performs the movements: he feels that he has cast his fly in the proper way. This merely means that, in spite of divergence, the series of movements corresponds to, and reproduces the memory-picture of the process sufficiently exactly for the divergence not to be appreciable. A certain possible limit of deviation from the memory-picture exists, within which the departure is unperceived. If, however, the divergence of the action from the memory-picture of this be too great, the fisherman is conscious of it, and feels that he has made a bad throw—a fact of which the loss of his fly probably adds further confirmation.

In just the same way, the actions of the vocal organs in speech, reproduce the memory-pictures approximately, though not always exactly. Here, again, if the movement-series deviates beyond a certain extent from the

mental picture, the divergence is recognised, partly by
the actual muscular sensation, but more generally by
reason of the divergence of the result from the memory-
picture of the sound.

But the memory-pictures themselves are not homogeneous, and composed of only one kind of impression;
for each repeated utterance of the sound leaves its trace
upon the mental picture. Upon the mind is recorded
each divergence from the original picture—that is, a new
impression of a slightly different character is made. Of
the various impressions recorded, the most recent are the
deepest and most potent; so that in the course of time the
new impressions outweigh the older in the memory-picture.
Thus in time the aggregate of impressions result in a
memory-picture which is of a slightly different character
from the old one. From this new memory-picture the
same degree of unperceived divergence is possible, this
degree being always constant; but since the memory-
picture itself has been modified, the starting-point of
divergence has also been shifted slightly further from the
original point of departure.

To put the matter in another way, if the change in
pronunciation is sufficiently gradual, if it does not proceed further than a certain point at a time, the individual
does not perceive the slight shifting which has taken
place, and the impression is unconsciously recorded. If,
however, the pronunciation at a given moment of utterance is too far from what the speaker instinctively feels to
be the normal, he at once perceives the difference, and
'corrects' the result as a 'mistake' or a 'slip of the
tongue.' Thus, on account of the inherent instability of

the organs of speech and the habits of using them, the pronunciation of each individual is continually liable to slight
variation, and therefore, gradually, to permanent alteration.

Variation in the speech of the individual is, according
to the above statements, in the natural and inevitable
order of things.   The speech basis is gradually modified,
and with it the sounds change.

This natural shifting of the speech basis is the cause of
all change in sound, when this is gradual and regular.

Sound changes are conveniently divided into two main
classes : *Isolative Changes*, which take place independent
of other neighbouring sounds in the word or sentence, and
uninfluenced by them ; and *Combinative Changes*, in which
sounds are modified by others which occur in close
proximity to them.   Both classes of changes depend
upon the shifting of the organic basis of speech.   It may
be well to give at once concrete examples from our own
language of each kind of change.

Isolative Changes.—Down to the end of the fifteenth
century, or the beginning of the sixteenth, the long
sound (ū), whether inherited from Old English or acquired
(in French words) during the Middle English period, persisted, so far as we can tell, practically unaltered, unless,
indeed, it was shortened by other *combinative* factors.
About the date above mentioned, however, in the South,
and far North into the Midlands, (ū) was gradually diphthongized by a process which we need not now discuss,
until it reached, probably by the middle of the eighteenth
century, its present sound of (*au*), as in 'house' (ha*u*s),
'ground (gra*u*nd), etc.   Another isolative change of
comparatively recent origin is that of the eighteenth-

century (ǣ) sounds to (ä). Almost all (ä) sounds which occur in Modern English, as in 'father' (fäðə), 'rather' (räðə), 'clerk' (kläk), go back to eighteenth-century (ǣ) sounds, the forms of these words in that century being (fǣðər, rǣðər, klǣrk). This change involves a gradual retraction of the tongue from a *low-front* vowel position to ⸱ that of the *low-back*, which has been subsequently raised, nearly everywhere, to the *mid-back*, the present sound. It is curious to reflect that during part of the eighteenth century the sound (ä) did not exist in the standard dialect of English. Foreign words, introduced during this period, which contained (ä) in the language from which they were borrowed, still retain the sound (ɔ̄), which was then substituted for the original (ä); thus 'brandy pawnee' = (pɔ̄ni), Scrt. *pāni*, 'water'; and the place-names Cabul (Kɔ̄bul) for *Kābul*, and *Cawnpore* (Kɔ́npɔ̄[ə]). In the same way the now slightly vulgar pronunciation (vɔ̄z) 'vase' represents, no doubt, an eighteenth-century attempt at the French sound (väz).

An old-fashioned pronunciation of 'rather' as (reiðə), which still obtains in America, and, curiously enough, in this country also, amongst school-boys, though only as form of peculiar emphasis, goes back to a different type, eighteenth-century (rēðər), which can be shown to have existed side by side with the type (rǣðər). This form must be still further derived from a M.E. type, *räðer* (räðer), whereas our modern form (räðə) is from a M.E. *rǎðer*, the first vowel of which was fronted to (ǎ) giving (ræðər) in the sixteenth, and (rǣðər), with vowel-lengthening before (ð), in the seventeenth or early eighteenth century. With the exception of this com-

binative lengthening, all the changes which the two
M.E. types *raðer* and *rāðer* have undergone are isolative
in character.

Combinative Changes.—The number of these in the
history of English, as, indeed, in that of most languages,
is very large. A few examples will suffice for the moment.

The two words '*cold*' and '*chill*' are both derived from
the same root (although they have different suffixes),
but different combinative factors have determined their
respective forms.

In O.E. these words appear as *cāld*, an Anglian form,
and *ċiele*, a West Saxon form. It is the difference of the
initial with which we are primarily concerned here. In
'*cold*,' from O.E. *cāld*, from Gmc. **kalda-*, the initial
consonant, a voiceless back-stop, is the original consonant,
and has undergone no change, being followed by a back
vowel; in '*chill*,' however, the O.E. *ċiele* presupposes an
earlier, primitive Old West Saxon **ċeali*, from a still earlier
*kœli, which comes from a Gmc. **kali-*. In this case the
original Gmc. back-stop has been fronted in West Saxon
to a front-stop, which has developed into the Modern
English 'ch-' (tʃ) sound. This is an example of the
fact that in prehistoric O.E. a back-stop was fronted to a
front-stop before a following front vowel—in this case (æ)
low-front. Wherever in Modern English what is popularly
called the ' ch- ' sound (tʃ) occurs in words of native
English origin, it is derived from an earlier *k*, fronted,
during the O.E. period, through the influence of a following
original front vowel,—one that is, which was already front
in the oldest English period.

Other examples of this combinative fronting of an

earlier *k* through the influence of a following front vowel are: O.E. *ċin(n)*, Mod.E. '*chin*,' with which compare Gothic *kinnus*, O.E. *cyċene*, an early loan - word from Latin *coquīna*, through an intermediate form, *kukina. In this O.E. word the second *k* was fronted before the front vowel *i*, whereas the initial remains a back consonant, because the following *y*, although also a front vowel, did not become so until the tendency for such vowels to affect preceding consonants had passed away. These processes will be described later on in more detail, in dealing specifically with O.E. sound changes.

Another combinative tendency which affects a large number of words in O.E. was that to round back vowels before nasal consonants. Thus we have reason to know that the O.E. *mōna*, 'moon,' came from an earlier form, *mānō, with the unrounded (*ā*) (mid- or low-back) in the first syllable. It is probable that the vowel itself was first slightly nasalized, and this nasal (*ã*) gradually tended to acquire a rounded pronunciation, just as the nasal vowel in *en*, *an*, in French, as in *enfant* (*ãfã*), is rounded, in the pronunciation of most French speakers, sometimes to a very considerable extent.

Now, it is characteristic of all tendencies of change in pronunciation, both Isolative and Combinative, that they obtain only for a period in the history of a language, and then pass away. Thus, for instance, as we have seen at a certain time, the speakers of Old English tended to pronounce back consonants before front vowels more and more forward, until at last they were uttered as wholly front consonants. But this habit died out, since we find that this modification of back consonants does not take place before those front vowels which were developed by a later process from earlier back vowels. We pronounce, to the present day, a back consonant in ' *kin*,' and therefore can have no doubt that the O.E. word *cynn*, ' race,' ' family,' also had a back consonant (k) initially, although the next sound in the word, *y* (high-front-round), is just as much a front vowel as *i* in O.E. *ćin*, ' chin.' But O.E. *y* in the former word was originally *u*, as we can see from a comparison with the Gothic *kuni*, which preserves the older form of the vowel. The O.E. *y* sound was developed by a fronting of original *u*, at a period at which there was no longer any tendency on the part of English speakers to advance the place of articulation of *k* when it came immediately before a front vowel.

According to the varying speech habits, the same combination of sounds is differently treated, not only in different dialects or languages, but in the same language at different periods. The so-called *Sound Laws*, or *Phonetic Laws*, therefore, are merely statements to the effect that at a given time, a given community tended to alter the pronunciation of such and such a sound, or combination of sounds, in such and such a way. This, of course, does not prevent the same tendency arising, independently, in totally unrelated languages, or more than once in the same language.

The problem of combinative changes is no less difficult than that of isolative changes. It is true that, in the former case, the immediate phonetic or physiological causes which determine the change are generally apparent; but these causes are not of universal operation, as we have seen from the fact that different languages, or the same language at different periods of its history, may treat the same combination of sounds in different ways, now leaving it unaltered, now altering it in this way or that.

This transitoriness of tendencies of sound change has already been illustrated by those combinative processes in the history of English to which passing reference has been made, but further illustration may be useful to show with what varying force they obtain, even among the different dialects of the same language.

A good example of this is the process known as '*u-ă-Umlaut*,' which began in O.E., probably early in the eighth century. Briefly stated, this process consisted in the development of a vowel-glide after a front vowel when a back rounded vowel follows in the next syllable. This vowel-glide apparently develops into a full vowel, which combines with the preceding to produce a diphthong. Thus an original *widu*, 'wood,' becomes **wi^u du*, then *wiudu*, whence *wiodu* in Northumbrian, and *weodu* (*wudu*) in Mercian and West Saxon.

The O.E. dialects vary considerably, both in the extent to which this diphthonging takes place, and also in the conditions which promote its occurrence.

In West Saxon, Northumbrian, and part of the Kentish area, *æ* remains unaffected by a following *u, o, a;* in Mercian, on the other hand, original *æ*, when followed by one of these vowels, is diphthongized, first to *æ^u, æu, æo, æa, ea*, the latter being the ordinary spelling. Thus in W.S. and Northumbrian the plural of *fæt*, 'cup,' 'vessel' (Mod.E. '*vat*'), is *fatu*, from **fætu*, with un-fronting of *æ* to *a* before the following *u*, but in Mercian *featu*.

The vowels *i* and *e* are diphthongized, to a certain

extent, in all dialects, but the conditions under which this occurs are far more limited in W.S. than in the other dialects; also *u* produces diphthongization much more readily in this dialect than *a* or *o*. Thus, after *w, i* became *iu < io < eo* quite normally, no matter what the intervening consonant may be: *cwicu*, 'living,' becomes *cweocu; widu < weodu* (whence, later, *c(w)ucu, wudu*), otherwise the vowel remains undiphthongized, except when *l, r,* or the lip consonants intervene: sicol, '*sickle*,' from **sikul*, *niȝun*, 'nine,' from **niȝun*, *sinu*, 'sinew,' *hnitu*, 'nit'; but *sweotol* (and *swutol*), 'clear,' from **switul*, meolc (earlier *miuluc*), from **miluk*, 'milk,' *seofon*, 'seven,' from **siƀun*, *cleopode*, 'called,' from **cliupode*, earlier *clipode*, pret. of *clipian*, and so on.

Under approximately the same conditions original *e* becomes *eu*, then *eo*: *eofor*, 'wild boar,' from *eƀur, heorot*, 'hart,' from earlier *herut*, *heolstor*, 'darkness,' from earlier *helustor;* but *regol*, 'rule,' an early loan-word from the Latin *regula, fetor*, 'fetter,' from **fetur*, *sprecol*, from earlier *sprecul*, 'loquacious.'

It appears, from the above examples, that in W.S. the tendency to diphthongization did not arise when the intervening consonant was a point-teeth or back, unless *w* preceded the *i* or *e*.

In the Kentish dialect of O.E., on the other hand, *i* and *e*, and, in some early texts, *æ* also, appear to be diphthongized, whenever *u* follows in the next syllable, whether *w* precedes or not, and no matter what the nature of the intervening consonant. Thus we find such forms as *reogol*, 'rule,' *breogo*, 'prince,' from **bregu*, *freoðu*- (in names), when W.S. has *friðu*-. Such Kentish forms as '*to nio-*

manne,' 'to take,' *forgeofan* (inf.), earlier *-*geƀan*, where *i*
and *e* are diphthongized by a following *a,* are quite foreign
to W.S., which has *nimanne*, giefan (also from *geƀan*, by
a process peculiar to W.S. (p. 236).

Mercian and Northumbrian also diphthongize *i* and *e*
freely ; the former *œ* as well, but before a following back
consonant (*c* or *g*) the diphthong is 'smoothed' or monophthongized again, in these dialects, by a tendency which
arose subsequent to the *u-, a-, o-Umlaut.* Thus in Mercian
dœgum, *dœgas* (dat. and nom.-acc. pl. of *dœg*, 'day')
apparently became *dœ^ugum*, etc., but were subsequently
smoothed to *dœgum, dœgas*, which are the forms actually
found in the principal Mercian text (*Vespasian Psalter*).

These processes of diphthongization did not arise, so far
as we know, in any of the O.E. dialects before the beginning of the eighth or, at earliest, the end of the seventh
century, and when once the above changes were complete,
the speech habit which produced them died out, never
again to be revived.*

It might appear that the problem of *Combinative
Change* differs essentially from that of *Isolative Change*,
since in the former case the 'causes' can be discovered and
stated, whereas in the latter case it is only possible to
state that this or that change occurs, undetermined, however, so far as we can discover, by the nature of the
surrounding sounds. But since, as we have seen, the
'causes' of *Combinative Change* depend for their effectiveness upon the natural speech tendencies which obtain at

* A very full account, and copious illustrations of every class of
Isolative and Combinative Sound Change, will be found in Paul
Passy's *Changements Phonétiques du Langage*, Paris, 1891.

the moment throughout a community, it is evident that the real determining 'cause' of this class of sound changes, as of isolative changes, is the speech basis. It is the general habit of speech which produces among a group of speakers the tendency to a given treatment of a combination of sounds, no less than to that of the isolated sound. Some German writers (*e.g.*, Sievers, in his *Phonetik*) employ the terms '*bedingt*,' or '*caused*,' sound change for combinative, as distinct from '*unbedingt*,' or '*uncaused*,' for isolative change. These terms are misleading, unless it be clearly borne in mind that both classes of change are ultimately caused or determined by the natural tendencies which are inseparable from a given speech basis. It is only by virtue of this that the pronunciation of a sound, at a given moment in the history of a language, tends to be influenced by the surrounding sounds.

We cannot explain the reason of the rise and passing away of these tendencies ; we can only shift the matter a stage further back, and say that they are inseparably associated with the speech basis of the community at the moment, and that, since this is unstable, so also the tendencies to variation must necessarily be in different directions at different times and among different communities.

The real problem of the causes of sound change, then, is put in the question, What factors determine the precise nature of the speech basis of a community at a particular period ? If we could answer this question, we should solve the question which is involved in it, namely, Why do the speakers of a community show at one period a set of tendencies in pronunciation, a group of speech habits, which are quite foreign to their ancestors or their descendants in

former or later ages?—we should be far nearer than we
are at present to solving one of the most important problems connected with the evolution of speech.

Many attempts have been made to account for the
general fact that the sounds of language change, but none
are wholly satisfactory. The simple question, What is it
that modifies the speech basis of a community? remains
unanswered, or, at best, only partially answered.

Formerly all sound change was ascribed to the inherent
laziness of men, who were said to be for ever striving after
increased ease of utterance. This was the view of the
eminent philologist Schleicher (*Deutsche Sprache*, pp. 50 and
following) and Whitney the Sanscrit scholar (*Language and
its Study*, 1875, pp. 42, 43, and *Life and Growth of Language*,
1886, p. 49, etc.). It must be urged against this theory
that ease and difficulty are very relative terms—familiar
sounds being, as a rule, easy, unfamiliar sounds difficult;
and although a certain absolute difficulty might, perhaps, be
asserted to exist in certain sound combinations, they are
nevertheless preserved in some languages. Some changes
which occur in language seem to be in the direction rather
of increased than less effort. The real answer, however,
is that the fact of ease or difficulty existing among a given
community in the pronunciation of certain sounds depends
upon their speech basis.

A desire for *Euphony* is another popular explanation,
which formerly received the support of authorities—*e.g.*,
Bopp, *Vgl. Gr.*, pp. 7, 77, 96, 274, etc.; *Vocalismus*,
pp. 18, 29; also Scherer, *Geschichte d. deutschen Spr.*,
pp. 136-138. This suggestion must be at once rejected
when we reflect that pronunciation changes gradually,

without the deliberate intention, or even the knowledge, of the speakers; and, further, that the deliberate alteration of pronunciation for the purpose of producing a more beautiful effect upon the ear would make sound change largely a matter of personal whim, which would result in endless diversity—to the extent of imperilling intelligibility—within the same community.

The influence of *Climate* was pressed by Osthoff (*Das physiologische und das psychologische Moment in der Sprachlichen Formenbildung*, 1879) as a means of accounting for the diversity of treatment of the same original sounds among the various groups of Aryan speakers. It cannot be denied that climate, since it determines so largely the general mode of life, the social organization, and the bodily habits of a community, and originally possibly even the racial characters must also, to some extent, at least, affect the language. And yet the sounds of a language go on changing throughout the centuries, while the people continue to live under the same climatic conditions. It would seem more probable that climate might help to predispose the speech basis of a community in a new direction, if a tribe migrated from its original seat to a new and very different geographical area, but that when the climatic conditions had once produced their effect, or continued to produce them upon each succeeding generation, they would rather tend to conserve than to alter the speech basis, unless, of course, some marked change of climate came about. At any rate, so far, no specific sound change has ever been related, with certainty, to any definite conditions of climate, and it seems as if the most that we can say is, that climate may contribute to produce a speech basis which inherently tends to vary along certain lines, although the connection between the two has never yet been shown.

Darmsteter (*La Vie des Mots*, 1887, p. 7) and Passy (*Changements Phonétiques du Langage*, 1891, pp. 230-235) maintain that sound change is primarily due to the 'mistakes' and faulty imitation of the pronunciation of their elders by children when learning to speak. This amounts to saying that children never perfectly master the sounds of their native language, a view which seems to be contradicted by experience; for the grosser 'mistakes' of children are soon corrected, and at seven or eight years of age the normal child is usually completely conversant with all the sounds in use among the community in which he lives. Besides, it is not explained how it comes about that all the children of the same generation make approximately the *same* 'mistakes'; or, in other words, why, if sound change has its roots in 'mistakes' of this kind, the pronunciation of a given community tends to vary on practically homogeneous lines. It is, of course, true that language changes from generation to generation, in the very process, as we have seen, of being handed on, but this is because the rising generation begins, as it were, where the former leaves off; their speech is the reproduction of the most recent developments of their parents' speech, and has, therefore, a slightly different starting-point of deviation. Thus, if the norm of the parents' speech be represented by a, with a possible, unperceived deviation represented by a^4, the children's norm will perhaps be a^3, with the range of possibilities of deviation, bringing the limit to a^7. There is also an element of variation in the

fact that individuals are differently constituted, mentally
and physically, so that the learner's speech can never be
an exact reproduction of that of his parents. But these
personal peculiarities in speech cannot, normally, exceed
the limits at which they are recognisable.

Lastly, in enumerating the various explanations proposed, we may mention the factor which has been emphasized by Hirt (*Indogermanische Forschungen,* iv.,pp. 36-45),
and quite recently, and more fully, by Wechssler (*Gibt es
Lautgesetze?* 1900), as chief among the influences which
modify the speech basis—namely, contact with foreign
speakers.

The nature of this influence is easily grasped. In
attempting to reproduce the sounds of a foreign language
we inevitably, as has been already pointed out, attempt to
imitate the strange sounds by uttering those sounds which
are nearest to them, according to our own perceptions, in
our own language. We never completely acquire the new
series of movements—that is, the speech basis of the foreign
tongue—but tend to modify the sounds, according to our
own familiar habits of articulation. Thus in time may we
indeed acquire a new speech basis, one different from our
own, but differing, also, more or less, from that of the
language we are trying to speak. The result is practically
a new form of speech which is neither one thing nor the
other. If we conceive of this process on a much larger
scale, as when two races come into social contact and acquire
each other's language, subsequently the speech of one will
predominate, that of the other dying out, with the result
that the speech basis of the whole area occupied by the
two groups of speakers has been shifted: first in the

mouths of the foreigners, and then, if these and their descendants are really assimilated, so that the two races are welded into a single community, by the reaction of the new manner of speech on the old. [In the primitive wanderings of races the process of the incorporation of peoples speaking different languages must continually be going on.

The further question of how far racial characteristics tell in moulding the speech basis, is also involved in the above hypothesis. Are we to add race mixture as a further influence on the language arising from foreign contact ? ?

It seems evident that such obvious points as the degree of thickness of the lips, the length and general size of the tongue, the facial angle, the shape and size of the nose, all of which are characteristic racial features, must play a considerable part in determining the original speech basis; and there may be subtler points of anatomical structure which play a part, as well as the general temperament and natural bodily habit.

But so far the anatomists have done but little to show the precise connection between the physical structure of races and the speech basis therewith associated.

In the absence of precise knowledge it is, perhaps, safer to assume that, within limits, the speech organs are so adaptable that an individual of any race can acquire the speech habits of any other, provided his linguistic training begins in childhood, and that the structural differences between the vocal organs of the various races are of less importance, on the whole, in determining the speech basis, than are those particular habits of using the organs, which are acquired in infancy by the unconscious and natural process of learning the mother-tongue, understanding by this phrase the language which a child learns first.

It seems that a change in the speech basis need not imply a modification in the structure of the speech organs themselves, but only of the mode of using them.

At the same time, it is a reasonable inference that the speech basis *is*, under normal conditions, related to the actual sh e and structure of the organs of speech, and therefore that the more two races differ in physical type, the greater will be the differences in their natural speech habits. In this sense, the effect of foreign speakers in modifying the speech basis of a community, will be in proportion to the degree of separation between the two races. The more unlike one race is to another in temperament and physical type, the greater will be the difference between the natural tendencies of their speech organs; the more considerable, therefore, the modification which the language of each will undergo in the mouths of speakers of the other race.

The views of Hirt and Wechssler are widely accepted at the present moment, and there can be no doubt that the suggestion which they contain is a most valuable one in explaining, for instance, the differences which exist between the several groups of the Aryan family of languages, or the different branches of the Latin tongues—Italian, Spanish, French, Provençal, etc., all of which have been developed from closely-allied forms of popular Latin; but the explanation does not always apply to the case where a single language in the course of its history develops, as we have seen is the case in English, quite different tendencies in succeeding periods, without it being possible to show the

connection between these tendencies, and any specific
characteristic in other languages which have come into
contact with it by conquest or otherwise. It might be
maintained that those well-marked sound changes which
distinguish Old English from the other West Germanic
languages are, in some obscure way, due to the influence of
native British speakers of Celtic origin, and later on of
Scandinavians, and that the impulse to the sound changes
which characterize the Middle English period had its
origin in the speech of the Normans; but even if such
a theory could be substantiated, which is in the highest
degree improbable, what foreign influence is responsible
for the very considerable changes which have taken place
in English pronunciation since the sixteenth century?

A factor which has hitherto hardly been considered, and
which has certainly not been systematically investigated, is
Occupation. There can be little doubt that the prolonged
use of certain parts of the body in a particular way tends
not only to affect the form and function of the parts
themselves, but also, indirectly, induces a certain general
bodily habit. There are many such modifications of the
individual which affect the organs of speech, and may predispose the person concerned to a particular mode of using
these. Thus it might be supposed that such work as
swinging a scythe or flail would develop the muscles of the
chest and throat, in such a way as to affect the utterance.
Again, the constant necessity to shout, which exists in
noisy occupations, such as that of the fisherman or sailor,
who has to make himself heard through the storm, or that
of the blacksmith or factory hand, who must make their
voices rise above the clang of the hammer on the anvil, or the

hum and clashing of machinery, can but produce a permanent habit of speaking loud, which may affect the quality
of the sounds uttered. Another point is that in speaking
from a distance or amid noise, certain speech sounds
become practically useless, because they are inaudible—
namely, voiceless consonants, especially the stops. Under
these conditions the vowels are all-important, particularly
those of the stressed syllables. These remarks are merely
thrown out as a suggestion of a possible source of the
modification of the speech basis. In any case, occupation
can hardly be omitted from the forces which affect the
development of language.

Of all the above factors which, it has been maintained,
modify the speech basis, none can be considered wholly
sufficient to explain all cases ; and, although we may admit
that race, climate, occupation, and foreign contact, each and
all play their part in determining the physical and mental
habits of a community, we must also recognise that the
whole question is still very obscure, and that at present we
know neither the precise way in which speech is affected by
these modifying factors, nor how any of them, while
remaining to all appearance constant, can yet produce
tendencies of change, now in this way, now in that, in the
pronunciation of a single language.

In fact, so far as the history of a single language is concerned, which is spoken for a long period by the same race,
in the same geographical area, and under identical climatic
conditions, unaffected, for long periods at any rate, by any
alien language, it is hardly too much to say that, although
we can understand why the pronunciation should indeed
be liable to change, we can, as yet, form no idea as to why

such a language develops just those specific changes in its sound system which, as a matter of fact, actually occur, nor why these arise at one period rather than another. For the present, the words of M. Paul Passy (*Changements Phonétiques*, § 617) remain true: 'En somme, ce que nous savons sur les causes premières des changements phonétiques est bien peu de chose. Nous constatons que dans tel dialecte, à tel moment, telle ou telle tendance phonétique prédomine; pourquoi prédomine-t-elle, nous l'ignorons, ou nous pouvons tout au plus le conjecturer.'

CHAPTER V

DIFFERENTIATION OF LANGUAGE: THE RISE OF DIALECTS

THE problem now before us is how, from an originally uniform and homogeneous form of speech, there are developed, in the course of time, innumerable varieties— dialects which differ in varying degrees one from the other in essential features of pronunciation, and languages which are so distinct that only the most searching historical investigation can reveal their original affinity.

We may say at once that there is no radical difference between a 'Dialect' and a 'Language.' From the moment that two forms of speech present what we somewhat vaguely call 'dialectal' differences, which mark them as separate, the potentialities exist for infinite divergence. Under favourable conditions the two dialects may grow wider and wider apart, until not only are the two groups of speakers mutually unintelligible, but their common origin could never be suspected without the application of rigid historical and comparative method.

The distinction between a 'Dialect' and a 'Language' is only one of the degree of differentiation from the original type.

We have seen that the starting-point of sound change

lies in the individual speaker. A change in the speech of
a community is the result of the tendencies of a host of
individuals. It has been pointed out that every individual
differs slightly from every other ; how, then, can we speak
of a community possessing a homogeneous language ?
Further, we may ask, What is the precise relation of the
speech of the individual to that of the community ?

It is as well to know clearly what we mean by the term
'community,' and it may be defined, for purposes of linguistic discussion, as a group of individuals who, by reason
chiefly of the frequency of their social intercourse, naturally use the same form of speech, and among whom the
individual differences are so slight that they are inappre-
ciable. We speak of the 'community at large,' generally
meaning thereby all persons who live in these islands.
But within this large group of human beings there are
many smaller groups and sections of the community.
The smaller the social division, the closer must be the
bond between the members of it, the more frequent and
intimate their intercourse. Thus the inhabitants of a
province, county, or large city form a little community or
State by themselves, whose members are to a great extent
independent of, and shut off from the influence of, other
counties and cities. Normally, the communication and
opportunities for social intercourse of such a group of
persons among themselves are greater than those between
them and the members of other similar groups outside
their own. But even within the limits of the county or
province, still smaller and more closely knit communities
exist, in the villages and the hamlets included within the
wider division. The hamlets and villages, again, are

made up of groups of separate families, and these, the narrowest and closest of all divisions of society, consist of individuals.

In the strict sense, the limits of a speech community are comparatively narrow. Only such persons who, by virtue of their place of abode, and their occupations, and their general conditions of life, are brought into constant, and more or less intimate social intercourse, can be said to constitute a speech community. In the country, the village is generally coextensive with the speech community; in large towns the population forms itself into speech communities in the narrow sense, on principles which are largely determined by class and occupation; but also to some extent by the actual distribution of the inhabitants throughout the various quarters and districts of the city.

Among the members of the community, in the narrowest sense, there exist not only actual differences of pronunciation, but also differences of tendency—one individual tends to vary his pronunciation in this way, another in that. But these differences of actual pronunciation, and of tendency to change, are usually so slight, that they are unperceived, both by the individual himself and by the community among whom he lives. They arise, as we have seen, quite naturally, from the differences of mental and physical organization; but they do not progress beyond a certain point, partly because of the unconscious effort of the speaker to reproduce exactly the sounds which he habitually hears, and partly because social intercourse, whereby the speech is acquired and handed on, no less than the fact that all the speakers of the community are under

practically identical conditions of life, naturally contributes
to produce approximately the same habits of mind and
body, therefore the same speech basis, and consequently
the same pronunciation, and the same tendencies of change,
in all the members of the community.

The majority of tendencies of variation in speech habit
which exist in the individual will be shared also by the
speech community at large, so that they will be strengthened and encouraged by social intercourse. Those tendencies, on the other hand, which are peculiar to the
individual, and which are not shared by the community,
will not gain ground, but will be eliminated.   The
strongest and most clearly marked of these individual
tendencies will be unconsciously suppressed, or, in some
cases even, will be deliberately checked in youth, by the
corrective ridicule of associates ; others, which are not
sufficiently marked to be generally noticeable, either disappear naturally with the definite acquirement of the
speech basis, or may continue to exist, so long as they do
not develop beyond the point at which they are recognisable by the speaker himself and by his companions.   Thus
there is in every community a certain body of tendency
which is common to all speakers, and this develops, unperceived and gradual, but also, for the time being,
unchecked.

Allowing, then, for the slight and unrecognised differences which exist between individual and individual, we may
say that the speech of a community, in the special sense
above defined, is homogeneous for all practical purposes ;
and, allowing for the elimination of the purely individual
tendencies, which do not jump with the general trend of

speech habit, we may further say that all the members of such a community will tend, at a given time, to change their speech basis, and therefore their pronunciation, in one and the same direction.

Now, it is clear that this uniformity of pronunciation, and this agreement in direction of change, presuppose the existence of a community in the sense in which we have defined it—namely, under such conditions that all the members have equal opportunities of intercourse with each other. If, however, this state of things be altered or upset, if circumstances arise which make this social intercourse less frequent, and less intense at any point within the community, or which create conditions in the mode of life which affect the community unequally; then we can no longer regard the groups of speakers thus unequally affected, and variously circumstanced, as one community in the terms of our definition, but must consider that there are as many communities as there are centres of disturbance of the original conditions. We may regard the groups of speakers thus formed as isolated the one from the other, the degree of isolation being measured by the degree of interruption of the social intercourse which formerly existed.

Now, when isolation occurs, which splits one community into two or more groups, the necessary conditions are present for the differentiation of the originally homogeneous speech into dialects. Each group will tend to develop its language along different lines, and the differences, slight enough in the beginning, may in time attain considerable proportions. The reason why the different groups of speakers necessarily grow further and further

apart as regards their language is not difficult to understand.   We must consider that every individual naturally
tends gradually to diverge from the norm in speech so far
as is possible within the limits already described.   But
the question of which of his personal tendencies are
allowed to develop, and which are eliminated, is determined by the general balance of habit and tendency in
the community as a whole.   So soon as the constitution
of the community is changed, the balance is upset, and
tendencies which would before have been checked may
now, among a smaller group of speakers find a wider echo:
—that is, there is a larger proportion of speakers who
share them.   These tendencies, therefore, are confirmed,
and may become general among the new and smaller community.   Again, tendencies which find encouragement, and
gain a firm footing in one community, are eliminated in
another.   Of course, unless the isolation be complete, it is
probable that all the groups of speakers will still have
certain lines of change in common, and will also agree, as
before, in suppressing, for the most part unconsciously,
certain other tendencies.

The formation of dialects depends, then, upon the
development of different groups or series of tendencies
among communities which are isolated one from the other.
The extent to which two or more dialects differ from, or
agree with each other, in fostering, or eliminating, this or
that tendency to variation, will depend upon the degree
of completeness of the isolation of the several communities.

We may now properly inquire what are the chief factors
of isolation, or modes of interruption, of social intercourse-

which split up a community and give rise to dialectal differences.

We may divide human society into groups of increasing size : the Family, a group of individuals naturally associated together by the fact of common parents and a common dwelling-place; the Hamlet or Village, or group of Families ; the Province, which includes numerous villages ; and the Nation at large, which embraces all— Provinces, Villages, Hamlets, Families, and Individuals.

Each of these divisions, while it typifies characteristic modes of isolation of group from group, necessarily involves also a characteristic association of the members of each group.   Individual is isolated from individual, even in the same family, as we have seen, by slight differences of mind and body.   These are the psychological and physiological, or Organic factors of isolation.   Among them we may also consider differences of Age and of Sex. Family is separated from Family by the barriers of Occupation, Class, and the fact of living in different houses—these we may call the Social factors ; Hamlet or Village from other Hamlets and Villages by the geographical features of the country—varying distance, rivers, mountain ranges, forests, moors, or lakes, and by what we may call Political conditions.   These are the geographical factors, which, of course, include also the Political, Social, and Organic factors.   Province is isolated from Province, and Nation from Nation, by the same kind of factors, only they are naturally intensified as the geographical separation becomes greater, until this often involves the further factors of Climate, Soil, the general mode of life, Religion, and Race itself.

7

The wider our Social divisions, the more powerful, important, and complete becomes the mode of isolation which is associated with it.   A community may gradually spread, by a process of natural and steady increase in numbers, over an immense area, until the outlying fringes of population attain to so great a geographical severance from the original centre that they reach an altogether different soil and climate.   These may involve a total change in mode of life and in the whole fabric of Society, and contact with new and very different races.   On the other hand, instead of the gradual spread of the population over wide tracts of country, the same results may be more rapidly, but just as completely, attained by a section of the community moving off from their original seats, and proceeding, within a comparatively short space of time, to a remote geographical area.

It will be readily recognised that the Geographical factors are the most powerful of all in the differentiation of speech, since not only do they involve the complete isolation which results from a total severance of all social intercourse, thus including, in a very thorough form, all that group of factors which we have called the Social group. but they also expose the speakers to new conditions of Soil and Climate, and all that follows therefrom, and in this way are active in modifying the physical and mental organization, and therefore the speech basis.   As we have repeatedly insisted, the speech basis of a people, even when they are living under the same conditions for a long space of time, tends to vary; but this process is greatly hastened and intensified if the community be subjected to such changed conditions of life and such different outward surroundings as those to which it is exposed by migration to other climes, far-distant lands, and among alien peoples. We can observe how great are the differences in speech in a single large town between the different classes—the Public Services, the Professions, Commerce in its various grades, the Artisans, the Slum-dwellers. The isolation between these groups is Social, partly the natural result of difference of occupation, partly, also, due to the more artificial barriers of Class or Caste which are closely associated therewith. Originally, prob-ably, the same, the divisions created by Occupation and by Class are now distinct in nature, although they cross each other and overlap at innumerable points.

But with all its differences of dialect, the speech of one large town, taken as a whole, may appear almost homo-geneous, if we compare it with that of another town in the same country which is a few hundred miles away. Such towns as Glasgow, Liverpool, and Bristol, all possess a number of what we may call class and occupational dialects, but the differences between such dialects are comparatively slight, by the side of those differences which will appear from a comparison of the speech as a whole, in each of the cities mentioned, with that of the others ; that is to say, that those speakers from Glasgow who differ most widely amongst each other, will have far more in common in their several pronunciations, than they will have with any speakers from Liverpool or Bristol. This statement does not, of course, include speakers of Standard English in these cities, whose speech is not appreciably modified by the Regional Dialect.

The social conditions at the present time are so complex

that, apart from the inhabitants of small country villages, practically no individual can be regarded merely as the member of a single community. From his position in society, the nature of his avocations, and the place of his abode, almost every one belongs, from these different points of view, to several communities; he is brought, with varying degrees of intimacy, into relations with people of every class, engaged upon all manner of employments, and coming from widely different parts of the country. The result is that the speech of almost every individual, unless, indeed, as we have said, he lives continuously in one small country village, where the social circle is extremely limited, and where communication with the outer world is inconsiderable and infrequent—the speech of every individual does not represent a uniform dialect, as spoken by any single class or community, but is, in reality, a compromise between the characteristics of several different dialects. Consider the case of a wealthy merchant or banker. He spends part of his time in the city, where he associates with persons employed in business similar to his own, some of them his equals in education and social status, others belonging to a different social class, and therefore, often, to a very different speech community. Our banker or merchant has been at a Public School, and at a University; he has spent, perhaps, some years in foreign travel as part of his general training; his wealth enables him to reside in London for part of the year, and also to live in baronial fashion in the country for the other part. Outside his hours of business he associates with his fellow merchant princes, but also with men of the liberal professions, with diplomats, members of Parliament, military men, country

gentlemen, peasants, and peers. It is impossible to classify
such a man merely as either a city merchant, a man about
town, a University man, or a country gentleman. He is each
and all of these in turn ; he belongs to several communities
at once, and his speech inevitably bears traces of his contact
with, and sojourn among, every one of them, though one
or other will preponderate in determining his mode of
utterance. It is probable that in the case of our hypothetical merchant prince, the speech of the more distinguished classes, among whom he moves as an equal, will
to all intents and purposes be his, especially if he has been
familiar with it from childhood ; but he will not entirely
escape the influences of the other class, occupational, or
regional dialects with which he is brought into contact.
In fact, every speaker of the ' standard ' English dialect is
subjected to the same complex linguistic influences, and his
speech necessarily bears traces, however slight these may
be, of other forms of English, whether they be the dialect
of a class, of a province, or a blending of both. In the
same way, no provincial dialect is completely uninfluenced
by standard English on the one hand, and by neighbouring
local forms of speech on the other.

It is a remarkable thing how comparatively homogeneous
the standard English dialect actually is, and how this form
of our language may be heard, with a uniformity of pronunciation and intonation in which minor differences
appear to be merged, in the mouths of the educated upper
classes in all parts of the country.

This degree of uniformity is due to the free intermixture
of all people of a certain amount of wealth, which is
rendered possible by the facilities of modern locomotion.

This process of unification is begun at those great meeting-places for the wealthy youth of England—the Public Schools and the older Universities.

This linguistic influence is further carried to all classes of the population, in every nook and corner of England, by the clergy, and to a lesser extent by the national schoolmaster.

The fact is that never, under any social conditions, whether these be the most simple and primitive, or the most complex imaginable, is the isolation of any group of speakers from outside influences absolutely complete. The members of a small linguistic group or community may— indeed, do—enjoy a far greater frequency of intercourse among themselves than do any of them with the members of communities outside. In a primitive state of society it is difficult to draw a distinction between the Homestead, which includes the members of one family and their dependents, and the Hamlet. But the influence of external communities, too, must of necessity be exerted to some extent—directly in some cases, in others indirectly. Thus, no dialect can possibly possess absolute uniformity, for the external influences do not affect all the members equally. New and 'foreign' tendencies are acquired by some members and not by others.

A group of families who reside in proximity, in the same hamlet, (or even the divisions of one and the same family) may represent so many separate communities. The isolation of one such family or division from another may not be great, but it is sufficient to allow of each being subject to slightly different external speech influences, or reacting in a slightly different way to the same influence. One family may acquire this peculiarity from the speakers of another village, while another family takes on quite a different habit or tendency. If we took as a test the possession, or the reverse, of these particular habits of speech, it would be necessary to classify the two families as forming two slightly distinct communities, speaking two slightly different dialects. On the other hand, the points in which there was linguistic agreement between the families of the same village would be far in advance, in number and degree, of those in which they differed; so that, bearing in mind the actual facts, we should be justified in asserting that the dialect of the village or homestead was uniform, in the relative sense that the members of that particular village community showed a greater linguistic affinity with each other, than with any other group or groups of speakers.

It is in this qualified and relative sense, that we speak of the uniformity and homogeneity of Primitive Aryan or Primitive Germanic speech. We cannot conceive of any considerable collection of human beings whose speech should not present at least that degree of dialectal differentiation, which must exist between the different families or households that make up the community as a whole. The two principles—individual variation and collective unity—are for ever contrasted in language. As Paul has said (*Principien*, p. 55), it belongs to the nature of language, as a medium of social intercourse, that the individual speaker should feel himself to be in agreement with his fellows.

Divergencies which originally arise in a single family may, in time, spread to one or more other families, and thence to the whole tribe. If a group of closely allied

families move off from the rest of the tribe, and migrate
to a distant area, the slight peculiarities which in their
original seats differentiated their speech from that of
their fellow-tribesmen may form the starting-point for
divergencies of considerable magnitude.

It is possible that the beginnings of the dissimilar
tendencies among the various Aryan languages in the
treatment of lip-modified back consonants, and of the
' palatalized' or partly-fronted consonants, may have arisen
as slight dialectal divergencies within Primitive Aryan itself.

It is important to realize that the gradual dying out of
the old local dialects, which is at present going on, and the
levelling up and down of speech, throughout our own
country, to a type which appears to offer but an insig-
nificant degree of variety, is not a purely natural process.
There is no natural tendency in a language which is
already differentiated into various dialects, to become
uniform ; nor do the impulses towards divergence become
weaker with the growth of civilization, and the spread of
education. The phenomenon which we are witnessing
in England to-day, is that of one dialect being gradually
substituted for others. That such a substitution should
occur is not a new thing in the history of language ; it
depends in our own case upon the prestige of the en-
croaching dialect, as well as upon social conditions. The
degree of uniformity with which the standard dialect is
spoken over a large area, depends upon the extent to which
the factors of geographical and social isolation can be
weakened. At the present day, this is undoubtedly effected
to a certain extent, partly by the mixture of classes, which
characterizes our social system, partly, also, by the great

development in means of communication between different parts of the country, which has taken place during the last fifty years, chief among which we must, of course, place railway extension ; but we must by no means disregard the influence of the bicycle and the motor-car.

Still, it is easy to over-estimate the degree of uniformity which exists in English speech, and a minute investigation by a trained observer, will reveal differences which are very real, but which easily escape the notice of the untrained ear.

The need of a uniform international language has of late years been forcibly urged, and to-day there are probably many thousands of persons all over Europe who can speak *Esperanto*. It is interesting to speculate as to the probable future of this movement. From what we know concerning the changes of languages, it seems probable that if this artificial language were really to become firmly established in all the civilized countries of the world, it could not long retain a sufficient degree of uniformity, either in structure, or in pronunciation, to serve the purpose for which it was originally created. At the present moment, there is a conventional pronunciation which can be approximately acquired, with fair ease, by the natives of most countries. But, already, every speaker must necessarily modify the sounds in a certain way, in accordance with the speech basis of his mother-tongue. Thus an Englishman will diphthongize (ō) and (ē) to (*ou*) and (*ɛi*) ; a Russian will make *ō* into (ɔ̄)—that is, low-back-tense-round ; a Swede will either over-round this sound, (ō), till the effect produced upon foreign ears is that of (ū), or will attempt to reproduce it by (ɔ). Again, such a sound as (ū), = high-back-tense-round, will be made by the Swede into the high-flat-tense-round or the mid-back-tense-over-rounded, and by the Frenchman into a high-back-tense-round with considerable advancing of the tongue; a Welshman will make (ō) and (ē) into (ɔ) and (ɛ), and so on. This for a beginning. But when once the language has been learnt, and has become a traditional form of speech, as is presumably hoped by those who advocate its use, its sounds will develop on different lines in every country, since, as they will be identical with the corresponding sounds in the native language, they will, of course, follow precisely the same path of change as that which these pursue. Thus we should expect that in a few generations *Esperanto* will be different in each country, so far as the sounds are concerned. Added to the difficulty of diffusing a uniform sound system among widely-separated peoples, each speaking a distinct language of their own, we must further consider the equally formidable difficulty of preserving a uniform system of *accent*, including thereunder both *stress* and *intonation*. Frenchmen will never, as a nation, acquire a system of strong stress on certain syllables of words, with weak stresses on the others, such as exists in Italian or the Germanic languages. A very slight error in the distribution of stress is sufficient to make a word unintelligible. The present writer has repeatedly heard a Frenchman pronounce the word 'literature' (litératjūr) instead of (lítərətʃə) or (lítrətʃə), with the result that a group of Englishmen who were present, were completely baffled as to what he meant. The same Frenchman also spoke of the works of (bɛrnártʃau), whom the writer took to be a Chinese author, until it appeared from the conversation that Mr. Bernard Shaw (bãnədʃɔ́) was referred to.

It is difficult, at present, to see how divergencies of this kind can be avoided, in the pronunciation of *Esperanto* ; and if they exist, not only will the new language lack uniformity from the beginning, but the subsequent divergencies in the different countries will be all the greater from the fact that the starting-points will be diverse to begin with, and the tendencies which mould the future destinies of the various forms will be different in each case. It may be argued that the facilities of international communication are rapidly developing, that the geographical isolation between even the mutually remotest countries of the world will, in time, be no more insuperable than that between the North and South of England at the present day, or again, that the increased use of telephonic communication may make it as easy to converse with a man in St. Petersburg as with one in the same room. We must admit that progress in the utilization of steam, electricity, and mechanical contrivances generally, has done much, and will doubtless do yet more, to break down the isolation imposed by distance ; but this can never wholly disappear—nothing can ever make social intercourse between persons who habitually live hundreds of thousands of miles from each other, as easy, intimate, and frequent as that between individuals living in the same village, or between communities separated only by a few miles of road or rail. Thus, while the differentiation of language may become increasingly slow, the process must always continue.

The general structure, the word-order, and form of the sentence in such an artificial language as *Esperanto* must of necessity be profoundly affected in the different centres in which it is cultivated, by the native idiom, since there

are no models, as in the case of Latin, to serve as guides.
Latin is no longer susceptible of development, so long as
the classical models are followed ; it is crystallized once for
all, and any departure from the old usage is jealously
avoided.   Nevertheless, in the Medieval Latinity the
language is so far a living and traditional instrument of
expression, that it was variously affected by the native
dialects of the different countries where it was written, so
far as structure and idiom are concerned.   Immutability
in speech is inconceivable, so long as it remains a living
expression of thought and emotion, which has its roots in
the national consciousness.   A language can only cease
to change, when it has ceased to live.   Change is the
necessary penalty which is paid for life, by any form of
speech.   If *Esperanto*, so it would appear, ever becomes
a living language, it will change, and change in different
ways among different groups of human beings.   In this
case it will no longer serve as a means of international
communication.   In fact, this purpose can only be realized
if *Esperanto* never actually quickens, but always remains
a mere artificial and lifeless collection of words, pronounced according to carefully-drawn rules (which must
be learnt afresh by each speaker, and rigidly adhered to),
and built up into sentences according to rules upon which
all the *Esperantists* must agree.   In this case, doubtless,
it will be possible for students from all parts of the world
to hold with each other a kind of restricted intercourse
both by word of mouth and in writing.   The interesting
and curious point will be, that from time to time, the
natural developments, which are bound to creep in with
extensive usage, will need to be deliberately suppressed by

congress after congress, as the heresies of the early Church
were by the Councils.

Such is what might be expected, from what we know of
the differentiation of language, to happen to *Esperanto*, as
to any other living form of speech, which has a wide
geographical diffusion.

In the last chapter we dealt with the way in which the
language of an individual changes, and also discussed
briefly the various determining causes of sound change
which various writers have suggested. The present chapter
has been an attempt to show how, when factors come into
play which bring a group of individuals into close social
relationship with each other, and at the same time cut
them off from other groups of speakers, sound change,
which is natural and inevitable, in the speech of all groups,
yet takes place in each group along lines more or less
different. It has been said that the origin of this differentiation, was the fact that in each group of speakers a different
set of tendencies gets the upper hand, while each group
also, unconsciously, eliminates on different principles. The
various interplay of individual tendencies produces, in each
community, a net result which is special and characteristic.

The relative agreement and homogeneity in the speech
of the members of the same community was attributed to
the unconscious subordination and elimination of idiosyn-
crasies, and the approximation by the individual of his
speech to that of the average of the community. It has
been further repeatedly pointed out that the line of development followed by the pronunciation of a community, is
determined by the particular line of gradual shifting of the

speech basis, and this in its turn is the result of a combination of those general factors already referred to. A few
words may be in place here as to the part which these
factors play in the speech of the community considered as
an association of individuals. It is well to observe that
a given set of factors—the Climatic or the Occupational—
may, and often do, affect, directly, and equally, all the
individuals of a community ; but it must not be forgotten
that this is not necessarily the case. In the case where
the modifying influences of occupation, for instance, act
directly, and to the same degree, upon a whole group of
individuals it is natural to expect that the results, allowing, of course, for the differences of individual temperament
and organization, so often insisted upon, will be the same
for all—that is, that the whole group will undergo the
same kind of modification of the speech basis.

On the other hand, it must be remembered that the
modifying factors may operate by affecting only a few
individuals of a group directly, and that the results of this
direct influence upon their speech may, through social intercourse, gradually spread to all the other members, although
the majority of them have never been directly exposed to
that particular source of modification which induces the
change in the speech basis. Thus, in the speech of the
individual, it is possible, theoretically, to distinguish on
the one hand, those alterations of his speech basis which
are the result of the direct modification of his habits of
speech, or of the actual organs themselves, by external
factors, such as occupation, climate, etc. ; and on the
other those which he acquires by the unconscious
imitation of other speakers. A single individual might,

under favourable conditions, be the originator of far-reaching modifications in the speech basis of a large community. For this to come about it would be necessary that the peculiarity gained ground, in the first instance, in a very restricted community, such as a family in which the individual, perhaps as father or chief, had considerable influence. Thence the change might easily affect an ever-widening circle. The smaller the social circle involved, and the more limited its relations with larger divisions of society, the less chance there is of the purely individual peculiarities being swamped and eliminated by the speech of the majority. Such considerations bring home to us how complex may be the question of the rise of this or that departure in a language from the former speech habit ; since, although, by the time a linguistic phenomenon comes under the observation of science, it may be wide-spread, and appear in a whole family of languages, it may, nevertheless, have had its origin in a remote past, in some obscure and subtle influence exerted upon a very small speech community.

It is probable that in the history of a language different groups of factors co-operate, with varying force, at different periods—now one group predominate in influence, now another. But at present our analysis of causes does not enable us to do more than suggest in a general way, the probable nature of the modifying factors at work ; we are for the most part unable to see the precise connection between the effects which we chronicle, and any specific one of the possible causes which may have produced them.

Before concluding this chapter, it may be appropriate to say something of the conception of ' *Laws of Sound*

Change,' '*Phonetic Laws*,' or '*Sound Laws*,' as they are variously called, which plays so important a part in modern historical linguistic study.

The phrase is used to express several slightly different ideas, but, reduced to the simplest form, a sound law is merely a statement of the observed facts of pronunciation of a given language at a particular period. The statement that at the present day in the South of England the *r*-sounds have no trill, but are varieties of a weak point-open consonant, is a sound law. This is the simplest form of sound law. Again, we may state more precisely the phonetic conditions within the word or sentence, under which a sound occurs at a certain period in the history of a language, as when we say that the definite article in English has the vowel (ī) when stressed : 'he is *the* one man I want to see' (hi *iz* ðī wan mæn *ai* wɔnt tə sī)—(i) when unstressed, before a word beginning with a vowel ; (ə) when unstressed, before a consonant. Both forms are shown in 'the earth is the Lord's' (ði ʌþ *iz* ðə lɔ̄dz). If we compare the form of a word in more than one period of the same language, we often note that the sound which was pronounced in the earlier has been replaced by another sound in the later period. The statement that O.H.G (ū) has 'become,' or been replaced by, (au) in Mod. H.G.—*e.g.*, O.H.G. *mūs*, Mod. Ger. *maus*—is a sound law which is revealed by historical grammar. Lastly, we apply the term 'sound law' to the facts of differentiation revealed by the comparison of the forms of the same word in more than one cognate language. The result of comparing Sanscrit *śatam*, 'hundred,' Gk. ἑκατόν, Lat. *centum*, Gothic *hund*, Lithuanian *szimtas*, is that we can formulate the law that a certain original sound, which we will for the moment call x, has become š (ʃ) in Scrt., k in Gk. and Lat., h ($=\chi$) in Gmc., sz ($=$ʃ) in Lithuanian.

This inquiry into the particular series of substitution of sounds, or 'sound changes,' which occur in languages at a given moment in their life - history is a very important part of the modern science of language in its historical and comparative aspects. This branch of inquiry, known as Phonological investigation, is at the base of all scientific linguistic study; and the reason for this is obvious when we reflect that unless we know the habits and tendencies to change which characterize a language, or family of languages, we cannot identify, with any degree of certainty, the same word in the various forms it may assume in different ages and in different languages. Until we can take this preliminary step, we cannot profitably compare the forms of one language with the cognate forms in another. We could not know that Irish *iasc* was cognate with Latin *piscis* and with English *fish*, unless we knew from other sources that initial p is lost in Celtic, but becomes f in Gmc.

We have repeatedly insisted in this and the foregoing chapters, that change in language takes place unconsciously —that there is nothing arbitrary or whimsical about it. It has been said that each speaker can diverge to a certain extent from the norm in pronunciation without the divergence being apparent to himself or his fellows. This means that every speaker has a certain group of slight varieties of sound, upon which he rings the changes, all of which, in his consciousness, to his muscular sensations, and to his sense of hearing, represent one and the same

8

sound. Every time he utters a word containing a particular sound, he produces one or other of the varieties which
represent his conception of the sound. He may utter now
this, now that variety, but he does not go outside the
limits imposed by his powers of discrimination of sound
and sensation. We may say, therefore, with the above
qualification, that the speaker will always pronounce the
same sound in the same way. What is true of the
individual is true also of the community ; and, with
qualifications of the kind just made, we may assert
that, in a given community, at a given period, the
same sound will be pronounced in the same way, whenever it occurs under the same conditions—that is, unless
it be affected by the neighbouring sounds in word or
sentence.

This is what is meant by the statement, which the
school of Leskien, Brugmann, Osthoff, Paul, and Sievers
have raised into a cardinal axiom of method, that ' *sound
laws admit of no exceptions*.' When apparent exceptions
are found it means either—(1) That there are combinative
factors at work which we have omitted from our calcula-
tion — that is, that the sound is affected by other
sounds in the same word, or sentence, or by accent.
(2) That the particular word in which the apparent exception occurs, contains a sound which is in reality different
in origin, or which has been earlier differentiated from
the other sounds with ; which we had classified it.
Cases (1) and (2) necessitate the restatement of our
law, or the formulation of a new law, as the case may
be. (3) A word may be borrowed from another dialect
or language, in which it is pronounced in a different

way from the ordinary form in the native dialect. 'Exceptions' of this order are found in all dialects, which is what we should expect from what has been said with regard to the influence constantly exerted by one dialect upon another. In standard or literary dialects loan-forms from a variety of dialects are particularly frequent. In fact, most literary forms of speech are, to a great extent, artificial products, and represent rather a mixture of elements from several dialects, than any one uniform dialect. Hence a literary language is a far less favourable field for the observation of the laws of the evolution of speech, than an unwritten peasant dialect. (4) The apparent exception may be a form which has not developed by the ordinary processes of sound change from an older form, but due to the *Analogy* of another form in the same grammatical category, or with which some mental association has been formed. The question of *Analogy* will be dealt with subsequently.

Having regard to the above facts, the mutual influence of dialects upon each other, and the consequent absence of absolute uniformity of speech, except within the narrowest limits of small communities,—while even here there are the 'dialects' of the individuals to be reckoned with,— it is clear that any statement that such and such a sound becomes such and such another, at a given period in a given dialect, can only be an approximation to the actual facts. Thus, when we say that the eighteenth-century English vowel (ǣ) became (ā) in the standard English of the next century—*e.g.*, eighteenth-century (pǣst, lǣf, pǣþ) = present-day (pāst, lāf, pāþ)—we select a particular average type from among several varieties of pronunciation. If we were to examine the pronunciation of these words by a hundred Englishmen at the present day, all from more or less the same class, and who had received the same kind of education, we might possibly find a dozen or more slightly different vowels among them, all of which might be roughly classified as varieties of long ($\bar{a}$), while some of the number might possibly retain some form of the eighteenth-century vowel. The individual varieties of the first class would come under our law, while the others would be classed as dialectal variants, due to the influence of provincial forms of speech, in which the law did not obtain—that is, in which the change of ($\bar{æ}$) to ($\bar{a}$) had not taken place. A full and complete history of a language would involve an account of the speech of every individual.

In the spelling of Middle English many dialectal varieties of pronunciation, and doubtless also of individual peculiarities, are expressed ; but in a highly-cultivated literary language the spelling is usually crystallized, and expresses merely a general average of the extant pronunciations, the same symbol being used by 'correct' writers without regard to differences. Thus we must be prepared to admit that such symbols as Greek ω, Latin $\bar{u}$, Gothic ai, which, for practical purposes of philological statement and investigation, we consider as representing severally the same sound, ($\bar{o}$, $\bar{u}$, ai) respectively, with perfect consistency, may in reality have been conventionally used, in the same words, by writers whose pronunciation differed more or less considerably. In all cases, however, until a spelling has become absolutely fixed, like that of classical Greek and Latin or Modern English, it is safe to assume that the use of the symbol is fairly consistent, and that it expresses, at the worst, a group of closely-related varieties of sound.

So much stress has been laid upon the varieties which exist in what is treated for scientific purposes as a unity—namely, that group of individual dialects which we call a single language, or homogeneous dialect—because these differences, although they are not lost sight of by philological scholars when they assert that the laws of sound change admit of no exceptions, and speak of 'uniform' languages and dialects, are yet very apt to be totally ignored by less experienced students, to the great detriment of method, and obscuring of ideas. Each individual, we must remember, pronounces the same sound, whenever it occurs, according to the character of his speech basis, and what is true of the individual is true also of the community. The net result of the regularity and consistency of individual habit and tendency, is consistency of general tendency in such a collection of individual dialects as goes to make up what we call a language.

With these considerations as a background of our consciousness, we may accept the statement that sound laws admit of no exceptions. Unless this were true, if, indeed, sound change were the result of chance or of whim, then, as Leskien said years ago (*Deklination im Slavisch und Deutsch*, 1877, p. xxviii), language, the subject of our investigations, would be incapable of scientific treatment, and there could be no science of language.

Sound laws are not of the nature of natural laws, since

they have not a universal application to human language in general, but only hold good of a specific dialect at a given time.   A sound law is merely a statement of a fact, or a sequence of facts, but does not include a statement of general conditions, under which these are bound to occur, nor an indication of the universal causes of the phenomena which are recorded.

CHAPTER VI

LINGUISTIC CONTACT

WE have already seen how the speech of each individual within a given community presents certain characteristic personal peculiarities. Every individual speaker affects, and is affected by, the speech of every other speaker with whom he comes into contact. Similarly, the language of a small community influences, and is influenced by, the dialects, more or less closely related, of neighbouring communities.

This process of action and reaction of one form of speech upon another goes on wherever two or more individuals or communities are brought into social relations with each other. If it is traceable in the case of communities whose forms of speech are closely related, or are merely dialects of the same language, the effect produced by widely different, or totally unrelated languages, upon each other, is still more considerable.

The contact between two languages may be either *direct*, by personal intercourse between the speakers, or *indirect*, through the medium of literature. Direct contact comes about on the frontiers of two speech areas; by the transference of considerable communities among foreign races, either by a peaceful migration and settlement or through

119

warlike invasion ; or, again, by means of individuals who travel among foreign speakers, and sojourn for a greater or less period in another country.

The larger the number of speakers between whom and the foreign speakers contact exists, the greater the influence upon both languages. Colonization and conquest offer the most favourable conditions for linguistic contact on a considerable scale, provided that the new race does not drive out or exterminate the old. When two races live side by side, each preserving their own language, but, from the necessities of life, compelled to know, or at least to understand, that of the other to a certain extent, as in the case of the Scandinavians in England, who were first piratical invaders, then settlers, the influence of each language upon the other is likely to be profound. Under such conditions, there grows up in time, a large section, in both communities, which is bi-lingual. Perhaps at last the condition of bi-lingualism is reached by practically all speakers in each community. When this happens, one or other of the languages will gradually die out. The question of which community surrenders its language, will be determined by various social, intellectual, and other conditions. Intermarriage welds the two races into one, and the speech which survives as the language of the community, bears traces of that which has died out. The language which has gone under, may leave traces of its existence upon the pronunciation, the vocabulary, and the general structure of the language.

We have already pointed out that when a language is acquired by foreigners, the original pronunciation is never perfectly preserved, owing to the difference of the speech-bases. Although, here and there, an isolated individual may be able to speak two languages with equal perfection of pronunciation, this is impossible in the case of a large bi-lingual community. The speech basis of the native tongue is transferred to the newly-acquired language, and, as a result, the sounds of the latter undergo considerable modification. In the case where the native speech is acquired by the incoming race, it is maintained that the modification of this is far less than that which follows from the adoption of the immigrant language by the original inhabitants of a country (*cf.* Wechssler, *Gibt es Lautgesetze ?* p. 97). The adoption of English by the Normans illustrates the former, that of the Romance languages by Teutons and Celts the latter.

The incorporation of any considerable proportion of foreign elements, into the vocabulary of a language, implies a certain amount of bi-lingualism—at least, for a time. A bi-lingual speaker will often introduce foreign words when speaking his own language, and *vice versâ*. At first, the words thus introduced from one language into another, are, chiefly, the designations of ideas or objects which are familiar to one people, but not to the other. The first reason for such loans is the actual necessity which is felt, to express a given conception, or to indicate some object for which no name exists in the language in use at the moment. The fact of a people possessing no name for a natural product does not imply any inferiority, though this may be inferred, up to a certain point, when the word borrowed is the name of some object of industry On the other hand, the necessity of borrowing words which express ethical, religious, or political conceptions, most certainly denotes inferiority of moral and civil development, on the part of those who are compelled to seek their mode of expression from foreign sources. As a rule the new word is adopted at the same time as the idea, or the object which it denotes.

There are two ways of enriching the vocabulary of a language, when the need for this arises from the introduction of fresh ideas, or new products of human ingenuity: one, that which we have hitherto been considering, by incorporating new material from another tongue; the other, by adapting and combining elements of the native vocabulary, on the model of the foreign name. An example of this is the German *vaterland* or the Russian *otíchestvo* (*atít∫εstvo*), which are translations of the Latin *patria*.

The introduction of foreign elements into a language in the first instance, usually starts, as we have seen, with an individual who is master of both tongues. In employing a foreign word, the individual has no intention to introduce a permanent element into the vocabulary: he merely supplies the necessity of the moment. For a word to become permanently fixed in a language, it is a necessary condition, as a rule, that it should be repeatedly used, and that it should be used spontaneously from several centres within the community. Foreign words gain a footing gradually. At first they are only used among a small group of individuals who are closely associated together by class, occupation, or nearness of geographical contiguity. Thence they may spread to other groups of a similar nature, and finally to the whole community. Some words may never come into general use, but may always be confined to the upper grades of the community.

By the time a foreign element has passed into general usage, it is no longer felt to be an alien, but has become part and parcel of the native language.

A foreign word generally gains currency in a form as near to the original as the natural pronunciation of the community permits. It is very rare that a word retains a sound which does not exist in the language into which it is borrowed. Still, foreign sounds are occasionally introduced into a language in isolated words, as, for instance, the initial (ž) of *génie* which is pronounced by the educated German, or the nasalized vowel in the French *envelope* which still survives in the pronunciation of some English speakers. Such foreign sounds, however, are confined to the more cultivated classes of a community, and in general use, the nearest sound in the native speech is substituted for them.

The original stress of foreign words is preserved long after their sounds have been replaced by the native sounds. Thus, while the numerous Norman-French words in Chaucer contain but few vowel or consonantal sounds which do not also occur in native English words, the original accent still persists in many, by the side however, of another form in which the accent is on the first syllable, as in English words—*e.g., vertúe* (Fr.), *vértue* (Eng.), *licoúr* and *lícour*, etc.*

* Sounds which do not occur in native English words, but which were maintained in French loan-words, are : (oi) in *joie, jointe,* etc. ; (aŭ) probably still pronounced with slight nasalization in Chaucer's day in *chaunce, chaunge,* etc. (tʃaŭnsɛ, tʃaŭndžɛ). Among consonants, the combination (dž) does not occur initially in English words, although common in Norman French : *juge, gentil* (džydzɛ, džɛntil), etc.

The Norman words which are found in English, won their way in through the prolonged direct, and intimate contact of the two races, which led to a final amalgamation. As the Normans were scattered throughout the length and breadth of the country, they affected all dialects equally. The Scandinavian invaders and settlers, on the other hand, were confined to certain districts. In those districts where they settled, the two races and the two languages were gradually fused ; here the contact was direct and intimate. But the Scandinavian elements are not found in equal numbers in all dialects. In those dialects which had no direct contact with Scandinavian speech these elements are scanty, and when they exist, have spread from other areas where the influence of the Northmen was directly exercised. Thus foreign influence may pass indirectly to speakers who have had no direct contact with the alien race, through the medium of other speakers of their own blood, with whom the foreigners came into direct relation.

Still more attenuated, is the influence which one language may exert upon another through travellers, or others who spend some time in foreign countries, and then return to their own country, bringing accounts of strange customs or institutions, or articles of native industry. Many Indian words have passed into English through the intermediary of our civil and military officials. These words gain currency partly by means of literature, partly through direct contact of Anglo-Indians with their countrymen. The number of persons, among the governing classes in England, who have no connection with India through members of their family, or their friends is small, so that probably a very large number of Indian words have become known to the upper classes of Englishmen, by word of mouth, from persons who acquired them direct from Indian speakers. On the other hand, the same words are known to other sections of the community in this country, only in their written form, from books and newspapers. Such words will be pronounced by the former class of persons with an approximation to their Indian form, and are thus in the same position as words acquired by direct contact; by the latter class, however, for whom they have never been living elements of a spoken language, they are uttered according to the nearest interpretation of the written symbols in harmony with their ordinary English values. Of course, as India and its institutions become more and more widely and directly known, the traditional pronunciation of Indian words obtains an ever-increasing diffusion.

The changes in pronunciation which words undergo in the process of their direct incorporation from living foreign languages, are in the nature of instantaneous substitution of the nearest native sound for the unfamiliar foreign sound. What are known as *Acoustic* changes, or changes due to faulty imitation, occur chiefly in foreign words. When once a word has been incorporated and thoroughly acclimatized, so that it is no longer felt as other than part of the language, it shares in all the changes of pronunciation which take place in the language.

We have now briefly to consider the influence of one language upon another as exerted through literature. When a foreign word gains a footing in a language, not from a living spoken tongue, but from one which is no longer spoken, which is *dead*, the only possible source from which it can come, is the written remains of the language as preserved in literature. The great culture languages of Greek and Latin have contributed, and continue to contribute, a large proportion of the vocabularies of every European language. Only next in importance, from this point of view is French, which, from the early Middle Age down to the present day, has been regarded as the chief vehicle among the modern languages of all that is distinguished and polite in Art and Letters. In the case of a living language, however, it is difficult to draw the line of distinction between influence which comes purely through the written form, and that which may be exerted directly by the uttered speech upon some individual or group, and which has spread from them, by word of mouth and by means of the pen, into the language of life and of literature. In the case of words borrowed from dead languages, however, there can be no doubt. Words from such a source acquire the sounds which in every respect are normal and natural in the language into which they are taken.

Many words borrowed from Latin into English are, and remain essentially, 'learned' as distinct from 'popular' words—that is to say, they belong to the language of books, and not to that of everyday life. We do not learn them as children in the ordinary course of social relations with our fellows, but acquire them later from our schoolmaster or our school-books.

But many words which had a 'learned' origin pass, in the course of time, into universal usage in the language of everyday life ; they are no longer felt as grand, important words,

but express homely and familiar things or ideas.   They cease
to be ' learned,' and become popular.   It has been well
pointed out that ' the true distinction between a " learned "
and a " popular " word depends not upon etymology, but
upon usage ' (*cf.* Greenough and Kittredge, *Words and
their Ways in English Speech*, p. 29).   Such words as
disaster, *contradict*, *humour*, are examples from among
many, of words of distinctly learned origin, which are
now in everybody's mouth.   *Telephone*, *Telegraph*, *Phonograph*, which are modern concoctions from the Greek,
have come to be, owing to the progress of scientific and
practical discovery, among the commonest words, just as
the inventions which they designate are among the most
familiar objects of modern life.

Another form of the process of borrowing words from
a dead language is the revival of archaisms, or even of
words which are completely obsolete, from earlier phases of
the native language.   This process is essentially artificial,
and the old-new words rarely pass beyond the pages of
the works in which their new birth takes place.   At best,
such revivals survive only in the mannered writing, or the
painful and studied utterances of an individual, or of a
literary clique.

CHAPTER VII

ANALOGY

THE power of variously inflecting words in order to express different shades of thought and syntactic relations, comes naturally, in speaking a language of which we have even a moderate command. But such a power of 'correctly' forming adverbs from adjectives, of expressing past action, or plurality, or possession, does not depend upon the capacity of calling up the recollection of every individual form which is used. No human memory is stored with the past tenses of every verb which the speaker uses, with the comparative of every adjective, with the plural of every noun.

Nor is this necessary, for in the moment of utterance the formative element required, rises naturally in the mind of the speaker, although he may have no recollection of ever having heard it in that precise combination in which he is using it. The speaker, in fact, remakes for himself the conjugations of verbs, the declension of nouns, and so on, by the 'correct' use of certain formative suffixes. Were an effort of memory required in each instance, fluent and rapid speech would be impossible.

The fact is that comparatively few types remain in the memory, and from these the rest of the forms which the speaker uses are generalized, are made according to the model of those forms which actually are stored in the memory. This process is known as *Analogy*. Certain formative suffixes are associated in our minds with certain syntactic functions, and, as occasion demands, these inflexional elements, rise quite naturally into the consciousness, along with the shades of thought and meaning with which they are associated.

Analogy, and not memory for individual forms, is the natural process which takes place in the course of living utterance. The greater number of forms produced by this process are—allowing, of course, for the changes in sound which have occurred—identical with those which the same process called into existence at earlier periods of the language—that is to say, they are historically ' correct.' But in some cases new associations have been formed, so that the forms which a given generation of speakers, habitually, and naturally, call into existence in speaking, may differ from those which the speakers of earlier periods were in the habit of using.

The question of whether a form is ' right' or ' wrong,' is decided by the speech habit of the community at the time being. Forms in general use are ' correct,' those which are not in use are ' wrong.'

An important point to bear in mind, however, is that, whether a form produced by a given speaker, by the process we are discussing, be ' right' or ' wrong,' in the sense in which we have just defined these terms, the actual process whereby the form is created, is the same in all cases. If a speaker makes use of a form which he has created according to some type which he has in his mind, but which is ' wrong' in the sense of not being the one in

general use in the speech community of which he is a
member, this arises from the fact that for some reason or
other his associations, in this particular case, are different
from those of the community at large.

The history of every language abounds with forms which
are new departures from an earlier habit, and which are
due to the formation of new association groups within the
minds of the speakers of the generation which gave them
birth.   Words are associated in the mind, in groups,
according to three main principles : their general affinity
of meaning; identity of grammatical function; similarity
of form.   When more than one basis of association exists
between a group of words, the association is doubly strong.

Examples of association by virtue of general affinity
of meaning are—*Natural Relationships:* Father, Mother,
Brother, Sister ; the names of the seasons of the year :
Spring, Summer, etc. ; names of animals : (*a*) *Wild Animals:*
Lion, Tiger; (*b*) *Domestic Animals:* Cat, Dog, Sheep,
Oxen.   In the same way we connect all the cases of an
inflected substantive, all the persons and tenses of a verb,
and so on.   From this point of view, every word in the
language naturally falls, in the mind of the speaker, into
a group of words, linked together, more or less closely, by
a general association of meaning.   Such natural groups
we may call *association groups.*

The second class of association groups, the members of
which are linked together in our consciousness, are those
whose basis of association is their community of grammatical or syntactical function.   In this way are connected
all plurals of substantives—*dogs, boys, trees,* etc.—which
agree further in expressing the idea of plurality by the

same formative element.   Even when this is not the case, and when the idea of plurality is expressed by different means, as in *mice, houses, children*, the association, though looser, still exists.   Similarly, while all adverbs are associated as possessing a common function, the relations are of various degrees of closeness.   In the most general way, simply as adverbs, *hardly, well, here*, are associated.   But we can distinguish more intimately related groups of adverbs, such as adverbs of manner—*hardly, bitterly, well, ill*.   Of these, the first two are peculiarly closely associated in possessing the same formative suffix—*ly*, and the last two have the further association of antithesis.   Again, we may make an intimate group of adverbs of place—*here, there, everywhere*, and so on.

Passing to verbal forms, all preterites are associated in that they express the idea of past action—*placed, told, rang, went, came*.   Within the large group of preterites, however, the weak past tenses, the strong past tenses, and the weak past tenses with change of vowel, form so many smaller and more closely related groups of association.   Thus *gave, came, wrote*, are more nearly associated with each other than they are with *sent, charmed*, and so on.   In the case of strong verbs there are small groups which have the same vowel sequence—*sing, sang, sung; ring, rang, rung*.

In speech, the way in which a past tense of a verb is formed, depends upon the associations which exist in the speaker's mind.   Thus, if a speaker had the association groups *sing, sang, sung, ring, rang, rung*, and *fling*, with past part. *flung*, he might quite naturally form a preterite **flang* instead of *flung*.   It would be incorrect to describe

9—2

such a process as '*false*' analogy, as is sometimes done. The actual process is 'correct' enough, although the result in this case is a form not commonly employed. The speaker who makes such a form, merely shows that he has not the past tense of *fling* in his memory, and that he forms one on the pattern of two other past tenses which happen to be the received forms. The 'correct' speaker who has heard the received form *flung*, has grown to isolate the word from the class of verbs which have the sequence of three vowels, and to form an association between it and such verbs as *stick*, *stuck*, and so on.

Whenever a speaker uses a form which strikes us as 'wrong'—that, is unusual—we may be sure that there is some reason for it; and the interesting thing is to discover the precise association which exists in the speaker's mind. If the association is different from that which exists in our mind, then the application of the principle of analogy, itself essentially the same in all cases, will lead to a different result.

The question of which is the 'regular' type within a given speech community depends partly upon the number of words which form the association group, and partly upon the frequency of occurrence. Sweet has pointed out (*New Engl. Gr.*, § 538) that in colloquial.language only common words, as a rule, present 'exceptional' forms. The plural *men* could never have been preserved had it been a word but rarely used. It is one of those isolated words which are, as it were, specially learnt at a very early age by constant repetition. But if the word *man* became obsolete, or fell into infrequent use, it is inevitable that we should form the plural according to the pattern of the thousands of other words in English which have -s-plurals. Young children, whose knowledge of, and experience in, the language is slight, constantly make such mistakes as ' foots,' ' tooths,' ' oxes,' and so on, simply because they have not learnt that these words are isolated from the vast majority of words which take -s-plurals.

Even in the case of common words, the attraction of larger groups often proves too strong, and the ' exceptional' forms tend to disappear.   Thus we now say *books*, and in the standard language at any rate, *cows*, although O.E. had *bēc̄*, which would have produced ' *beech* ' in Mod. Eng., and *cȳ*, which would have given ' *ky* ' (kai), which latter form, indeed, persists in Scotland and in some English dialects. Hence, it is frequently necessary to assume some additional association in order to explain the retention in Mod. Eng. of forms which differ from the common type.   The O.E. neuter plural *scēāp* (Angl. *scēp*) persists in the modern plural 'sheep'; and here we may perhaps assume an association with 'flock' or 'herd,' and regard a 'flock of sheep' as a kind of collective noun in which the individual animals are lost sight of.   Another inevitable association of ' sheep ' is with ' cattle.'   We may contrast this view of sheep, *en masse*, with that of ' *lambs* and their *dams*,' when the comparative isolation of the individual mothers scattered over a field, with their offspring skipping round them, and the plurality of the individuals is forcibly brought home to the spectator.

A curious case is that of the plural *fish* applied chiefly to an article of diet, when the association is probably with ' flesh ' or ' food.'   This is a new plural, since the O.E. form was *fiscas*, and therefore demands the assumption of

some new association such as that suggested. The form
fishes, the descendant of the old plural, is applied more
usually to the living creatures, especially when enumerating, or dealing with different species, as in the title of
Couch's famous book on *British Fishes*.

Words which constantly occur in the same phrase are
often so closely associated in the mind that one suggests
the other. Such pairs are : *male* and *female* ; *king* and
queen ; *mother* and *father* ; *here*, *there*, and *everywhere* ; and
so on. The reason, in the first place, for these phrases
is that an intimate association of meaning exists between
the words thus linked together. The result of such association is that the words influence each other formally.   The
word *female* is from an Old French *femelle*, Latin *fēmella*,
which normally would appear in Mod. Eng., as (fīmɛl),
a form heard in Scotch ; but the association with *male* has
influenced the second syllable, until many speakers believe
the word to be a form of *male* with a prefix : hence the
still   further   popular   new   formation ' *shemale*,' used
jocularly.

In Scotch *king* is pronounced with a short, tense (i), the
origin of which can scarcely be other than its association
with *queen* (Scotch kwin). *Mother* in O.E. was *mōdor*,
and the *d* continued into late M.E. The modern (ð) is
undoubtedly due to the association with *brother*, O.E.
brōðor, where the (ð) is original. The association between
these two words is twofold—they both are names for
family relationships, and they both have, and have always
had, the same vowel. When once the open consonant
was established in *mother*, this word influenced the word
father, which in O.E. is *fœder* and in M.E. *fāder* and *făder*.

The pronunciations (ðīr, wīr) for *there* and *where* are established for the eighteenth century (*cf.* Ellis, *Early English Pronunciation*, p. 104), and the same pronunciation of these words occurs in many popular dialects of the present day (*cf.* Wright's *English Dialect Grammar*, under *there* and *where* in Index). It can hardly be doubted that we have here, not a normal phonetic development, but the result of the association of *there* and *where* with *here*, in which word the (ī) has arisen by regular sound change: (O.E. *hēr*, but *hwǣr*, *þǣr*).

A group of words of cognate origin are sometimes so far differentiated in form by different phonetic conditions that they cease to be felt as etymologically identical. In this case we say that a word has been isolated from its original association group. The words *doom*, *-dom* (in king*dom*, etc.), and *deem*, are all derived from the same original root, *dōm-*, but probably no one but a student of the history of English associates them together in his mind at the present time. *Deem*, from O.E. *dēman* (vb.), shows a vowel changed by the process of i-mutation from an older *ō*, and *-dom* has sunk to the level of a mere formative suffix, and has no independent existence. From the substantive *doom* a new verb has been formed, which, however, has a different meaning from that of the original verb *deem* at the present time. It is generally the case that when two words have become isolated from each other by change of form, the meanings also grow further and further apart, till at last there is absolutely nothing which leads to an association between them. No English speaker now connects for-*lorn* with the verb *lose*, and yet the former was originally the regular past participle of the latter verb. The old verb *forlose* is lost except in the solitary surviving form just quoted, and the uncompounded verb *lose* has a newly-formed past participle, which is now, however, of some antiquity. The analogy of such a participle as for-*sworn* has maintained the fossil *lorn;* but its meaning has diverged considerably, and has grown further and further away from that of the simple verb *lose*, until there is nothing left, either in form or meaning, which should serve to connect them together in the mind of an ordinary speaker.

It often happens that before the association between a group or pair of words is quite broken by change of form, Analogy intervenes, and, eliminating some of the deviating forms, levels the group all under one type.

Take the words *cool* (adj.); to *cool, cool*ness. Here O.E. has *cōl*, the normal ancestor of *cool;* but *cēlan* (vb.), and *cēlnesse; (cf. dōm, dēman)*. In this case Analogy came into play in time to prevent a further differentiation of form and meaning, which might have broken all connection between the words, and has formed a new verb and a new abstract noun. The formal connection, as well as that of meaning, between these words and *cold* is possibly still felt by some speakers, but the association is not strong enough for them to affect each other formally. In the case of the further cognate *chill*, the association is probably entirely one of affinity of meaning. In the last case the differentiation is very far back indeed, and consists in a very primitive, pre-English difference of vowel and of formative suffix, and subsequent English combinative changes.

In cases where cognate forms which have been considerably differentiated by sound changes have resisted the tendency to isolate them from their original association group, as in the case of *foot*, which retains its plural *feet*, this is due, as has been said, to the frequency of occurrence, but also to the close association of general meaning which exists between the singular and plural of the same word.

It is sometimes said that Analogy *hinders* normal sound change, but this is scarcely accurate. What actually occurs is that, although the change is carried out regularly enough, yet, in certain cases, some stronger association works, with the result of re-creating a form identical with the old, on the analogy of some cognate which has not undergone the change. In such a case both forms, the new creation and that produced by the ordinary processes of sound change, are often preserved side by side, not infrequently, however, with a differentiation of meaning. The wider apart the two forms become, the greater the likelihood that each will be specialized for a different function. We have seen this to a certan extent in the two verbs *deem* and *doom*. Another case of a similar kind is seen in the two words *ghostly* and *ghastly*. The latter is the normal phonetic development of the O.E. adj. *gāstlīc*, which in M.E. appears in the form *găstlich(e)* and *găstli*, with a normal shortening of O.E. *ā* before such a consonantal combination as *-stl-*. This word underwent a fronting of the vowel in the seventeenth century (gæstli). Then in the eighteenth (æ) was lengthened before *-st-*, giving a form (gǣstli), and this (ǣ) became (ā) in the late eighteenth or early nineteenth century. *Ghostly*, on the other hand, is a M.E. new formation from the substantive *gōst*, when the *ō* for O.E. *ā* is perfectly normal.

Another example of a similar process is seen in the
adjectives formed by the suffix *-like*. This is originally
cognate with the adjectival and adverbial suffix *-ly*, both
being forms of the O.E. *līc*. The O.E. suffix is itself
derived from the old substantive *līc* = body, form. Thus
originally *wīflīc*, ' womanly,' ' feminine,' meant ' having the
body or form of a woman.' Already in O.E. when used
as a suffix, the word had doubtless been completely isolated
from the substantive in the consciousness of the speakers,
and had become a mere formative element, although the
association with *ġelīce*, 'like' (literally ' having the same
form '), was probably still maintained. Then in M.E. the
suffix *-līk*, *-līch* or *-li*, was shortened through lack of stress,
became isolated even from ȝ*elīch*, ȝ*elīk*, and was still
further emptied of its original independent meaning.
When this had come about, a fresh class of adjectives
arose, formed from *-līk*. Thus at the present time *-ly*, *-like*
both exist as living suffixes, the former being principally
adverbial, and we have the doublets *wifely*, *wifelike*, *manly*,
manlike, and so on. The two suffixes, it will be noted,
express different shades of meaning ; the older being purely
formative of adjectives or adverbs, the latter having the
more definite sense of ' like a wife ' or ' beseeming a wife,'
etc. No doubt the association with the independent word
like tends to preserve the diphthong (*ai*) even in the unstressed position.

The process of Analogy is operative in every period of
linguistic development, and although attention is usually
only called to it when it produces a new and strange form,
it nevertheless comes into play in every utterance of connected speech. The history of any language shows that

Analogy, besides working as a conservative factor by producing forms that are historically 'correct,' is also perpetually causing new departures, due to the gradual shifting of association groups which is ever taking place with every language which is alive, on the lips, and in the minds, of living speakers. These new associations are formed, in the first instance, within the individual consciousness, and their chance of becoming permanent parts of speech depends upon whether they are shared by the community at large. If this is not the case, the new departures of individual speakers are eliminated by social intercourse with that majority of other speakers who have different association groups. Just as each community has its own tendencies of sound change, which are different in some respects from those of other communities; so also each community has its association groups, which are different from dialect to dialect. When we come across a dialect whose speakers have a different series of associations from those which exist in our own minds, we are apt to consider the result as 'ungrammatical' and 'wrong,' forgetting that there is absolutely no test whereby we can gauge the inherent 'correctness' or 'falseness' of mental associations as expressed in speech. The human mind plays freely around and among the phenomena of speech; and we cannot control the subtle conditions which establish links between idea and idea, between word and word.

Within a given dialect certain associations are current, and practically universal, and therefore 'correct' so far as that dialect is concerned. The power to speak the dialect of a community 'correctly' — that is, in the same way as the members of that community speak it—

depends upon possessing the same association groups as they.

In tracing the history of a language, we are constantly confronted by forms which are the result, not of natural phonetic development, but of analogy, and in this case it is our business to endeavour to discover the group of forms with which the new association has been established. There is no limit to the period, nor to the dialect, in which these new formations arise; and experience teaches us that they did, as a matter of fact, come into existence and gain a permanent footing in the classical languages of antiquity, nay, in Primitive Aryan itself; just as they do at the present day, alike in polished literary speech, and in peasant dialect.

CHAPTER VIII

METHODS OF COMPARISON AND RECONSTRUCTION

THE science of language is often divided into two main branches, General Comparative Philology of the Aryan languages (not to go beyond these for the moment), and the special History of the several Families of Aryan speech, or of individual languages. The Comparative Philologist, as such, is mainly concerned with that original unity which has been dissolved ; with the original forms from which those of the various families and individual languages spring—that is, with the Primitive Aryan mother-tongue. The Comparative Philologist in the special sense is chiefly occupied with the reconstruction of this mother-tongue, and therefore is concerned primarily with the points of agreement between the different languages. But before he can reach the final unity, the primitive mother-forms, he must needs observe how great is the diversity among the groups of languages with which he deals ; and this can only be accounted for from a knowledge of the special speech habits of the speakers of each language.

The investigation of these habits is the business of special students of the history of a single language, or of a group of closely allied tongues, such as the Germanic or

Slavonic. By comparing the cognate forms of such a group,
it is possible to form some idea of a phase of speech-life
which is more primitive than any actually preserved—to
reconstruct, in fact, Primitive Germanic or Primitive
Slavonic.

But before we can compare words in different languages,
with any profit, we must be quite sure that those forms
we are comparing are really cognates—that they really are
the descendants of the same original form.   The closer the
languages are in relationship, the less difficulty will there
be in recognising their cognate forms.   Thus the merest
beginner would hardly doubt the affinity of O.E. *fōt*,
'foot,' Gothic *fōtus*, O.Norse *fōtr*, O.H.G. *fuoz*.   Even
if he went further, and ascertained that 'foot' in Scrt.
was *pād-*, *pad-*, in Greek πούς, in Latin *pēs* he might
surmise that these were all forms of the same word which
is found in the Germanic languages.   The tests of identity
of origin, are form and meaning.   But, since related
languages often develop on widely differing lines, the form
frequently undergoes very remarkable changes, and the
meaning may vary so greatly, that it is not always easy
to see how this or that particular shade of significance
becomes attached to a particular root.

The science of Comparative Philology has been gradually
built up, until we are now often able to assert with confidence, the original identity of words, which, a few years ago,
no one would have dreamed of connecting with each other.
This is made possible by our ever-increasing knowledge of
the laws of sound change within the individual languages.
By this means it is possible gradually to divest a form of
its more recent peculiarities, and to reconstruct its earlier

phases, so that many old friends emerge, as it were, from
disguise. ₰ But in the beginning it was necessary to start
with such words as from their nature, admitted but little
change in meaning, and whose form in several tongues was
sufficiently recognised to prohibit any reasonable doubts of
identity. The classes of words most suitable for purposes
of comparison, in the beginning, are words which express
concrete and familiar objects, such as the natural relationships—father, mother, brother, etc. ; names of parts of the
body—head, eyes, ears, feet, etc. ; names for the earth, the
sky, water, the wind, heat, cold, snow ; names of the most
widely distributed plants and animals. Further, we should
expect to find the designation of the numerals, at any rate
up to ten, the common property of men whose ancestors
had, in ages however remote, spoken one and the same
language. These are the kind of words upon which the
foundations of Comparative Philology are laid, and when
these are built with care and thoroughness, the way is
paved for further progress. Now, when, in the case of
words in different languages of whose identity there can
be no reasonable doubt, even from the beginning, we
observe a regular permutation of sounds constantly re-
curring throughout a series of languages, when the differences between the languages are always of the same nature,
we are able to lay it down as a general principle, based on
observation, that such and such a sound in this language
corresponds with such and such a sound in that. ₰ We
proceed upon the assumption that the same changes will
always occur, under the same conditions, in the same
language ; if we find in a large number of cases that when
Greek, Latin, etc., have *p*, Germanic shows *f*, we expect

that this will always be the case, when the conditions are the same. In those cases where Greek p does not correspond to f in Germanic, we assume, either that the p in question does not represent the same original sound as that which we know becomes f in Germanic, or that there are conditions present which differentiate the case from others with which we are familiar. These conditions it then becomes our business to discover.

We do not believe that Greek and Latin are derived from Sanscrit; nor Germanic from Greek or Latin; but rather, that they are all derived from a common ancestor now long dead. Therefore, we do not state our sound law in the form of saying that Sanscrit, Greek, and Latin p becomes f in Germanic; but that a *Primitive Aryan p* is retained in the former three languages, but has become f in Germanic. Having gained, then, some knowledge of the precise way in which the groups of languages we are comparing, agree with, or differ from each other, and, further, a knowledge of some of the principal laws of sound-change of each of the derived languages, we ask what were the original forms from which those forms which we know have developed. In other words, the question we try to solve is, which of the forms before us is most primitive, which preserves most faithfully the features of the original common mother. The reconstructed forms of Primitive Aryan or Primitive Germanic which, according to present philological method, figure so largely in comparative and historical studies must not be taken too seriously therefore; these merely record the opinion that this or that feature in this or that language is primitive and original, and in assigning such and such a form as

the common ancestor of a group of forms from various
languages we must be prepared to show how each is
derived from it.

In tracing the history of a word, root, or grammatical
form in a single language, we get, as a rule, more light
upon it the further we can go back ; and by allowing for
the various isolative and combinative sound changes which
have affected it, we are gradually able to show the original
identity of the root with that which occurs in a considerable number of words. But so long as we keep to
one language we can only discover the principle of those
changes the conditions of which were present at some
time during the period of which we have an historical
record of that language. Thus if we were dealing with
the history of the word *seek* in English compared with
be-seech, we should first inquire what was the oldest
recorded form of these words. A glance at an etymological dictionary, or, better still, at an ' Anglo-Saxon '
dictionary, would reveal the fact that in both cases the
infinitive was *sēc(e)an*, with nothing to show that the
present difference between the final consonants of the two
words existed. In Middle English we find that *sēken*,
sēchen, *besēken*, *besēchen*, all occurred ; and, further, that in
the present-day English dialects *seek*, *seech*, *beseek*, *beseech*,
are in use in different parts of the country. Now, the
Mod. Eng. ' *ch-* ' (tʃ) sound presupposes a different sound
in O.E. from that which has become *k* in Mod. Eng.,
and that sound, we should find, if we consulted an O.E.
grammar, was certainly pronounced in the O.E. *sēc(e)an*.
It was probably a *front-stop consonant*, and it invariably
develops into the Mod. Eng. ' *-ch* ' (tʃ) ; at any rate, in the

10

South and Midlands. At this rate the M.E. *sēchen* would appear to be normally developed from O.E. *sēċ(e)an*. How are we to account for the M.E. and Mod. Eng. forms with *-k*? Certainly not by assuming an 'exceptional' change of *-ċ* (front-stop) to (k). If we look at the paradigm of the O.E. verb, it appears that in West Saxon it ran as follows in the Pres. Indic. Sing.: *iċ sēċe, þu secst, hē secþ;* and in M.E. the same texts which have *ich sēche* in 1st person singular, and *sēchen* in the Inf., not infrequently have *sēkst, sēkþ* in the 2nd and 3rd persons. The O.E. spelling does not express any difference of pronunciation; but the M.E. spelling shows a back-stop in the two last forms, and this implies a corresponding distinction in O.E., although this is not expressed in the written forms of that language. What conditions have these two forms in common, which distinguish them from the 1st Pers. and from the Inf.? They both have voiceless open consonants, *s* and þ respectively, immediately after the *ċ*. May we not, then, formulate tentatively the law that in O.E., before *ċ* had developed into its present sound,—perhaps even before it had reached the pure front-stop stage,—when it was followed immediately by a voiceless open consonant, it became a *back-stop* (k)? This is borne out by other examples. We have thus accounted for the existence of two forms with *k*-sounds in the conjugation of the O.E. verb *sēċan*. But we have still to explain how this sound got into the 1st Pers. Pres. Indic. and the Inf.

We are perfectly justified, from what is known of the habits of speakers, in assuming the possibility that a whole verb might be formed *on the Analogy of two persons,* especially when these are so frequently used as were the 2nd and 3rd persons singular in O.E. and M.E. We should explain M.E. *sēken*, etc., and Mod. Eng. *seek* in this way. For some reason the analogy has not taken place in *be-seech*, which retains the O.E. *ċ-* form unaffected by the other persons. In the case of the dialects above referred to, the Analogy affects sometimes the compounded, sometimes the uncompounded verb.

This digression from the general statement is intended to show that reference to the earlier forms of a language may tell us something which cannot be gathered from its latest forms. The varying conditions which subsequently differentiated O.E. *ċ* into *k* on the one hand, and on the other to '*-ch*' (tʃ), were present, and expressed in the spelling of English itself. But if we now proceed to inquire the reason of the differences of vowel between *seek* or *seech*, on one hand, and that of the past tense *sought*, on the other, we can get no light, so long as we confine our attention to English. As far back as we can go in the history of that language, we find this difference of vowels, but nothing to account for it. O.E. has *sēċan—sōhte*, and here we can note that the variation is *ē—ō*, an interchange which occurs in a large number of associated pairs of words in O.E., it is true; but this fact does not help us to explain the change.

The next step, therefore, is to inquire what is the corresponding form to O.E. *sēċan* in the other Gmc. languages. It is possible that some of these may retain some feature which O.E. has lost, and which may explain the interchange of vowels. The corresponding verb in Gothic is *sōkjan*, in O. Sax. *sōkian*, in O.H.G. *suohhan*. From these forms we learn that O.E. is peculiar in having ē in the root of the Inf. It appears that both Gothic and O. Sax. have ō, which vowel, as we have seen, also occurs in O.E. in the Pret. O.H.G. *uo* appears in a large number of words in which Gothic and O. Sax. have ō. We are, therefore, justified in assuming that ō is the most primitive form of the vowel in the inf. Why has O.E. ē here? Now, both Gothic and O. Sax. possess a feature which does not appear either in O.H.G. or in O.E., and that is that they preserve a suffix *-jan or -ian* in the inf.; that is to say that *j* or *i* appears in these languages immediately after the *k*. The sound of *j*, we have reason to believe, was that of a front-open consonant, closely related, from the position of the organs of speech and the area employed in its articulation, to *i*, which is a high-front vowel. Now, *-jan* is a very common verbal suffix in Gothic, and in all cases where O.E. and Gothic agree in possessing certain verbs, we find that the vowel of these verbs, if ō in Gothic, is ē in O.E.; if *a* in the former language, *e* in the latter; if ŭ in Gothic, then ў̃ in English—that is, that where Gothic has a back vowel English shows a front in the inf. of corresponding verbs, when there is reason to believe that a *j* originally occurred in the suffix. For example: Goth. *drōbjan*, 'disturb,' 'trouble,' O.E. *drēfan*; Goth. *fōdjan*, 'feed,' O.E. *fēdan*; Goth. ga-*mōtjan*, 'meet,' O.E. *mētan*, and so on. Examples of Goth. *a* = O.E. *e*, under the same conditions, are: Goth. *namnjan*, 'name,' O.E. *nemnan*; Goth. *satjan*, 'set,' O.E. *settan*; Goth. *warjan*, 'defend,' O.E. *werian*. Examples of Goth. *u* = O.E. *y* are: Goth. *bugjan*, 'buy,' O.E. *byċgan*; Goth. *fulljan*, 'fill,' O.E. *fyllan*; Goth. *huggrjan* (= huŋgrjan), 'to hunger,' O.E. *hyngr(i)an*.

In all these cases Gothic shows consistently a back vowel
in the root, followed by *j*; O.E. invariably has in the
same words a front vowel in the root, but has usually no
j or *i* following. We need not pause here to discuss
under what circumstances *j* is also preserved in O.E., but
may note that when it is lost in that language the preceding consonant is doubled, provided that the sound
immediately preceding the consonant is not a long vowel
(*cf. settan* and *byċġan*, where *ċġ* is the O.E. mode of
writing a *long* voiced stop).

In all the above cases, although only Gothic forms are
here given, O. Sax. and O.H.G. agree in showing *ō* (O.H.G.
uo), *a*, and *u* respectively where O.E. has *ē*, *e*, and *y*. The
inference we draw is that ō, a, and u are more primitive than
the English vowels in these words, and that the special
quality of these, front instead of back, is due to a change
in the earlier sounds produced by the following *j* or *i*. This
is still further borne out by the fact that ō, etc., are preserved in O.E. itself, in cases where the root is, not followed
by *j* or *i*. Thus by the side of *mētan* we have in O.E. the
substantive *ġe-mōt*, by the side of *fēdan*, *fōda*, ' food,' just
as we have *sōh-te* by the side of *sēċ(e)an*. With O.E.
nemnan we may compare the sub. *nama*, and with *fyllan*
the adj. *full*. The comparison of the other Germanic
tongues, in deciding the question of the difference of
vowel in *sēċ(e)an—sōhte*, showed us that O.E. must also
once have had an inf. **sōkjan*, since it enabled us to
supply the lost *j* which effected the change from the more
primitive vowel ō, preserved in Gothic and O. Sax. The
forms in the cognate languages also made it certain that
the original vowel was the same as that preserved in the

unchanged forms in O.E. itself. Another fact which emerges from our examination of the above forms is that the particular change in question, which has already been referred to in an earlier chapter of this book, although it took place before the earliest English documents, yet occurred after English had developed into a dialect, or group of dialects, independent from the parent Germanic. Had the change affected Primitive Gmc. before its differentiation, we should find traces of it in Gothic; whereas we find none, and only signs of its beginning in O. Sax. and O.H.G. This process of *i-* or *j-mutation*, as it is called, arose independently in English, and, at a later date, in most of the other Gmc. languages. It affects all back vowels in O.E. which occur in the roots of words containing originally *j* or *i* in the next syllable or suffix; not only in verbs, as in the examples given above, but in all words whose suffix fulfils, or once fulfilled, the necessary conditions.

When once the knowledge of such a process has been gained by a comparison of the cognate languages, it can be utilized for purposes of reconstruction, without a further appeal to the comparative method. Thus, if we find the O.E. forms *betst*, ' best,' *fyrst*, ' first,' compared with *fur-ðor*, we should be justified in assuming the possibility of an old superlative suffix *-ist*, which has changed *a* and *u* to *e* and *y* in these words, even if we had not, for the moment, the confirmatory evidence of Gothic *bat-ist-s*, ' best.'

We see that a knowledge of the sound changes peculiar to the individual languages helps us to reconstruct primitive forms which may be of use in a wider comparative survey; but this special knowledge of an individual language can only be gained, at first, by knowing what was the starting-point of the language we are considering, and this knowledge, again, can only be acquired with certainty by the help of the cognate languages. Our Primitive Gmc. forms, which we may reconstruct from English alone, must be tested by comparing them with the other Gmc. languages. If from our knowledge of the laws of each, we reach the same result in reconstruction, no matter from which we start, then we may have a very fair conviction that our reconstruction is right.

But it sometimes happens that the consideration of the Gmc. languages alone leaves us in the lurch, and that we are stopped by what are insuperable difficulties, so far as the light shed from these alone reaches.

If, for instance, we compare the Gmc. forms of so common a word as 'tooth,' we find that in O.E. we have *tōþ*, in Goth. *tunþus*, in O.H.G. *zand*; and we may well ask what is the relation of these forms to each other. Gothic and O.E. agree in the initial and final consonants of the root *t* and þ; there is, therefore, the a priori reason of greater frequency, for assuming that *t* and þ are more primitive than the O.H.G. *z* and *d*. On the other hand, Gothic and O.H.G. agree in having a nasal consonant after the vowel, and we must assume either that O.E. has lost an *n*, or that Gothic and O.H.G. have both introduced one in this word. According to the same general principle of relative frequency of occurrence, it is more reasonable to assume that these languages preserve an original nasal here, where O.E. has lost it. It is improbable that two languages so far separated geographi-

cally as Gothic and O.H.G., should have developed,
independently, a habit of infixing nasals. We naturally
next inquire why, in this case, O.E. has lost an original
nasal which is preserved by Gothic and O.H.G. There are
plenty of examples of words in which the latter languages
have a nasal, but in which O.E. has not : O.H.G. *gans*,
'goose,' O.E. *gōs* ; Goth. *munþs*, O.H.G. *mund*, ' mouth,'
O.E. *mūþ* ; Goth. *sinþs*, ' road,' ' journey,' O.H.G. *sind*,
also Goth. ga-*sinþja*, O.H.G. *gi-sindo*, ' travelling companion,' ' servant '; O.E., *sīþ*, *ge-sīþ* ; Goth. *anþar*, O.H.G.
andar, ' other,' O.E. *ōþer* ; Goth. and O.H.G. *hansa*,
'host,' O.E. *hōs* ; O.H.G. *samfto*, 'soft,' O.E. *sōft*. These
examples suffice to show the conditions under which the
nasal is lost in O.E. It will be observed that in all the
above cases, there is in Gothic, immediately after the
nasal, and in O.E., following the vowel, one or other of
the three consonants, *s*, *f*, or *þ*—that is to say, a *voiceless
open* consonant.

The agreement of Gothic and O.E., as regards the consonants, is a strong indication of these being primitive, so
that we can formulate the law that O.E. loses a nasal
(n, or m) before voiceless open consonants, and we can reconstruct for prehistoric O.E., forms with the nasals as
they occur in Gothic.

It is further to be noticed that the vowel which
precedes the nasal undergoes in O.E. a compensatory
lengthening, and that in cases where Gothic and O.H.G.,
and therefore presumably the parent Gmc. also, have the
combination -*an*+voiceless open consonant, O.E. has *ō*—
that is to say that in this case, the original *a* has been
rounded as well as lengthened. We may now return to

O.E. *tōþ*, and in the light of the above examples and remarks, we see that we shall be justified in reconstructing therefrom an earlier form *tanþ-*, which, allowing for the regular differences of the consonants, agrees entirely with the O.H.G. *zand*. The Gothic form, on the other hand, as we have seen, is *tunþ*-us instead of *tanþ-*, as we might have expected on the analogy of *anþar* compared with O.E. *ōþer*.

Is there any process of change peculiar to Gothic whereby a form *tanþ*- could become *tunþ-* ? There is none ; and the Gothic forms with -*un*-, such as *munþs*, quoted above, and *kunþs*, 'known,' O.E. *cūþ*, O.H.G. *chund* ; juggs (=juŋg-), 'young,' O. Fris., O.S., O.H.G. *jung* ; *hund*, 'hundred' ; O.E., O. Sax. *hund*, O.H.G. *hunt*, etc., show that Gothic, as a rule, agrees with the other Gmc. languages in preserving the combination -*un*- in cognate words. Indeed, the agreement is so complete, and so widely extended among the Gmc. languages ; that, following the ordinary method, we must assume that Gmc. -*un*- is *preserved* in all the languages ; and, conversely, that when the derived languages all agree in showing this combination it is original. The result of this is that we must regard the Gothic form *tunþ*- as original : preserved from the parent language, and not derived from any other form of the same 'root.' We are therefore compelled to conclude that there were in Gmc. two forms of this root : one, *tunþ-*, preserved in Gothic, and another, *tanþ-*, from which the O.E. and O.H.G. forms, and the O. Norse *tannr*, from *tanþ-r*, from *tanþ-az*, were derived. How are we to account for the differentiation of an original 'root' into two

forms, *tanþ*- and *tunþ*-? The fact itself is common
enough in Gothic and the other Gmc. languages, and the
so-called strong verbs offer plenty of examples. The
following table will illustrate this ·

		Inf	Pret. Sing.	Pret. Pl.	Past Partic	
O.E.	...	bind-an	band	bund-on	bund-en	'bind '
Goth.	...	bind-an	band	bund-um	bund-an-s	,,
O.H.G.	...	bint-an	bant	bunt-um	bunt-an	,,
O.E.	...	wind-an	wand	wund-	wund-	'wind'
Goth.	...	-wind-an	wand	wund-um	wund-ans	,,
O.H.G.	...	vint-an	vant	vunt-um	vunt-an	,,
O.E.	...	winn-an	wann	wunn-	wunn-	'struggle
Goth.	...	-winn-an	wann	wunn-um	wunn-ans	,,
O.H.G.	...	vinn-an	vann	vunn-um	vunn-an	,,

Numerous examples also occur of the same 'root'
appearing in different forms.

Gothic has *-hinþ-an*, 'to catch,' *hand-us*, 'the hand,'
originally 'that which seizes,' and *hunþ-s*, 'that which is
seized,' or 'booty'; O.E. has *hand*, and *hūþ*, 'booty,'
from *hunþ*-, with the loss of the nasal before -þ-, as in
mūþ, from *munþ*- ; O.H.G. *hant*, 'hand,' and heri-*hunda*
(=O.E. *hūþ*), 'war plunder.' Side by side with *sinþs* and
ga-*sinþa*, Goth. has the vb. *sand-jan*, 'send,' and O.E.
sīþ >*sinþ*-, and *send-an* >*sand-*jan, with the *j*-mutation
of *a* referred to above. Besides the changes which occur
in the strong vb. *bindan*, Gothic has and-*bund*-nan, 'to
release'; *bandi*, 'a fetter' (exactly corresponding to O.E.
bend, where *e* is the *i*-mutation of *a*); and ga-*binda*,
'bond,' etc.

These examples show that this interchange of vowels
within the same 'root' was an established fact in Gmc.
before its differentiation, since it occurs in all the derived

languages. We can, therefore, learn nothing of its origin from Gmc. alone. If we go beyond Gmc., and compare the forms in the other Aryan languages which are cognate with *tunþus*, etc., we find a curious variety of forms. Latin *dent-*, Gk. ὀ-δόντ-, Scrt. *dant-*, Lith. *dant*-ìs, are the forms in the principal Aryan languages which we have to compare with each other, and with the two Gmc. types *tanþ- and *tunþ-*, which we have found ourselves justified in reconstructing. The question now before us is : What are the Primitive Aryan types from which the above forms are derived, and what is their precise mutual relationship? Our comparison of the Gmc. languages yielded two types for parent Gmc. ; to what does a wider survey lead us? In the first instance, we may settle the question of the consonants. We note that Scrt., Gk., Latin, and Lith. all agree in having *d-* as the initial, and *-t-* as the final consonant of the root; and in the face of this unanimity we must conclude that sounds which all these languages have preserved, are the original Aryan sounds. Gmc. *t* = original *d-*, and þ = original *t*, are the result of a characteristic ' shifting' of the older consonants, which, with the reservation formulated in what is known as *Verner's Law*, hereafter to be discussed, invariably produces the same results ; so that wherever the other languages agree in having *d*, Gmc. has *t*, and where they have *t*, Gmc. has þ, except under the special conditions stated by Verner.

We may now return to the vowels, and for this purpose it will be convenient to deal here with the group of vowel +*n*,—*on*, *en*, *an*, etc. It might be contended that since Scrt., Lith., and Gmc. all agree in possessing a form of

the above root with -*an*-, this must be regarded as a primitive form ; let us see whether this can be upheld. If -*an*-is to be regarded as a primitive Aryan form, it can only be on account of the agreement in the three languages which we have just noted. This assumption would imply that we regard a primitive -*an*- as having been preserved in Scrt., Lith., and Gmc. We shall do well to examine severally the claims of each language to the primitiveness of its -*a*- and -*an*- sounds. Let us take Scrt. first. Although this language agrees with Gmc. and Lith. in this case, it is at variance with Gk., which has -*ov*-. The same disparity is observable in Scrt. *jambha*-, ' tooth ';
Gk. γόμφος, γομφίος, ' molar ' (which correspond to O.E. *camb*, ' comb '), and in *tam*, ' this ' (acc.) ; Gk. τόν ; Goth. þan-a ; Scrt. *damas*, ' house '; Gk. δόμος ; Lat. *domus*. Here we have Scrt. and Gmc. *an*, *am* by the side of Gk. -*ov*-, -*oμ*-.

But in Scrt. *janas*, ' race,' we have -en- both in Latin and Gk.—*genus*, γένος ; and the same divergence appears in Scrt. *bandhus*, a 'relative,' compared with Gk. πενθερός. Lith. also shows disagreement with Scrt. here, for its cognate is *bèndras*, ' companion.' This is the same root which in Gmc. has, as we have seen, the three forms *bind*-, *band*-, *bund*-. In Scrt. *ánti*, ' against,' Gk. ἀντί, Lat. *ante*, Scrt. agrees with Gk. and Latin.

These examples show that Scrt. -*an*- is represented in Gk. sometimes by -*ov*-, sometimes by -*ev*-, more rarely by *av*-.

If we compare the correspondences of simple *a* in Scrt. without a following nasal, we find the same divergence in some, at least, of the cognate languages.

1. Scrt. *a* = Gk. *a* in *ájami*, 'drive'; Gk. ἄγω, Lat. ago: *ajras*, 'ground'; Gk. αγρός; Lat. ager; Goth. *akrs*.

2. But Scrt. *a* = Gk. *o* in *pati*, 'husband'; Gk. πόσις : *avi-*, 'sheep'; Gk. ὅις (from *ὅϝις); Lat. *ovis*: katara, 'which of two'; Gk. πότερος : *dadarśa*, 'he has seen'; Gk. δέδορκε, etc.

3. Scrt. *a* = Gk. ε in *asti*, 'is'; Gk. ἐστί; Lat. est; Lith. *ěsti*.

Scrt. *aśva*, 'horse'; Lat. equus : Scrt. *ca*, 'and'; Gk. τὲ; Lat. que.

Scrt. *páta-ti*, 'he flies'; Gk. πέτε-ται; Lat. petit, etc.

We see that the three vowels *a, e, o* in Latin and Greek are all represented in Sanscrit by *a*; in fact, *e* and *o* do not exist at all in this language. If, then, Scrt. *a* be in all cases primitive, we must assume that the other languages which possess a more varied vowel system have differentiated an original vowel *a* into three distinct sounds, *a, e, o*. The alternative is that the three vowels existed in the mother-tongue, but were all levelled in Scrt. under one sound, *a*.

Passing to Lithuanian, this language agrees with Scrt. in having *a* where Gk. and Latin show *o* : nakt-is, 'night,' Lat. *nox* (= *nokt-s*); *-patis*, 'lord'; Gk. πόσις; *avis*, 'sheep'; Gk. ὅ(ϝ)ις, Lat. ovis.

On the other hand, Lithuanian agrees with Gk., Lat., Gmc. in showing *e*, thus differing from Scrt.—esmi, 'am'; Gk. ειμι (= εσμι) : medùs, 'honey'; Gk. μεθυ; O.E. medu (= *medu); O.H.G. *metu;* but Scrt. *madhu*: *sĕnas*, 'old'; Gk. ἔνος (= *σένος); Lat. *senex*. Again, the closely-allied Slavonic languages, such as Old Bulgarian (or Old Church Slav.), agree also with Gk. in having *o* in

cases where Lith. has *a* : O. Slav. *nosti*, 'night'; Lith. *naktis*.
O. Slav. *ovi-tsa*, 'sheep'; Lith. *avis*. This makes it probable
that *o* existed in Primitive Lith. also, but was unrounded
to *a* in the independent life-history of the language.

Last we have to deal with Germanic, which, like Scrt., had
already, in its earliest literary period, no original *o* sound ;
at any rate, not in stressed syllables. It can be shown that
when this vowel appears in the Old Gmc. languages, it is
either derived by a secondary process from an earlier *u*, or
has been preserved in late loan words from foreign languages.
In all cases where Gk. has *o*, Gmc. has *a* in cognate words.
But it can be established that the sound *o* underwent a
change to *a* within the historic period, since foreign proper
names which contained the former sound appear in Gmc.
speech, when borrowed, with *a*. Thus the Gallo-Roman
Moguntiacum, 'Mainz,' is *Maginza* in O.H.G.; and *Vosegus*,
' the Voges, appears with *a* in O.H.G., as *Wascono walt*.
The inference generally drawn from these facts is that up to
a certain period, parent Gmc. preserved *o*, which it inherited
from Aryan ; but that then a tendency arose to unround
o to *a*, which tendency naturally affected the loan words
also. Those words which were borrowed subsequent to this
change, preserved their *o*-sound in Gmc. speech (*cf.* O.H.G.
kocchōn, ' to cook,' from Lat. *coquere*).

If the above reasoning be correct, then Gmc. originally
possessed the vowel *o ;* its *a* is not primitive in those cases
where it corresponds to *o* in Gk. and Latin, and therefore
proves nothing when compared with the *a* of Scrt. and Litn.

We have now briefly examined the claims of *a* in Scrt.,
Lith., and Gmc. successively, to be regarded as primitive
in cases where Gk. and Latin have the vowel *o*. We have

seen that Scrt. *a* corresponds not only to *a* in Gk. and Latin, but also to *e* and *o;* and we are therefore forced to admit, either that Gk. and Latin preserve the three original sounds, or, at any rate, an original diversity, whereas Scrt. has lost it ; or that in the former languages, one original sound, without any discoverable difference of conditions, has been treated in three different ways. The latter possibility we may reject at once on general grounds. For the former view there are overwhelming arguments. Of these, that which establishes beyond any reasonable doubt the primitiveness of Gk. *e,* is the strongest ; and to it is due the conviction, now universally shared by all philological scholars, that the Gk. vowel system is far nearer to that of the original Aryan than are the Sanscrit vowels.

There are certain words which have a variety of back-stop in Latin, Celtic, and Lithuanian, but which in Sanscrit have a sound, expressed in transliteration by the symbol *c,* and usually pronounced (tʃ), but which is classified as a 'palatal,' and was originally, almost certainly, a front-stop. The vowel which follows it is always *a* in Scrt. In Gk. these words have π or τ, which, for reasons into which it is needless to enter here, are known to have developed from a back-stop with lip modification.

This 'palatalization' in Sanscrit was for a long time unaccounted for, since, in other words, Sanscrit agrees with the languages above mentioned in also having *k*—that is, a back consonant.

The explanation was discovered independently by several scholars about the same time (see Bechtel, *Hauptprobleme,* p. 62). It is this : In cases where the European languages (Gk., Latin. etc.) have *a* or *o* following the consonant,

Sanscrit agrees with them in having a back consonant; in those cases where the former languages have *e*, Sanscrit has *c*, the front consonant. A natural inference is that in Sanscrit also, *e* formerly occurred in those cases where it is found in Gk., Latin, etc., and, *e* being a front vowel, fronted the preceding consonant. After the fronting process was complete, Sanscrit levelled *e* under *a*, the series of changes probably being: *e—œ—a*. If this is so, then prehistoric Sanscrit must have agreed with all the European tongues in possessing *e*, and thus the last argument against accepting this as the original sound disappears.

Examples are: Scrt. *panca*, 'five,' Gk. πέντε (from **penkwe*); Lat. *quinque* (from ** kwenkwe*, from **penkwe*). Scrt. *catvâras*, 'four,' Gk. τέσσαρες and πέσσαρες (Bœotian), Lith. *keturi*, Old Irish *cethir*. On the other hand, Sanscrit has *kákša*, 'hip-joint'=Lat. *coxa*; also kakúd, 'summit'=Lat. *cacūmen*.

When it was thus established that Sanscrit *a* was not original in cases where the other languages had *e*, it was further asked, Why should Scrt. *a*, which corresponds to *o* in Gk. and Lat., etc., be original either? No reason could be shown for the development in these languages of *o* from an earlier *a*; but, on the other hand, belief in the primitiveness of the Scrt. vowel system was seriously shaken. Henceforth, it was regarded as, at the very least, highly probable that the three vowels *a*, *e*, *o* all existed in the Aryan mother-tongue; a view which, as has been said, scholars now regard as established. Of all the Aryan languages, the Hellenic group are now considered to preserve the primitive vowel system most faithfully. Greek is by far the richest in vowel sounds, and hence, instead of attributing, as was formerly done, a poor vowel system to the mother-tongue, it is now the universal practice to credit it rather with the wealth and variety which is found in that group of dialects, than with the poverty and comparative monotony of Sanscrit.

After this long discussion, which it is hoped may have afforded some illustration of the methods of comparison and reconstruction, we may return to a consideration of the various forms of the root 'tooth' in the different Aryan languages.

We had established (see p. 154) the existence of two forms of the root in Gmc.—*tunþ-, which is found in Gothic, and *tanþ-, which is the ancestor of O.E. tōþ and O.H.G. zand. The forms enumerated from other languages were—Scrt. dant; Lith. dant-is; Lat. dent-; and Gk. ὀ-δόντ-. From what has just been said, it will be seen that we are now in a position to regard Gk. -δοντ- as primitive, and practically identical with the ancestral form. We are further justified in equating it with the Gmc. *tanþ (see p. 158), and with the Lith. dant-is (pp. 157, 158).

As regards the Scrt. form, the a might represent either an original o, in which case the Scrt. form may also be derived from the form *dont-, or it might be derived from an earlier *dent-. Since, however, the former is so well established for several branches of the Aryan family, it is on the whole, perhaps, more probable that the Scrt. form also goes back to this, in common with Lith., Gk., and Gmc. We may now pass on to discuss the Latin form dent- and the Gothic tunþ-us. What are the mutual relations of these, and what connection have they with the Aryan *dont- which we have established?

11

Lat. *dent-* might, if taken by itself, be an original form, representing an Aryan **dent-* ; just as Gk. πενθ-ερός, Lith. *bend-ras*, represent an original **bhendh-*. This form occurs in Gmc. as *bind*-an, with Gmc. change from *e* to *i* before *n*+consonant. At this rate, original **dent-* would produce in Gmc. **tenþ-*, and thence **tinþ-*, but this form of this particular word is not found in any Gmc. tongue.

There are other cases, however, when Lat. *-en* corresponds to Gmc. *-un* : for instance, Lat. *cent-um*, Goth. *hund-*, '100'; to these forms there correspond ἐ-κατόν in Gk., *szimtas* in Lith., and *śatám* in Scrt. Again, Lat. *ment-*, 'mind'; Goth. ga-*mund-s*, 'remembrance,' corresponds to Scrt. *mati-*, 'thought.' In these cases we see that Lat. *en*, Gmc. *un*, correspond to forms in Scrt. and Gk. which have no nasal. In this case Lat. *en* cannot be derived from an original *en*, since, as we have just seen, that is preserved in Gk. and in Scrt. becomes *an* (πενθερός, Lat. *of-fendix*, 'tie,' 'band'; Scrt. *bandhus*, etc.) ; further, original *en* equals Gothic *-in-*, and not *-un-*. We may formulate our results so far thus :

$$\text{The Series} \begin{cases} \text{Scrt. } \textit{-an-} \\ \text{Gk. } \textit{-ov-} \\ \text{Lat. } \textit{-on-} \\ \text{Gmc. } \textit{-an-} \end{cases} = \text{Idg. } \textit{-on-}. \qquad \text{The Series} \begin{cases} \text{Scrt. } \textit{-an-} \\ \text{Gk. } \textit{-ev-} \\ \text{Lat. } \textit{-en.} \\ \text{Gmc. } \textit{-en} \text{ (in)} \end{cases} = \text{Idg. } \textit{en}.$$

$$\text{The Series} \begin{cases} \text{Scrt. } a \\ \text{Gk. } \textit{-a-} \\ \text{Lat. } \textit{-en-} \\ \text{Gmc. } \textit{-un-} \end{cases} = \text{Idg. } ?$$

That is to say that by the side of the forms *-en-* and *-on-* of roots with a nasal, we must assume that a third form existed—a form which, whatever it was, acquired various sounds in the separate development of each Aryan language. It is generally assumed that this third form was a weakened form which possessed, originally, no definite vowel sound, but contained a syllabic nasal very similar, probably, to the second syllable of the English word ' *button* ' (batn). Comparative philologists usually write this hypothetical sound ꬼ, to distinguish it from the consonantal *n*, or ꬺ in the case of *centum*, etc.; *cf.* Lith. *szimtas*, from Aryan *$\check{k}$ꬺtóm.* We have thus established a strong probability that Gothic *tunþ-* and Latin *dent-* are both from an original form *$dn̥t$-*, whereas the various other forms of this word, including the O.H.G. *zand* and O.E. *tōþ*, are all derivable from a primitive *dont-*.

Although only two forms of this root have survived, other similar roots preserve all three forms, thus : πενθερός, *bendras* and *bind-*, from *bhendh-* ; *band* and *bandhus*, from *bhondh;* *bund* and of-*fend*-ix, from *bhn̥dh-*. This differentiation of an original vowel, which goes back to the mother-tongue, is known as *Ablaut* or *Gradation*. The supposed causes of this phenomenon will be treated later on.

We have endeavoured in the above discussion to illustrate the method, and line of reasoning whereby the reconstructed forms of the mother-tongue are arrived at.

The principles upon which our method is based are briefly stated by Brugmann (*Techmer's Zeitschrift*, Bd. I., pp. 254, 255). They may be summarized as follows :

The probability that any given feature in a language is primitive increases with the number of languages in which it can be traced.

The greater the geographical separation of those languages in which the same feature occurs, the greater the likelihood that it is inherited from the mother-tongue.

Geographical separation limits the probability that the

11—2

occurrence of the same peculiarity in several languages is due to contact between them at a late period, or to borrowing.

In cases where we find diversity of form in the derived languages, we assume diversity in the mother-tongue, unless we are able to show that this diversity is due to special conditions in individual languages—that is, to particular laws of sound change which we can state definitely.

It is desirable to take as wide a survey as possible, and to check the results and conclusions at which we arrive, from several sides.

In all reconstruction we must be guided by common-sense; we must bear in mind that we are dealing with sounds, and not with symbols, and must not overstep the limits of what is reasonable and probable in the sphere of actual change of sound.

CHAPTER IX

THE ARYAN OR INDO GERMANIC MOTHER-TONGUE, AND THE DERIVED FAMILIES OF LANGUAGES

SINCE even the most elementary books on the History of English contain at least some statement to the effect that there once existed a language, long since extinct, which is now known as the Aryan mother-tongue, from which various groups or families of languages sprang, together with an enumeration of these, a very brief account of the present views on this subject will suffice in this place. All that need be attempted here is a short and, if possible, a clear account of what is meant by the phrase *mother-tongue*, an enumeration of the principal groups of languages into which this was differentiated, the supposed relationship in which they stand to each other, with a more particular account of one group—the Germanic, of which our own language is a member.

Among the numerous general authorities on the questions with which we are about to deal, there may be mentioned: Isaac Taylor, *The Origin of the Aryans*, 1890; Sweet, *History of Language*, 1900; Schrader, *Sprachvergleichung und Urgeschichte*, 1890; and, above all, Brugmann, *Grundriss der Vergleichenden Grammatik der Indogermanischen Sprachen* [2nd ed.], Bd. I. (Lautlehre), 1897 ; and *Kurze Vergleichende Grammatik der Indo-germanischen Sprachen*, Bd. I. (Lautlehre), 1902, by the same author. The introductory chapters of the last two works deal with the classification and other general problems connected with the Aryan languages. The larger book should be constantly consulted by advanced students of Comparative Philology, while even beginners might with advantage consult the smaller. Brugmann's works are standard text-books of the best kind ; they are masterpieces of method, and display the latest results of modern research, more especially in so far as it deals with such problems as are settled and no longer under discussion. Brugmann represents the solid, safe, conservative wing of the new science of language, of which, together with Osthoff, Paul, Sievers, and one or two more, he was the founder more than thirty years ago. Students of the history of the Science of Comparative Philology will recognise Scherer and Leskien as the intellectual fathers of the band of scholars of whom Osthoff and Brugmann are now the distinguished and venerated chiefs.

The Conception of a Family of Languages.

The resemblances and agreements in the forms of words, in vocabulary, and in inflections, which exist between such languages as Mod. Eng., Dutch, Danish, and German, are so striking that they cannot fail to impress even the least instructed student of two or more of the above languages. The farther back we go in the history of these tongues, and the earlier the forms of them which we compare, the closer becomes the resemblance. That there is an intimate connection between them is obvious. They

are commonly classed together under the general name of
the Germanic or Teutonic languages. We may take a few
points of resemblance for consideration : (1) The modern
Continental languages of the so-called Germanic group
have, in a large number of cases, practically the same
group of sounds associated with the same meaning.
German *kommen*, 'come,' Dutch *komme(n)*, Swedish *komma*,
German *tag*, 'day,' Dutch *dag* (dāh), Danish *dag* (dæȝ);
German *ein, zwei, drei, vier, fünf*, Dutch *een, twee, drie,
vier, vijf*, Swedish *en, twå, tre, fyra, fem*= 1, 2, 3, 4, 5 ;
German *mutter*, Dutch *moeder*, Swedish *moder*, ' mother.'
And so on throughout the vocabulary, we find that these
languages have in common thousands of words identical
in meaning, and differing but little in pronunciation.
The resemblances of Mod. Eng. to the other languages
are in many cases not so close, but none the less unmistakable. (2) We find that all of these languages agree in
possessing a class of so-called weak verbs, which form their
past tense by the addition of the suffix *-de, -te, -ed,* or *-ede*,
to the root of the verb.   Eng. *hear, hear-d ;* Swedish *höra,
hör-de ;* Dutch *hooren, hoor-de ;* German *hören, hör-te*, and
so on. (3) These languages all possess groups of so-
called strong verbs, which form their past tenses and past
participles by series of changes in the vowels of the
'root': Eng. *sing, sang, sung;* Danish *synge, sang,
sunget;* Dutch *zingen, zong, ge-zongen ;* German *singen,
sang, ge-sungen*, etc.

Now, agreement between languages which includes
sounds, vocabulary, inflection, and such deep - rooted
features as vowel change within the 'root' itself, cannot
be mere coincidence.   Neither, when we find such common

features equally among widely-separated groups of speakers, such as the Germans, Swedes, Danes, and English, can the agreement be the result of wholesale borrowing; for in this case it would naturally be asked, from whom have all these languages borrowed their characteristic features? Again, there is no reason for assuming that any one of these languages is the surviving ancestor of all the others.

There remains only the possibility that English, Dutch, the Scandinavian languages, and German, are each and all the descendants of the same original language; that they represent, in fact, the various forms into which a parent language, which no longer exists, has been differentiated, by virtue of such factors of isolation as those we have already discussed. *Cf.* p. 96, etc. This extinct form of speech, out of which we assume all these languages to have developed, along more or less different lines, we call *Primitive Germanic, Parent Germanic,* or simply *Germanic.* If we wished to compare the Germanic languages systematically, we should take the oldest forms of each which are preserved in writing. The above examples are drawn from the modern languages, partly because these are, on the whole, more familiar and accessible to the general student, partly also to show how close the resemblance still is, even after all these centuries of separation. The oldest considerable body of ancient Germanic speech is the fourth-century translation of part of the Bible in Gothic, a language long extinct.

By applying to the other ancient and modern languages or dialects of Europe and India tests similar to those briefly suggested above, similar results are obtained by scholars—namely, that at various points languages resolve themselves into groups of closely-related forms of

speech. For each of these groups it appears necessary to
assume a primitive ancestral form which no longer survives,
and from which the various members of the group have
been differentiated, in the same way as the Germanic
languages sprang from parent Germanic.

Thus we are able, from this point of view, to distinguish
the following groups or *Families of Speech :* (1) *Indian,*
of which the best-known ancient representative is *Sanscrit,
Iranian,* which includes *Old* (*and Mod.*) *Persian* (West
Iranian), and *Zend,* the dialect in which the *Avesta*—that
is, the collection of the ancient sacred books of the Parsees
—is written (*East Iranian*). This dialect is also known as
Old Bactrian. Indian and Iranian dialects are usually
grouped under the general head of *Indo-Iranian.* The
earliest remains of Sanscrit are the hymns of the Rig-Veda,
the language of which is approximately 4,000 years old.
(2) *Armenian,* whose written records go back to the fifth
century of our era. (3) *Hellenic,* or Greek dialects.
(4) *Albanian,* now recognised as a member of an independent
group. (5) *Italic,* which consists on the one hand of *Latin,*
and on the other of the *Oscan* and *Umbrian* dialects.
(6) *Celtic,* of which ancient *Gaulish* was a member, but
which is best known from *Old* and *Modern Irish* and *Scotch
Gaelic* on the one hand, and from *Welsh* in all its stages on
the other. (7) *Germanic.* (8) *Baltic-Slavonic.* The last
represents two nearly-related divisions of one original group.
The *Baltic* division is known to us from *Lettish* (still
spoken), *Old Prussian* (which died out in the seventeenth
century), and by *Lithuanian,* spoken at the present day by
something between one million and a half and two million
persons in Russia and East Prussia. Lithuanian records

go no further back than the tenth century. The *Slavonic* division consists of *Russian, Bulgarian, Servian* (Eastern), *Bohemian* or *Chekh* (tʃɛh), *Sorbian,* and *Polish* (Western). The oldest form of Slavonic known is preserved in a translation of the Bible and other religious writings from the ninth century. The dialect is known as *Old Bulgarian, Old Church Slavonic,* or simply *Old Slavonic.*

The Aryan Family of Languages.

A comparison of the common characteristics of each of the above families of languages with the others reveals the fact that there are many features shared by the whole group of families. These consist of fundamental elements of vocabulary, such as the numerals, the substantive verb, the pronouns, the names for the natural relationships. Further innumerable suffixes and formative elements appear, under varying forms, it is true, in all the above families. They all show the same principle of vowel gradation, or differentiation of vowels in the same root, and the main outlines of sentence-structure and syntax are common to all.

Here, again, the points of agreement are too numerous and too deeply seated to be fortuitous; and the same inference is drawn with regard to the mutual relations of the various families, as were drawn from facts of the same order, in connection with the relationship of the different languages which go to make up a given family.

The assumption is made, that each of the now separate families of languages is sprung from a common parent language, the characteristics of which are preserved with varying degrees of fidelity in the derived languages. This common parent, the undifferentiated ancestral form of speech, from which it is assumed that *Indo-Iranian* and *Slavonic*, and *Greek* and *Latin*, and *Celtic* and *Germanic*, have all been developed, is known as the *Aryan Mother-Tongue*, *Primitive Aryan*, or *Indo-Germanic* (Idg.), etc. This form of speech is, of course, nowhere spoken at the present time, nor has it ever been within the historic period. Authorities differ as to the length of time which has elapsed since the differentiation of the mother-tongue into dialects, but we may take it at something between ten and twelve thousand years.

Where was Primitive Aryan spoken?

The answer to this question, down to twenty-five years ago, was generally given in the words which the late Mr. Max Müller used, in dealing with the subject, to the end of his life—'somewhere in Asia.' With the exception, however, of Mr. Max Müller, and the distinguished Berlin Professor, Johann Schmidt, who died two or three years ago, probably no other responsible authority would have given such an answer—at least, not in a dogmatic manner—any time during the last quarter of a century. The question is discussed at length in the works mentioned above by Taylor, Schrader, and Sweet; and among recent contributions to the subject, the reader may also refer to Schrader, *Reallexikon der Indogerm. Altertumskunde*, 1901, under heading, '*Urheimat der Indogermanen*'; Hirt, *Indogerm. Forsch.*, i., p. 464; and Kretschmer, *Einl. in die Gesch. d. griech. Spr.*, 1896. It is sufficient here to say that the universal view now held by scholars is that the '*Home of the undivided Aryans*' was 'somewhere' in *Northern or Central Europe*.

In favour of the old view no serious argument ever has been, or ever could be, advanced, while all the evidence derived from archæology, ethnology, and comparative philology, makes for the probability of the ' *European hypothesis.*'

It is to be deplored that the writers of elementary text-books, or ' cram-books,' as they too often are, should still continue to copy, out of the works of an earlier generation, among other views now obsolete, this particular view of migration in successive waves from Asia, which often appears in modern books of the class alluded to, not as a tentative and possible account of what happened, but in the form of a categorical statement of undisputed fact. Unfortunately, the theory has been discredited for more than thirty years.

The Aryan Race.

It used formerly to be assumed that, since affinity of language had been proved between Indians, Slavs, Germans, Greeks, Italians, and Celts, it therefore also followed that ' the same blood flowed in the veins' of all. At the present time probably no impartial observer would suggest such a view. The Aryan languages are obviously spoken at the present day by men of very different physical types, and certainly of distinct race. Which of the existing races who speak Aryan languages represents the original race? Perhaps none. On the other hand, it is maintained by many writers that the blonde, long-headed races of Northern Europe are nearest in physical type to the original Aryans. This question, however interesting in itself from many points of view, has but little bearing upon the problems of speech development with which we are here concerned.

Whether the original speakers of Primitive Aryan were fair, like some Swedes and Russians; or dark, like other Slavs, and like some of the speakers of Irish and Welsh at the present day; or whether the mother-tongue was spoken both by fair and dark races, does not primarily concern us. We are content to know that there was a mother-tongue, which, in the course of time, spread over an immense geographical area, and was acquired by people of various racial types, who lost their own language in consequence; a fact which was probably of significance in determining the particular line of deviation from the original form, which Aryan speech followed in different areas (see *ante*, pp. 86 and 87).

The Relative Primitiveness of the Divisions of Aryan Speech.

As regards the preservation of inflections in their original fulness and variety, the general principle seems to be that those languages which longest preserved their old '*free*' accent of the mother-tongue, such as Sanscrit, Greek, Baltic-Slavonic, retained also for a long time a large proportion of the original suffixes and formative elements following the root; those, on the other hand, which, like Latin, Celtic, and Germanic, developed a fixed and stereotyped accent at a comparatively early period, suffered a greater loss of inflections through the weakening of that part of words which was habitually unaccented.

When we come to consider sound changes, however, no special claim to superior general fidelity to the original quality of the sounds, in other than final syllables, can be advanced in favour of any particular group of languages.

A sound is here subject to numerous changes, both
Combinative and Isolative; there it appears to enjoy
immunity from change. Thus, for instance, ancient
Greek has preserved the rich and varied vowel system
of Primitive Aryan with remarkable fidelity, but the old
consonantal system undergoes many striking changes in
this language: *s*, except when final, becomes *h*, and
is often lost; the old back consonants with lip modification become, according to the conditions in which they
appear, pure lip stops, or pure point-teeth stops; the
old voiced aspirates are all unvoiced; if two aspirates
of any kind follow each other in successive syllables of the
same word, the first loses its aspiration.   This last change
is known as ' *Grassman's Law*,' and applies also to Sanscrit.
All final consonants are lost, and *t* before *i* becomes *s*.
Sanscrit has a poor and monotonous vowel system compared with Greek; but the consonants, with the exception
of the back series (back, back-outer, and back-lip-modified),
are on the whole primitive.   The outer varieties of back
consonants become š (ʃ) and ž respectively.   Latin preserves
in many cases the simple vowels intact, but they are liable
to various combinative changes; the diphthongs *oi, eu, ou*,
are all levelled under *ū* (though O. Lat. still has *oe* for the
first); *ai* becomes *ae* (*ae*), and then *ē; ei* becomes *ī*.   Latin
preserves faithfully the lip-modified back consonants which
Greek changes so completely; but gets rid altogether of
aspirated stops, which become under various conditions
b, d, and *f*.   Germanic preserves the old vowel system
fairly well, but levels *ā* under *ō*, *o* under *a*, *ei* under *ī*,
and *oi* under *ai*.   All the stop consonants undergo change;
the voiced stops are unvoiced, the voiceless stops are

opened in the corresponding areas of articulation; the
voiced aspirated stops also become the corresponding
voiced open consonants.

Such are a few of the principal characteristic changes which
take place in four important families of the Aryan languages.
Clearly the paths of development are very various.

The Mutual Relations of the Chief Groups of Aryan Speech.

The problem of how to group the Aryan languages, or
families of languages, among themselves in such a way as
to express the degree of relationship in which they stand
to each other has occupied a number of eminent scholars.
Schleicher (*Deutsche Sprache*[2], p. 29) remarks, in somewhat general terms, that when two or more members of
a family of languages resemble each other closely, we
naturally assume that they have not been so long separated from each other, as have other members of the same
family which have already diverged from each other much
farther. On the grounds of this principle, and guided by
what he assumed to be decisive points of resemblance,
Schleicher formulated his famous ' *Stammbaum*,' or genealogical tree, which expresses his conception of the inter-
relations of the Idg. languages and the relative periods
at which they differentiated from the mother-tongue and
from each other (see *Compendium*[2], 1866, p. 9). He con-
ceives that Idg. first split into two branches ('durch
ungleiche entwickelung')—that is to say that the ancestral
form of Slavonic and Germanic (' *Slavo-deutsch* ') deviated
from the remaining *Ursprache*. Then this remaining stem,
which Schleicher calls ' *Ariograekoitaloceltisch*,' divided

into Arian (that is, the Indian group) on the one hand, and a dialect from which was subsequently differentiated Greek, Italic, and Celtic, on the other.

This *Stammbaum* theory was ruthlessly attacked by Johann Schmidt in 1872 (*Verwandtschaftsverhältnisse der Idg. Spr.*), who altogether rejects the old explanation of the Idg. differentiation, and substitutes for it what is known as the ' *Wellen-*, or *Übergangstheorie* ' —that is, the theory of gradual transition. Schmidt's investigation embraced at once all the various points of agreement which exist among all the groups of Idg. speech.   As a result, he believed himself justified in giving the following account of the process of the breaking up of the primitive speech.   Indo-Germanic speech extended over a geographically unbroken area, in which arose from the earliest times, at different points, slight beginnings of incipient dialects in the shape of sound variation, which extended more or less far from their starting-place into the neighbouring districts.   These differences grew up gradually among the speakers of what was once a homogeneous speech, and formed the proto-types of the subsequent families of languages.   These dialects, however, Schmidt regarded as, in the first place, forming a continuous series, and shading one into the other.   Then, here and there, the speech of one area gained in importance and strength, and absorbed those on either side which differed only slightly from it, thus destroying several links in the chain and leaving a gulf. This process happened in various centres, with the result that *speech-islands* were left, which differed widely from the surrounding forms.   This was the origin of the great

families of Idg. speech.   (For good account of Schmidt's
theory *cf.* Schrader, *Sprvgl.*, p. 89, etc. ; and Brugmann
in *Techmer's Ztschr.*, i., p. 226, etc.)

This explanation entirely swept away Schleicher's original
'speech unities' of 'Slavo-Germanic,' ' Graeko-Italo-Cetic,'
etc.   Schmidt showed that if the Slavonic languages could
not be widely separated from the Germanic, on account of
certain resemblances, too strong and too numerous to be
due to coincidence, neither could the Slavonic languages
be separated from the Indo-Iranian group.   Greek, on the
other hand, had undoubtedly close affinities to Sanscrit ;
but also other, equally strongly-marked characters in
common with Latin.   Thus the old division of the
European and Asiatic branches, supposed to represent
two main dialects of the Mother-Tongue, was done away
with.   The Gmc. family in Schmidt's scheme comes between
Slavonic and Celtic, and the latter forms the connecting-
link between Gmc. and Latin, thus completing the circle
of affinities.   This ingenious view of gradual transitions,
and the subsequent dying out of intermediate varieties,
was accepted by Schrader (*loc. cit.*) and by Paul (in the
Chapter 'Sprachspaltung,' *Principien d. Sprgesch.*).

Modifications of the ' Übergangstheorie.'

In 1876 *Leskien* published his *Deklination im Slavisch-
Litauischen und Germanischen*, in the Introduction to which
he discusses the question of Idg. classification at some
length.   On p. x of the Introduction he criticises Schmidt's
statement of his case, and contrasts the new views with the
Stammbaumtheorie.   He points out that the ' *Übergangstheorie* ' by itself, involves the gradual spread of popu-

lation, by mere increase, over a slowly but ever increasing area. Schleicher's explanation involves migrations of considerable magnitude, a process which would accomplish the work of differentiation far quicker and more completely. Leskien, however, does not by any means reject Schmidt's hypothesis, but proposes to modify it, and to combine it with the theory of genealogical development. It is possible for a large community, whose speech had already two slight dialectal varieties, to migrate from their original seat and settle down, still as one community, for a long time. In this case we assume three sections, as it were, of Schmidt's community—A, B, C, of which B's speech forms the connecting-link between A and B, and his different points of agreement with both. Thus in their original seat A and B have had, as it were, a common speech life, so have B and C, but not A and C. Then B and C move off together, and in their new home continue their common life. Any developments subsequently undergone by A must be quite distinct from B; and, on the other hand, B may develop on lines common to C, but in which obviously A can have no share. Leskien applies this argument to the relations of Indo-Iranian, Slav.-Lith., and Gmc., and considers the treatment of Aryan $\acute{k}$ and of bh-m; for this latter example I propose to substitute that of bh = Gk. ϕ, Gmc. and Slav. b. Indo-Iranian shares with the Baltic-Slavic languages the change of one of the original k sounds to š ($\int$), but Gmc. shows no such tendency; on the other hand, Indo-Iranian (originally, at any rate) preserves the old aspirate bh, while both Gmc. and Slav. get rid of the aspiration.

With this modification, then, Leskien's diagram (Einleit-ung, p. xi) may be reproduced as follows:

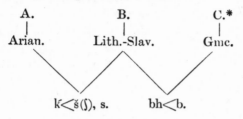

A.   B.   C.*

Arian.   Lith.-Slav.   Gmc.

k < š(ʃ), s.   bh < b.

Recent Views.

If we accept Hirt's view of the importance of foreign influence in differentiating language, (*cf.* p. 85) it would seem that some such modification of Schmidt's theory as that proposed by Leskien is necessary ; since, on the one hand, it accounts for the points of resemblance between different families of Idg. speech, and, on the other, allows also for the possibility of contact with speakers of non-Idg. languages, which may explain the great diversity which also exists. With regard, how-ever, to the features which several languages have in common, but which others do not possess, on the basis of which Schmidt postulated his system of continuous contact, Brugmann has taken up a very sceptical attitude. In an elaborate article in *Techmer's Zeitschrift für allge-meine Sprachwissenschaft*, i., p. 226, etc. (*Zur Frage nach den Verwandtschaftsverhältnissen der Idg. Spr.*), after dis-

---

* The similarity between Slav.-Lith. and Gmc. in their treatment of original *bh* consisted primarily in the loss of aspiration ; since although, later on, the individual Gmc. languages developed a voiced lip-stop (b) under certain conditions, there is reason to believe that this sound did not exist in Gmc. itself, and that *bh* became at first a lip-open-voice consonant.

cussing one after another, all the special points of development which two or more groups of Idg. speech have in
common, he comes to the conclusion that the majority of
them prove nothing in support of the assumption of the
peculiarly close relationship claimed between those groups
of languages in which they occur (*loc. cit.*, pp. 252-254).
The only exception to this destructive conclusion admitted by Brugmann is the close relationship of Celtic
and Italic (p. 253). The same views are maintained in
the most recent pronouncements of the same author (*cf.*
*Grundriss*², i., pp. 22-27 ; and *Kurze-vergleichende Gr.*,
pp. 3, 4, 18-22). The agreements which exist then, as
they unquestionably do, between two or more speech
groups, are not necessarily to be explained by assuming
with Schleicher a common '*Slavo-Germanic*' language,
or a common '*Graeko-Italic*' period.

Brugmann suggests possibilities other than the genealogical theory. The ancestors of two or more groups may
have lived side by side, in a remote prehistoric period, before
the breaking up of the mother-tongue, and may have
developed the same tendencies in common. In such a case
we should have to deal with dialectal variation originating
within Aryan itself. It matters little whether, in their
subsequent life-history, the languages remain in geographical contact, or become widely separated ; for in the race-
migrations of ages, original contiguity may be broken and
joined again more than once. In grouping the languages
of the Aryan stock, Brugmann arranges the families in
the order suggested by their mutual resemblances ; this is
the most practical method of arrangement so long as it
is remembered that nothing beyond resemblance is implied

thereby, and that the question of how to interpret the resemblance is left open. It is possible that examples of original dialectal character are afforded by the treatment of $k̂$ (forward k), which becomes s or ($ʃ$) in Indo-Iranian and in Baltic-Slavonic, but which in all the other families is levelled under the full-back stop.

The Sounds of the Mother-Tongue.

By applying methods similar to those illustrated in the last chapter, the following sounds are now believed to have existed in Primitive Aryan:

Consonants.

	Back.	Back-lip-Modified.	Back-outer.	Front.
Open...	—	—	—	j
Stop ...	k, kh, g, gh	k^w g^w	k̂, k̂h, ĝ, ĝh	-—
Nasal...	ŋ	—	—	—
Divided	—	—	—	—

	Blade.	Point-teeth.	Lip.	Lip-back-Modified.
Open...	s, z	—	—	w
Stop ...	—	t, th, d, dh	p, ph, b, bh	—
Nasal...	—	n	m	—
Divided	—	l	—	—
Trill ...	—	r	—	—

Vowels.

	Unrounded.			Rounded.
	Front.	Back.	Flat.	Back.
High ...	ĭ	—	—	ŭ
Mid ...	ĕ	ă	ə	ŏ
Low ...	—	—	—	ɔ (?)

Also syllabic ḷ, ṛ, ṇ, ṃ ; and the *diphthongs :* ĕi, ĕu, ăi, ău, ŏi, ŏu.

The Relations of Vowels to each other in Aryan—Ablaut, or Vowel Gradation.

Cf. Brugmann ; *Grundr.*[2] i., p. 482, etc., and *Vgl. Gr.* p. 138, etc. ; Hirt *d. Idg. Ablaut,* 1900, and *Griech. Gr.,* ch. *ix.* and *x.* ; *Streitberg Urgerm. Gr.,* p. 36, etc. ; Noreen *Urgerm. Lautlehre,* p. 37, etc. ; and the references given in these works.

In all Idg. languages, certain vowel changes occur within groups of etymologically related words, both in ' *roots* ' and in *suffixes—e.g.* : in Gk., λέγω, 'I speak'; λόγος, 'word'; φāμί, 'I speak ' (*Doric*), φωνή, ' voice '; πατήρ, ' father,' Acc. πατέρα; φεύγω, 'I fly,' Aorist ἔφυγον, etc. In Latin, *tego*, ' cover,' perf. *tēxi ; moneo,* literally ' cause to remember,' *me-min-i,* = **men-* ; *dāre,* 'give'; *dōnum,* 'gift'; *dătus,* ' given,' etc. In Gmc., vowel changes of this nature take place regularly in the strong verbs—*e.g.* : Gothic, *giban,* ' give,' pret. sing. *gaf,* pret. pl. *gēbum, kiusan,* ' choose,' pret. sing. *kaus,* pret. pl. *kusum,* etc. ; also in other etymologically related words : O.E., *dæg*, 'day,' *dōgor* ; Goth., *hinþan*, 'catch,' *handus*, 'hand' (literally, 'that which seizes'), etc.

The above changes cannot be explained by sound laws peculiar to the particular languages in which they occur ; their explanation must be sought in the common *mother-tongue*. The phenomena of these primitive vowel alterna-tions are all included under the name *Ablaut*, invented by Grimm, although they are of various nature, and the causes which produced them must have been of several kinds ; according to the present view however, it is probable that they were in all cases associated with primitive conditions of accentuation. Although the differentiation of vowels by *Ablaut* was made use of in Idg. to express differences of meaning, these latter are only indirectly related to the vowel changes. If a vowel originally recurred in a parti-cular form in a particular grammatical category—as, for instance, in the Germanic strong verbs—this was because the phonetic conditions were present upon which that form of the vowel depended. The origin of Ablaut distinctions, then, is a phonological problem. Even in Idg. itself there must have been cases like that of the suffix in Gk. ῥη-τήρ, compared with ῥή-τωρ, in which the variation of the vowel performed no semasiological function at all.

The full explanation of this difficult question will prob-ably always remain hidden, since we are here dealing with a portion of the earliest history of the *Ursprache* itself.

No single sound law produced all the phenomena with which the historical period of Idg. speech presents us in this respect, but a considerable number of laws, which were active at different periods, possibly widely separated in time.

The *Ablaut* as we know it in the earliest historic period is the result of the stratifications of the speech of different ages.

We have to distinguish two fundamentally distinct kinds of *Ablaut* : a *Quantitative* and a *Qualitative*. The latter kind consists in the interchange, within cognate '*roots*' and *suffixes*, of vowels of different *Quality*—e.g., ĕ-ŏ (*cf.* ῥητήρ-ῥήτωρ). The causes of this Ablaut are the most obscure.

Quantitative Ablaut, on the other hand, consists in the *shortening* or *lengthening* of vowels. This kind of *Ablaut* is associated mainly with the position of the accent in *Primitive Aryan*. By *accent* here may in all probability be understood *stress*.

It should be remembered that Idg. consisted, not of ' *Roots*,' but of *words*. ' *Roots*,' which are mere grammatical abstractions, had no existence in *Idg.* any more than in *Modern English*. Since, however, it is necessary to make some kind of abstraction in dealing with groups of cognate words, it is better to call these ' *Bases*.' Aryan words were monosyllabic and polysyllabic, and so we speak also of monosyllabic and polysyllabic *Bases*.

The accent in Aryan was '*free* '—that is, the chief accent might rest, theoretically, upon any syllable in a word. In a word of several syllables only *one* syllable can have full stress ; the other syllables have varying degrees of stress. It is enough to distinguish, from this point of view, *Strong*, *Medium*, and *Weak* syllables, all of these being, however, relative terms—*Strong* implying the *chief stress* in any given word, *Weak* implying the *least stress*, or what is also called *absence of stress* (*cf.* pp. 45 and 46 above).

Now, at a certain period in primitive Idg. vowels were very sensitive to the influence of stress. According to the degree of strength with which any syllable was uttered, so its original vowel or diphthong was either preserved in its full volume, or was *weakened* or '*reduced.*' If the syllable was altogether unstressed, it might lose its vowel completely. The only vowels which, after the period of this weakening in unaccented syllables, could stand in strong syllables were *ă*, *ĕ*, *ŏ*, and diphthongal combinations of these with *i̯*, *u̯*, *r̥*, *l̥*, *m̥*, *n̥*.

We distinguish, then, three main '*grades*' or '*stufen*' of vowels, one of which every syllable of an Aryan word must necessarily contain : the *Full* grade in strong syllables, the *Reduced* grade in *Medium* syllables, and the '*Vanishing*' grade in *Weak* syllables.

The 'Dehnstufe' or Lengthened Grade.

So far we have only considered the weakening or total disappearance of a vowel ; there remains to be dealt with the further case in which an original short vowel is *lengthened*. To this grade German writers give the name of *Dehnstufe* or '*stretch grade.*'

It does not follow that *all* long vowels in Idg. are of this origin ; there are original long vowels, which were long before the beginning of the Ablaut processes. But in word series (*Ablautsreihen*) in which we find long vowels side by side with short vowels, the short vowels occurring, not in the *Reduced* grades, but in *Full* grades, showing that they are original, then, in these cases, we may assume that we are in the presence of the '*Stretch*' grade

Compare, for instance, Latin *vĕho* with perf. vēxi (Idg. e-ē) ; O.E. *sĕt*, pret. sing. of *sittan* (= Idg. *sod), with *sōt*, 'soot'—literally, 'that which settles down' (= Idg. *sōd). The explanation of this lengthening has been formulated by *Streitberg* (*I. F.*, iii. 305, etc.), and has gained fairly general acceptance.　Briefly stated, his law runs : 'The short vowel of an accented (*Strong*) syllable is lengthened in Idg. when a following syllable is lost (*cf.* also Brugmann, *Vgl. Gr.*, p. 38, and Hirt, *Idg. Ablaut*, p. 22, etc.).　This, of course, is merely the general explanation of the origin of the lengthening in Idg. itself ; it does not follow that we are always able to trace the loss of a syllable in all cases where the *Dehnstufe* occurs in the derived languages.

The Vowels of the Weakened Grades.

The fate of the Aryan full vowels when weakened under the conditions described above (p. 185) is clearly a matter of hypothesis.　It is, however, our business to endeavour to form some idea of what happened by a comparison of all the derived languages.　The reduced forms of *ā, ē, ō* appear in *Indo-Iranian* as *i*, and in all the other families of Aryan speech as *a*.　It is therefore assumed that the original sound was an ' obscure' vowel, which is written *ə* in philological works.

NOTE.—Thus *Brugmann, Grundriss,*[2] *loc. cit.*, and *Vgl. Gr.*, § 127 ; *Hirt*, on the other hand (*Idg. Ablaut*, p. 5, etc.) assumes that these vowels did not lose their original quality in Idg. when reduced, but were merely unvoiced, and, instead of *ə*, writes *ẹ ạ ọ*.　Hirt's reason for so doing is that in Greek θετός compared with τίθημι, στατός compared with ιστᾱμι, δοτός compared with δίδωμι, the

original *quality* of *e*, *a*, *o* reappears. He argues that the
whispered vowel has emerged in Greek with mere shortening, while the other languages have lost the original quality
of *ę* and *ǫ*, and levelled them under *a*. This view is also
shared by *Fick*, *Bechtel*, *Wackernagel*, and *Collitz* (see
references in *Hirt*). Brugmann, however, and probably
most other scholars, explain the above Greek forms as new
formations from θατός, etc.

The reduction of short *a*, *e*, *o* cannot be proved, from
any historical indications, to have altered these vowels at
all, since the original vowels reappear intact in positions
where, theoretically speaking, reduction must have taken
place—that is, in weak syllables. Brugmann writes these
theoretical reduced vowels $_{a,\ e,\ o,}$ but does not discuss
their nature. Hirt, again, assumes that these were *voiceless*
('*tonlose*') vowels. In the derived languages this grade is
indistinguishable from the full grade short vowels.

NOTE.—The modification by accent of the long and short
vowels cannot have been synchronous. We may accept
Hirt's hypothesis concerning the reduction of the short
vowels, since it appears to jump with the facts. But the
long vowels certainly appear to have lost their characteristic quality altogether. If this is so, then the two processes cannot have taken place at the same time, since it
is scarcely conceivable that a short vowel, when unaccented,
should retain its quality more completely than a long, at
a period when *all* vowels in weak syllables were affected.
We may, perhaps, assume an early period of vowel reduction
which only affected *short* vowels, which were either unvoiced
or whispered in weak syllables, but which left long vowels

unaltered. Then in a subsequent period *long* vowels were reduced under the same conditions, only more completely than the short vowels in the former period, since they lost their quality and became an indeterminate sound (ə). We must suppose that in this period the whispered or voiceless a̯, e̯, o̯ which had been produced in the former age of reduction remained without further alteration. At a later period the latter class were again fully voiced, thus being levelled under the unreduced *a, e, o*, while ə remained until the breaking up of Aryan into dialects, and was then levelled under *a* in all groups except *Indo-Iranian*, where it became *i*.

Qualitative Ablaut.—Under certain conditions, which are by no means clear as yet, primitive ĕ in *Full-Grade* syllables became ŏ, and ē in the same grade became ō. Therefore, when we have a base in which primitive ĕ or ē occur, we may also expect to find cognate forms with ŏ or ō. This ŏ underwent lengthening in the *Dehnstufe*.

We may summarize the foregoing statement as follows

	D.	D°.	F.	F°.	R.	V.
e Series ...	ē	ō	e	o	e	—
o ,, ...	ō	—	o	—	o	—
a ,, ...	ā	ō	a	o	a	—
ē ,, ...	—	—	ē	ō	ə	—
ō ,, ...	—	—	ō	—	ə	—
ā ,, ...	—	—	ā	ō	ə	—

Note.—*D.* = *Dehnstufe* ; *D.°* = *Dehnstufe* in which ō from ē occurs; *F.* = *Full Grade* ; *F.°* that in which *o* from *e* occurs; *R.* = *Reduced Grade* ; *V.* = *Vanishing Grade*.

Diphthongal Combinations in Ablaut.

Each and all the above vowels of the *F. Grade* occurred in Aryan in combination with *i, u,* and the vocalic consonants *l, m, n, r.*

The long diphthongs were levelled under the original shorts, or were monophthongized in all Idg. languages except Scrt., in which there are still traces of the long (*cf.* Brugmann, *Grundr.,*[2] i., p. 203, etc.).

For the *-i-* and *-u-* long diphthongs we assume a *R. grade* *ǝi̯, ǝu̯,* which appear to have been levelled already in Idg. under the *F. Grade* before vowels. In the *V. Grade* the first element entirely disappears, leaving *i̯, u̯.* In all grades *i̯* and *u̯* are vowels before consonants, but become consonants before following vowels.

The combinations of *l, m,* etc., are treated in the same manner: F. el, ol; R. ǝl; V. l̥, etc. The 'liquids' and nasals in the V. Grade are consonantal before vowels, otherwise they are syllabic. The Reduced grades *ǝi̯, ǝu̯,* of long diphthongs appear as *ī, ū* before consonants; as *ai̯, au̯* before vowels.

The reduced grades of the short diphthongs *ei̯, ai̯, oi̯* are either levelled under the V. grade, or, when they receive a secondary accent are lengthened to *ī, ū.*

Although theoretically, each vowel in every word might, under the necessary conditions, appear in every grade, it does not follow that, in the derived languages, all the original possible forms of a word, '*root,*' or suffix survive; they are very rarely all found in any one language, and some have apparently disappeared from all languages.

Examples of Aryan Ablaut.

Idg. e Series.

F.		D.		V.
e ‖ o		ē ‖ ō		
Ar. *sĕd-, 'sit':				Idg. -sd- :
Lat. sedēre	Lat. sodālis	Lat. sēd-imus	O.E. sōt	Lat. nīdus
Gk. ἕξομαι	Goth. sat	Goth. sētum		>*nisdos
O. Sl. sedeti		O.E. sæton		O.E. nest
O.E. sittan				
>*set-jan				
Ar. *bher- :				Idg. *bhr- :
Lat. fero	Lat. for-s,	Goth. bērum	Gk. φώρ	Gk. δι-φρ-os
Gk. φέρω	for-tūna	O.E. bæron	Lat. fūr	(chariot-
Goth. bairan	Gk. φορά			board for
O.E. beran	Goth. bar			two)
	O.E. bær			Idg. bhṛ :
				Goth. baur
				O.E. boren
				(= Gmc.
				*bur-)
Ar. *ped :				Idg. pd- :
Gk. πέζα	Lith. padas	Lat. pēs	Gk. πῶς	Gk. ἐπί-
Lat. pĕdem	Gk. ποδός	>*pēds	(Doric)	βδ-αι-
	Lat. ap-		Goth. fōtus	=*epí-pd-
	pod-ix			
Ar. *-ter :				
Lat. pater	Lat. auc-tor	Gk. πατήρ	Gk. φρά-τωρ	Lat. pa-tr-is
O.E. fæder	Goth. brō-þar	Gk. φρά-τηρ		Gk. φρα-τρ-ά
				Goth. bro-þr-
				ahans

The symbol < in this book means ' becomes,' or ' develops into ';
> means ' derived from.'

Idg. o Series.

F.	D.	V.

o.
Ar. *ŏkʷ- :
  Gk. ὄσσε = *οκε;
  ὄψομαι
  Lat. oculus
Ar. *ŏd- :
  Gk. ὀδμή
  Lat. odor
	ō.
	Gk. ὄπ-ωπ-α ; ὤψ
	
	Gk. ὀδωδή
		—
		
		—

Idg. a Series.

F.	D.	V.

a.
Ar. *ak- :
  Scrt. ájras
  Gk. ἀγρός
  Gk. ἄγω, ἄκτωρ
  Lat. ago, actor
  Goth. akrs
  O.E. æcer
Ar. *năse :
  O.H.G. nasa
  Scrt. (Instr.) nasá
	ā.
	Gk. ἦχε (η from ā)
	Lat. exāmen
	  (>-āg-men)
	Lat. amb-āges
	O. Ir. āg
	
	Lat. nāres
	Lat. nāsus
		Scrt. pári-jman
		
		—

NOTE.—According to Hirt, the forms ἀγρός, ájras, ager, akrs, also nasa and nasá, are R. grade (cf. Idg. Abl., §§ 761-764) ; but the reduced grade of the e, a, o series are indistinguishable from the F. grade in the derived languages.

Idg. ē Series.

F.	R.	V.
ē.	ə.	
Ar. *sē, ' sow ':		
Lat. sēvi	Lat. satus	Scrt. s-tri,
Lat. sēmen		' wife '
Goth. mana-sēþs		
Ar. *dhē, ' place ':		
Scrt. dadhāmi	Scrt. hitás	Scrt. da-dh-
Gk. τίθημι	(h from dh)	mas
Lat. fēci	Gk. τιθεμεν	
Goth. gadēþs	Lat. facio	
O.E. dǣd		
Ar. *lēd, ' let,' ' grow tired ':		
Gk. ληδεῖν	Lat. lassus	--
Goth. lētan	>*lad-to-	
O.E. lǣtan	Goth. lats	

Idg. ō Series.

F.	R.	V.
ō.	ə.	
Ar. *dō-, ' give ':		
Scrt. dadāti	Scrt. a-ditas	dēvá-t-tas
Gk. δίδωμι	Scrt. ditiš	(-t- from -d-)
Gk. δώσω	Gk. δίδομεν	Lat. dē-d-i
Lat. dōnum	Lat. datus	
Lat. dōnare	Lat. datio	
Ar. *bhōg-, ' roast ':		
Gk. φώγω	Gk. φαγεῖν	--
O.E. bōc (pret. of bacan)	O.E. bac-an	
	O.E. bæcere	

Idg. ā Series.

F.	R.	V.
ā.	•.	
Ar. *sthā-, ' stand ':		
Gk. ἵστημι	Scrt. sthitás	Scrt. gō-ṣṭh-á
Gk. στήσω	Gk. ἵ-στα-μεν	(' standing-
(η from ā)	Gk. στατός	place for
Lat. stāre	Lat. status	cows ')
Lat. stāmen	Lat. statim	Goth. awistr
Goth. stōls	Goth. staþs	(= *oui-st-
		tro) 'sheep-
		fold '
		O.H.G. ewist
Ar. *bhā, ' speak ':		>*awist
Gk. φημί (*φᾱμί)	Gk. φαμεν	
Lat. fāri		—
Lat. fāma		

For an account and full examples of the Ablaut in original polysyllabic bases, see Brugmann and Hirt, *loc. cit.*, especially the latter. In dealing with these bases, it is necessary to distinguish the vowel gradation in each syllable. A few examples may be given here (*the numbers refer to syllables*):

Aryan * *genewo,* ' knee.'

Scrt. jánu, Gk. γόνυ, have F. in 1st, R. in 2nd; Goth. kniu (= *ǵnewo-), O.E., cneō, have V. in 1st, F. in 2nd; Scrt. abhi-jnú, ' down to the knee,' Gk. γνύξ, πρόχνυ, Goth. knussjan, have V. in 1st, R. in 2nd.; while D. grade appears in Gk. γωνιά, in 1st.

13

Aryan *$\acute{g}en\bar{e}$, *$\acute{g}on\bar{e}$, *$\acute{g}en\bar{o}$, *$\acute{g}on\bar{o}$, ' know.'

Goth. kann has F. (Idg. *$\acute{g}$on-) ; Lith. žinóti, Goth. kunnaida, have R. or V. in 1st (Idg. *$\acute{g}$ṇ-) and F. in 2nd ; Scrt. a-jña-sam, jñā-tás, Gk. γι-γνώ-σκω, Lat. nōsco, O.E. cnāwan, have V. in 1st (Idg. $\acute{g}$n-) and F. in 2nd ; O.H.G. kunst (Idg. *$\acute{g}$ṇ-t-to) has R. in 1st and V. in 2nd.

Aryan *$pel\bar{e}$, ' fill.'

Scrt. parīnas (r from l) has F. in 1st and 2nd ; Scrt. pṛnāti, Lat. plēnus, etc., Gk. πλῆ-ρες, etc., have V. in 1st, F. in 2nd ; Scrt. pūrnás, Lith. pílnas, Goth. fulls, have R. in 1st, V. in 2nd.

Aryan *$per\bar{o}$, *$perem$, ' forward.'

Gk. πρωί, O.H.G. vruo (=*frò), have V. in 1st, F. in 2nd ; Lith. pirmas, O.E. forma (= *furma > Idg. *pṛmo-), have R. in 1st, F. in 2nd (or 3rd if we assume pre-Idg. *peremo); Goth. fruma, O.E. from (=*pṛmo), have R. in 1st, V. in 2nd (*peremo), and F. in 3rd.

The phenomena of Ablaut are to be regarded as a series of *Combinative Changes* which took place in the mother-tongue. They are among the most characteristic features of Aryan speech. If primitive Aryan be a dialect of a still older language, then we may consider that its characteristic independent life as Aryan begins with the first Ablaut changes.

CHAPTER X

THE GERMANIC FAMILY

THIS Family, which is of special importance to students of English, falls into three divisions—the *North Germanic* or *Scandinavian;* the *East Germanic*, represented by *Gothic* and the language of the *Vandals*, both long extinct, and the latter only preserved in proper names; *West Germanic*, the earliest forms of which are *Old Saxon*, the *Old English* dialects, *Old Frisian*, all of which belong to the so-called *Low German* group, and *Old High German*, the name given to a group of West Germanic dialects in which the voiceless stops of Germanic, preserved in all other dialects and languages of this family, underwent a change to open consonants or affricated sounds respectively, during the sixth and seventh centuries. Other consonants also underwent change, but less universally than Gmc. p, t, k, though even in the case of k the opening or affrication was not carried out with perfect uniformity, in all positions, in every H.G. dialect. Within the *West Germanic* branch itself, it is now usual to assume an *Anglo-Frisian* group, which subsequently differentiated into *Old Frisian* and *Old English*. (For statement and arguments in favour of this view, see especially Siebs, *Zur Gesch. d. engl.-friesisch. Spr.*, 1889, and Bremer, *Ethnographie der germ. Stämme*², 1900, p. 108, etc.

The latter is a reprint from Paul's *Grundr.*[2], in which see p. 842, etc.) This assumption of an original Anglo-Frisian unity is based upon certain very close agreements in vocabulary, and in the treatment of the vowel sounds, which exist between O.E. and O. Fris.   At the same time, the *Anglo-Frisian* unity, although a very plausible hypothesis, is contested by some scholars (*e.g.*, Morsbach, *Beibl. zur Anglia*, vii., and Wyld, *Engl. Studien*, xxviii., pp. 393, 394, *Otia Merseiana*, iv., pp. 75, 76), and a further critical examination of the points of agreement between the two languages is desirable in order to determine how far these are really due to a common, and how far to an independent, development.

[On the classification of the Germanic languages, their mutual relations and characteristics, the best authorities are : Kluge, *Vorgeschichte der germanischen Sprachen* in Paul's *Grundriss*[2] ; Streitberg, *Ur-germanische Grammatik*, pp. 9-18 (the latter book is perhaps the best introduction to the study of Germanic Philology which exists); *Einleitendes* in Dieter's *Laut- und Formenlehre d. altgermanischen Dialekte*, vol. i., 1898.   The above works contain full references to the special grammars of the several languages, and to authorities on the various questions of general and special bearing connected with Germanic Philology.]

Primitive Germanic.

By this term is meant, as already indicated, that undifferentiated form of speech, distinguished from *Primitive Aryan* by possessing the characteristic Germanic features, and containing the germ of those peculiarities which subsequently appear in those languages, already enumerated, which spring from this source.   The sources of our knowledge of *Parent Germanic* are of a twofold character: *Direct* and *Indirect*.

The *direct* sources of knowledge are scanty, and consist (1) of Gmc. words mostly occurring in proper names mentioned in the works of Greek and Latin writers from the time of Cæsar; and (2) very early loan-words from Gmc. still preserved in *Finnish*, which in many cases retain down to the present day the original full Gmc. form.   The *indirect* sources are (1) the earliest Runic inscriptions in *Primitive Norse*, some of which are as old as the first century of our era, and the language of which is therefore but a stage removed from *Primitive Gmc.*; and (2) the reconstructions which are made according to the strict methods of modern Comparative Philology (*cf.* Chapter VIII.).

Characteristics of Germanic.

At what point of the original Aryan dialectal differentiation does *Germanic* come into existence?   Can we say that when a certain group of features have developed within a speech area this ceases to be *Primitive Aryan* any longer, but has now an independent existence with the definitely-marked features of the ancestor of the Germanic languages?

Probably the most characteristic and typical Germanic characteristics are the consonantal changes, the so-called sound-shifting processes, known to the readers of text-books as *Grimm's Law*.   We might perhaps say that from the moment that original t, p, k, have become open consonants, here is the beginning of Gmc.   Since none of the readers (and few of the writers) of the ordinary small primer

which discourses glibly of *Grimm's Law* have any idea
where that Law is to be found in the works of Grimm,
nor how he states it, it may be of interest to mention that
in vol. i. of the *Deutsche Grammatik*, p. 584, etc. (I quote
from the edition of 1822), the immortal grammarian discusses, with numerous examples, the relations of the consonantal sounds of Sanscrit, Greek, and Latin, etc., with
those of Gothic and Old High German. Grimm also
notes that in certain Gothic words ' exceptions' occur to
the usual correspondences of Gk., Lat., Scrt. *p*, *t*, *k*, to
Gothic *f*, *þ*, etc. These exceptions were to be explained
some fifty years later by *Verner*.

The statement of these facts of consonantal change
which would be accepted at the present day is very different from Grimm's statement, as the reader may see by
comparing the treatment of the subject by Streitberg, for
example, with the above passages in Grimm's Grammar.

The Consonantal Shiftings in Germanic.

I. Aryan *p*, *t*, *k* were aspirated to *ph*, *th*, *kh*, being thus
levelled under the original voiceless aspirated stops.

II. All the voiceless aspirated stops, both old and new,
were opened, and became the corresponding voiceless open
consonants.

Examples :

Aryan
{
ph (original); O. Sax. and O.H.G. *fallan*, ' fall ';
Gk. σφάλλω.

ph (from earlier *p*); Goth. *-faþs*, ' lord,' ' master ';
Scrt. *páti*-, ' master '; Gk. πόσις (from **potis*),
' husband '; Lat. hos-*pit*-is (gen.), ' guest-
friend.'
}

Aryan
- *th* (original); Goth. *skaþjan*, 'to harm'; Gk. *ἀ-σκηθής*, 'blameless.'
- *th* (from earlier *t*); Goth. *munþs;* O.E. *mūþ*, 'mouth'; Lat. *mentum*, 'chin.'

Aryan
- *kh* (original) ;   ?
- *kh* (from earlier *k*); Goth. *hairtō*, 'heart'; O.E. *heorte;* Gk. καρδία; Lat. *cord-is* (gen.).

These changes invariably take place *initially; medially,* however, when the accent in Aryan fell on any other syllable than that *immediately preceding* them, the Gmc. consonants *f*, *þ*, *h* (back-open cons.) were *voiced* to ð (lip-open-voice), ð (point-teeth-open-voice), and ʒ (written *g* in most old Germanic languages, but = back-open-voice). These were the '*exceptions*' to his law which puzzled Grimm, but which were explained as above by Verner (*Kuhn's Zeitschrift,* xxiii., pp. 97-130) in 1877. Sanscrit and Greek often preserve the original accent, so that where we find *b, d, g,* in Germanic, instead of the voiceless sounds, the Greek forms often show the accent on some other syllable than that immediately preceding the consonant. This habit of voicing in the Germanic languages, under the above conditions, proves that parent Germanic retained the original system of 'free' accent, since the same root shows voiceless or voiced forms according to the shifting position of the accent.

Examples of Verner's Law :

Aryan *p* (or *ph*) = Gmc. ð (written *b*); Goth. and O. Sax. *sibun*, '7'; Scrt. *saptá ;* Gk. ἑπτά.

Aryan *t* (*th*) = Gmc. *đ* (written *d*); Goth. *fadar*, 'father'; O.E. *fæder* ; Scrt. *pitár* ; Gk. πατήρ.

Aryan *k* = Gmc. ȝ (written *g*) ; O.E. *sweger*, ' mother-in-law '; Scrt. *svašrū* ; Gk. ἑκυρᾶ, from *σϝεκυρᾶ.

NOTE.—The old Germanic languages do not distinguish *b*, *d*, *g*, according to whether they represent open conso-nants or stops. Originally these consonants were all *open* in Gmc. It is usual for philologists, for purposes of accuracy, to write these original open consonants ƀ, đ, ȝ. The popular expression that ' *h* became *g* by Verner's law ' is most mischievous, and gives a false impression. We are dealing with changes which took place hundreds of years before writing was known to the Gmc. peoples—with pure sound changes. The facts are simply and accurately stated by saying that the *lip, point-teeth, and back voiceless open consonants were voiced*. That is the process which took place under the conditions described by Verner.

The Third Germanic Consonant Shifting.

The Aryan aspirated voiced stops, *bh*, *dh*, *gh*, are opened in Gmc. to the corresponding voiced open con-sonants.

The ƀ, đ, ȝ thus produced are indistinguishable from the same sounds which arose according to the conditions of Verner's Law ; they share in each language the sub-sequent development of these, and are also written *b*, *d*, *g* in the old languages.

These voiced aspirates survive, as such, only in Sanscrit ; in Gk. they remain as aspirates (apart from certain com-binative changes), but are unvoiced, and are written φ, θ, χ.

Examples :

Aryan *dh*, Gmc. ð : Goth. ga-dē-þ-s, 'deed'; O.E. dǣd ; Scrt. dá-dhā-mi, 'set, place'; Gk. τί-θη-μι.

Aryan *bh*, Gmc. ƀ : Goth. brōþar, 'brother'; O.E. brōþor ; Scrt. bhrā́-tar ; Gk. φράτωρ.

Aryan *gh*, Gmc. ʒ : Goth. steigan, 'climb, ascend'; O.E. stigan ; Scrt. stighnutē ; Gk. στείχω.

The Fourth and Last Consonantal Shifting in Germanic.

The Aryan voiced stops *b*, *d*, *g*, were unvoiced in Gmc. to the corresponding breath-stops *p*, *t*, *k*.

There is an indication of the approximate date of these processes of shifting in place-names. The mountain name *Finne* was borrowed by the Suevi from the Gaulish *penn*, after they crossed the Elbe in the fifth century B.C. Therefore the change from *p* to *f* was subsequent to this. On the other hand, the Gmc. *Dōnavi*, 'Danube,' from Latin *Dānuvius*, preserves the *d* unchanged, which shows that the change from *d* to ð had already taken place before the incorporation of this name in Gmc. speech, which occurred about 100 B.C. (On the relative chronology of the shifting processes, see Kluge, *Paul und Braune's Beitr.*, ix., 173, etc., and Streitberg, *loc. cit.*, § 126.)

Examples of Fourth Shifting of Voiced Stops :

Aryan *b*, Gmc. *p :* Goth. *paida*, 'coat'; O.E. pād ; Gk. (Thracian) βαίτη, 'shepherd's coat of skins.'

Aryan *d*, Gmc. *t :* Goth. ga-tamjan, 'tame'; O.E. temian ; Gk. δαμάω ; Lat. dom-are.

Aryan *g*, Gmc. *k :* O.E. *cran*, 'crane'; O. Sax. crano ; Gk. γέρανος.

Characteristic Treatment of the Aryan Vowels in Germanic.

A. Isolative Changes.

Aryan o *is unrounded to* a *in Gmc.*: Lat. *ovis*, ' sheep ';
Gk. ὄις, from *ὄϝις ; Goth. *awis-tr*, 'sheepfold'; Lat. *hostis*,
' enemy,' ' stranger '; Goth. *gast-s ;* O. Sax., O.H.G. *gast*,
' guest.' Thus original o and a are indistinguishable in Gmc.

Aryan ā *is rounded to* ō *in Gmc.*, and is thus levelled
under original ō : Gk. φράτωρ, ' brother'; Lat. *frāter ;*
Goth. *brōþar ;* O.E. *brōþor ;* Lat. *sāgire*, 'perceive quickly
and keenly '; Goth. *sōk*-jan, ' seek.'

Aryan ē *is lowered to* ǣ *in Gmc.* This ǣ is again raised
to ē in Goth; in West Gmc. it becomes ā, and in O.E.
this ā is again fronted to ǣ : Gk. τί-θη-μι, ' place,' etc. ;
Goth. *ga-dēþs*, ' deed '; O.H.G. *tāt ;* O.E. *dǣd ;* Gk. νῆ-μα,
' thread '; Lat. *nē-re*, ' sew '; Goth. *nēþla*, 'needle'; O.H.G.
nādala ; O.E. *nǣdl*.

Aryan oi *is levelled under* ai *in Gmc.*: Gk. οἴνη, ' one,
upon a die '; O. Lat. *oinos* (later *ūnus*) ; Goth. *ains ;* O. Lat.
moitare (later *mūtare*), ' change '; Goth. *maidjan*, 'alter.'

Aryan ou *is levelled under* au *in Gmc.* : Gk. οὖς, from
*οὔος, from *οὔσος, ' ear '; Lat. *auris*, from *ausis, from
*ousis ; Goth. *auso ;* Gk. ἀ-κούω, from Aryan * sm̥-kous-jō,
' hear '; Goth. *haus-jan*, 'hear.'

Aryan ei *becomes* ī *in Gmc.*: Gk. πείθω, ' persuade ';
Lat. *fīdo*, from *feido ; Goth. *beidan*, ' expect ' (*ei* in
Goth. = ī) ; O.E. *bīdan ;* O.H.G. *bītan*.

[Aryan ēi is probably the origin of an ē sound which
appears as such in the Gmc. languages.]

The other Aryan vowels are unaffected by isolative
change in Gmc.

B. Combinative Changes.

Aryan *e*, which is otherwise preserved in Gmc., is raised to *i* in Gmc. under the following conditions: (1) *Before* i *or* j *in the following syllable:* Gk. μέσσος (from *μεθ-jος); Lat. *medius;* Goth. *midjis;* O.E. *midd;* O. Sax. *middi*, Gk. ἕζομαι (from *σεδjομαι), 'sit'; Lat. *sed-ēre;* O. Sax. *sittian;* O.E. *sittan* (from *sett-jan); O.H.G. *sizzen*. (2) e *becomes* i *when followed by a nasal +* another consonant: Gk. πενθερός, 'father-in-law' (literally, 'relation'); Lith. *bendras,* 'companion,' from Lat. of-*fend*-ix, from root *bhendh- ;* Goth., O.E., O. Sax. *bindan*.

[*e* also becomes *i* in Gmc. in unstressed syllables; *cf.* O.E. pl. *fēt,* 'feet,' from *fōtiz* (nom. sing. *fōt*), Lat. *ped-es*.]

Apart from these conditions, *e* remains in Gmc.. Gk. ἔδω, 'eat'; Lat. *edo;* O.E., O. Sax. *etan;* Gk. ἔργον, 'work' (from *ϝέργον); O. Sax. *werk;* O.H.G. *werc;* and so on.

West Germanic Characteristics.

The Gmc. sound system underwent but few changes in W. Gmc., but these few are important.

The change of *ǣ* to *ā* has already been mentioned. In addition, the combinative treatment of *i* and *u* must be noted.

Gmc. *i* remains in W. Gmc., unless followed in the next syllable by *ă* or *ŏ*, in which case it was lowered to *e* . O.E., O.H.G. *nest,* 'nest,' from *nizdo* (*cf.* Lat. *nĭdus*, from *nizdos).

Of course, if n + consonant intervened between *i* and *ă, ŏ,* *i* remained. Gmc. *u* also remained, apart from the presence

of a following *ă*, *ŏ*, in which case it was lowered to *o* in
W. Gmc. : O.E. *oxa* ; Goth. *auhsa* (= *uhsa*) ; Scrt. *ukṣan* ;
O.E. *gold*, 'gold,' from Gmc. *gulđo* ; *cf. kulta*, 'gold,'
a very early Gmc. loan-word in Finnish.

The above account of the treatment of Aryan sounds in
Germanic is the merest outline.   The question of the lip-
modified back consonants, of consonantal combinations,
and of the special W. Gmc. treatment of *i* and *u* between
vowels, have not been dealt with ; on all these points the
reader should consult Streitberg's *Urgerm. Grammatik*.

CHAPTER XI

THE HISTORY OF ENGLISH : GENERAL REMARKS ON
THE SCOPE AND NATURE OF THE INQUIRY, AND
THE MAIN PROBLEMS CONNECTED WITH IT

IF it were necessary to answer as briefly as possible the
question, What does the history of English involve ? it
might be said that, given the English language as it now
exists, in all its forms, spoken and written, historical inquiry should attempt to trace the origin and development
of the characteristic features of each.

This is the ideal of completeness ; practically the
history of English is mainly concerned with the rise, on
the one hand, of present-day polite spoken English, and,
on the other, with that of the literary dialect. The
problems herein involved are sufficiently complicated, and
the history of the modern *dialects*, or forms of popular
speech, at any rate in its minute detail, is held to be the
work of the special investigator. At the same time, it is
important to have some conception of the popular dialects,
and to understand as clearly as possible their mutual
relations, as well as their relation to, and influence upon,
the more cultivated and artificial forms of English speech.

Two methods of procedure are open to the student.
He may either start with the language as he knows it,

and trace it backwards, step by step, to the earliest forms preserved in the oldest written documents; or, starting with these, he may work forwards to the present day. Whichever method be chosen, it is necessary to have at least some knowledge of the language at each stage of its development, and, further, it is of the highest importance that the student should endeavour to realize as far as possible each stage as a living language which was actually spoken. In fact, every step we take into the past of a language involves a process of reconstruction : first, an interpretation of the written symbols, and then the gradual realization of the consciousness of the part, so that the sentences begin to pulsate with life, and become for us the living expression of the thoughts and emotions of the men who uttered them. There can be no doubt that the best way to cultivate this power of getting into sympathetic touch with the speech of a bygone age is to train the perceptions and the sensibilities in the school of modern speech, and for this reason, as well as for others repeatedly argued in these pages, the study of the spoken language of our own time is the best training-ground for historical study.

Each period of the development of English presents special problems to the investigator—problems which depend partly upon the nature of the changes which the language itself undergoes, partly upon the social conditions and general historical and political events which affected the linguistic conditions, and partly, also, upon the form in which the records of each age have come down to us. The minute investigation of the dialectal varieties in Old and Middle English is the business of the specialist, and many of the details which are of great interest and importance for him have but little bearing upon the development of present-day English.

The solution of one and the same kind of problem may demand a different method at different times. Thus the reconstruction of the pronunciation, which is necessarily our first care in dealing with the written records of all periods earlier than our own, offers difficulties of quite a different kind in Old English from those which meet us in attempting to realize the sounds of Shakespeare. In the latter case we have a considerable body of direct contemporary testimony, sometimes, it is true, rather contradictory, as to the phonetic values expressed by the symbols in ordinary spelling ; in the former the precise sound which the letters were intended to express can only be inferred indirectly from the spelling of foreign words of whose pronunciation at the time something is known, by the help of comparative philology, or by considering the later developments, since the O.E. period. On the other hand, in dealing with the written language of periods which had no stereotyped orthography, we have, at any rate, the advantage of being warned by a change in the spelling of a probable change in sound, whereas for the last 400 years—although, as can be shown from other sources, considerable changes in English pronunciation have taken place—the spelling during this period has varied so little that, were there no other means of information, we might suppose that sound change had been arrested since early in the sixteenth century.

Probably the best course for the student of the history of English to pursue is first to make himself acquainted with the chief characteristics of each period, and then to construct for himself as complete a picture as possible of the gradual passing of the speech of one period into that of the next, until the whole space of time covered by the records is filled in. A narrative which should thus set forth in outline the changes through which our language has passed during the last 1,200 years, might with advantage, in the first instance, be limited to the history of the modern literary language, and that form of spoken English which most closely resembles it. The question would thus be, What is the relation of these modern forms to the earlier forms of English ? The scope of this inquiry might be extended, especially by Scotch students, so as to include the rise of Scots, as a form of speech so distinct from English, that it deserves to be ranked as another language. No other group of English dialects, except those out of which the literary and polite spoken English grew, possesses the distinction which Scots achieved of being for centuries the speech of kings and scholars, of poets and historians ; the language at once of the Court, the Government, the Church, and of Literature.

Besides the problems connected with changes in sound, the student of the history of English must naturally trace the modifications in the inflexional system which have taken place, many of which are also associated with sound change. The impoverishment of the English grammatical inflexions has been due very largely to phonetic changes which have occurred in the unstressed syllables of words, whereby many final syllables have been lost altogether, while others have been very considerably altered from their original form. The changes in our accidence, especially the loss of many case-endings, have brought about very marked changes in the form and structure of the sentence.

Inseparable, too, from the growth of culture, and from a general expansion of a nation's genius, is the development of the vocabulary. It is natural that the meaning of words should change as the group of ideas associated with a given word is now widened, now contracted, but perhaps the most considerable modifications of our vocabulary at all ages have come from without, by the incorporation of altogether new material from other languages. Every text-book upon the history of English contains more or less reliable lists of foreign words which have passed at various times, and from different sources, into usage in the English tongue. It will be convenient to deal with the question of loan-words under a separate heading within each section which is devoted to a period in the growth of English. Points of interest in connection with this subject are: to distinguish words of foreign origin which have got into English, through the spoken language, from those which have been incorporated from merely literary sources; to determine the period at which any given word or class of words passed into English. One of the chief popular fallacies in dealing with loan-words is the assumption that the latter question can be settled out of hand by an appeal to history. Thus, for instance, it is commonly assumed by popular writers that all Latin words which occur in Old English, and which refer to ideas or objects connected with the Christian religion, were incorporated into English at the time of the mission of St. Augustine. As a matter of fact, some of these words

14

are centuries older, and were certainly acquired by the heathen English, already in their Continental homes. The one sure test of the immediate source of an early loan-word, and the date of its importation, is its form, and the consideration of the changes which it has undergone *in common with* the native element of the language into which it has been borrowed. If this test cannot be applied, as is sometimes the case, there always remains a certain dubiety as to the precise period of borrowing.

In studying the various forms of English preserved in the literary remains of the Old and Middle periods, it is important to keep the several dialects distinct, and, further, not to confuse the language of different ages. It often happens that a work comes down to us in several manuscripts, copied at different times by a variety of scribes, whose native dialect is not always the same as that of the original. In such cases there is naturally a mixture of dialectal forms, and not infrequently, also, a mixture of forms which belong to the period of the original with those which are contemporary with the copy. This confusion arises from the fact that the scribe sometimes faithfully copied his text, but sometimes also wrote the form which was current in his own speech, instead of the more archaic form of his model. .·

Therefore the study of the dialect of a given area, at a given period, must be based, in the first instance, upon texts whose date and dialect can be fixed beyond any doubt. Although the spelling in Old and Middle English texts is on the whole fairly consistent and regular, there is always the apparently exceptional spelling, which occurs here and there, and which deserves attention. The questions raised by the occasional departure of scribes from the conventional spelling are : Do they represent a new tendency which is springing up within the dialect, a new departure from the older mode of speech which the traditional spelling records, and which the scribe from time to time, either deliberately or unconsciously, expresses in a phonetic spelling ? Are they mere careless scribal errors ? Do they represent another type of pronunciation in use within the dialect, due to class or other differentiation, or to the influence of another dialect ? While it is unwise to attach too much importance to sporadic eccentricities of spelling on the part of a scribe, they should all receive consideration, and anything like repeated deviation from the tradition should be carefully investigated, since if it can be shown to express some reality of pronunciation, it is certainly of value, and may throw great light upon the speech habits of the period.

Chief Points of General Method.

There are certain general principles of method which should be constantly borne in mind in the historical study of language, and these may now be summarized, even at the risk of repetition, for they follow logically from that view of language which this work has attempted to set forth, and some of the principles have already been formulated in this and in earlier chapters.

1. We must not be misled by the inconsistency of the written representation of sounds in early records, into assuming an inconsistency of pronunciation. Such inconsistency of spelling may occur while the pronunciation itself is perfectly constant. A fluctuation in the graphic

14—2

representation of sounds is particularly likely to occur in a period in which a series of sound changes are in process of being carried out, or have just been completed. The fluctuation in spelling may make it appear as though, in the same text, there were traces both of the beginning and the end of a particular process of sound change. Even when a spelling is to a great extent phonetic, as in O.E., it will generally be slightly behind the actual pronunciation.

2. Apparent anomalies in the development of sounds, or 'exceptions' to well-established sound laws, may result from a mixture of dialectal forms; and the 'exception' may prove to be merely an importation from another dialect in which that particular line of development is quite normal. The mixture of dialects is especially common in literary forms of language, which represent historically the pure form of no single dialect, but a conglomeration of several. The higher the development and cultivation of a literary dialect, the more artificial it is likely to be, and the further removed from any naturally-developed form of living speech. Good examples of artificial literary dialects are the Greek κοινή, Classical Latin, and Modern Polite English. In O.E. and early M.E. the various forms of written English each represent pretty accurately the dialect of the province in which the text was written. But Chaucer's English is no longer the dialect of a particular geographical area, but rather a fully-developed literary or official form of speech which shows considerable dialectal mixture. These literary or official dialects often become, with certain modifications, the traditional mode of speech of a social class, or even of a whole country.

3. Many apparent 'exceptions' are the result of Analogy, and not of Phonetic development at all. The history of every language has numerous examples of forms of this nature. In Mod. Eng. the preterites of 'break' and 'speak' are not the representatives of O.E. *bræc*, *sp(r)æc*, but are formed on the analogy of the p.p. *brok*-en, *spok*-en. This process of forming new associations, as we have seen (Chapter VII.), is always at work at all periods of every language. In postulating Analogy in explanation of a form which has not followed the ordinary phonetic development, it is our business to discover the group of forms associations with which has caused the new departure in question.

4. After a sound has changed, within the dialect of a given community, to something quite different from its original form, the same sound may reappear within the same dialect from some other source, and may then remain, the tendency to change it having passed away. The Southern and Midland dialects of English rounded all O.E. *ā* sounds to *ō* (ɔ) in early Transition M.E., O.E. *hām*, etc., becoming *hōm*, etc. But in M.E. *ā* reappeared again from two sources: (1) O.E. -*ă*- in open syllables was lengthened—O.E. *sċ(e)amu* < M.E. *schāme*. (2) Norman-French *ā* in loan-words—*e.g.*, *dāme*, 'lady.' This new *ā* survived during the whole M.E. period, until it was fronted in the sixteenth century to (ǣ), which later became (ē), whence Standard English (ɛi) as in '*shame*' (ʃɛim) and '*dame*' (dɛim).

5. Where diversity of sound exists, we assume it to represent original diversity, unless the conditions whereby one sound was differentiated into several, can be clearly

shown.   Thus in O.E. the vb. 'to bear' has the following
forms of the root: Inf. *ber*-an, pret. sing. *bær*, pret. pl.
bǣr-on, p.p. *bor*-en.   Here we assume that there were
originally four distinct forms of the root in Gmc., since
nothing that we know of the habits of O.E. leads us
to believe that any conditions are present in these cases
to split up one sound into four; and, further, a comparison of the other old Gmc. tongues points also to the
conclusion that so far as Gmc. is concerned, there were
always four distinct forms of the root (*cf.* examples of *e*-
series of Aryan Ablaut, under **bher*- in Chapter IX.).   On
the other hand, if we take the three vowels *a*, *e*, *ea*, in the
O.E. *racu*, 'narrative'; *reččean*, inf. 'to narrate'; *reahte*,
pret. 'narrated,' we have every reason to assume that in
this case one original Gmc. sound *a* has been differentiated
into three sounds in O.E. itself, and the conditions of that
differentiation can be stated (*cf.* Chapter XII., sections on
i-mutation and Fracture).   Thus we should reconstruct the
earlier forms **raka*-, **rækk*-jan, **rah*-ta, respectively, to
correspond to the three O.E. forms above.

6. The same sound, as we have just seen, may have a
various development in the same dialect under different
phonetic conditions.   Later on, when the tendencies of
combinative change which produced the variety have passed
away, the different forms may be used promiscuously, and
without regard to the original conditions under which
they severally arose.   It should be remembered that combinative change may operate not only within what we
call the 'word,' but also within the breath-group, or, as it
often is, the sentence.

The two words 'of' and 'off' in Modern English. were

originally doublets of the same word, the *voiced* final consonant occurring in cases where the word was unstressed in the sentence, the *voiceless* final when it was stressed. Now the two forms are independent and distinct words, each specialized to express a different meaning; and although ' of,' as it happens, is usually without stress, ' off' may be used equally in stressed or unstressed positions. In the same way the word *seint*, ' saint,' had two forms in M.E. : (sin) in unstressed positions, (saint) when stressed. The latter strong form has become Mod. Eng. ' saint ' (sɛint) ; the former has become (sən or sənt), as in *St. Andrews* (sənt ændrūz) or *St. John*, the name of the Apostle (sən džɔn). But in the family name St. John, pronounced (sindžən), the stress has been shifted to the first syllable, which, however, still preserves the original form which it acquired in unstressed positions; and the same is true of the name *St. Leger* (silidžə) as regards the vowel, although here the -*n* has been lost. The substantive ' saint,' however, always preserves the strong or stressed form, even when it occurs with weak stress in a sentence.

The principles of modern philological method have been formulated on various occasions, notably by Brugmann— *e.g., Morphol. Untersuch.*, i., p. xiii, etc. ; *Zum heutigen Stand der Sprachwissensch.*, p. 53, etc. ; *Grundr.*², pp. 63-72 ; *Griech. Gr.*³, pp. 2-9.

CHAPTER XII

HISTORY OF ENGLISH: THE OLD ENGLISH PERIOD

THE designation *Old English* is applied to that period of the history of our people which extends from the first settlement of Germanic tribes in these islands down to the coming of the Normans. The O.E. period of the language may roughly be estimated as reaching down to 1050, after which period the chief features of the next, or *Transition* period from Old to Middle English, begin to be fairly well established, and expressed in the written forms which have come down to us.

Within the O.E. period of the history of the language it is possible to distinguish, from the documents, three stages of development, which are known respectively as the *Earliest*, down to 750; *Early*, down to 900; *Late*, down to 1050. The dates here given are, of course, only approximate, since neither the imperfection of the series of records, nor the slow and gradual mode of growth in language, permit us to make a precise hard-and-fast division between different periods.

There are three chief types of dialectal variety distinguishable from the records : *Saxon*, of which *West Saxon* became the principal dialect of literature ; *Kentish*, the dialect of the *Jutes; Anglian,* which includes both *North-umbrian* and *Mercian.*

Sources of our Knowledge of O.E.

Practically everything of value from a literary point of view is preserved in W.S., having been either written in that dialect originally or copied into it at a later period. There are a certain number of Charters, which possess great historical interest, in other dialects, especially Kentish. There is little original prose, except Homilies and Laws, which are mainly W.S. in form ; and of the translated literature the greatest part, and that which is of the chiefest interest, the authentic works of King Alfred, is in the same dialect— the other dialects, apart from charters, being represented almost entirely by translations of the Psalms and inter-linear versions of the New Testament. There are glossaries, which are of great value to students of the language, in Saxon, Kentish, and Mercian dialects. The poetical literature, with the exception of a few fragments in Early Northumbrian, exists in manuscripts of the tenth and eleventh centuries in a dialect which, while it is largely W.S., yet shows numerous characteristics of other dialects, the result, probably, of late copying from Anglian by W.S. scribes.

The following is a list of the chief remains which are important for the study of the several dialects. It will be noticed that very little *Earliest W.S.* has been pre-served.

A. Earliest Texts.

1. NORTHUMBRIAN.—*Northumbrian Fragments,* in Sweet's *Oldest English Texts,* p. 149, etc. *Liber Vitæ,*

O.E.T., p. 153, etc. Northumbrian Genealogies, *O.E.T.*, p. 167, etc. Names in Moore MS. of Bede s *Eccl. Hist.*, *O.E.T.*, p. 131, etc.

2. MERCIAN.—*Epinal Glossary (circa* 700), *Corpus Glossary* (*circa* 750), in *O.E.T.* Charters of eighth century (Latin, containing Eng. words and names), *O.E.T.*, p. 429, etc.

3. KENTISH.—*Charters* (Latin, but containing Eng. words and names), *O.E.T.*, p. 427, etc. These documents belong to seventh and eighth centuries ; the earliest of these, No. 4 in *O.E.T.*, is the oldest *written* document we possess containing English forms.

4. WEST SAXON.—*Charter* No. 3 in *O.E.T.*

B. Ninth-Century Texts (Early).

1. NORTHUMBRIAN.

2. MERCIAN.—*Vespasian Psalter and Hymns*, *O.E.T.*, p. 183, etc. ; the Hymns also Sweet, A.S. Reader, p. 117, etc.

3. KENTISH.—*Numerous Charters*, mostly English, *O.E.T.*, p. 441, etc. ; three in A.S. Reader[7], p. 189, etc. *Bede Glosses* (MS. Cott., C. II.), *circa* 900, *O.E.T.*, p. 179, etc.

4. WEST SAXON.—*Works of King Alfred : Cura Pastoralis,* Sweet, 1871 ; *Orosius*, Sweet, 1880. *Parker MS. of Anglo-Saxon Chronicle down to* 891, Ed. Plummer. *Two of the Saxon Chronicles.* 2 vols. Oxford, 1892-1900.

C. Late Texts.

1. NORTH-
UMBRIAN

Northern Area

Durham Ritual : Surtees Soc., vol. iv., 1840. *Cf.* also Skeat's collation, *Tr. Phil. Soc.*, 1879. *Durham Book* or *Lindisfarne Gospels :* Skeat, *Gospels in Anglo-Saxon*, 1871-1887.

Southern Area

Rushworth MS : Interlinear version of SS. Mark, Luke, John, known as *Rushworth²*, *Matthew in this MS. being in Mercian. Cf.* Skeat's ed. of Gospels above.

2. MERCIAN.—*Rushworth² :* Interlinear Gloss to Matthew, second half of tenth century. *Cf.* Skeat above. *Glosses from MS. Royal*, 2 A. 20. Ed. by Zupitza in *Zeitschrift für deutsches Altertum*, Bd. xxxiii., p. 47, etc. (*circa* 1000).

3. KENTISH.—*Glosses :* Zupitza in *Ztschr. f. d. A.*, xxi., p. 1, etc., and xxii., p. 223, etc. ; also in *Wright-Wülker's Vocabularies*, p. 55, etc., 1884. *Hymn*, known as ' *Kentish Hymn*,' in Kluge's *ags Lesebuch* and Sweet's *A.S. Reader. Psalm L.*, known as ' *Kentish Psalm*,' in Kluge's *Lesebuch*.

4. WEST SAXON.—*Ælfric's Grammar and Glossary* (*circa* 1000), Zupitza, 1880. *Ælfric's Homilies*, Ed. Thorpe, 1844-1846. *West Saxon Gospels*, MS. Corpus, Cambridge (written at Bath, *circa* 1000). *Cf.* Skeat's Ed. of *Gospels in Anglo-Saxon* above.

5. Another *Saxon Dialect*, but not the West Saxon of

Ælfred nor of Ælfric, is represented by a Gloss. (*Harleian MS*. 3,376; printed Wright-Wülker, 1, 192, etc.) and a set of Homilies, known as the *Blickling Homilies* (Ed. Morris, E.E.T.S., 1880). Both of these texts are tenth century, the latter MS. being dated 979 in the text itself.

Authorities on O.E. Grammar.—The best general authorities on O.E. Grammar are *Bülbring, Altenglisches Elementarbuch, Heidelberg,* 1902; and *Sievers, Angelsächsische Grammatik,* Halle, 1898. These works deal with all the problems of O.E. Grammar, the latter entering into the discussion of dialectal differences with considerable minuteness. A brief but reliable outline is found in the Grammatical Introduction to Sweet's *Anglo-Saxon Reader,* seventh edition.

The following special monographs will be found useful for advanced, detailed study of O.E. dialects:

Northumbrian Texts.

Lindelöf, V.: *Die Sprache d. Rituals von Durham,* Helsingfors, 1890. *Wörterbuch zur interlinearglosse des Rituale Ecclesiae Dunelmensis, Bonner Beiträge zur Anglistic* ix., 1901. *Die Südnorthumbrischen Mundart* (Die Spr. d. gl. Rushworth²), *Bonner Beitr.,* x., 1901. *Glossar zur altnorthumbrischen Evangelienberzetzung die sogenannte Glosse Rushworth,*² Helsingfors, 1897.

Lea, E. M.: *The Language of the Northumbrian Gloss to the Gospel of St. Mark, Anglia,* xvi., 62-206.

Füchsel, H.: *Die Sprache d. northumbrischen interlinear-*

version zum Johannes-Evangelium, Anglia, xxiv., 1-99.

[Both of the above, Lea and Füchsel, deal with the *Lindisfarne Gospels,* or *Durham Book.*]

Cook, A. S.: *A Glossary of the Old Northumbrian Gospels* (*Lindisfarne*), Halle, 1894.

Mercian Texts.

Dieter, F.: *Die Sprache und Mundart, der ältesten englischen Denkmäler* (Espinal and Corpus Glossaries), Göttingen, 1885.

Chadwick, H. M.: *Studies in Old English* (deals with the old Glossaries), 1899.

Brown, E. M.: *Spr. d. Rushworth Glossen* (Rushw.[1]), Part I., Göttengen, 1891. *The Language of the Rushworth Gloss to Matthew,* Part II., Göttingen, 1892.

Zeuner, R.: *Die Spr. d. Kentischen Psalters* (Vespas. A. 1), Halle, 1881.

[This text (*Vespasian Psalter*) was formerly supposed to be Kentish, though now universally recognised as Mercian.]

Thomas, P. G., and Wyld, H. C.: *A Glossary of the Mercian Hymns* (in Vespas. A. 1) in *Otia Merseiana,* vol. iv., Liverpool, 1904.

Grimm, C.: *Glossar. z. Vesp. Ps. und d. Hymnen,* Heidelberg, 1906.

Kentish Texts.

Wolf, R.: *Untersuchung d. Laute in d. Kentischen Urkunden,* Heidelberg, 1893.

Williams, Irene: *Grammatical Investigation of the Old Kt. Glosses* (MS. Vespas. D. vi.), *Bonner Beitr.,* xix., 1906.

West Saxon.

Cosijn, P. J. : *Altwestsächsische Grammatik*, Haag, 1888.

> [This is practically an exhaustive monograph based upon Alfred's *Cura Pastoralis*. It treats also, though less fully, with the forms of the Parker Chronicle. It is invaluable for the study of Early West Saxon.]

Fischer, F. : *The Stressed Vowels of Alfric's Homilies*. Publications of Mod. Lang. Assoc. of America, vol. i., Baltimore, 1889.

Brüll, H. : *Die altenglische Latein-Grammatik des Alfric*, Berlin, 1904.

Trilsbach, G. : *Die Lautlehre d. spätwestsächsischen Evangelien*, Bonn, 1905.

Harris, M. A. : *Glossary of the West Saxon Gospels*, Boston, 1899.

Saxon Patois.

Hardy : *Die Sprache d. Blickling-Homilien*, Leipzig, 1899.

Boll, P. : *Die Sprache d. altenglischen Glossen in Ms Harley 3,376, Bonner Beitr.* xv., 1904.

Numerous articles on special points are referred to in the works here enumerated, and in the grammars of Sievers and Bülbring.

Pronunciation of Old English.

This is established by the following considerations : (1) Old English was first written, after the introduction of Christianity, in the British form of the Latin alphabet. The contemporary pronunciation of Latin is therefore important in settling the probable value of the symbols in O.E., since the English would naturally use the symbol which represented in Latin the nearest sound to their own. (2) Phonetic considerations based (*a*) upon the West Germanic origin of the English sound, (*b*) upon the subsequent history of the sound in Middle and Modern English. (3) A comparison of varieties of spelling of the same word, representing different scribal attempts to express the same sound, or unconscious lapses from the traditional mode of spelling, in favour of one more phonetic. (4) Accents in the manuscripts indicating quantity ; length is also sometimes expressed by doubling the vowel.

In spite of everything, however, there must always remain some uncertainty and difference of opinion on certain points.

The following table shows the probable value of the O.E. symbols of the vowels :

	Unrounded Vowels.		Rounded Vowels.	
	Back.	Front.	Back.	Front.
High ...	—	ĭ	ŭ	y̆
Mid ...	a	ĕ	ŏ	œ̆ (< ĕ̆)
Low ...	ā (or mid ?)	æ̆	—	—

There are also combinations of above in the diphthongs ēā, ēū (ēŏ<) ; ĭū (<W.S. ĭē or ēō ; Kt. ēŏ or ĭō ; North. ĭō ; Mer. ēō). [The marks of length are only occasional in the manuscripts.]

As regards the question of whether the above vowels were 'tense' or 'slack,' it is probable that the High and Mid vowels in the front series (unrounded) existed in a ' *tense* ' form, both long and short, and, further, that a short mid-front-slack also existed, having a different origin. It is usual among English scholars to write this vowel ę, a symbol which is found in some manuscripts.

The symbol ŏĕ (mid-front-round) hardly occurs in W. Saxon texts, ĕ being the symbol used already in Early W. Saxon. This probably implies that unrounding took place earlier in this dialect than in the others. In Northumbrian æ is used during the whole O.E. period. On the whole, it is possible that all the round vowels were tense.

Originally, doubtless, (ɔ) low-back-tense-round, and the same vowel short and slack, existed, but the long at any rate seems to have been levelled under the mid-back-round, by, or soon after, the historic period.

Pronunciation of Old English Consonants.

In addition to the ordinary Latin consonantal symbols, certain letters of Runic origin are habitually used from the ninth century onwards to express English sounds which did not exist in Latin. Thus þ ('*thorn*') is written to express the point-teeth-open consonant, whether voiced or voiceless, and ƿ ('*wēn*') to express that of '*w*' (lip-back-open).

Before the historic period, the old *k* (back-stop-breath) was differentiated in O.E. into a back and a front stop. The latter was the ancestor of the Mod. Eng. ' ch '- sound (tʃ). The manuscripts occasionally write *k* for the former, but more often *c*, which does duty both for the back and the front sounds. It is convenient to distinguish the two sounds by writing *ċ* for the fronted consonant. It is a disputed point how soon the full (tʃ) sound, as in Present English, developed. Most German scholars insist that this sound was fully established quite early in the O.E. period. Sweet has always held that the O.E. sound was a front stop, which view is shared by the present writer. It is merely a question of probabilities, and cannot be definitely settled one way or the other. The really important thing is to realize that there were two sounds in O.E., a back and a front, and to express this fact in pronunciation.

Another symbol whose pronunciation is doubtful is *g*. The O.E. form of this letter is always ȝ, or ᵹ, down to the middle of the eleventh century, after which the Continental *g* is used. There were originally two sounds in West Gmc., which were inherited by O.E., and expressed by the symbol ȝ, etc., a back-open-voice and front-open-voice, (*i.e., j*). The back-open, before the historical period, was differentiated into a back and a front sound, the latter thus being levelled under original *j* to all appearances. These sounds continue to be written ȝ without any distinction during the O.E. period. It is probable that by the year 1000, or thereabouts, the back-open was stopped initially, but remained an open consonant medially and finally.

The O.E. symbol, cȝ, which represents the doubling of old *g* before *j*, was, in Sweet's view, pronounced as a voiced front stop during the O.E. period. Here again opinions are divided, German scholars, Sievers, Bülbring, and Kluge, maintaining that the Mod. Eng. sound -'dge' (dž) was already established.

For a full account and discussion of O.E. pronunciation, *cf.* Bülbring, *Elementarbuch*, pp. 13-31 ; Sweet, *History of*

15

English Sounds, pp. 101-149 ; and for an additional discussion of O.E. c, g, cg, also Kluge in *Paul's Grundriss*, pp. 989, etc.

The most practical book for beginners who want to learn the language is probably Sweet's *First Steps in Anglo-Saxon*, which should be followed up with his *Anglo-Saxon Reader* (seventh edition). Both works contain a short, practical account of the pronunciation, a practical grammar, accidence and syntax, as well as well-chosen texts, and a glossary. Another book, which may be recommended to beginners is A. S. Cook's *First Book in Old English*, Athenæum Press, 1903 (third edition), which, in addition to phonology, grammar, vocabulary, and texts, contains also a useful bibliography.

Old English Sound Changes.

The vowel system of O.E. is distinguished from that of the other West Gmc. languages, notably from Old High German, by a number of characteristic changes which took place in the former group of dialects, mostly before the period of the documents. These changes are of both the Isolative and Combinative classes, and a knowledge of them is of importance to those who wish to pursue the history of the language in a systematic way, further back than Old English itself, and to inquire into its precise relationship with the other West Gmc. languages.

For those whose main object, however, is to trace the growth of the Modern Language, and to relate it to the earlier forms, a detailed knowledge of the minutiæ of O.E. sound change is out of place for this particular purpose.

In the same way, the specialist is deeply interested in

the dialectal differences of O.E. The most important of these consist in the different treatment, in different geographical areas, of the original vowel sounds. But these early differences are but faintly reflected, even in the full M.E. period of the language, and in the Modern speech hardly any of the primitive dialectal distinctions can be traced.

The various local treatment of sounds which we find in M.E. seems in the light of our present knowledge of O.E. to be but of recent growth, and as for the English dialects of to-day, their peculiarities, so far as we can trace their origin, would appear for the most part not to be more than two, or at the most three, hundred years old.

As in a work like the present space is necessarily limited, it will be best in dealing with the phonology of O.E. to consider mainly, such typical sound changes, whether of common O.E. origin or subsequently developed during the O.E. period, within the several dialects, as have left their traces upon the language of the present day, of which some knowledge is necessary in order to understand the phenomena of Mod. Eng. grammar. For this purpose we shall endeavour to make a judicious selection in the following account.

Changes in the West Germanic Vowels which affected Old English generally.

A. *Isolative Changes.*

1. W. Gmc. *a* < O.E. *æ*: O.E. *dæg*; Gothic *dag-s*; O.H.G. tac; O.E. æcer, 'field'; O. Sax. *akkar*; O.H.G. *acchar*.

2. W. Gmc. *ā* < O.E. *ǣ*: O.E. *mǣþ*, 'mowing'; O.H.G. *mād*; O.E. *wǣpn*, 'weapon'; O.H.G. *wāfan*.

15—2

3. W. Gmc. *ã* (*i.e.*, nasalized *a*) < *ō*, then, with loss of
nasalization, O.E. *ō*: *þōhte*, pret. of *þenċan*, from
þãhta, *cf.* Goth. *þãhta*; O.H.G. *dãhta*, 'thought.'
> [NOTE.—This nasalized *ã*, which was developed
> already in Germanic itself (*cf.* under Com-
> binative Changes, pp. 231-233), appears
> rounded to *ō* in the earliest English texts,
> of all dialects. It is probable that originally
> it was a *low-back-tense-round*, though it may
> have been raised to the mid position quite
> early.]

4. W. Gmc. *ai* < O.E. *ā*: O.E. *hām*; Goth. *haims*;
O.H.G. *heim*; O.E. *gāt*, 'goat'; Goth. *gaits*;
O.H.G. *geiz*.

5. W. Gmc. *au* < O.E. *ǣū*, whence *ǣō*, *ǣā*, and finally
ēā in nearly all dialects: O.E. *ēāge*, 'eye'; Goth.
augō; O.H.G. *ouga*; O.E. *hēāfod*, 'head'; Goth.
haubiþ; O.H.G. *houbit*.

B. *Combinative Changes.*

1. *Rounding of W. Gmc. a to o before Nasals.*—In O.E.
texts of all periods, from ninth century onwards, such
double forms as *mann*, *monn*, *land*, *lond*, *nama*, *noma*,
'name,' etc., are found. The oldest texts have only *-an-*
in these words, and a comparison with the other Gmc.
languages leaves no doubt that this is the original form.
In ninth-century texts, however (King Alfred's period), the
forms with *-on-* largely predominate, while later on, in the
tenth and eleventh centuries, those with *-an-* are again in
the majority

In M.E. the *-on-* forms again become frequent, but in
Mod. Eng. they have almost entirely disappeared, the
preposition *on* being the only form which has survived in

the polite language, apart from cases where lengthening has taken place (see below).

It might appear that such words as '*strong*,' '*long*,' etc., were examples of the preservation of the -*on*- forms; but this, as we shall see, is not the case, and these forms require a different explanation (see p. 273).

It is impossible to believe in the alternate change of -*an*- to -*on*-, and of this to -*an*- in late O.E., and again of this back to -*on*- in M.E., and finally in a return to -*an*- in Mod. Eng. At any rate, there cannot have been an alternate process of rounding and unrounding going on for centuries. As Sweet pointed out long ago (see Introduction to *Cura Pastoralis*, p. xxii), in all dialects, at all periods, both -*an*- and -*on*- forms are found; sometimes one is in the majority, sometimes the other. It looks as if a double pronunciation existed at the same time amid speakers of the same dialect, just as nowadays we hear both (æs) and (ās) = ' ass,' and so on, among persons who otherwise have no dialectal peculiarity. The preponderance of this or that form may have been quite artificial, and a question of fashion.

2. *Rounding of W. Gmc. ā to ō before Nasals.*—This is universal in all O.E. dialects from the earliest period. Examples are: O.E. *mōna*, ' moon '; O. Sax. and O.H.G. *māno;* O.E. *nōmon*, pret. pl. of *niman*, ' take'; O.H.G. *nāmum*, etc. This sound (ā), as we have seen, otherwise than before nasals, becomes *æ* in O.E., and its subsequent non-W. Sax. development is important in the history of the language.

3. *Fracture or ' Brechung.'*—This is the name given to the diphthonging of original O.E. front vowels before

certain consonants or combinations of consonants. This change is not, in all its forms, strictly 'common O.E.,' since it is more fully developed in W. Sax. and Kentish than in the Anglian dialects. The dialectal differences in this particular will, however, be discussed subsequently, and we may now content ourselves with describing the process itself, and the conditions under which it occurs in those dialects in which it is most observable.

The Primitive O.E. front vowels *i*, *e*, *œ* are diphthongized respectively to *iu*, *eu*, and *œu* before *h* or *h* + another consonant, *rr* or *r* + another consonant; *œ* undergoes the same change before *ll* or *l* + another consonant, and *i*, *e* before *l* + *h* or *c*.

The process depends upon the character of the following consonants: *h* was a back-open-voiceless, and *ll*, *rr*, or *l* and *r*, when followed by other consonants, appear to have been pronounced either as back consonants, or, as is more probable, as strongly inverted consonants— that is, with the point of the tongue turned upwards and backwards. This mode of articulation is heard to-day in the pronunciation of *r* throughout the whole of the Saxon part of England, and also in Oxfordshire. Inverted *l*, or *l* formed with considerable hollowing out of the front part of the tongue, is also common in the Southern dialects. The result of this method of articulation was that a strong glide vowel was developed between *i*, *e*, *œ*, and the following h, ll, etc., and rr, etc. At the present day in such a word as '*ale*' we often hear (*ai*ᵘl) with a fairly distinct *u*-like glide before the ' thick ' *l*.

The glide in O.E. would appear to have been of *u* quality. In the ninth century *œu* had become *ea*, and *eu* eo—in West Saxon at any rate. In an early North-umbrian text (*Bede's Death Song*) *iu* is still preserved in *wiurþiþ*, later *wiorþeþ*.

Examples are:

(1) of *æ*: O.E. (W.S. and Kt.) *eahta*, 'eight,' O. Sax., O.H.G. *ahto*; O.E. *earm*, 'poor,' O.H.G. *arm*; O.E. (W.S. and Kt.) *ceald*, 'cold,' O.H.G. *kalt*.

(2) of *e*: O.E. *feohtan*, 'fight,' vb., O.H.G. *fehtan*; O.E. *eorþe*, 'earth,' O. Sax. *ertha*, O.H.G. *erda*; O.E. *eolh*, 'elk,' *cf.* M.H.G. *elch*.

4. *Loss of Nasal Consonant before Voiceless Open Con-sonants* (*h, f, þ, s*), *and the Result on Preceding Vowel.*— (*a*) Before *h*: Since all the Gmc. languages show a loss of *n* and *m* before a following *h*, we may assume that this loss took place in the common Gmc. period. Before disappearing, however, the nasal consonant nasalized the preceding vowel, and in O.E., at any rate, the nasalization was preserved down to the beginning of the English period. Examples: Goth. *þagkjan* (=*þaŋkjan*), 'think,' pret. *þāhta*; O.H.G. *denken*, *dâchta*, with originally nasalized *ă*. The preterite form is from earlier **þaŋk-ta*, which became **þaŋh-ta*, with the common Gmc. change of *-kt-* to *-ht-*. The O.E. form *þōhte* shows the characteristic rounding of this nasal vowel, and compensatory lengthen-ing after the loss of nasalization. The Primitive O.E. distinction between this *ā* and W. Gmc. *ā* is shown by the difference of the subsequent treatment in O.E., the latter being fronted to *ǣ*.

Another example of this rounding and lengthening in O.E. is *brōhte*, pret. of *bring-an*, which stands for earlier

*$bra\eta hta$, which became *$br\bar{a}hta$. Other vowels than a are merely lengthened in compensation for the loss of nasality; thus O.E. $\bar{p}\bar{u}hte$, pret. of $pyn\dot{c}ean$, ' seem,' from $p\bar{u}hte$, from *$pu\eta hta$; O.E. $p\bar{e}\bar{o}n$, ' prosper,' is from *$pi\eta han$, which in Prim. O.E. was *$p\bar{\imath}han$, whence *$p\bar{u}han$ with Fracture, which in W. Sax. became *$piu(h)an$, *$p\bar{\imath}on$, and finally $p\bar{e}\bar{o}n$, with change of $\bar{\imath}o < \bar{e}\bar{o}$. In O. Sax. this vb. appears as $th\bar{\imath}han$, and in O.H.G. $d\bar{\imath}han$. The original n is seen in another form preserved in O.E., $gepungen$ (originally a participial form), in which earlier h has been voiced to g (back-open-voice) by the process known as Verner's Law, which depends upon the place of the accent. Before g the nasal consonant is not lost.

(b) *Loss of Nasal before* f, p, s.—This is a Primitive Old English change, but is precisely similar in nature and in results to the foregoing.

O.E. $s\bar{o}fte$, ' soft,' O.H.G. $samfto$; O.E. $t\bar{o}p$, ' tooth '; O.H.G. $zand$, both from earlier *$tanp$ (see *ante*, pp. 152-3); O.E. $s\bar{\imath}p$, ' journey,' Goth. $sinps$, O.H.G. $sind$; O.E. $g\bar{o}s$, ' goose,' O.H.G. $gans$; O.E. $\bar{u}s$, ' us,' O.H.G. uns.

It is probable that the $\bar{o}$ in these words, as well as in the class before mentioned, which show an earlier loss of the nasal, was originally different from the other O E. $\bar{o}$ (in $f\bar{o}t$, ' foot,' etc.), which represents an original Gmc. $\bar{o}$. The former may have been the *low-back-round*. In any case, there is no graphic distinction made between the two sounds in O.E., and their subsequent history has been identical. The levelling under one sound almost certainly took place early in the O.E. period.

In words like O.E. $g\bar{o}s$, $t\bar{o}p$, etc., the process of change was apparently as follows · *$gans$, *$g\bar{a}ns$, *$g\bar{a}s$, *$g\bar{o}s$, *gōs.* The rounding of the nasalized *ã* was earlier than that of *a* before a nasal consonant, since the earliest texts invariably have *ō* in *gōs*, etc., whereas, as we have seen, *monn*, etc., appear in the earliest records of English with *a.*

5. *i- or j- Mutation.*—This process, often called by the German name, *i*-Umlaut, is common to all the O.E. dialects, and there is no O.E. sound change whose traces are so perceptible in Mod. Eng. It consists in the fronting of an original back vowel, or diphthong, which contained at least one *back* element, by the influence of a following *-i-* or *-j-* in the following syllable. It is generally held now that the *-i-* or *-j-* first fronted or front-modified the intervening consonant or group of consonants, and that this in turn fronted the vowel immediately preceding them.* The only front vowel affected is *æ*, which is raised to *e*. In this case it was possible for the fronting of the vowel not to take place until after the *i* or *j* had disappeared altogether. All that was necessary was that, before being dropped, it should have fronted to a greater or lesser extent the intervening consonant. The fronting of the vowel was a comparatively late process, taking place about the beginning of the seventh century, shortly before the earliest manuscripts which we possess in O.E. were written. It can be shown that *i*-mutation was later than Fracture, for instance, since diphthongs produced by the latter process are further affected by the former. In cases where the *-i-* or

---

* When the fronting was caused by *-j-*, as in *-ja-* or *-jo*-stem nouns or *-jan* verbs, the *-j-* was assimilated to the preceding consonant, which was thus not only fronted, but lengthened—as in *cynn*, from **kunja*, etc. *r* was not doubled, and *-j-* remained (after short vowels). When final, *-j-* became *-i-* and the *e* in O.E. *Cf. here* > *heri* > **hærj* > **harja.*

-j- have disappeared in O.E. its original existence can usually be established by referring to the cognate word in Gothic or Old High German.

The following examples illustrate the effect of this mutation upon the various vowels :

The mutation of *æ* is *e :* O.E. *þeċċean,* ' to cover,' from **þækk-jan* (*cf.* O.E. *þæc,* ' roof ').

,,   *a* is *æ :* O.E. *ġe-slægen,* 'struck,' p.p. from **slag-in-*.

,,   *o* is *e* (earlier *œ*): O.E. *ele,* ' oil,' loan-word from Latin *oleum,* W. Gmc. **olja*.

,,   *w* is *y :* O.E. *cynn,* 'race,' ' family,' from **kuññj, cf.* Gothic *kuni* from **kunja*.

              O.E. *fyllan,* ' fill,' from **fulljan* (*cf.* O.E. *full*).

,,   *ā* is *ǣ :* O.E. *sǣlan,* 'bind,' from **sāljan* (*cf.* O.E. *sāl* ' rope ').

,,   *ō* is *ē* (earlier *ǣ*): 1. Original *ō :* O.E. *fēt,* from **fōtiz,* pl. of O.E. *fōt*.

              2. *ō* from *ō :* O.E. *gēs,* pl. of *gōs,* from **gōsi*.

              3. *ō* from W. Gmc. *ā :* O.E. *fēhþ,* ' takes,' from **fōhiþ, *fōhiþ, *faŋhiþ* (*cf.* O.E. *fō,* ' I take,' from **fōha, *fāha, *faŋha*).

,,   *ū* is *ȳ :* 1. W. Gmc. *ū :* O.E. *fȳlþ,* ' filth,' from **fūliþ,* O. Sax. *fūliþa* (*cf.* O.E. *fūl,* ' foul ').

              2. O.E. *ū :* O.E. *dȳstiġ,* ' dusty,' from **dūstig* (*cf.* O.E. *dūst,* O.H.G. *dunst*).

The *i*-mutation of the O.E. diphthongs will be best treated under the head of Dialectal Divergences.

In some words it might appear that *y* was the mutation of *o*—*e.g.*, *gylden,* ' golden,' compared with *gold,* the substantive ; *fyxen,* ' vixen,' feminine of *fox; gyden,* ' goddess,' compared with *god.* The fact is that the *o* in the above words is a W. Gmc. change from an earlier *u* before a following *a* in the stem ending. The original *u* was, however, preserved unchanged when followed by *i*, so that **gulđin-, *fuhsiʳ-, *guđin,* remained unchanged until the period when the following *-i-* fronted the root vowel to *y*.

Lengthening of Short Vowels.—During the O.E. period original short vowels were lengthened before the consonantal combinations *-ld*, *nd*, *mb*: *cīld*, ' child '; *fīndan*, vb. ' find '; *cāmb*, ' comb.' These lengthenings are important for the subsequent history of the language, their later development being similar to that of original long vowels. When these combinations are followed by another consonant, such as *r*, which occurs, for instance, in the plural suffix, *-ru—cīldru*, *lămbru*, etc.—the lengthening does not take place, or is subsequently got rid of. This explains the interchange of diphthong and short vowel in (tʃaild—tʃildrən), and also the short vowel in Mod. Eng. (læm), which must be explained from the plural type with a short vowel in O.E.

Many later shortenings took place in cases where a third consonant follows the vowel in compounds—*e.g.*, *hănd*, *hăndfull*, etc. (*cf.* p. 272, etc., below).

Dialectal Divergences in the Old English Vowel System.

Each of the O.E. dialects possesses certain characteristic phonological features peculiar to itself alone. The West Saxon dialect has more individual peculiarities than any of the others which, in a large number of cases, agree in those respects in which they differ from West Saxon. Thus it is often sufficient to describe a characteristic as West Saxon on the one hand, or as *non-West Saxon* on the other, implying by the latter phrase that Northumbrian, Mercian, and Kentish agree in that particular respect.

In Modern English it is comparatively rare that a form can be derived only from the exclusively West Saxon type, though this sometimes happens. On the other hand, the survivals of Anglian peculiarities, common to both North-

umbria and Mercia, are numerous; a few specifically Northumbrian, exist, and a few which are specifically Kentish.

The following are the chief O.E. dialectal differences
which can still be traced in Modern Polite English:

A. Features Common to all the non-West Saxon Dialects.—
1. Primitive O.E. *ǣ*, which remains in W.S., is raised to *ē*
in the other dialects: W.S. *dǣd*, ' deed,' non-W.S. *dēd;*
W.S. *sǣd*, 'seed,' non-W.S. *sēd*. The forms with *ē* are the
ancestral forms of the Mod. Eng. (ī) forms, *seed, deed*, etc.
The other O.E. *ǣ*, the *i*-mutation of *ā*, is preserved in all
dialects except Kentish, which raises it to *ē : clēne*, 'clean';
in other dialects *clǣne*, from *clāni*.

2. The *i*-mutation of Pr. O.E. *ēa* (Gmc. *au*) is *īe*, later
ȳ in W.S.; but in the other dialects *ē : W.S. hīeran*, later
hȳran, ' hear,' from *hēārjan. Cf.* Goth. *hausjan*>Gmc.
hauzjan, non-W.S. *hēran.* This is the origin of Mod.
Eng. ' *hear* ' (hiə(r)). The W.S. form, had it survived,
would have given (haiə(r)).

3. After front consonants, (*ċ, ġ, sċ*), *ǣ*, and *e* are diphthongized, in W.S., to *ēā* and *ie* (later *y*) respectively.
This diphthonging does not take place in non-W.S.—
e.g., sċeld, 'shield,' W.S. *sċīeld, sċȳld;* non-W.S. *sċēld*,
whence Mod. Eng. (ʃild). On the other hand, Mod. Eng.
chill is apparently from W.S. *ċi(e)le*, and not from non-
W.S. *ċele*. The W.S. form is from *ċæli*, whence *ċeali*,
and then *ċiele, ċyle*, with *i*-mutation of *ea*.

B. Common Anglian Features.—1. Pr. O.E. *a, æ* is not
diphthongized to *ea* before *l, ll*, or *l* + another consonant,
in Anglian as in W.S., but remains as *a*, and is subsequently
lengthened to *ā : W.S. eald*, ' old,' Ang. *āld;* W.S. *ċeald*,
' cold,' Anglian *cāld;* W.S. *beald*, ' bold,' Anglian *bāld;*

W.S. *weald*, ' forest,' Anglian *wāld*. The long *ā* in these words, together with all other O.E. *ā* sounds, was rounded to *ō* in M.E. in the South and Midlands, and is the origin of Mod. Eng. (*ou*). Thus the Anglian forms of above words gave rise to Mod. Eng. *old, cold, bold, wold*. The W.S. form of the last word appears to be also preserved in the modern doublet form *weald*.

C. **Distinctively Northumbrian Features.**—1. In Late Northumbrian the combination *weo-* appears as *wo-*. The same combination in Late W.S. appears as *wu :* W.S. *weorþ*, later *wurþ*, Late Nth. *worþ* ; W.S. *sweord*, ' sword,' later *swurd*, Late Nth. *sword*, etc. Mercian and Kentish preserve *weo* unaltered. 2. *īu* does not undergo change to *ēo*, but preserves the first element unaltered during O.E. period.

D. **Kentish Features.**—In Kentish, by the middle of the ninth century, the earlier *y̆*-sounds, the result of *i*-mutation of *ŭ*, had been unrounded and lowered to *ĕ*. All the other dialects preserve *y̆* during the whole O.E. period. In M.E., as we shall see, the Saxon dialects alone preserved the old sound ; the Anglian unrounded it to *ĭ*. Thus, such forms as *gelt*, ' guilt,' W.S. *gylt ; senn,* ' sin,' W.S. *synn ; snetor*, ' wise,' W.S. *snytor*, etc., are typically Kentish. In the modern language a few of these forms with old Kentish *e* occur—*e.g., merry*, from Kentish *meriġ* = W.S. *myriġ*. The cognate substantive *mirth*, on the other hand, is Anglian as regards its spelling, while the actual pronunciation might be from either the W.S. or the Anglian type. In a few cases the modern forms preserve the M.E. spelling *u*, which is Norman French manner of expressing the old Saxon *y* sound—*e.g., church*, from W.S. *ċyrċe ; bury* (vb.), W.S. *byrġean*, M.E. (Southern) *burien*. In the latter word it is

interesting to note that, although we retain the Southern
(Saxon) spelling, we pronounce the Kentish vowel *e* (bɛri).
Such words as *ridge* and *bridge*, O.E. *hryċġ*, *bryċġ*, are
Middle Anglian in spelling and pronunciation, but the
Southern or Saxon variants occur in dialectal forms, such
as Somersetshire *burge*, with metathesis, and in proper
names, such as *Rudge*.

[NOTE.—The original O.E. form of *ċyrċe* is *ċir(i)ċe*; the
y, which is represented by M.E. *u*, must be due to the
influence of *r*.]

The Old English Vocabulary.

The native vocabulary closely agrees with that of the
other W. Gmc. languages, and more particularly with that
of the Continental Angles, with O. Frisian and O. Saxon.
The foreign elements are, in the main, from three sources,
Celtic, Latin, and Old Norse.

Celtic Loan-Words in Old English.

The number of these is far smaller than was formerly
supposed, and it is probable that a thorough investigation
of Welsh would reveal the existence of a larger number of
words borrowed from English in the early period into that
language.

Among those words of undoubted Celtic origin which
are found in O.E., it is possible to distinguish at least two
strata : those which were passed into the vocabulary during
the common Germanic period, and which survived in the
several Germanic languages after the separation, and those
which came independently into the English vocabulary
through contact of the Germanic settlers in these islands
with the Celtic inhabitants.

One of the earliest of the former class is O.E. *rīce,* 'kingdom,' 'rule,' which is found also in Gothic *reiki,* 'kingdom,' *reiks,* 'ruler,' O.S. *rīki,* O.H.G. *rīhhi* (Mod. Germ. *reich*). This word in the form **rīg-* must have been borrowed from Celtic sources before the Pr. Gmc. 'shifting' of the original voiced stops *b, d, g,* to *p, t, k;* hence the *g* was unvoiced along with the original Aryan voiced stops. In O. Irish the word is *rī,* with genitive *rīg,* which is cognate with Latin *rēx* (*rēk-s,* from **rēg-s*) and *reg-o,* etc. Mod. Eng. still preserves the word in *bishop-ric.*

Other words for which this Pr. Celtic origin is sometimes claimed are doubtful, since, instead of being loan-words borrowed before the Germanic consonant 'shifting,' they may equally well be cognates possessed by Germanic and Celtic alike.

Among words borrowed in Britain in the O.E. period may be mentioned *drȳ,* 'magician,' in common use in poetry, borrowed, apparently, from a form resembling that found in O. Irish *drui.* Mod. Eng. *druid* is related to this word, but has reached us through the French, from Gaulish sources. Another word is O.E. *dunn,* 'dun,' 'dark brown,' from a Celtic type, *donnas. Cf.* Welsh *dwn* (= dun), 'dusky,' Irish *donn,* 'brown.' *Brocc,* 'badger' (*cf.* O. Ir. *brocc*), occurs already in the Epinal Glossary, and is still in dialectal use.

Latin Element in Old English.

This forms by far the most considerable part of the foreign element in the O.E. vocabulary. The question is not so simple as might appear from the lists of Latin loan-words which are given in some books on the history of

English. It is possible to distinguish at least three classes of words of Latin origin in O.E : (1) Words which formed part of the common West Germanic, or common Germanic, vocabulary; (2) words acquired first in this country, before the conversion of the English to Christianity, (3) words which passed into O.E. at a later period, after the introduction of Christianity, through the influence of the Church and the spread of learning.

The only true test of the period at which any particular word was borrowed is its form. It is certain that some words relating to Christian ideas and beliefs were adopted by the Germanic peoples long before they were converted from heathendom; while, as is natural, the actual adoption of the Christian religion, its forms and ceremonies, its ideals and its culture, led to the introduction of a host of fresh words to express new ideas. It is therefore unsound and inaccurate to mix up in one class all the words of Latin origin which relate to Christianity, and label them ' words of Christian origin.' O.E. cyrċe, ċiriċe, ' church,' from Gk. κυριακά, ' belonging to the Lord,' is a very early loan, which goes back at least to the W. Gmc. period (cf. O.H.G. chirihha.)

1. As regards the earliest class of Latin words, those acquired in the Continental Period, it is possible that some may have passed into W. Gmc. through the medium of Celtic ; and, again, it is not always possible, apparently, even for Celtic experts, to distinguish with absolute certainty between words in Celtic which are Latin loan-words and those which are genuine Celtic, cognate with the Latin forms.

The best tests of a Latin word having been adopted in the

Gmc. or W. Gmc. period are, first, the retention in genuine popular words of the Latin intervocalic *p*, *t*, *c* (k), unaffected by the later Neo-Latin voicing: O.E. *nǣp*, 'turnip,' Lat. nāpus; *mynet*, 'coin,' Lat. *moneta; fīc*-beām, 'fig-tree,' Lat. *fīcus*; secondly, its occurrence in several Gmc. tongues with the characteristic treatment which it would have undergone in each language had it belonged to the native element of Gmc. or W. Gmc.   Thus O.E. *strǣt*, compared with O. Sax. *strāta*, O.H.G. *strāzza*, Mod. Eng. *street*, from Latin *strāta via*, ' paved way,' clearly belonged to the common W. Gmc. vocabulary, for the *ā* has been fronted to *ǣ* in O.E. like original W. Gmc. *ā*, and the O.H.G. form shows the High German change of W. Gmc. *t* to *zz*. In the same way O.E. (W. Sax.) *cīese*, later *cȳse*, non-W. Sax. *cēse*, is a W. Gmc. loan from Latin *cāseus*, whence we may assume a form **kāsjō-*, **kāsi*, which gave rise on the one hand to O.H.G. *chāsi* (Mod. Germ. käse), and on the other to the English forms.   (W. Sax. *cīese* is from earlier **ceāsi*, from **cǣsi*, with diphthongization of *ǣ* to *eā* after a front consonant, and subsequent i-mutation to *īe*, whence *ȳ* in Late W. Sax.)   Mod. Eng. ' *cheese* ' is from the non-W. Sax. form.   Latin *Cæsar* was adopted into Gmc. speech at an early period, the sound of the old diph thong being approximately preserved : Gothic *kaisar*, O.H.G. *cheisar*.   In O.E. the diphthong underwent, in common with W. Gmc. *ai*, the characteristic change to *ā*; hence we get O.E. *cāsere*.   It is, of course, possible that this word was independently borrowed by Gothic and by W. Gmc.

It must be borne in mind that in these loan-words we are not dealing with words *written down*, with the *spell-*

16

ing of classical Latin, but with words actually used in living popular speech. In popular Latin, *b* between vowels was early weakened to an open consonant, at first a pure lip-open, like Gmc. *ƀ*. This sound is generally written *f* in O.E., though the spelling *b* is found in early texts. In O.H.G. it is written *b;* hence Lat. *cucurbita,* 'gourd,' O.E. *cyrfet* (with i-mutation), O.H.G. *churbizz;* Lat. *tabula,* 'plank,' 'writing-table,' O.E. *tæfl,* 'table' (for games), O.H.G. *zabal,* and so on.

2. **Words from Popular Sources acquired in Britain.**— Wright, in his *The Celt, the Roman, and the Saxon,* propounded the view that the people in the towns in this country continued to speak Latin long after the Romans had withdrawn from the island, and expresses his belief that if Britain had not been settled by the English ' we should have been now a people talking a Neo-Latin tongue, closely resembling French.' He thinks that the Angles and Saxons found the inhabitants of this country speaking Latin, and not a Celtic dialect. Pogatscher, in his important book, *Zur Lautlehre der Griechischen und Lateinischen und Romanischen Lehnworte im Altenglischen,* 1888, accepts this view in the fullest possible way, going further, indeed, than Wright, who, in the passage quoted by Pogatscher himself (*loc. cit.,* p. 3), expressly says : ' I have a strong suspicion, from different circumstances I have remarked, that the towns in our island continued, *in contradistinction from the country,* to use the Latin tongue long after the Empire of Rome had disappeared, and after the country had become Saxon.' Subsequently, however, Pogatscher's views were, to a certain extent, modified by the arguments of Loth (*Les Mots Latins dans les Langues Brittoniques,*

1892), and in an article, *Angelsachsen und Romanen* (*Englische Studien*, xix., p. 3, etc.), he apparently contents himself with Wright's view that Latin was spoken in cities, without insisting that it had become the national language. The important point, however, is that it seems to be well established that a form of Latin—a popular dialect which had begun to undergo some of the changes characteristic of the Neo-Latin languages—actually was spoken in this country for some time after the coming of the Angles, Saxons, and Jutes. This form of spoken Latin was the source of the numerous popular words of Latin origin which passed into English during the period between the settlement of Britain and the acceptance of Christianity, as preached by St. Augustine. But this spoken Latin had undergone certain important changes in pronunciation by the middle of the fifth century. It no longer retained the form of old classical Latin, but had advanced in many respects in the same direction as the popular forms of Latin on the Continent, which were the ancestors of the modern Romance languages. The words borrowed from this source into O.E. had naturally already undergone the characteristic changes of early Romance, and the O.E. forms of them retain, as far as is possible, the pronunciation which they had in Brito-Romance at the date of the borrowing. When once these words had passed into O.E. speech they became part and parcel of that speech, and underwent the same subsequent changes as native O.E. words.

Among the most characteristic changes of popular Latin, which was developing into Romance, is the voicing of *p*, *t*, and *c* (*k*), between vowels. We have seen that those woıds borrowed from Latin in the Continental period retain the above consonants, in this position, unaltered. The later words, however, acquired in England, show a change of *p* to *f* (= v), of *t* to *d*, and of *c* to *g*. It should be noted that O.E. *f* represents a Romance *b* (voiced stop), a sound which did not occur medially in O.E. in the earliest period ; *g* was also pronounced as an open consonant in the medial position.

Examples.—Lat. *p: capistrum*, 'halter,' O.E. *cæfester*, from Brit.-Rom. **kaƀestr-; prǣfost*, 'officer,' Lat. *prǣpositus.* Lat. *t: ruta*, O.E. *rūde*, 'rue'; *moraþ*, 'sweetened wine,' Lat. *morātum*, represents a further Romance development of intervocalic *d* from *t* to *ð*, a voiced open consonant. Lat. *k: fœnuculum*, O.E. *finugl*, 'fennel '; Lat. *cuculla*, O.E. *cugele*, ' cowl, monk's hood.'

The loan-words of early Brito-Latin origin, as well, of course, as those of Continental origin, undergo, as has been said, such ordinary O.E. sound changes, as took place after the date of borrowing. A few examples are :

(1) *Change of* a *to* æ : O.E. non-W. Sax. *ċæster*, from **castr.*

(2) *W. Sax. diphthonging after front cons.:* W. Sax. *ċeaster.*

(3) *Fracture: Wyrtġeorn*, from **Vortigern; męarm*-stān, Lat. *marmor ; sealm*, Lat. *(p)salmus.*

(4) *i-mutation: cyċene*, from Lat. *coquina ; Wyrt*ġeorn, from **Vorti-* < **Wurti-*.

The oldest English form of *Lincoln* on record is *Lin(d)cylene* (A. Sax. Chron., 941, 942, Parker MS.), and other manuscripts have *-cylne, -kylne.* Now, this, the genuine O.E. form of the Latin *colonia*, shows unmistakable signs of having passed through Celtic speech. *Cylene* presupposes a pre-mutation form *culīne, from *colīne; the change of *o* to *u* when *i* follows in the next syllable being normal in O.E., and observable in many Brito-Latin loan-words. It can be shown that a change of *ō* to *ū* and of this to *ȳ* (high-front-round) took place in Celtic. But if this word came into English, in the place-names or otherwise, from the form *colȳna before the period of the O.E. i-mutation, (ȳ) would be an unknown sound to English speakers, and the nearest approach to it in English would be (ī). Hence we may assume that the earliest English form was *colína*, whence *cúlina, and finally, with mutation, *cyl(e)ne*. The O.E. variant -*colne*, whence our spelling -*coln*, is a later form taken direct from literary Latin.

To show how important is the *form* of the word in determining the date of its importation into the language, we may instance the two O.E. words *ynče*, ' inch,' and *yndse*, or *yntse*, ' ounce,' which are both derived ultimately from the Latin *uncia*. Both show i-mutation, and must therefore both have been introduced before 600 or thereabouts. Which is the earlier form? Obviously *ynče*, for the following reasons : Latin *uncia*, if borrowed in Gmc., would undoubtedly assume some such form as *unkjō-, which would normally become *ynče* in O.E. and *inch* in Mod. Eng. As a matter of fact, *unkja* occurs in Gothic, but this may well be an independent loan. In Romance speech *uncia* became (*ontȿja), whence later (*ontʃia), with assibilation of *č* before *i, j*, similar to that which developed also in English, and has given us our pronunciation (intʃ). But the English process was far slower than the Romance change; hence by the fifth or sixth centuries the latter language had already developed a sound not far removed from (tʃ), whereas O.E., although it had begun to front *k* before *i* and *j*, had not progressed so far. We may therefore regard the -*ts*- in O.E. *yntse* as an English approximation to the Brito-Romance sound in the word, the earlier loan *ynċe* having at this period probably the form (*unċi) with a front stop.

In cases where Latin words contain no test sounds such as intervocalic voiceless stops, there cannot be absolute certainty as to whether they belong to the earliest Continental class of loans, or whether they were acquired early in the English period, and even the fact that the same word exists in O.H.G. or O. Sax. does not necessarily settle the matter in favour of the former class, since each language may have adopted the words independently. On the other hand, words which retain the Latin intervocalic *t*, etc., might belong either to the Continental period or the late English, if their vowels are not such as are liable to early English sound changes.

Enough has perhaps been said to show that the question of Latin words in O.E. is fraught with difficulties, and one that presents some problems which cannot be definitely solved.

3. **Latin Words chiefly from Ecclesiastical or Learned Sources, borrowed after Conversion of the English to Christianity.**—After the introduction of the Christian religion, and with it Latin culture, into England, the vocabulary was further enriched by words both bearing directly upon the Church, its government and ideals, its officers, the functions of the ministers of religion and their

vestments, etc., and also by others expressing the circumstances and objects connected with the everyday life of
Christians both clerical and lay. The new culture affected
the language of Englishmen in two ways : by introducing
words direct from classical Latin, and by calling into
existence fresh adaptations and combination of native
words to express hitherto unknown objects and ideas.

The Latin words which passed into English after the
introduction of Christianity are chiefly from literary and
not spoken popular Latin ; hence they had not undergone
the characteric changes of the latter. Again, most of the
characteristic English sound changes had already been
carried out by the beginning of the seventh century,
so that from the English side they underwent, as a rule,
comparatively little change. Further, it is probable that
during the Old English period these words remained, for
the most part, the linguistic property of the clergy and
learned classes ; they were derived from literary sources,
and preserved, to a great extent, the form in which they
were borrowed.

A few examples of learned words are : *Discipul,* ' dis-
ciple '; *martyr ; pæll,* ' pallium '; *pāpa,* ' pope '; *sācerd,*
' priest,' from *sacerdos.* Words of more popular origin
and use are : *Abbod,* ' abbot '; *ælmesse,* ' alms,' from
alimosina ; domne (applied to a Bishop or Archbishop) ;
mæsse, ' mass,' from **messa,* Lat. *missa.*

Many native words were adapted to Christian uses.
Such are : *hūsl,* applied to the Blessed Sacrament, but
originally meaning ' sacrifice ' in general, *Cf.* Goth.
hunsl ; scearn, ' the tonsure,' related to *scieran,* ' to cut ';
ān-buend and *ān-setl,* ' hermit ' and ' hermitage '; *fulwian,*

'baptize' = *ful-*wīhan*, 'consecrate'; *fulluht* and *fulwiht*, 'baptism,' -wiht being probably associated in popular etymology with the word meaning creature; *godspellere*, 'evangelist'; *hūsl-þegn*, 'acolyte'; *ġelaþung*, 'the Church' —literally, those who have received the 'call' or 'invitation.'

The Picardian form *market*, from Latin *mercātum*, occurs in the Laud MS. of the Chronicle under the year 963, but this text was written in the first quarter of the twelfth century.

[In addition to the works by Kluge and Pogatscher, cited above, the reader should also consult *The Influence of Christianity on the Vocabulary of Old English*, Part I., by H. S. MacGillivray, Halle, 1902.]

The Scandinavian Element.

It is well known that the language of the invading Norsemen, usually known to us as the 'Danes,' has left considerable traces upon the vocabulary both of the literary language and of that of the dialects of English. Although the process of the blending of the two languages was undoubtedly carried out during the O.E. period, it is not until the M.E. period that this linguistic element finds its way, to any considerable extent, into the written records so far as they have come down to us. The reason for this is that for a long time English and Scandinavian were spoken side by side by two separate communities in those districts which were settled by the Northmen. Not until the two races had amalgamated, and Norse had given way altogether to English, did many Scandinavian words become part and parcel of English speech. It is pointed out by Björkman, in the introductory remarks to his excellent book, *Scandinavian Loan-Words in Middle English*, Part I., Halle, 1900, that the words from this source found in O.E., which, indeed, are few in number, and which have mostly died out by the M.E. period, refer for the most part to things connected with the life and institutions of the invaders, such as *cnear*, ' war-ship '; *fylcian*, ' to collect '; *ōra*, the name of a coin ; and so on. Those words and expressions which appear at a later date, on the other hand, reveal something very different from the superficial relations between the two peoples, such as the above words point to. The later words include several adverbs, pronouns, and other words which show a close and intimate connection between English and Scandinavian speakers.

The fact that practically no prose literature of the early period has survived in any but a West Saxon form no doubt also accounts to a certain extent for the paucity of Scandinavian words actually recorded in O.E. itself. The list of these words given by Kluge, *Paul's Grundr.*², p. 932, etc., includes many words whose Scandinavian origin is doubtful. The close affinity of sounds and vocabulary between the two languages makes it in many cases practically impossible to be certain whether the word in question is really a Norse loan-word or an original English word. The question of the linguistic tests of true Scandinavian words will fall to be discussed in the next chapter.

CHAPTER XIII

THE MIDDLE ENGLISH PERIOD

A COMPLETE account of the various forms of English speech, which should trace the development of each and show their mutual relations, would be a most complicated task, and one which in the present state of knowledge would be impossible.

The difficulty arises partly in the number of M.E. texts, and the great dialectal variety which they display; partly also in the fact that the remains of O.E. outside the West Saxon dialect are so scanty.

The modern dialects are not, as a rule, the representatives of the M.E. dialects, except in certain of their most pronounced features, such as the Northern (ē or ī, etc.), as contrasted with South and Midland (*ou*), which both represent Common O.E. *ā*. Most of the peculiarities of the modern dialects are of quite recent development, and afford but little help in elucidating the problems of the M.E. period. It is quite possible, of course, that many features of the present-day dialects, which it is impossible to discover from the texts of the earlier period, may already have been developed, but could find no adequate expression in the spelling. On the other hand, there is no doubt whatever that the majority of the most characteristic features of Middle Kentish and Middle Southern (from Somersetshire to Sussex) have completely vanished from the modern speech of those areas.   The Middle English dialects, therefore, stand to a great extent isolated ; of some, we cannot watch the early development, owing to the loss or absence of records of the oldest period ; while there are others whose subsequent career we cannot trace, because they have perished.

Towards the end of the fourteenth century there emerges, from among the many provincial forms which had hitherto been used for literary purposes, a dialect, chiefly Midland in character, but containing some elements at least of all the other chief dialectal types, which henceforth serves as the exclusive form of speech used in literature, and from which Modern Standard English is descended.   This, with certain variations, is the English of Chaucer, of Wycliff, and of Gower.

The precise area in which the literary dialect arose is still disputed, but there can be little doubt that, whatever may have been its precise antecedents, it was a real living form of speech, not a literary concoction, and that the English of Chaucer is the flexible, racy speech of a class, if not of a province, most probably that of the upper strata of English educated society—the language at once of the nobles and officials of the Court, and of the scholars and divines of the University of Oxford.

It is true that in a few cases the Modern Standard English form of a given word cannot be traced directly to that particular M.E. type which is found in Chaucer's language ; but, speaking generally, we may say that the literary English of to-day is the lineal representative of the dialect in which Chaucer writes. This being the case, the most practical course for the student of the history of the English language is to consider M.E. as culminating in the dialect of literature as found in Chaucer, and to take that as the M.E. type from which he traces Modern English.

But in order to understand, even approximately, the development of Chaucer's English from the older forms, the beginner must become acquainted with the chief general M.E. characteristics. of sound change, inflexional system. and vocabulary.

He must, further, consider the main characteristic features of the principal M.E. dialectal types, in order that he may recognise their forms in Chaucer's language and in that of the modern period.

General Authorities on the Middle English Period.

So far there is no complete and minute M.E. Grammar, and we have largely to rely upon monographs of particular texts. The principal M.E. Grammar is that of Morsbach, *Mittelenglische Grammatik*, 1 Theil, Halle, 1896. This is minute, and deals with the phonology of all the dialects. So far as it goes, this is a most valuable book for the advanced student, but, unfortunately, it breaks off in the middle of a paragraph, without having dealt with the whole vowel system. In this work the texts and authorities of each dialect are enumerated, and the problems of *accent* and *quantity* are exhaustively treated. In the second volume of Kaluza's *Historische Grammatik der Englischen Sprache*, Berlin, 1901, the main features of M.E. are dealt with in a short space, and in a manner which is practical and convenient for beginners, especially those whose main object is to trace the history of the standard language. Sound and suggestive, though difficult to use on account of lack of systematic arrangement, is Kluge's *Geschichte d. Engl. Spr.* in *Paul's Grundriss*. The development of M.E. sounds from O.E. is dealt with in Sweet's *History of English Sounds* (H.E.S.), Oxford, 1888, pp. 154-198; and the same writer's *New English Grammar*, Part I., Oxford, 1892, *Shorter English Historical Grammar*, and *Primer of Historical English Grammar* (the latter a masterpiece of concise and accurate statement), all give a short but clear account of the main characteristics of M.E. in their relation both to the earlier and the later forms of English. An exceedingly useful sketch of M.E. Grammar for beginners is also prefixed to *Specimens of Early English*—Part I., from 1150-1300 ; Part II., 1298-1393.

Other general works and monographs dealing with specific texts will be referred to in the course of this chapter.

Chronological Divisions of Middle English.

We may adopt Sweet's divisions, which are : *Transition O.E.*, 1100-1200 ; *Early M.E.*, 1200-1300; *Late M.E.*, 1330-1400.

Dialectal Divisions of Middle English.

It is possible to distinguish four chief dialectal types, which correspond to the O.E. divisions, although within each of the original dialectal areas numerous sub-varieties are recorded in M.E. The principal dialect groups are :

(1) *Northern*, descended from *Old Northumbrian*. By the beginning of the fourteenth century it is possible to

distinguish between *Scots* and *Northern English*, although the former *name* (M.E. *Scotis*) appears to have been applied only to Gaelic speech down to the sixteenth century.

(2) *Midland*, which corresponds to the old dialects of Mercia and East Anglia. The Midland area reaches as far south as the Thames.

(3) *The Southern, or Saxon Dialects ;* and

(4) The Dialect of *Kent*

Texts representing the Chief Dialects.

It will be unnecessary here to do more than enumerate a few of the chief M.E. texts, of which the date of the manuscript and the place in which it was written is well established.

A. **Transition Texts**— *East Midland.*—*A.S. Chronicle, Laud MS.*, from 1122-1154, probably written about 1154 at *Peterborough.* Extracts from this are to be found in Skeat's *Specimens*, Part I. The whole text may be read either in Thorpe's Ed. of A.S. Chronicle (Rolls Series) or in Plummer's *Two Saxon Chronicles*, Oxford, 1892.

Southern.—*History of the Holy Rood-tree, circa* 1170, Ed. Napier, E.E.T.S., 1894.

B. **Early Middle English**—*Northern.*—*Metrical Psalter*, Yorkshire, before 1300. Extracts in *Specimens*, Part II., Ed. Surtees Soc., 1843-1847 ; *Cursor Mundi, circa* 1300 ; *Specimens*, Part II.

Midland. — *The Ormulum*, written in *Lincolnshire* in 1200. Extracts occur in Sweet's *First Middle English Primer* and in Skeat's *Specimens.* The most recent complete edition is that of Holt, Oxford, 1878.

Southern.—*Ancren Riwle* (*A.R.*), *Dorsetshire, circa* 1225. Extracts in Sweet's *Middle English Primer* and the *Specimens*. In the latter book other Dorsetshire texts of about the same period, and perhaps by the same author, may be studied. The standard edition of *A.R.* is that of Morton, Camden Soc., 1852.

Kentish.—Various Sermons and Homilies in the Kentish Dialect, from 1200-1250, are to be found in Skeat's *Specimens*, Part I.

C. Late Middle English—*Northern.*—*Prick of Conscience* (Hampole), *Yorks*, before 1349 ; *Specimens*, Part II., Ed. Morris, E.E.T.S.

Midland.—*Alliterative Poems, Lancashire, circa* 1360 ; *Specimens*, Ed. Morris, E.E.T.S., 1869 ; *Earliest Prose Psalter, West Midland*, 1375, Ed. Bülbring, E.E.T.S., 1891.

Southern.—*St. Editha, Wilts*, 1400, Ed. Horstmann, 1883.

Kentish. — *Ayenbite of Inwyt*, 1340 ; see *Specimens*, Part II., Ed. Morris, E.E.T.S., 1866.

We have, unfortunately, no Northern texts of this period earlier than the two mentioned in A above—that is to say, nothing to bridge the gulf of more than two hundred years, and no texts produced in Scotland till the *Bruce*, 1375.

General Characteristics of Middle English compared with Old English.

A. Middle English Orthography.—The changes in spelling which distinguish the period with which we are dealing with that which went before are of a twofold nature. There are, firstly, the changes introduced in an attempt

to express the changes which were taking place in pronunciation; and, secondly, those due to the application
of an entirely different system of sound notation, which
was in the main Norman French. The former class will
be more fully treated in enumerating the M.E. sound
changes.

The influence of French spelling is present in various
degrees even in very early M.E. texts, and even before the
Conquest. Thus *u*, instead of the English intervocalic *f*
to express a voiced sound, occurs in an eleventh-century
manuscript. Later on *u* is universal in such a Southern
text as *A.R.*, although Northern texts retain *f* much later
even in French words. The Midland Orm writes *serrfenn*
usually, but *serruen* only once (*H.E.S.*, 602).

The spelling of the *Ormulum*, which is so remarkably
consistent and methodical as to call for special notice,
shows only very slight touches of Norman influence, but is
partly the English traditional spelling, with modifications
introduced by the writer Orm for purposes of greater
phonetic exactitude.

As the knowledge of French and French documents
became more and more widespread among educated
Englishmen, the French mode of expressing sounds became
fixed, so that, instead of the orthography being English,
slightly influenced by French, as in the case of some early
M.E. manuscripts, that of the late M.E. period is principally basally French, with a certain residue of traditional
English spellings.

In the South, where we find the largest proportion of
Anglo-French loan-words in the early period, French
orthography begins earlier than in the North and Mid-

lands. French loan-words retain their regular French spelling, and this system is then transferred to English words containing sounds approximately the same as those occurring in French. Thus already in *A.R.* we find French *c* (=s) transferred to English words, as in *seldcēne*, ' seldom-seen.'

The following is a list of some of the chief novelties in M.E. spelling ; many of them have survived in the English spelling of the present day :

Vowels.—*o* written for O.E. *u* in the neighbourhood of *n, m, v, w;* a purely graphic attempt to distinguish letters which resemble each other in shape : *sone,* ' son, O.E. *sunu.* The sound itself (u) remains during the M.E. period.

u written for O.E. *y* when this sound is preserved, otherwise for A.-Fr. u, which had the sound of y (*i.e.*, high-front-round) ; *cf. wurchen,* O.E. *wyrċan.* When long, the same sound is written *ui* (in the South), to represent O.E. *ȳ* : *huiren,* ' hear,' O.E. *hȳran.*

ou for O.E. *ū,* and for A.-Fr. (ū)-sound : *hous,* ' house, O.E. *hūs; court.* This spelling is very rare for the short (u)-sound.

ie occurs in Gower and other texts to express a long tense (ē), as distinct from the slack (ē), written *e: hieren,* ' hear,' O.E. (non-W.S.), *hēran.*

y is written for (ī). It never expresses the rounded (y) in M.E.

Consonants.—*ch* is written for O.E. *ċ* already in the middle of the twelfth century (*cf.* the so-called *Kentish Gospels,* for instance) : *chester,* O.E. (Kentish, etc.) *ċester ; chēke,* O.E. *cēāc,* ' cheek.' Medially *cch* or *chch* occur. *-tch-* is rare before the fifteenth century.

17

gg is written for the O.E. *ċġ*: *brigge*, *brugge*, O.E. *bryċġ*, 'bridge.' The spelling -*dg*- for this sound is not common before the fifteenth century.

j is written *initially* for the same sound, which only occurs in this position in French words: *jugement*, etc.

The O.E. symbol ȝ, slightly modified in shape, is retained in M.E. to express the front-open voiced consonant: *ȝiuen*, 'give,' O.E. *ġiefan*; *weȝ*, 'way,' O.E. *weġ*. The use of *y* for this sound belongs to the later M.E. period.

The symbol *g* is a new symbol imported by French scribes. Prior to the Conquest, ȝ was the only form of the letter, and did duty for both back and front consonants. The new symbol appears first about the first quarter of the twelfth century. At first the scribes use the English symbol ȝ and the Continental *g* indiscriminately for either the back or the front sound. From the thirteenth century onwards, however, the distinction is usually consistently made, the modified form ȝ of the old letter ȝ being used for the latter, the new for the former sound. Orm makes the distinction most carefully, and further introduces a symbol of his own, a combination of the Continental *g* and English ȝ, to express a back stop, in words like *ȝod*, etc.

[NOTE.—This interesting and important discovery was made by Professor Napier. *Cf. Academy*, 1890, p. 188, and the reprint of the article in *History of the Holy Rood-tree*, E.E.T.S., 1894, p. 71.]

gu, the French symbol for a back stop before front vowels, is still retained in *guest*. In M.E. it is sometimes written in *guod*, ' good,' and *kingue*.

gh is written for a back - open voiceless consonant, O.E. *h* : *inogh*, 'enough,' O.E. *ġenōh*.

sch, ssch, sh, are written for O.E. *sĉ,* and less commonly *ss* and *s : schip, ssip, flessch, fless,* etc.

th replaces þ and ð : *thinken,* etc., in Late M.E.

qu replaces O.E. *cw : quēne,* 'woman' (kwéne), O.E. *cwĕne ; queen,* 'queen' (kwēn), O.E. *cwēn.*

c is used for *(s)* in French words, as at present in *face,* etc., and occasionally, as we have seen, in English words as well.

u, and later *v,* are used medially, instead of O.E. *f,* to express the voiced sound : *lauerd,* O.E. *hlāford,* 'lord'; *euel* and *evel,* 'evil,' O.E. (Kentish) *efel.* In Southern texts, where O.E. *f* was voiced initially, *u, v* are written in that position : *uorþ,* O.E. *forþ.* In *A.R. f* is still written finally, to avoid confusion with the vowel, as in *līf,* 'life'; also before voiced consonants, as in *hefde,* 'had,' O.E. *hæfde.*

B. Middle English Sounds.—The *quality* of M.E. sounds is established partly from historical considerations of their origin and subsequent development, partly from the various phonetic attempts to render them made by the scribes, partly by the rhymes of the M.E. period.

By the last means we are able, for instance, to show the existence of two long '*e*'-sounds, although the M.E. spelling does not in all cases distinguish. Chaucer, a careful and accomplished maker of rhymes, never rhymes M.E. ĕ, the result of a M.E. lengthening of O.E. ĕ, as in *bĕren,* O.E. *bĕran,* with the other ē inherited from O.E., as in *hēren,* 'hear,' O.E. hēran. Further, we still distinguish between the sounds of the two words 'hear' and 'bear.' There can be little doubt that in M.E. the sound in *hēren* was a mid-front-tense, whereas that in '*bēren*'

17—2

was mid-front-slack. This M.E. distinction is still further confirmed by the scribal distinction, already noted, of *ie* for the former class of words, and *e* for the latter.

The *quantity* of vowels is established by the means just described, which are, however, even more conclusive in settling the quantity than they are in determining the precise quality of a vowel.

For the quantities of early M.E. the Ormuium is invaluable, since the writer invariably doubles the consonant after short vowels, or, in the few cases where this is not practicable, marks the short quantity thus: *năme*, 'name,' etc.

We may assume that when Orm does not double the consonant, the preceding vowel is long. Thus he distinguishes between the singular *lamb*, with long *ā*, already in O.E., and the plural *lammbre*, where the combination of consonants (*mbr*) has prevented lengthening.

Marks to show that a vowel is long are rare in M.E., but the doubling of vowels for this purpose, although not consistently practised in early M.E., is very common, and fairly regularly carried out in later M.E., as in Chaucer's *stoon*, 'stone'; *heeth*, 'heath,' etc.

Qualitative Sound Changes in Middle English.

1. O.E. *ā*, which includes both original *ā* and *ā* lengthened from *ă* during the O.E. period, before -*ld*, -*mb*, -*nd*, *hānd*, *lāmb*, and Anglian *āld* (M.E. *lōmb*, *hōnd*, *ōld*), is rounded to *ō* (ɔ) in the *South and Midlands*: O.E. *hām*, 'home,' M.E. *hōm*; O.E. *sār*, 'sore,' M.E. *sōr*, etc.

In the North, except before *l* + another consonant,

ā is gradually fronted to *ē* through intermediate stage of *ǣ*. This sound is written *a* in the North of England, but in Scotland often *ai*. Its front character can be shown from the M.E. rhymes, and also from the Mod. Scots and Northern Eng. dialect forms, which show (ē, īə), etc.

The Southern and Midland rounding must have begun very early, since no N.-Fr. word with *ā*, such as *dāme*, 'lady,' *fāme*, etc., ever shows any trace of the process. Therefore, before the period of the earliest loan-words from Norman sources, O.E. *ā* and Fr. *ā* were already distinct. The early manuscripts are by no means consistent in writing *o* for the old *ā* sound. The *Kentish Homilies* (MS. Vespas., A. 22, before 1150) occasionally writes *ō* by the side of the usual *ā*. The *Laud MS*. of the Chronicle has one example, *mōre*, under the year 1137 (*cf.* Skeat's *Specimens*, I., p. 11, l. 42). This manuscript was probably written after the year 1154. *Orm* (1200), though such a careful orthographist, writes *a* in all cases, never *o*. This probably indicates that the change had not gone far enough in his dialect, to be recognisable as a new sound. *Genesis and Exodus*, also E. Midl. fifty years later, has plenty of *ō* spellings. The so-called *Lambeth Homilies* (before 1200) has no *ō*, but always *ā*; while the collection of *Homilies* of the same date in Trinity College, Cambridge, have *ō* universally, and apparently no *ā*'s. *Ancren Riwle* (1225) has *ō*, *oa* in hundreds of cases, *a* occurring only once in an unequivocal word, *wāt*; *lātes*, from O.N. *lāt*, *lǣte*, is thus written five times. [On this text, *cf.* Ostermann, *Bonner Beitr.*, 1905.] It is therefore clear that the rounding of *ā* had been

carried out in the South and in some Midland dialects
by the second half of the twelfth century, even although
the scribes do not consistently express this in their
spellings. On the other hand, it can be proved by an
examination of the rhymes of Barbour's *Bruce* (1375) that
by that date the Northern fronting was fully complete.
ansuér—mar, O.E. *māra*, ' more ' (Book I., 437, 438) ; *war*,
' was,' O.E. (Northern) *wēron*, rhymes to *mar* (Book II.,
59, 60) ; *war* to *rair*, ' roar,' O.E. *rāran* (Book IV., 422,
423). The front quality of the vowel in *war*, in spite of
the spelling, is proved by the rhyme of *wer*, with different
spelling, to French *manér* (Book IV., 7, 8), and by that
of *ere*, O.E. *ǣr*, to *were* (Book IV., 402, 403). The vowel
in all these words is certainly front, either (ǣ) or (ɛ̄), or
even possibly (ē), which is suggested by the rhyme *neir*,
' near,' *manéir* (Book IV., 377, 378). In the sixteenth
century the rhyme *drēme*, ' dream,' O.E. *drēām*, with *hāme*,
is noted by Professor Gregory Smith in *Specimens of
Middle Scots*, p. xx ; *cf.* also *ibid.*, p. 174, lines 13, 14, in a
poem by Sir David Lindsay.

2. O.E. *ǣ* (1), when original, was very early in the O.E.
period raised to *ē* in all dialects but W. Saxon. This
sound is represented in the earliest M.E. (Southern) texts
by the spellings *œ* or *ea*, the levelling of *ǣ* with the old
long diphthong having already taken place in O.E. Later
on this sound seems to disappear altogether, even in
Southern, the non-Saxon *ē* penetrating from the other
dialects.

O.E. *ǣ* (2), which was the *i*-mutation of *ā*, survives, in
all dialects but Kentish, throughout the O.E. period. In
M.E. it was gradually raised to (ɛ̄), written *œ*, *ea*, *ee*.

In Mod. Eng. this sound, in common with Anglian *ē*, has become (ī), but its origin is often expressed by the spelling *ea*, as in *heath*, O.E. *hǣþ*, from *hāþi, as distinguished from *deed*, from non-W.S. *dēd*, earlier *dǣd*, with original *œ*. This M.E. (ɛ) was not raised to (ī) in Mod. Eng. until much later than the M.E. tense sound, and is still preserved as (ɛ), etc., in Irish English (*cf* pp. 320, 321).

3. O.E. *ō*, often written *oo* in M.E., was pronounced with increased rounding, and by the period of Chaucer had probably reached a sound closely resembling Swedish *ō*, which to the ear is almost like *ū*. In the sixteenth century the full (ū) sound was developed. In the North O.E. *ō* had a different development, as is shown by such rhymes in Northern Eng. and Scotch texts as *fortóne—sóne*, 'soon' (*Pricke of Consc.*, 1273-1274, *circa* 1340); *auentūre—forfūre*, 'perished,' O.E. *forfōr* (*Bruce*, Book X., 528, 529); *blūd—rūde* (*Schir W. Wallace*, 1488, Book II., 91, 92). In the same poem, Book II., we find *fūde*, 'food,' O.E. *fōda* (308), *blūd* (311), *gūd* (312), all rhyming with *conclūd* (314). There are numerous examples of such rhymes in Scotch texts. Here we find, then, O.E. *ō* written *o*, *u*, *oi*, etc., rhyming with French *ū* (ȳ), which is also spelled in exactly the same ways as the former sound. The inference is that in Northern Eng. and Scotch, by the fourteenth century, at any rate, the two sounds were felt as identical. Whatever may have been the precise sound intended, it is clear that its acoustic effect was approximately that of a high-front-round vowel, or perhaps a high-mixed-round, that it was the ancestor of the various sounds representing O.E. *ō*, which we find in the modern dialects of Scotland and the North of England, and that

it evidently did not pass through the (ū) stage which is universal in the South and Midlands.

4. O.E. ȳ is unrounded everywhere but in the South to ī, which shares the same development as original ī, and becomes (ai) in Mod. Eng. In the South the ȳ sound is preserved, and is written u or ui. The Southern forms have died out, with the exception of 'bruise' (brūz), O.E. brȳsan, which has preserved the characteristic M.E. Sthn. spelling. It must be noted that ȳ became ē in *Kentish* already in the middle of the ninth century, and this sound, together with all other O.E. ē's, is preserved in M.E. in that dialect.

5. O.E. ē, ī, and ū were preserved unaltered, unless affected by a M.E. process of shortening (see p. 270, etc.), so far as the evidence goes, during the whole M.E. period. (ē) was raised to (ī) in the early Modern period ; ū was diphthongized in the South and Midlands about the same time, to a sound which subsequently became (au). The Norman spelling ou to express ū has been retained, and is now popularly regarded as the natural symbol of the modern diphthong. (ī) was diphthongized to (əi) in the sixteenth century, and from it (ai) has developed, with slight variations, in all dialects.

The Short Vowels.—With the exception of O.E. ǽ, these undergo no qualitative change during the M.E. period.

6. O.E. ǽ appears already in O.E., as e in Kentish, and to a certain extent in Mercian. In W. Sax. and Northumbrian æ is preserved. In M.E., Southern texts, especially Kentish, preserve e, but otherwise a is the usual form. Chaucer has *fader*, 'father,' O.E. *fæder ; water*, O.E. *wæter*, ' water,'

In the later language the *e*-forms disappear altogether. In combination with ʒ, *e* forms in Kentish a diphthong, written *ei*.

Those dialects which have *a* combine this sound into the diphthong *ai* with the following ʒ, as in *dai*. Sometimes *i*, sometimes ʒ is written. In early texts the O.E. distinction between the sing. and pl. of such words as *dæʒ*, pl. *dagas*, etc., is preserved: *dai*, *dawes*, etc. (on change of O.E. *g* to *w*, see p. 274 below). Chaucer has *dai*, *day*, *dayes*, etc., with the ʒ of the sing. generalized throughout. On the other hand, he has the vb. *dawen*, 'dawn,' from O.E. *dagian*, earlier **dagōjan*. Apparently, the diphthongs *ei* *ai* were scarcely distinguishable in M.E. The vowel in *wei*, 'way,' *rein*, 'rain,' O.E. *weʒ*, *reʒn*, has had precisely the same development as that in *dai*, O.E. *dæʒ*, and *wain*, O.E. *wæʒn*, 'wain.'

O.E. *a* when preserved, is, of course, indistinguishable from *æ* in M.E.

The O.E. Diphthongs.—Such of these as survive the various O.E. combinative factors in the different dialects, which tend to monophthongize them, are completely monophthongized in the M.E. period, except in Kentish, where the spellings *dyath*, 'death,' O.E. *dēaþ*, *þyef*, 'thief,' O.E. *þēof*, seem to imply a diphthongal pronunciation. But with the dying out of the Kentish dialect all trace of the original diphthongs, as such, disappears.

Otherwise, O.E. *ēa* is monophthongized to (ǣ) in early M.E., and *ēo* to (ē). The diphthongal spellings, are, however, common in early texts, in spite of the undoubted change of sound. Similarly, the short diphthongs *ea* and *eo* become (æ) and (e) respectively. This is proved by the fact that ēā, ēō are not infrequently written for old ǣ, ē, and conversely ; while the original short œ and e are often expressed by ea and eo respectively.   In fact, in early texts ĕǎ is a regular symbol for, and proves the existence of, the sounds (ǎ̆).   This (ǎ̆), representing the original diphthongs, was, together with original ǣ, raised to (ɛ̆).   The new (ē) sound was completely levelled under original O.E. ē, and the original O.E. ĕ, when preserved short, was levelled under the new ɛ̆.

Mod. Eng. *weald*, side by side with *wold*, appears to represent the Saxon *weald*, E.M.E. *wǣld*, whence *wēld* (ɛ), Early Mod. (wēld).   *Wold* is, of course, the old Anglian *wǎld*.   The early Middle Kentish *chold*, ' cold,' is apparently a mixture of Southern *c̆æld*, *c̆hæld*, and Anglian *cǎld*, *cōld*.

The Development of New Diphthongs in Middle English.

The various diphthongs which came into existence during the M.E. period are the result either of the vocalizing of O.E. *ġ* (front-open voice consonant) after a preceding *œ* or *e*, as has been already indicated above, as in *dei*, *dai*, *rein*, etc. ; of the development of a front vowel glide before fronted *h*, as in *heih*, ' high,' O.Angl. *hēh*, etc. ; or the development of a back vowel glide between a back vowel and a back-open consonant, as in *douhter*, O.E. *dohter*; *inōuh*, ' enough,' O.E. *ġenōh*, *plōuh*, ' plough,' O.E. *plōh*.   In late O.E. the last two words become *inūh* and *plūh* respectively, by the over-rounding and raising of (ō) to (ū) through the influence of the second element of the diphthong, and the subsequent contraction of (ūu) to (ū).   The literary English (pl*au*) and the archaic (*inau*) 'enow' are the result, not of the old nom., which in Late O.E. had *h*, but of the oblique cases, where the voice sound was retained—O.E. *genōge*, *plōges*. This O.E. *g* became *w* in M.E.—*inōwe*, *plōwes*, etc., where *ōu* or *ōw* had the same sound as in the Nom. The sometime existence of the actual diphthong (ōu) is confirmed by the Modern dialect form (plōh), in which the second element has been lost. The standard English (inaf), 'enough,' represents the old nom.; and so do the dialect forms (plūh, plūf, inūh), etc. The O.E. combination *ag-* before vowels produces M.E. *aw-au* (*cf.* O.E. *dragan*, M.E. *drawen*).

In O.E. *af-* the consonant is sometimes weakened to a vowel, thus forming the second element of a diphthong— O.E. *hafoc*, M.E. *hauk ;* and the same thing may happen to O.E. *ef-*, as in M.E. *eute*, 'newt,' O.E. *efete*.

The combination *au-* in Norman French words was pronounced (*a*un) by some speakers, presumably in imitation of the original nasal vowel. Such spellings as *daungerous*, *aungel*, 'angel,' are frequent, and they survive in many cases in Mod. Eng.—*e.g.*, *haunt*, *haunch*, *aunt*, *iaundice*, *laundry*, etc. Here the fluctuation of the Mod. Eng. pronunciation between (ō) and (*ā*) makes it evident that two types, one (*a*u) and the other (*a*un), existed in M.E. The Mod. Eng. (hōntʃ, džōndis, lōndr*i*), etc., go back to M.E. (hauntʃ, džaundis), etc.; while the Mod. Eng. pronunciations (hāntʃ, džāndis, ānt), etc., are descended from M.E. forms without diphthongization. In the same way Mod. Eng. *al-*, pronounced (ōl-), also presupposes an earlier (*a*ul-), as in Mod. Eng. (ōl, sōlt, bōl) = 'all,' 'salt,' 'bawl,' from (*a*ul, s*a*ult, b*a*ul). This is apparently the result of the development of a parasitic (u) between *a* and the following *l.*

Quantitative Vowel Changes in Middle English.

1 *Lengthening of Original Short Vowels.*

(*a*) *Early Lengthening before Consonantal Combinations.*
—As we have seen, all short vowels were lengthened in late O.E. before certain consonantal combinations. Unless conditions arise to shorten these vowels again, their length is preserved in M.E. In the case of the lengthened *a* before -*ld*, *mb*, *nd*, *ng*, the survival of the new quantity is made certain by the spellings *hōnd* (Orm *hānd*), *strōng* (Orm *strang*), etc., which show that the lengthened *ǎ* is rounded to *ō* together with original O.E. *ā*, in *hām*, M.E. *hōm*, etc. In other cases we have to depend upon Orm's spellings (*ante*, p. 260), the occasional marks of length in the manuscripts, rhymes of the new long vowels with original longs, and the later history of the words in English. Thus from the latter point of view Mod. Eng. *find* (faind) *field* (fīld), *hound* (haund), can only be derived from M.E. types with the long vowels *ī*, *ē*, and *ū* respectively. Orm's spellings, *findenn*, *feld*, *hund*, corroborate the assumption of the existence of such types, as do the other M.E. spellings, *field* (ē), *hound* (ū), which have survived to the present day.

In certain words, such as *hand*, *lamb*, etc., where we should expect a M.E. lengthening, on account of the presence of the combinations -mb, -nd, etc., the Mod. Eng. forms nevertheless presuppose M.E. forms with a short vowel. In these cases we must assume that both

long and short forms existed in M.E., the latter types produced by inflexion. (On this point see pp. 271-273 below.)

(b) *Later Lengthening of Vowels in an Open Syllable.*—
By the first half of the thirteenth century, the typical
M.E. lengthening of the vowel *a, œ, e, o* in open syllables
was complete, and had taken place in all dialects.

This is shown by the frequent rhyming of original short
vowels in this position, with original longs : *swēte—eðgēte,*
O.E. *swēte, ēaðgēte ; ōre—vorlōre(n)*, O.E. *ār, forlōren*
[*cf.* Morsbach, *M.E. Gr.*, p. 86]. Such rhymes at least
prove agreement in quantity, if not in the quality of the
vowels.

Again, already in Orm we find *faderr,* 'father,' O.E.
fæder, and *waterr,* O.E. *wæter,* with (ā) ; *etenn,* 'eat,'
O.E. *ĕtan ; chele,* 'cold,' O.E. (non-W.S.) *cĕle,* both
with (ɛ̄) ; *chosenn,* p.p. of *chēsenn,* 'choose,' O.E. *cŏren,*
(Orm's p.p. has *s* on the analogy of the inf. and pres.
indic.) ; *hope,* O.E. *hŏpu,* both with (ō). The Mod. Eng.
spelling ' *eat* ' implies a long slack (ɛ̄)—at any rate down
to the sixteenth century, when the corresponding tense
sound was written *ee*, and was raised to (ī). The lengthened *ō* must also have had a different sound in M.E. from
the original *ō*. The latter became (ū) in the sixteenth
century ; the latter was still (ō), and was later, in the seventeenth century, raised to (ō). (See below, pp. 323, 324,
on development of the two *ō*-sounds in the sixteenth and
seventeenth centuries.) The sounds in Mod. Eng. *water*
and *father* (ō and ā) do not represent the normal independent development of this M.E. *ā*. The vowel in *water*
is influenced by the *w,* and that in *father* is from a M.E.
doublet with a short vowel. (See below, pp. 271 and 317.)

M.E. $\bar{a}$, whether due to lengthening of older $\breve{a}$, or whether it be a N. Fr. $\bar{a}$, develops in standard Mod. Eng. into the diphthong (ɛi), with the same sound as the *name* of the first letter of the alphabet. Thus O.E. *năma*, M.E. *nāme*, Mod. Eng. (nɛim) ; N. Fr. *dāme*, Mod. Eng. dɛim. The dialectal (fɛiðər or feðər) exactly represent M.E. *fāder*, so far as the long vowel is concerned.

2. *Vowel Shortening in Middle English.*

The chief factor of vowel shortening in M.E. is the presence of a long or double consonant, or a group of consonants, immediately after the vowel.

From the above statement, those consonant groups which, as we have seen (*ante*, p. 235), tend to lengthen a short vowel, must, of course, be excepted.

It is immaterial whether the shortening group occurs in the body of a simple word or arises in composition, provided that the combination existed before the shortening process began. Examples:

A. *Before double consonants :*

1. *Mette*, ' met,' O.E. *mětte*, from *mēt-de, from *mētede*.

B. *Before other consonant groups :*

1. *Two stops: keppte*, 'kept,' O.E. *cēpte; sleppte,* ' slept,' O.E. *slēpte.*

2. *Stop + divided, or nasal: ŭtmōst*, O.E. *ūtmest ; little,* O.E. *lȳtle ; chappmenn*, O.E. *cēāpmenn.*

3. *Stop + open cons.: děpthe*, O.E. *dēpþu or **dēopþu ; Ĕdward*, O.E. *Eādward.*

4. *Open cons. + stop: sǫffte*, ' soft,' O.E. *sōfte ; wissdōm,* O.E. *wīsdōm ; sohhte*, O.E. *sōhte*, ' sought.'

5. *Open cons.* + *divided or nasal cons.* : *gŏsling*, dimin.
of *gōs; deffles*, 'devils,' O.E. *dēōfol; wimman*, from wīfmann.

6. *Open cons.* + *open cons.* or *h* : hŭswīf, Mod. Eng.
(hazif) ; *gŏshauk*, O.E. *gōshafoc*.

7. *Nasal cons.* + *stop* : *flemmde*, ' put to flight,' O.E.
(Angl.) *flēmde*.

8. *Divided or nasal cons.* + *open cons.* : *hallghenn*,
'hallow,' later M.E. *hălwen; fillthe*, ' filth,' O.E. *fȳlþ*;
mŏnthe, ' month,' O.E. *mōnaþ* ; obl. cases, *mōnþe*, etc.

9. *Nasal* + *divided cons.* : *clennlike*, O.E. *clǣnlīce*.

[NOTE.—The words with doubled consonants above are
Orm's spelling, which proves the preceding vowels to be
short.]

It will be observed that under the conditions enumerated
not only are original O.E. long vowels shortened, but also
that the new (M.E.) long vowels, developed in open
syllables, do not arise here, in close syllables.

The occurrence in the declension, conjugation, or other
inflection of a word of both open and close syllables is
of great importance for the subsequent history of the
language. In this way doublets arose of the same word,
one with a long, the other with a short. Thus the nouns
fāder and *wāter* were long, but in the inflected forms the
combinations -dr-, -tr- arose by the syncope of the *e* of
the second syllable. The genitives were *fădres, wătres*.
Similarly, words which had original long vowels underwent shortening in inflection as a result of syncope.
Thus *dēvel* in nom. form, O.E. *dēōfol*, had pl. *dĕvles*
(*cf*. Orm's *dĕffles* above) ; from this shortened type, which
gave rise to a new nom., Mod. Eng. (dɛvil) is derived.

Shortening was apparently normal before -*st* and -*sch* (ʃ).

O.E *sĉ*. Words with original long vowels before these combinations show, however, some fluctuation of quantity in M.E. Thus O.E. *brēost* became M.E. *brēst*, whence *brĕst*. *Brēst*, however, is also found, and this type is probably due to the inflected forms, where the syllable division was *brē-stess*, etc. Modern dialect forms, such as (brīst, brēst), also exist (*cf.* also '*priest*,' M.E. *prē-stes*). In the same way Standard Mod. Eng. *flesh* goes back to a type (fleʃ) in M.E. But the M.E. form with the long vowel (Orm has *flǣsh*) must be due to the syllable division of Gen. *flǣ-shes*, etc.

The Late O.E. lengthenings before -*nd*, -*mb*, etc., are also liable to show short forms in Standard Mod. Eng. In many cases here, too, doublets arose in inflection, since the lengthening either never took place or was got rid of before a third consonant. Thus Mod. Eng. *lamb*, compared with M.E. *lōmb*, clearly goes back to a M.E. type with a short vowel, such as occurs in the plural *lămbre*. Mod. Eng. *hand* (hænd) perhaps arose from such compounds as *handful*. Mod. Eng. *friend* (frɛnd), by the side of M.E. *frēnd*, from O.E. *frēond*, is from a shortened M.E. type, which arose, perhaps, in the compound *frĕndschipe*. The Scotch dialects preserve the representative of the long M.E. type here, as does Standard English also in *fiend* (fīnd), M.E *fēnd*, O.E. *fēond*. Mod. Eng. *child*—*children* (tʃaild–tʃildrən) preserve the normal interchange of long and short seen in Orm's *child*, pl. *chilldre*. There are some short forms in Mod. Eng. which it is difficult to account for, unless we assume that shortening could take place within the longer breath group or sentence under the same conditions as those which caused it in the inflected

word or compound. Such are *land* (lænd) compared with
M.E. *lōnd*, Orm *lānd;* and *band* (bænd) compared with
bond. The latter represents a much later shortening of
M.E. *bōnd*, O.E. *bānd*, similar to that which has taken
place also in *long*, M.E. *long; strong*, M.E. *strōng*.
Against the latter form Standard English has *hang*, *sang*
(hæŋ, sæŋ), etc.

In most cases where O.E. short vowels were lengthened
and O.E. longs shortened, the possibility of doublets
existed from the inflectional or other conditions of M.E.
In a vast number of cases, by comparing Standard English
with the Modern dialects, it will be seen that both long
and short forms have been perpetuated in modern speech.

The original rise of the doublets had nothing to do
with dialectal idiosyncrasy, but the subsequent generaliza-
tion of the long or short type, as the only form in use,
depends upon the speech habit of the particular community. As we have seen, Standard English is by no
means consistent in this respect, but uses now the
descendant of a M.E. long, now of a short vowel.

The best general accounts of the quantitative and
qualitative vowel changes in M.E. are to be found in
Sweet's *H.E.S.* and Morsbach's *M.E. Gr.* The latter is
particularly elaborate, though as regards the qualitative
vowel changes it is unfortunately still awaiting completion.

The Treatment of the Old English Consonants in Middle English.

1. *The Back Consonants.*—O.E. *g* remained as a back
stop *initially* before original back vowels and before
consonants. Orm, as we have seen (p. 258), invented a

18

special symbol to express this sound.   Non-initially, O.E. *g* was an open voiced consonant, which in M.E. acquired considerable lip modification, together with a weakening of the back consonantal element, the tongue being lowered to a vowel position.   The result is the Mod. Eng. *w*, in words like *draw*, M.E. *drawen*, O.E. *dragan*.   Orm writes the O.E. symbol ȝ followed by *h* for this sound, implying probably that the back element still predominated in his pronunciation.   Medially and finally M.E. *w* combined with the preceding vowel to form a diphthong.

O.E. *c* remained as a back stop in all positions.   The O.E. *cn-* in *cnāwan*, etc., remained in the Standard pronunciation down to the sixteenth or early seventeenth century.

O.E. *h*, a voiceless back consonant, medially between before or after back vowels, remained as such in M.E. The same tendency to lip modify *h* existed as in the case of the voiced sound, the result in the case of *h*, however, being the development of a lip-teeth (f) sound, as in Mod. Eng. *tough* (taf), O.E. *tōh*.   This is the normal development in Standard English and in many dialects.

In the Northern dialects the old back-open voiceless consonant remains to this day, as in Scotch (plūh), etc. Standard (pl*au*) is, as we have seen, a doublet, formed from the oblique cases which had *g* in O.E. and *w* in M.E. ᚄ Before *t*, *h* also became (f) in M.E., *brofte*, O.E. *brōhte* occurs in Lagomon, while the Modern dialects have forms like *broft*, 'brought' (in Cornwall), and *thoft*, 'thought,' in Kent, Devon, and Cornwall.   For other examples see Wright, *Dialect Gr.*, § 359.   The more usual development in this position, however, seems to have been either the voicing of *h*, in which case it formed the second element

(u) of a diphthong, as in the types from which Standard English (dōtə, brōt, pōt), etc., sprang, or the preservation of the back-open voiceless consonant unchanged, as in Sc. (poht), etc.

O.E. *hw* was apparently preserved as a voiceless *w* in the Lower Midlands and South ; in the North and part of the Midlands the back element was strongly consonantal. This is expressed in Northern texts by the spelling *qu*, as in *quāle*, ' whale,' O.E. *hwæl ; quēt*, ' wheat,' O.E. *hwǣte*, etc. The pronunciation (kw) is apparently unknown in the Modern dialects, and probably never developed.

Initially before vowels *h* remains in M.E. as a rule, though it is very early lost in the neuter pronoun *hit*, which already in Orm is *itt*. Modern Scotch still preserves the strong form *hit*, which is, indeed, the only form in the Sc. dialects.

The Front Consonants.—The O.E. front stops *ċ* and *ċġ* were fully assibilated to (tʃ) and (dž) early in the M.E. period. The methods of representing these sounds have already been described (*ante*, pp. 257, 258). For the former, the M.E. spelling *ch*, later *tch*, are conclusive, but for the latter the M.E. spellings *gg* are of doubtful significance, being also used for the stop, as in the Scand. *legges*, ' legs.' We have therefore to rely chiefly on the evidence of the Modern dialects to establish the existence of the (dž) sound in M.E. Unlike *ch* (tʃ), (dž), with the exception of one or two much-discussed words, never occurs initially in English words, though common in words of French origin, where it is usually written *j* in Mod. Eng., as in *judge, joy, jest*, etc.

The development of *ċ* and *ċġ* in M.E. and Mod. Eng. presents much difficulty, since in many cases where we should expect (tʃ and dž) we get instead back stops—*dick* by the side of *ditch*, *flick* by the side of *flitch*, *seg* by the side of *sedge*, *rig* by the side of *ridge*, and so on.

The orthodox view is that in the North, O.E. *ċ* and *ċġ* were not as fully fronted as in the South, and that in M.E., or perhaps earlier, instead of developing into the full assibilated sounds, they were unfronted and became back stops. Thus words like *seg*, *brig*, and *flick* are looked upon as typically Northern forms, like *sedge*, *bridge*, *flitch* as normal Southern products.

Unfortunately, this theory, simple as it looks, will not bear investigation. It is true that M.E. texts and Modern dialects have, on the whole, more (-k and -g) and fewer (tʃ and dž) forms in the Northern, while the proportions are reversed in the Southern ; but numerous assibilated forms actually do occur in the Northern, and many forms with back stops in the Southern, which on the ordinary theory can only be accounted for by the assumption of a system of wholesale borrowing. Some of the Southern *k*-forms, such as *seek*, compared with *be-seech*, are admittedly due to the second and third person singular : O.E. *sēcst*, *sēcþ*, M.E. *sēkst*, *sēkþ* in the Southern, where *s* and *þ* have unfronted *ċ* ; others may be due to Scandinavian influence, though this cannot be invoked in the case of dialects which never had direct contact with Scandinavian speech. On the other hand, the occurrence of (tʃ and dž) forms in Northern dialects would seem to disprove the assertion that the O.E. front stops were not fully fronted in the North.

Fleck or *flick*, ' flitch,' in Somerset, Wilts, Hants, and Isle of Wight ; *seg*, ' sedge,' in Gloucester, and, on the other hand, *midge* in Northumberland, Cumberland, West-

morland, Durham, and East Yorks; *cletch, clutch,* ' brood
of chickens,' in Northumberland, Durham, North Yorks,
are troublesome forms to explain on the received theory.
None of the attempted explanations of these facts are
wholly satisfactory, but some are less so than others.

Initial *k* representing O.E. *c̆*, as in *kettle,* O.E. *c̆ietel,*
c̆etel; kirk, O.E. *c̆yrc̆e,* etc., are universally supposed to be
of Scandinavian origin. The *k*-forms are well established
in M.E., though the normal English *chetel,* and of course
chirche, etc., also occur, the former being comparatively
rare. M.E. *caf,* ' chaff,' compared with O.E. (W. Sax.)
c̆eaf, is explainable as due to the analogy of pl. O.E. *cafu.*

O.E. *g̊* initially offers further difficulties. Before *ĕ* it
normally appears written as ʒ, *y, yh,* etc., in M.E., without
change of sound. Thus: for-ʒ*ete*(*n*), *yete*(*n*) ' forget';
ʒ*elle*(*n*), *yelle*(*n*), ' yell '; ʒelpe(n) ; yelpe(n) ' boast'; ʒ*ēre,*
yēre, etc., ' year,' and so on.

Before *i,* ʒ is often lost in M.E., and in some words the
Modern Standard language and the dialects show the same
loss quite regularly; thus O.E. *g̊if,* ' if,' M.E. *if ;* O.E.
g̊icel, M.E. *ikyl,* etc., Eng. ic-*icle,* O.E. *g̊icc̆an,* M.E.
icching, icche(*n*), Mod. Eng. *itch ;* also in the prefix *g̊e-,*
M.E. *i-cume,* ' come,' p.p. Mod. Eng. ' *yclept,' hand-i-work,*
O.E. hand-*g̊e*-weorc. M.E. also has *ylde,* ' guild,' *ym-stōn,*
' gem,' O.E. *g̊*im-*stān.*

But M.E. has far more cases of ʒ*if,* ʒ*im,* etc., and, what
is still more difficult to explain, many with *g.* The appearance of *g-* is equally difficult to understand whether it
occur before *i,* where we should expect to find it lost
altogether, or before *ĕ,* where we should expect M.E. ʒ, *y,*
Mod. Eng. *y.* Here, apparently, we have the strange

phenomenon of a front-open consonant becoming a back stop. The words in which this occurs in Standard English are: *give*, O.E. *ġiefan, ġefan; gift; get*, O.E.- *ġietan, ġetan; guest* (with Norm. Fr. spelling *gu-*), O.E. *ġiest, ġest; begin*, O.E. be-*ġinnan*. To these may be added such Modern dialect forms as *gif*, 'if,' *gilpie*, 'a young spark,' related to O.E. *ġielpan*, 'boast,' and one or two others of more doubtful origin.

Now the back stop is established for M.E. in each of these words, since spellings with *g* occur, often by the side of those with 3 or *y*, in texts from every part of the country, and Orm uses his new symbol for the back stop once at least, in *gǣfen* (pret. pl.). Further, the evidence of the Modern dialects shows that in all cases two, in a few three, M.E. types must have existed—one with *g*, one with *y*, one with the initial consonant lost. For instance, *give*, meaning 'give way,' 'thaw,' is found, apparently, in Norfolk, Surrey, Kent, and Somerset; *yeave*, verb, with same meaning, and *yeavey*, adjective, though now obsolete, existed a hundred years ago in Devon, and were still preserved even later in the English dialect of a West-Country colony in Wexford; *eave*, (*h*)*eave*, 'to thaw,' 'grow moist,' is found in West Somerset, Cornwall, and Dorset.

The modern forms are given here to supplement and confirm the evidence for the existence of three types in M.E. What is the explanation of the apparent triple mode of treatment of the same original sound in the same dialects? Clearly, we do not assert that we have here an 'exception' to the ordinary laws of sound change in English. Either the three forms arose under different conditions which we have failed to discriminate, or the 'anomalous' forms are due to some external influence.

As usual in cases of great difficulty, the influence of the Scandinavian settlers has been called in to account for the forms with stops—*give*, etc. It is quite possible, of course, that in districts where Norse was spoken side by side with English, and where people knew both English *ġiefan* or *ġefan*, and Norse *geva*, English speakers might, when speaking their own language, substitute the initial consonant which they used in addressing the foreigners : this is possible, but it is not very likely to have taken place in such a common word. Moreover, the widespread distribution of the *g*-forms, which exist even in M.E. in all dialects, makes it impossible to account for them, in all cases, on the hypothesis of Scandinavian influence.   In such a word as *begin* we might attribute the *g* to the pret. and p.p. O.E. *began, begunnon, begunnen,* and this is probably the right explanation of that form.

On the other hand, it is possible that in *give* we have a perfectly normal English development of a stop under conditions of strong stress, whereas with weak stress the open consonant remained. It is to be observed that it is only those O.E. *ġ*'s which represent original Gmc. *g* which are stopped in M.E. and the Modern dialects ; those which represent Gmc. *j*, as in O.E. *ġear*, never become *g*, but remain as *y*, or disappear altogether. This may imply that O.E. *ġ* had two different pronunciations in O.E., according to its origin. If this were not the case, it is a strange coincidence that there should not be some examples of *ġ* = Gmc. *j* being stopped in subsequent times.   This whole question is discussed at length in an article by the present writer in *Otia Merseiana*, vol. ii., *History of O.E. ġ in the Middle and Modern English Dialects*, in which examples are given of the distribution of each of the three forms in more than fifty M.E. texts and all the chief Modern dialects.

O.E. *f* and *s* were pronounced as voiced sounds in the South, especially in Kent in M.E., as is shown by the spelling *uader*, 'father,' *zēchen*, 'seek.' This pronunciation still survives in the Modern Southern dialects, and Standard English *vat*, O.E. *fœt* (*cf. wine fat* in New Testament), and *vixen*, O.E. *fyxen*, are isolated examples of forms from a Southern dialect.

Summary of Dialectal Differences.

We may summarize the chief characteristic differences of dialectal treatment of the O.E. vowels.

O.E. *ā*
{
In Midland, Southern, and Kentish is rounded to *ō* (ō) written *o, oo, oa*.
In Northern is gradually fronted to (*ǣ, ē, ē*), written *a, ai*.
In Northern, before l + cons., *ā* is diphthongized to *au*, which becomes *ō* in Modern period.
}

O.E. *ǣ*¹
(Pr. O.E. *ǣ*)
{
Becomes *ē* already in O.E. period in the Anglian dialects and Kentish.
This *ē* remains in M.E.
Is preserved during O.E. period, and in M.E. in Saxon dialects; this *ǣ* becomes (*ē*).
}

O.E. *ǣ*²
(*i*-muta-
tion of *ā*)
{
Preserved in all old dialects except Kentish; becomes *ē* there, and is retained in M.E.
In all dialects of M.E., *except* Kentish, becomes (*ē*).
}

O.E. *ō*
{
In Midland, Southern, and Kentish is gradually over-rounded and raised towards (*ū*).
In Northern is fronted or 'mixed,' and rhymes in M.E. with French *ū* (=*ȳ*).
This sound is written *u, ui, oi*, in Northern and Sc.
}

O.E. *ȳ*¹
(*i*-muta-
tion of *ū*)
{
Is retained only in Southern, written *ui, u*.
In Northern and Midland is unrounded to *ī*.
In Kentish appears as *ē*, which had developed already in O.E. period.
}

O.E. *ȳ*²
{
The Late W. Sax. *ȳ*, from *īē*, is peculiar to this dialect; it is levelled under *ȳ*¹ in M.E. in Southern: *huiren*, 'hear,' Late W. Sax. *hȳran*.
All the other dialects have *ē* already in O.E., and this remains in M.E. *hēren*, etc.
}

The Foreign Elements in Middle English.

1. (*a*) *The Scandinavian Loan-words.* — As we have already seen, this element appears in O.E. to a certain extent, though in that period the words from this source are chiefly those which denote things and institutions belonging to the Norsemen, and more particularly such as refer to those habits, possessions, or institutions which would naturally come under the notice of a people who were in that unfortunate relation to them in which the English continued for so long. A terrorized community who were constantly expecting the attack of rapacious pirates, in which expectation they were not disappointed, might naturally know the names which their enemies gave to their vessels—' *barda*,' ' *cnear* '; and would not be unfamiliar with the name of the coins, ' *ōra*,' with which their foes may occasionally have paid for those treasures or articles of food, which were not extorted at the point of the sword. Such words as the above and others of the same nature appear, though late, in O.E. literature.

But the real influence of the Danish language upon our own was exercised when the foreigners had become permanent settlers within our country, after they had mingled their blood with our own—when they had ceased to be regarded in the light of aliens. While the amalgamation of races, through intermarriage, was taking place, there would naturally be several generations of bi-lingual speakers : persons who sprang from mixed unions between Scandinavians and English. Among such families, both tongues would be equally familiar, and when speaking English it would be an unconscious process to introduce from time to time a Norse word instead of an English one ; especially as the two languages were of such close affinity that their forms were in many cases practically identical ; in others, though slightly different, were yet recognisable and intelligible to English and Norse alike. To the bilingual period succeeded the age in which English definitely got the upper hand ; the younger generations no longer spoke Norse, but the English which remained, had incor porated, and made its own, many elements from the vocabulary of the language which had died out. In some cases these loans ousted the original English words altogether.

The very closeness of the resemblance between the two languages, makes it often a matter of difficulty to determine, with absolute certainty, whether a given word is English or Norse. Björkman, in the work already quoted (*ante*, p. 249), points out that words could be introduced from one language into the other without either side recognising that they were foreign words. Cognate words in the two languages, which were identical in form, though slightly different in meaning, often acquired in English the sense which they possessed in Scandinavian. An example of this is O. Norse *soma*, ' befit, suit,' which is cognate with the O.E. *sēman*, ' settle,' ' satisfy.' In M.E. the word *sēmen* appears in the sense of ' befit, suit, beseem,' etc., which last is, of course, the modern form of the word. We may compare also the adjective *seemly*, M.E. *sēmelich*, *sēmli*, etc.

The phonological tests which we should naturally apply to settle the origin of a word as definitely English or Norse, are not always to be relied upon, since from the similarity of the two languages, it was possible, in adopting a word from Norse into English, to give it a thoroughly English form. Scandinavian words were changed to their phonological English equivalent by an unconscious etymological instinct. Thus O.E. *sċ-* was recognised as identical with Norse *sk-*, and there were a large number of words which existed in both languages, and which differed only in having *sk-* in one, *sċ-* in the other. Bi-lingual speakers who used both forms of these words could easily substitute *sk-* when speaking English, and might even introduce the sound into English words which had no Scandinavian equivalent. M.E. *scatteren*, 'scatter,' side by side with the genuine English form *shatteren*, may well be due to such a process. Again, the etymological identity of Scandinavian *ei* with O.E. *ā* was clearly perceived, and we find the Scandinavian name *sveinn* appearing as *swān*, a word which was not normally used in O.E. as a proper name, and whose Norse form is often transliterated phonetically in that language as *Swegen*. Similarly, the technical term *heimsōcn*, 'an attack on the house or home,' is translated literally into O.E. as *hāmsocn*.

The question of the precise original affinities between Northern English and Scandinavian is obscure, on account of the absence of early records. Hence in many cases it cannot be determined with certainty which points of resemblance are due to primitive affinity, which to independent parallel development, and which to later contact.

(*b*) Scandinavian Suffixes in English.—Many M.E. verbs in *-l-* and *-n-* appear to be loan-words, and words with these suffixes are much more frequent in M.E. than in O.E. It seems probable that these suffixes may have spread from Scandinavian words to stems of English origin. When the

suffixes occur attached to native words, doubt may exist as
to whether the forms with the suffixes are wholly Scandinavian or only the suffix. Examples of -*l*- suffix are :
M.E. *babblen*, 'babble,' Swed. *babbla*; M.E. *bustlen*,
' wander blindly,' O. West Scand. *bustla*, 'splash about';
Mod. Eng. dialect *daggle*, with various meanings, such as
'to drizzle' and 'to trail in the dirt,' etc.; *dangle*, Swed
dialect *dangla*. The -*n*- suffix is used in Scandinavian
speech to form weak intransitive verbs, generally inchoative,
from verbal roots and adjectives (*cf*. Sweet, *New English
Grammar*, p. 467). The -*n*- verbs in O.E. (*cf*. Sievers'
list in his *As. Gr.*,[3] § 411, Anm. 4) are not inchoative,
and are formed from adjectives or substantives which
already possess an -*n*- suffix, such as *wæcen*, 'watching,'
whence *āwæcnian*; *fæstenian*, 'fix,' 'fasten,' is from
fæsten, 'fortress,' and so on. Examples of Scandinavian
verbs with this suffix are *hvītna*, 'whiten,' *i.e.*, 'become
white.' *Ancren Riwle* has *hwīten* used intransitively,
p. 150, l. 7 (Morton's Ed., *cf*. Skeat's *Etymological
Dictionary*, sub '*whiten*'), but the *Metrical English
Psalter*, p. 50, l. 9, has '*And over snawe sal I whitened be*,'
where the word is used transitively.

Such transitive verbs as *gladden, redden, frighten*, etc.,
are new formations of M. or Mod. Eng. Most of the -*n*-
verbs in O.E. are transitive. The intransitive usage, as
well as many of the verbs themselves of this class, would
appear to be of Scandinavian origin. Examples are :
batten, O. Swed. *batna*, from root *bat*-, which we have in
better, O.E. *beter*, Goth. *batiz*; M.E. *bliknen*, 'turn
pale,' O. West Scand. *blikna*; M.E. *dawnen*, 'dawn,'
O.E. *dagian*. On the other hand, O.E. *costnian*, M.E.

costnen, 'tempt,' which occurs in Ælfric, is probably native. (On the above, see also Skeat, *Principles of English Etymology*, i., p. 275 ; Kluge, *Grundr.*², p. 939.)

A trace of the O.N. nom. case ending *-r* is seen in O.E. *þræll*, where the *ll*, which in true O.E. words, we should expect to be simplified after a long vowel, is borrowed from Norse and preserved. This long *l* is due to the O.N. change of *-lr* to *ll*.

The neuter suffix *-t* is still preserved in *scant*, from O.N. *skamt* (neuter), 'short,' and in M.E. *wiȝt*, Modern dialect *wight*, 'strong,' 'nimble.'

In spite of the doubts that may arise in specific cases from the reasons already mentioned, the most reliable tests of the Scandinavian origin of words in English are those based upon phonological characteristics. In cases where the forms in M.E. or Mod. Eng. cannot be explained by any known law of English sound change, whereas the Scandinavian sound laws are in complete agreement with the form, we are justified, pending fresh information, in assigning a Scandinavian origin. There are, indeed, some words for which the evidence is particularly conclusive, since it can be shown that their form has been determined by prehistoric sound changes which distinguish the North Germanic, to which the Scandinavian dialects belong, from the West Germanic group, of which O.E. is a member.

A good example is the class of words which illustrate the development of Gmc. -$\bar{w}$- after original short vowels. In West Gmc. this sound became a vowel, and formed a diphthong with the preceding vowel. In West Gmc., on the other hand, it was stopped to -*gg*(*w*-), and in this form remains in Scandinavian. Mod. Eng. dialect *dag*, 'dew,' also 'to bedew,' appears in O. West Scand. as *dogg*, and in N. Swed. as *dagg*. This represents an original *daῶa, which regularly appears in O.E. as *dēā(w)*, M.E. *deu*, Mod. Eng. dew, O.H.G. *tou*.

Similarly, M.E. *haggen*, 'cut, hew,' represents O. West Scand. *hoggua*, from *haῶan. In W. Gmc. this is regularly represented by O.E. *hēāwan*, O.H.G. *houwan*, Mod. Eng. *hew*. Again, Mod. Eng. dialect *scag*, ' to hide, take shelter,' and *scug*, 'a place of shelter,' is from a Scandinavian *skuggi*, ' shade,' Danish *skygge*, 'overshadow.' The Gmc. form would be *skuῶjan, **skaῶ(j)an*, whence O.E. *scēāwan*, German *schauen*. Other examples of this class of words are : *egg*, O. West Scand. *egg*, but O.E. *ǣġ*, M.E. *ei*, German *ei*; *trig*, 'safe, tight, trim,' etc.; O. West Scand. *tryggr*, 'trusty, true,' but O.E. *trēōwe*, *ġe-trīēwe*, Mod. Eng. *true*, O.H.G. *gitriuwi*, German *traüe*, etc.

As examples of Mod. Eng. words whose form is at variance with what must have been the fate of the genuine O.E. forms had these survived, but which may be explained on the assumption of borrowing from Scandinavian, we may take the words *weak*, *bleak*. In O.E. we have *blāc*, 'pale,' and *wāk*, 'weak,' which in Mod. Eng. must have become 'bloke,' 'woke' respectively—in fact, the M.E. ancestors of these forms *blōk*, *wōk* are actually found.

The Mod. Eng. forms, however, are clearly from O.N. *bleikr*, *veikr*. It must be admitted that the development of the vowel in the English words (ī) is not quite clear, on the assumption that they preserved the diphthong into the M.E. period, and diphthongized forms are found in M.E. On the other hand, it is possible that in some English dialects an early monopthongizing of Norse *ei* to (ē or ẹ) took place.

Another good reason which justifies us in claiming a M.E. or Mod. Eng. word as Scandinavian is the fact, if it be a common word in familiar use, that it is not found in O.E., although the usual word in Norse. Orm is particularly rich in words of this kind, and has, among many others, the following, most of which are still in use : *takenn*, 'take,' the O.E. word is *niman*, and 'nim' is still found in our dialects ; *til*, 'to,' *cf.* un-*til*, and the common use of *til* for 'to' in the Northern dialects; *skinn*, 'skin,' O.E. *hȳd*, 'hide'; *occ.*, 'and'; *skill*, instead of the genuine Eng. *cræft*; *ille*, instead *yfel*, 'evil'; *mēōc*, meek,' O.N. *mjūkr ; gate*, 'way,' 'gait.' The English pronouns *they*, *their*, *them*, are all of Scandinavian origin, and have entirely replaced the O.E. *hie*, *hira*, *heom*, of which the last two are still found in Chaucer in the form *hir*, *hem*. (In addition to the authorities already quoted, see also Brate's useful article, *Nordische Lehnwörter im Ormulum*, Paul and Braune's *Beitr.* x.

2. **The French Element.**—The problems connected with the influence of French upon English during the M.E. period have been exhaustively treated by Mr. Skeat in his *Principles of English Etymology*, vol. ii. The student should further consult the *Anhang* (Supplement) on this subject, by Behrens, incorporated with Kluge's *Geschichte d. Engl. Spr.* in Paul's *Grundriss*, pp. 950, etc.; and Appendix III. in Mr. Bradley's edition of Morris's *Historical Outlines of English Accidence* contains a list of Norman French words from the principal English works from the twelfth to the early fourteenth century.

As the question of Norman French influence has been so thoroughly and clearly treated in the above, and is, on the whole, familiar to students of the history of English, no more need be done here than to summarize a few of the chief points of importance in this connection.

Norman French was a Northern French dialect. This dialect was spoken for about 300 years in England as a living, everyday language, at first by the official, noble, and governing classes, whose native language it was, later on by Englishmen also, even of the well-to-do sort generally. By the middle of the thirteenth century, probably, most educated persons were bi-lingual, those of Norman origin speaking at least some English, while the natives acquired the language of the foreigners. With the fusion of the races came, as we saw in the case of Norse, a fusion of vocabularies also. The Norman laws contain many technical words of English origin, while French words begin to be used in ever-increasing numbers by English writers from the year 1100 onwards.

Norman French, or, as, following Mr. Skeat, we may call it, Anglo-French, naturally had a development of its own in this country. Besides being the language of everyday life among the upper classes, this dialect was also the official dialect of the law and of Parliament down to 1362, and it continued to be taught in schools down to 1385.

With its death as an official vehicle there followed the rapid dying out of Anglo-French as a spoken language. In fact, English must have already obtained a very strong hold upon all classes before French was abolished by law as the dialect of officialdom ; but the latter occurrence gave it its death-blow. We may conclude, therefore, that soon

after the middle of the fourteenth century the direct source
of French words of this particular origin was running low.
By this time, however, hundreds of Anglo-French words
had passed into the speech of Englishmen, a very large
number of which have remained to this day in universal
use. Chaucer's language shows how deeply the new element
had penetrated into the texture of English vocabulary ; it
was no longer felt as strange by his time : it was part and
parcel of English.

By the side of Anglo-French words derived direct, in
England itself, many others were borrowed during the
fourteenth century from the French of the Continent,
mostly from the *Central French* or Parisian dialect of
the Île de France, but others also from the Picardian
dialect.

The influence of Central French, both direct and
through literature, which began in the M.E. period, has
continued ever since, and was especially strong during the
seventeenth century, as may be seen from such a comedy
as Dryden's *Mariage à la Mode*.

Middle English Inflections.

The changes wrought during the Transition and M.E.
periods in the O.E. inflectional system are the result
partly of natural sound change, partly of analogy.

As a result of the former, we may say generally that all
unstressed vowels—that is, therefore, all the vowels of the
endings—were levelled under *e*—*e.g.*, O.E. stānas, M.E.
stōn-es ; O.E. ēagena (gen. pl.), M.E. ēȝ(e)ne ; O.E. wudu,
M.E. wode, etc. Final *m* was levelled under *n*, which was
subsequently dropped altogether.

An account of M.E. inflections is to be found in *The Introduction* of Morris and Skeat's *Specimens of Early English*, vols. i. and ii. ; and the development from O.E. is briefly traced in Sweet's various works, already cited, upon Historical English Grammar, and in Morris's *Historical Outlines of English Accidence* (Ed. Bradley).

We select here some of the leading features of the M.E. inflectional system for enumeration.

Declensions.

Substantives.—The O.E. substantives, like those in all other Gmc., or, for the matter of that, in all Aryan languages, are classified for purposes of declension, according to the nature of their stems. We distinguish vowel stems and consonantal stems. In the former case the characteristic vowel of a class followed the 'root' or base, and was immediately followed by the case ending : Nom. sing. Gk. λυκ-ο-ς, Gmc. *wulf-a-z, Goth. wulf-s (the stem vowel being lost in the historic period in Gmc.), O.E. wulf (with loss not only of stem vowel, but of case-ending as well) ; instr. pl. Lith. *av-i-mis*, ' sheep,' Goth. (dat.) *gast-i-m*, ' guests,' O.E. (dat.) *sun-u-m*, ' sons.' The stems even in Gmc. had undergone some levelling through analogy, and in O.E. all stems take the ending *-um* in dat. pl., the vowel in this case representing at once *u* and *o*, and the *m* being all that was left of the original instr. pl. case-ending *-mis*, fully preserved, as seen above in Lithuanian.

Consonantal stems are those which end in consonants, which sometimes, as in the case of Latin *pes*, ' foot,' from *ped-s*, was the final consonant of the ' root ' itself ; in other cases, such as *hom-in-em* or πατ-έρ-α, was preceded by a vowel.

Of the consonantal stems, the most important class in O.E. is that of the -*n*-stems, usually known as the 'Weak' declension. O.E. *nama*, gen. sing., etc., *naman*, gen. pl. *namna*. The O.E. declensions, already greatly dilapidated by change and loss of final or other unstressed syllables, and considerably confused by analogy, as compared with that system which Comparative Philology enables scholars to reconstruct as the original Aryan, underwent further dilapidation and confusion in M.E. through the continued operation of similar factors of change. It is still possible to distinguish *a*-stems, *u*-stems, *i*-stems, etc., among the 'strong' declensions of O.E. In M.E. these are very soon all levelled under one 'strong' type, that of masculine *a*-stems. The full M.E. form of this declension runs·

	Singular.	Plural.
N.A.	stōn.	stōnes.
G.	stōnes.	stōne.
D.	stōne.	stōnen.

Before the end of the M.E. period, however, all that survived in the sing. was the gen. -*es*, and in the pl. -*es* was used throughout for all cases. A weak gen. pl. in -*ene* also occurs.

The old weak declension included all three genders. Masculines have -*a* in nom. sing. and -*an* in the other cases; the pl. ran nom. and acc. -*an*, gen. -*ena*, dat. -*um* (like strong nouns).

The neuter weak declension was the same, except that nom. and acc. sing. ended in -*e*; the feminine had -*e* in nom. sing., otherwise was declined exactly like the masculine. In M.E. the sing. of all genders has -*e* in nom., -*en* in the other cases; the pl. -*en* in all cases but the gen., which ends in -*ene*.

Here, again, we soon find the suffix -*en* used simply to express plural number.

The weak gen. pl. -*ene* was sometimes retained for convenience, *fairly late*, and is often used in early texts with nouns which otherwise took the strong pl. suffix -*es* in the nom. pl.—*alre Kingene King* occurs in a twelfth-century homily (Morris, *O.E. Homilies*, second series, p. 89, *l.* 16).

Of the two types of declension, the strong predominates greatly in the North and Midlands, while the weak is far more frequent in the South, where it is extended to words which were originally strong. At the present day the Berkshire dialect uses *primrosen* and *housen* in addition to the other scattered waifs of this declension which survive in the Standard language.

Verbs.—Among the most characteristic dialectal distinctions in M.E. are the personal endings of the pres. indic. of verbs. They are as follows:

North : -*e* or -*es* in first, and -*es* in all other persons sing. and pl.

Midlands : first -*e*, second -*est*, third -*eth* ; pl. -*en* in all persons.

Southern : first -*e*, second -(*e*)*st*, third -(*e*)*th* ; pl. -*eth* in all persons.

The *present participle* ends in -*and*(*e*) in the North, -*end*(*e*) in the Midlands, *ind*(*e*) in the South.

The suffix -*ing*(*e*), originally that whereby verbal nouns were formed (O.E. -*ung*, as in *leornung*, etc.), gradually replaces the older -ind(e) as the suffix of present participles, although the former continued to be used in the South down to the middle of the fourteenth century, while the old ending -and was still preserved in the North considerably later—*e.g.*, *syngand, sayand, plesand,* etc., are still used by Sir David Lyndsay in a passage of some twenty verses given by Mr. Gregory Smith in *Specimens of Middle Scots,* pp. 162, 163, by the side of forms in -*ing*.

Pronouns.—The distinctions of gender and case expressed by the O.E. demonstrative pronoun, also used as a definite article, *se, sēō, þæt,* were considerably impaired in M.E.   The Northern and Midland dialects very early use the new form *þe* (where the *þ* is due to the analogy of the other cases and genders) as an indeclinable article in all cases and for all genders of the sing. the pl. is *þa*.   In the South, however, the distinctions of gender and case are preserved much longer.   A new fem. nom. sing. *þēō* was formed to replace the old fem. *sēō* by the side of masc. *þe,* and *þet,* corresponding to O.E. *þæt,* was used before neuter words.

In the North *þet* was used as a demonstrative pronoun, indeclinable, with a pl. *þās*.

Traces of the original inflections still survive in a few fossilized forms, *e.g.,* the proper name *Atterbury*—M.E. *at þer(e) bury,* O.E. *æt þǣre byriġ,* the change from *at þer* to *atter* being quite normal in M.E. ; *for the nonce* = M.E. *for þe nōnes* = *for þen ōnes,* where *þen* is properly a dative, O.E. *þǣm,* levelled under the accusative, O.E. *þone, ōnes* being a genitive in form, used first adverbially, but here as a substantive.   The neuter article survives in Sc. *the tane and the tither,* originally M.E. þet āne, þet ōþer.   *The t'other* was perfectly polite colloquial English a hundred years ago, though now felt as a vulgarism when used seriously.

The Rise of Literary English.

The works written in this country down to the third quarter of the fifteenth century show more or less strongly marked points of divergence in the form of language, according to the province in which they were written. These differences are observable in the vocabulary, more strongly still in the inflexions, and most characteristically of all in the sound system, so far as this can be reconstructed from the spelling.

From the period at which Caxton's activities begin (1475), the dialectal variety, which had hitherto been so remarkable a feature, disappears, to all intents and purposes, from literature.   Henceforth the language of books becomes uniform, the spelling, owing to the necessity for comparative consistency felt by the printers, rapidly crystallizes, and the form of language thus displayed differs but little *in its written form* from that of the present day, of which it is, indeed, the lineal ancestor.

This literary dialect, to which Caxton by his copious industry gave wide currency and permanence, was not a bogus form of speech, deliberately vamped together from various written or spoken sources.   It represents a living, spoken form of language, that of the Capital.

The London Dialect.—This dialect can be traced from the middle of the thirteenth century, in proclamations, charters, and wills—that is, both in public and private documents. The earliest forms are distinctly Southern in character, but Midland influence gains ground, and even Northern features find their way into the latest charters of the fifteenth century. Kentish influence is considerable, but the Saxon elements are more and more eliminated.

The language of literature and the Standard spoken English of the present day, while mainly Midland, or, rather, traceable to a M.E. Midland type, yet preserve Northern, Saxon, and Kentish elements in isolated cases. It is contended by Morsbach (*Über den Ursprung der neuenglischen Schriftsprache*, Heilbronn, 1888)—(1) that this composite dialect developed naturally in the Metropolis owing to social and political conditions; (2) that this is proved by an investigation of the official and legal documents in English emanating from London during the fourteenth and fifteenth centuries; (3) this dialect gradually spread its influence as a literary medium far and wide, until it became the only recognised form for writers from all provinces. Caxton, who translated several important works, such as Trevisa's version of Higden, into the London dialect, greatly contributed to the spread of this form of speech.

Dibelius, in *John Capgrave und die englische Schriftsprache*, Anglia, xxiii., p. 152, etc., argues that not only in London, but in Oxford also, the tendency arose to set up a fixed literary form of English. Wycliffe, a Yorkshireman by birth, who became Master of Balliol, chose the Oxford type as his literary vehicle. The differences between the London and Oxford types persisted

down to the third quarter of the fifteenth century. Both
types were imitated throughout the country, and documents
from Norfolk, Suffolk, and Worcester all show, by the side
of local peculiarities, certain points of agreement with both
the Oxford and the London forms of English. These
points of agreement become stronger as time goes on,
showing that the standards of both places were followed
over a wide area. The knowledge of the London English,
before printing, would naturally spread through the influence of the law and legislature; that of Oxford would
be carried far and wide by the clergy. In this way the
path was prepared for the universal acceptance of a literary
form which combined the features of both the Oxford and
the London models. Such a form, Dibelius maintains, is
to be found in the printed works of Caxton, and such a
form exists in Present-day English, which is the descendant of the dialect employed by Caxton. The great
writer of the Oxford type of English was Wycliffe, whose
translation of the Bible contributed to give currency to
that form, and this influence may be detected among some
of the writers of the Paston Letters. Dibelius, while laying
stress upon the English of Oxford as an important element
in the literary dialect, admits freely that the London type
predominates, and that its influence is found everywhere,
even in writings which show no trace of Oxford influence.
Caxton's English is far more that of London than of
Oxford, and probably what of the latter element is found
in his works is due to literature rather than to direct contact.

The language of Chaucer deviates in many respects
from the typical London dialect of the charters, and the

modern English literary language is nearer to the latter than to the former. The explanation probably is that, although Chaucer certainly wrote in one form of the London speech of his day, the particular variety of this which he employed was the courtly language of the upper strata of society. His writings seem to represent an actual contemporary form of language rather than a literary tradition. The language actually preserved in the London wills and charters is most probably, to a certain extent, stereotyped, and the same may well be true of the Oxford type as represented by Wycliffe. Chaucer's language contains more Southern (Saxon), and probably also more Kentish elements than that form which was to become the ancestor of Present-day English. Strong though the literary influence of Chaucer was, it was not sufficient to found a permanent type of literary language, in spite of his numerous imitators and followers. We must, indeed, suppose that a Court dialect is a more transitory type of speech, more liable to the modifying effects of fashion, than the speech of the educated middle class. It would appear that the form adopted by Caxton in his writings was so vigorous and full of vitality, *as a spoken language also*, that it was confirmed, consolidated, and, when necessary, subsequently rejuvenated from the spoken form. Just as the written forms of this dialect rapidly ousted and replaced the other English dialects for purposes of public and private written documents, such as wills, letters, and documents of all kinds, no less than in purely literary productions, so also, though this was a slower process, and one not yet complete, the spoken form became the standard language of the learned, the polite, and the fashionable, to the gradual elimination of provincial speech.

In addition to the authorities referred to above, the student may, with great profit, consult Ten Brink, *Chaucer's Sprache und Verskunst*, Leipzig, 1899, and the remarks on pp. 20-29 of Kaluza's *Historische Grammatik der englischen Spr.*, vol. i., Berlin, 1900.

CHAPTER XIV

CHANGES IN ENGLISH PRONUNCIATION DURING THE
MODERN PERIOD—THE DEVELOPMENT OF ENGLISH
SOUNDS FROM THE FIFTEENTH CENTURY TO THE
PRESENT DAY

The Problem.

IT is proposed in this chapter to attempt to trace the
development of the English language, more particularly
of the Standard dialect, so far as the pronunciation is concerned, through the sixteenth, seventeenth, and eighteenth
centuries, and to inquire by what paths of change the
sounds of late M.E. passed into those forms which they
now have in English speech.

During the five hundred years which have elapsed since
the death of Chaucer very remarkable and far-reaching
changes have taken place in the Standard language, and
of these we may distinguish two main features. Firstly,
the actual sounds, especially the vowels, have undergone
considerable shifting; and secondly, from the materials at
our disposal, it is possible to establish the fact that in
most words more than one type of pronunciation of the
vowels has always existed, and that that type which at
one period is considered the 'correct' one, at a subsequent
date is often discarded in favour of another type, or its

descendant, which a former age would have regarded as
'ill-bred,' 'vulgar,' or 'incorrect.'

The task of the reconstruction of the pronunciation of
English during the different epochs of the Modern Period
is of a different nature from that of establishing the sounds
of Old and Middle English. In the latter case we have a
variegated orthography which differs from dialect to dialect,
in some cases from scribe to scribe, in the efforts to express
the sound. The problem is to interpret the written symbols:
in the former case we have a conventional spelling which
is practically fixed, and such varieties as exist throw but
little light upon the changes of pronunciation. On the
other hand, we have in the Modern Period, for the first
time, a series of systematic attempts, from various motives,
to describe the actual sounds used and their distribution.
The problem, therefore, is mainly how to interpret rightly
the accounts given by contemporaries of the pronunciation
of the various generations. It is unquestionable that in
this task we obtain help from knowledge gathered indirectly by a study of the changing spelling of M.E.,
just as this knowledge is itself often supplemented and
confirmed by the categorical statements of sixteenth or
seventeenth century writers.

The Sources of our Knowledge of the Pronunciation of the Sixteenth, Seventeenth, and Eighteenth Centuries.

From the year 1530 onwards there exists a series of
works by English writers in English, French, Welsh, and
Latin which deal directly or incidentally with the pronunciation of English during the age in which the writers
lived. These men belonged to several different classes of

society ; there were Divines, some of whom were Bishops and Court Chaplains, Oxford and Cambridge Professors and Heads of Houses, Schoolmasters of various ranks; there were Poets, Scholars, and Men of Science.

The late A. J. Ellis, to whom belongs the glory of having first made use of such writers as the above for our present purpose, and of having ferreted out many a long-forgotten tract, gives in Part I. of his wonderful work on *Early English Pronunciation*, Chapter I., an interesting account of his first struggles to interpret the accounts given by the above-mentioned phonetic authorities. His first certain guide to sixteenth-century pronunciation was derived from the works of William Salesbury, who in 1547 published a Welsh and English Dictionary, in the Introduction to which, according to Ellis, 'about 150 typical English words' are transcribed 'into Welsh letters.' The same writer also produced in 1567 a tract upon the pronunciation of Welsh, in which he refers to many other languages, thus establishing for the modern reader the pronunciation of sixteenth-century Welsh. It can thus be shown that the pronunciation of Welsh has changed very little since Salesbury's time, and his transliterations of English words into Welsh spelling are therefore of the highest value in ascertaining the English pronunciation of his day. Salesbury's essays are published *in extenso* by Ellis, together with an English translation of the Welsh treatise, in *E.E.P.*, p. 743, etc. An even earlier phonetic transliteration of English into Welsh spelling, that of a *Hymn to the Virgin*, made about 1500 (*cf.* Sweet, *H.E.S.*, p. 203), was published in the *Transactions of the Philological Society*, 1880-1881.

The following is a selection of the principal authorities,
a fuller list of which is given in Ellis's *E.E.P.*, Part I.,
p. 31, etc., and Sweet's *H.E.S.*, p. 204, etc. :

Sixteenth-century Authorities.

1530. PALSGRAVE: *L'esclarcissement de la langue Francoyse.*

> [Palsgrave was a graduate of Cambridge, and tutor
> to Princess Mary, sister of Henry VIII., and later
> on a Royal Chaplain. He died in 1554. He
> spoke the form of English in vogue at Court.
> His book contains an elaborate account of French
> pronunciation, elucidated by reference to English
> and Italian.]

1545. MEIGRET: *Traité touchant le commun usage de
l'escriture francoise.*

> [This book deals with French pronunciation, and
> makes the pronunciation of Palsgrave's English
> analogues more secure.]

1547. SALESBURY : *A Dictionary of Englishe and Welshe.*

> [Salesbury was born in Denbighshire, and studied
> at Oxford. See reference to this book and to
> Ellis's account of it above.]

1555. CHEKE (SIR JOHN): *De pronunciatione Græcæ.*

> [Cheke was born at Cambridge in 1514, and moved
> in the best literary society. He was Secretary
> of State in 1552, and died in 1557. In his trea-
> tise several Greek sounds are illustrated by Eng-
> lish words spelled phonetically in Greek letters.]

1567. SALESBURY: *A playne and familiar Introduction
teaching how to pronounce the letters in the
Brytishe Tongue, now commonly called Welsh.*

> [All the important portions of this book reprinted
> by Ellis; see references above.]

1568. SMITH (SIR THOMAS): *De recta et emendata linguæ anglicæ scriptione.*

[Smith was born in 1515 at Saffron Walden, Essex. He was a Fellow of Queen's College, Cambridge, public orator, and in 1536 became Provost of Eton. He was a Secretary of State in 1548, Privy Councillor in 1571. He died in 1577. The object of the above book was to improve English spelling. It contains tables of words printed in a phonetic alphabet.]

1569. HART: *An Orthographie:* conteyning the due order and reason, howe to write or painte thimage of mannes voice, most like to the life or Nature. By J. H. Chester.

[Hart was the real name of the writer of this book, according to the catalogue of the British Museum. Hart was, according to Ellis, probably a Welshman. Phonetic symbols are used in the above work, and the author was acquainted with several languages. He favours a pronunciation which was in his day only coming in. Gill, writing more than fifty years later, says of Hart: 'Sermonem nostrum characteribus suis non *sequi* sed *ducere* meditabatur.']

1580. BULLOKAR: *Booke at large for the Amendment of Orthographie for English Speech.*

[Bullokar uses phonetic spelling. The pronunciation which he records is archaic, and agrees more with that of Palsgrave than with that of his own immediate contemporaries.]

1619 and 1621. GILL: *Logonomia Anglica.*

[Gill was born in Lincolnshire in 1564 (same year as Shakespeare); member of C.C.C., Cambridge; Headmaster of St. Paul's School, 1608; died

1635. He transcribes passages from the Psalms
and from Spenser in his phonetic alphabet, and
discusses pronunciation at length. Gill is old-
fashioned, and has a horror of modernisms. The
pronunciation described is, on the whole, that of
the middle of the sixteenth century. The work
was reprinted in 1903 by Jiriczek in the series
' *Quellen und Forschungen*,' Strassburg.]

BUTLER : *The English Grammar . . . whereto is annexed
an Index of Words like and unlike.*

[Butler was a member of Magdalen College, Oxford,
and a country clergyman. He uses phonetic
spelling. His pronunciation is that of the end
of the sixteenth century, and he opposes the new
pronunciation.]

Seventeenth-century Authorities.

Ben Jonson's *English Grammar* is of interest on account
of its author, but is of little value for our purpose.

1651. WILLIS (THOMAS, of Thistlewood, Middlesex) : *Vesti-
bulum Linguæ Latinæ. A Dictionarie for Children.*

[Contains upwards of 4,000 words, supposed to be
arranged according to rhyme, but in most cases,
in reality, grouped according to spelling. There
are a certain number of genuine rhymes which
are useful.]

1653–1699. WALLIS : *Grammatica Linguæ Anglicanæ
Cui præfigitur De Loquela ; sive de sonorum
omnium loquelarium formatione : Tractatus Gram-
matico-Physicus.*

[This book went through six editions between the
above dates. Wallis was born at Ashford, in
Kent, in 1616 ; appointed Savilian Professor of

Geometry at Oxford in 1649 ; died, 1703. The introduction is of great importance, and establishes, with considerable certainty, the value of all the symbols. This work is the chief authority for the middle of the seventeenth century.]

1668. WILKINS : *An Essay towards a Real Character, and a Philosophical Language.*

[Wilkins was born in Northamptonshire in 1614 ; graduated at Oxford in 1648 ; elected Warden of Wadham, 1648 ; Bishop of Ripon, 1668 ; died, 1672. This '*Essay*' contains an admirable treatise on Phonetics. Wilkins makes use of a phonetic alphabet, into which he transliterates the Lord's Prayer and the Creed. The book is not infrequently to be met with in booksellers' catalogues of the present day.]

1668. PRICE : *English Orthographie* is the beginning of a very long title, which includes, among other things, ' Also some Rules for the points and pronunciation.'

[The book, when used by the side of other authorities, is useful ' in discriminating the exact sounds of the different vowel digraphs of the seventeenth century.']

1685. COOPER : *Grammatica Linguæ Anglicunæ.*

[This book contains a treatise on speech sounds, a discussion of peculiarities of orthography and pronunciation, and long lists of words illustrating the several vowel sounds.]

1688. MIEGE : *The Great French Dictionary.*

[Valuable information as to pronunciation prefixed to each letter.]

Eighteenth-Century Authorities.

1701. JONES (JOHN): *Practical Phonography.* (The first words of an immense title.)

> [A kind of pronouncing dictionary, in which all kinds of pronunciations of the same words are given, and therefore valuable as recording what actually occurred in English speech at the beginning of the eighteenth century.]

Circa 1713. ANONYMOUS: *Grammar of the English Tongue.*

> [Useful in corroboration of the statements of other authorities of the period.]

1725. LEDIARD: *Grammatica Anglicana Critica,* in which English words are transliterated phonetically into German spelling. Ellis gives a full account of results (Part IV., p. 1040, etc.).

1766. BUCHANAN: *Essay towards establishing a standard for an elegant and uniform pronunciation of the English Language throughout the British Dominions.*

> [The work of a Scotsman, this book bears some traces of this in the pronunciation described. Ellis notes that on the whole, however, this does not differ materially from that heard in the middle of the nineteenth century, except inasmuch as certain pronunciations of certain words are given as 'learned and polite' which would not now be so accounted.]

> A tract by Dr. Benjamin Franklin, entitled *A Scheme for a New Alphabet and Reformed Mode of Spelling,* in the form of a correspondence between himself and a lady, is given by Ellis (pp. 1058, etc.). The correspondence was carried on in the proposed alphabet, and the tract contains a table of sounds and symbols, and remarks by

Franklin thereupon. Ellis prints the paper in full, but unfortunately turns the whole thing into his own very clumsy *Palæotype*.

Method of using the Authorities.—By comparing the statements of a considerable number of contemporary authorities with regard to the pronunciation of a given sound, weighing one against another, and checking and interpreting one by another, we attempt first to arrive at a conclusion as to what is the precise sound which the various writers are trying to describe. The result of such an investigation often leads to the conclusion that at the same period there was more than one pronunciation of the same word; the writers are manifestly describing different sounds, though dealing with the same symbol. We thus establish the existence of two or more types of pronunciation at the same period. These varieties may arise from several causes. They may be the descendants of doublets which arose at an earlier period; they may represent different *dialectal* treatments of the same original sound; they may represent the pronunciation of the older and younger generation respectively. When the existence of the several types at a given period is once definitely established, the next problem is to inquire which earlier type each represents, and into which later form it subsequently develops. Until we have done this we can form no true idea of the development of any particular sound. Hence it is of the highest importance to know *all* the pronunciations of a given word which existed at a given time If we find that 'blood' was pronounced (blūd) in the sixteenth and seventeenth centuries, we are not justified in concluding, without further evidence, that the modern

20—2

form (blad) is its lineal descendant. This would be tanta-
mount to asserting that seventeenth-century (ū) appears as
(a) in the nineteenth, a statement which would at once be
disproved by further examination. The problem resolves
itself into showing (1) what sixteenth-century sound was
the ancestor of Present-day (a), and (2) what is the
Present-day representative of the sixteenth and seventeenth century (ū). When we find that a very large
number of words which now contain the sound (a) were
pronounced with (ŭ) in the sixteenth century, and with
that sound alone, we should be inclined to say that the
former sound has been developed from the latter, and
further to postulate a sixteenth-century pronunciation
(blŭd) as the ancestor of the Present-day polite form of
the word. As a matter of fact, the pronunciation (blŭd)
can be shown to have existed in the sixteenth century by
the side of (blūd). Similarly, although we can show that
in the eighteenth century, in good society, people said
(Kwæliti) and (Kwæntiti), it would be quite erroneous to
suppose that these particular forms developed into the
Present-day (Kwoliti) and (Kwontiti). The former types
have simply been discarded, and their places have been
taken by others whose predecessors existed in the
eighteenth century side by side with those first mentioned,
although at that time they did not happen to be the
forms in fashionable use.

In a word, when tracing the history of a language we
must always bear in mind the twofold problem : first,
the development of the actual sounds themselves, and,
secondly, the changing fashion of using them in a given
dialect in a particular group of words.

Ellis and Sweet both give the statements of the various authorities, so that the student can draw his own conclusions, in which he will, however, receive great help from the discussion of every point by the above-mentioned scholars. Ellis, besides the words in the text, has copious pronouncing vocabularies of the sixteenth, seventeenth, and eighteenth centuries, compiled from the whole body of Orthographists, Phoneticians, and Dictionary-makers of those centuries. In these lists all the variants in each period are given, and they are of the greatest use as affording convenient material for phonological investigation.

The Sounds in Detail.

In the present case the most convenient way of dealing with the subject will be to start with the M.E. sound and trace it downwards to the present day.

By way of illustration of the kind of material upon which our conclusions are based, and also of the method of dealing with it, it will be as well to give the full statements of the contemporary authorities concerning M.E. *a* and *ā*. The development of the remaining sounds will be given without reference to these, but each statement is based upon the same kind of material as that given in the case of *a* and *ā*.

The rules of pronunciation as given by the authorities are always based upon the uses of the letters.

PALSGRAVE (1530): ' The soundyng of *a* which is most generally used throughout the frenche tonge is such as we use with vs, where the best englysche is spoken, whiche is lyke as the Italians sound *a*, or as they with vs, that pronounce the latine tonge aryght.'

This points to a mid-back-slack for 'the best English.' Possibly the other sound of *a* which Palsgrave implies also existed in his day was a fronted form—almost our (æ).

SALESBURY (1547): ' A in English is of the same sound as *a* in Welsh, as is evident in these words of English—*all*, aal, *pale*, paal, *sale*, sal.'

The double vowels here imply length, and the last word should have been transcribed saal.   The sound of *a* in Welsh at present is (*a*) mid-back-slack, whether long or short.   He invariably transcribes M.E. *ā* with *aa*, and M.E. *a* with *ae*, apart from occasional inconsistencies like the above : *babe* he writes *baab*, *bake*, *baak*, *plague*, *plaag*, etc.   Examples of short *a* are *papp*, *nag*, *fflacs* (flax), etc.

SMITH (1568) says the only sounds of English *a* are those of long and short Latin *a*.

As samples of short *a* he has : *man*, *far*, *hat*, *mar*, *pass* , examples of the long are : *mane*, *farewell*, *hate*, *mare*, *pace*, *bare*, *bake*.   Since Salesbury gives the last word with (*ā*), there can be little doubt what sound Smith implied by ' sonus *a* vocalis Romanæ longæ.'   The first group had the same sound short.

HART (1569) identifies English *a* with that of German, Italian, French, Spanish, and Welsh, which is to be pronounced ' with wyde opening the mouth, as when a man yauneth.'

BUTLER (1633): '*A* is in English, as in all other languages, the first vowel, and the first letter of the Alphabet ; the which . . . hath two sounds, one when it is short, another when long, as in *man* and *mane*, *hat* and *hate*.'

This is the first indication of a distinction in quality between long and short *a*, and it is not repeated till fifty

years later, by Cooper. It seems clear that Butler must
have heard a difference, however, and since both long and
short are certainly fronted a little later, it seems probable
that one may have been slightly in advance of the other
in reaching (æ). Again, since M.E. long *a* has not only
been fronted, but also raised to (ē, ē, ɛi) in later English,
we shall perhaps be justified in assuming that Butler pronounced (hat) *hat*, but (hæt) *hate*. If so, he must have
been rather in advance of other contemporary writers, and
must have described the pronunciation just coming in.
Palsgrave's implied statement of the existence of another
sound of *a*, than of full-mid-back sound, may have referred
to this fronted form, which in his day was apparently not
highly esteemed, and may have originated in provincial
speech.

The net result of the above statements seems to be that
M.E. *a*, long or short, was retained throughout the sixteenth and well into the seventeenth century. The fronting tendency began in the sixteenth century, but was
considered first as a vulgarism, and then as new-fangled,
until the first quarter of the seventeenth century.

Middle English 'a' in Seventeenth-Century Pronunciation.

Ben Jonson (1640): 'A with us in most words is pronounced lesse than the French à, as in *art, act, apple,
ancient*. But when it comes before *l* in the end of a
syllable, it obtaineth the full French sound, and is uttered
with the mouth and throat wide open'd, the tongue bent
back from the teeth, as in *al, smal, gal, fall, tal, cal*.'

The first of these statements, that *a* 'is lesse than the
French à,' seems to indicate that Ben Jonson followed the

(then) new fashion, and pronounced a fronted (*a*), though perhaps not yet (æ). The *a* before *l* was clearly a full-back vowel, whether mid or low it is impossible to say. The pronunciation of *all*, *small*, *gall*, etc., here described is not that which produced Present-day Standard English (ɔl, smɔl), etc. We shall deal with that under the M.E. *au*. WALLIS (1653-1699) represents fully-developed, typical seventeenth-century pronunciation. He describes English *a* as ' *a exile*,' and goes on : ' Quale auditur in vocibus, *bat*, vespertilio ; *bate*, discordia ; *pal*, palla episcopalis ; *pale*, pallidus ; *Sam* (Samuelis contractio) ; same, *idem* ; *lamb*, agnus ; *lame*, claudus ; *dam*, mater (brutosum) ; *dame*, domina ; *bar*, vectis ; *bare*, nudus ; *ban*, exsecror ; *bane*, pernicies, etc. Differt hic sonus a Germanorum â *pingui* seu aperto ; eo quod Angli linguæ medium elevent, adeoque aërem in Palato comprimant ; Germani vero linguæ medium deprimant, adeoque aërem comprimant in gutture. Galli fere sonum illum proferunt ubi *e* præcedit literam *m* vel *n*, in eadem syllaba ut *entendement*,' etc.

This vowel (*a*) has previously been classified by Wallis as one of those of which he says : ' Vocales Patinæ in Palato formantur, aëre scilicet inter palati et linguæ medium moderate compresso '; and distinguishing the particular vowel he says : ' Majori apertura formatur Anglorum *a*, hoc est *á* exile.'

This description must refer to the same sound as that which Ben Jonson says is ' lesse than the French *à*,' and is pretty clearly fixed by Wallis as the low-front, being made by the ' middle of the tongue ' and with ' a greater opening ' than the other front vowels. It will be noticed that the English words in the passage quoted above are alternately short and long, and must therefore be (æ), as in (bæt), and (b͞æt), as in (b͞æt), respectively.

WILKINS (1668) says of *a* 'that it is framed by an emission of the breath, betwixt the tongue and the concave of the palate ; the upper superfices of the tongue being rendered less concave, and at a less distance from the palate.'

Wilkins' pairs of words to illustrate the short and long form of this sound are—

| Short : | bat | val-ley | fat | mat | pal | Rad-nor |
| Long : | bate | vale | fate | mate | pale | trade |

These examples and the remarks of Wilkins which have been quoted point to the same results as in the case of Wallis.

COOPER (1685): Cooper's account of the pronunciation of *a* must indeed have been considered 'new-fangled' by the older generation of his contemporaries. He distinguishes two sounds for original long *ā*, using the phrase '*a exilis*' to designate a different sound from that referred to by previous writers when they use the expression. The following are his remarks : 'A formatur a medio linguæ ad concavum palati paululum elevato. In his *can* possum, *pass* by prætereo, *a* corripitur; in *cast* jacio, *past* pro *passed* præteritus, producitur. Frequentissimus auditur hic sonus apud Anglos, qui semper hoc modo pronunciant *a* Latinum ; ut in *amabam*. . . . Hunc sonum correptum productum semper scribimus per *a ;* at huic characteri præterea adhibentur sonus unus et alter: prior, qui pro vocali ejus longa habetur ut in *cane* . . . posterior ut in *was* sect. septima sub *o* gutturalem.'

This seems to imply that *can* and *pass* had (æ), *cast*,

past (ǣ). Further, the symbol *a* also expresses a sound which is generally held to be the ordinary long sound (ǣ), but which is not the same; this other sound occurs in *cane*. Incidentally we may notice that Cooper pronounced *was*, not (wæz), but (woz). What was the third sound expressed by *a*?

Writing of ε, he says: ' ε formatur à linguâ magis elevata et expansa, quam in *a* proprius ad extremitatem, unde concavum palati minus redditur sonus magis acutus; ut in *ken* video. . . . Vera majusce soni productio scribitur per *a* atque *a* longum falso denominatur; ut in *cane*, canna; *wane*, deflecto; and ante *ge* ut *age*, ætas; in cæteris autem vocabulis (*ni fallor*) omnibus ubi *e* quiescens ad finem syllabæ post *a*, adjicitur; *u* gutturalis . . . inseritur post *a* ut in *name*, nomen, quasi scriberetur *na-um* dissyllabum.'

Here we have the statement that the sound in *cane*, *wane* was the long of that in *ken*, and that in the two former words it was falsely called ' long *a*.' This clearly implies that the third vowel sound expressed by the symbol *a* was a mid-front, presumably, since it is the long of that in *ken*, a slack vowel = (ē̆). A further statement is that when this long sound stood before certain consonants a vowel glide ' *u* gutturalis,' was developed after it. Writers of this period nearly always mean by short *u* an unrounded vowel, probably very similar to that in Present-day *but*, and this sound, whatever it may have been when stressed (probably high-back-tense), may have actually existed in Cooper's day as a glide vowel, or, as is, perhaps, more probable, the sound actually intended here is the mix-mixed-slack (ə). This implies a pronunciation (kē̄ən) (nē̄əm), etc.

Cooper's lists illustrating the different sounds of *a* are as follows :

a brevis (= æ).	*a longa* (= ǣ).	*a exilis* (= ē̆).
bar, vectis.	*barge*, navicula.	*bare*, nudus.
blab, effutio.	*blast*, flatus.	*blazon*, divulgo.
cap, pileum.	*carking*, anxietas.	*cape*, capa.
car, carrus.	*carp*, carpo.	*care*, cura.
cat, catus.	*cast*, jactus.	*case*, theca.
dash, allido.	*dart*, jaculum.	*date*, dactylus.
flash, fulguro.	*flasket*, corbus gluus.	*flake*, flocculus.
gash, cæsura.	*gasp*, oscito.	*gate*, janua.
grand, grandis.	*grant*, concedo.	*grange*, villa.
land, terra.	*lanch*, solvo.	*lane*, viculus.
mash, farrago.	*mask*, larva.	*mason*, lapidarius.
pat, aptus.	*path*, semita.	*pate*, caput.
tar, pix fluida.	*tart*, scriblita.	*tares*, lolia.

Among words which have the diphthong (ɛə), Cooper includes many which in M.E. had a diphthong *ai*, which was evidently levelled, in his speech under M.E. *ā*. The ɛə list is :

bain, balneum.	*hail*, grando.	*maid*, virgo.
bane, venenuum.	*hale*, traho.	*made*, factus.
main, magnus.	*lay'n*, jacui.	*pain*, dolor.
mane, juba.	*lane*, viculus.	*pane*, quadra.
plain, manifestus.	*spaid*, castratus.	*tail*, cauda.
plane, lavigo.	*spade*, ligo.	*tale*, fabula.

Miege (1688) confirms Cooper's account of *ē* in certain words :

' Dans la langue Anglaise cette voyelle A s'appelle et se prononce *ai*. Lorsqu'elle est jointe avec d'autres lettres, elle retient ce même son dans la plupart des Mots ; mais il se prononce tantôt long, tantôt bref. L'a se prononce en *ai* long generalement lorsqu'il est suivi immediatement d'une consonne, et d'une *e* final. Exemple: *fare, tarɩ, care, grace, fable*, qui se prononcent ainsi *faire, taire, caire, graice, faible.*'

Miege notes that '*regard* se prononce regaird. . . . Dans le mot de *Jane* l'a se prononce en *e* masculin, Dgéne.'

The eighteenth - century authorities are very unsatisfactory in their statements regarding the fate of the three seventeenth-century sounds (æ, ǣ, ɛ̄). Apparently they were all preserved, (ɛ̄) becoming tense late in the century, and ǣ tending to be retracted towards ā, which sound it has to-day in Standard English. In Sheridan's Dictionary, however (1780), we still find only (pǣþ), etc., and no (ā) sounds. In the course of the nineteenth century (ē) was diphthongized in Standard English to (ɛi), in which the first element is half tense. In the Cockney dialect of London, and often in Liverpool and Manchester, this has become (æi) or (ai), according to the social class of the speaker.

We may now summarize the results of the foregoing inquiry. M.E. *a* and *ā* were preserved on the whole throughout the sixteenth century, although the fronting process may have begun here and there before the end of the century. In the seventeenth century the fronting process was completed, (*a*) becoming (æ), as at present, (*ā*) becoming (ǣ). In the course of the century (ǣ) was raised to (ɛ̄). Before certain combinations (æ) was lengthened during this century. This lengthening does not affect all words of the same class, therefore we must suppose that in some cases forms from other dialects were adopted by speakers of the Standard language. It seems to take place chiefly before *s* and *r* followed by another consonant, and before (þ and ð)—*e.g.*, (kǣrt, gǣsp, pǣþ).

This new long (ǣ) was not levelled under the old long (from M.E. ā), since this had already become (ē). Concrete examples of the development of M.E. ǎ are :

M.E. *a* $\begin{cases} bat \\ raðer \\ baþ \end{cases}$ = 17th cent. $\begin{cases} (bæt). \\ (æ) \end{cases} \begin{cases} (ræðer) \\ (bæþ) \end{cases} \begin{cases} (rǣðer) \\ < (bǣþ) \end{cases} \}$ 18th cent. (ǣ); 19th cent. (ā) $\begin{cases} (rā̆ðər). \\ (bāþ). \end{cases}$

M.E. *ā* $\begin{cases} fāce \\ nāme \\ rāðer \end{cases}$ = 17th cent. $\begin{cases} (fǣs) \\ (nǣm) \\ (rǣðer) \end{cases} < \begin{cases} (fēs) \\ (nēm) \\ (rēðer) \end{cases} < \begin{cases} 18th (fēs) \\ cent. (nēm) \\ ɛ < ē (rēðer) \end{cases} \}$ 19th (feis). cent. (neim). *ei* (reiðə).

The origin of the M.E. doublets *raðer, rāðer, faðer, fāðer,* have already been explained in the chapter on M.E. sound-changes (*ante,* p. 271). Present-day (ā) is never derived from M.E. ā, which is always (ɛi), but from M.E. *a* with seventeenth-century lengthening.

The seventeenth and eighteenth century sound (ǣ) is still preserved in many of the Southern English dialects, and in the Irish brogue, where such pronunciations as (kǣrd), (bǣþ) are usual. In the Northern dialects the fronting of M.E. *a* was never fully carried out, and (*a*) is either preserved as a full-back or is only slightly advanced. The seventeenth-century lengthening does not seem to have affected these dialects, which have the same vowel in (man, baþ, ka(r)d), etc.

The Present-day forms ' *clerk* ' (klāk) ; ' *Derby* ' (dābi) ; (hāþ) *hearth ;* (hāt), *heart,* may be discussed here. Originally, both of these words had M.E. *er*—*clerk, Derbi.* But in M.E. *e* before *r* was often made into *a,* doubtless through an intermediate stage (æ). This has happened in *star, far,* where the old spelling has been retained. In these

words we have the sixteenth-century (*a*), seventeenth-
century (æ), then (ǣ), which, as we have seen, becomes (*ā*)
in Late English. Our pronunciation of *clerk* and *Derby*,
heart, *hearth*, etc., goes back, in each case, to a M.E. (*a*),
which has regularly become (*ā*) in Late English by the
stages mentioned. The spelling in these words is that of
another M.E. type, with (ɛ) or (ɛ̄), which before *r* becomes
(ʌ̄) quite regularly in Late English. The provincial or
'vulgar' (dāb*i* klʌ̄k, hʌ̄þ) go back to the M.E. (ɛr) type.
In other words, Standard English preserves this type ; thus
(sʌ̄vənt), *servant;* (hʌ̄d), *heard;* (lʌ̄n), *learn,* are derived from
M.E. pronunciations with (ɛr, ɛ̄r). In eighteenth-century
colloquial literature these words are sometimes spelled *larn,*
sarvant, which expresses a then common pronunciation (lǣrn,
sǣrvənt), etc., and these forms are established by seventeenth and eighteenth century authorities. In polite speech,
however, only the (ʌ̄) forms survive in these words. The
spelling *Clark* in the proper name, of course, implies the
same type as that which is now received as 'correct.' It is
one of those sports of fashion so common in the history of
a Class Dialect that (klʌ̄k, dʌb*i*) should now be considered
vulgar, and (sāvənt) equally so.

M.E. (ɛ) *and* (ɛ̄) *and* (ē̆).—The short, slack M.E. (ɛ) has
survived in English pronunciation to the present day. It
occurs in such words as *men, better, set,* etc., and in *friend*
(frend), where it is the result of a M.E. shortening of *ē̆,*
which subsequently lost its tenseness, probably also in
breath, from M.E. (brɛþ) from (brɛ̄þ), from earlier *brǣþ.*
The unshortened form is heard in 'breathe,' M.E. *brē̆ðen.*

The symbol *e* in M.E. also denoted two distinct long
vowels, as we have seen (above, p. 259, etc.).

1. (ę̄), which had two origins: (a) O.E. ǣ, M.E. hēþ, from O.E. hǣþ; (b) O.E. e, lengthened during M.E. period in open syllables: bēren 'bear,' O.E. beran; mēte, 'meat,' O.E. mete.

2. (ē), which sprang from—(a), O.E. ē, whatever its origin, as in hēr, 'here'; hē, 'he'; sēd (now W. Sax.), 'seed'; quēn, O.E. cwēn; (b) O.E. ēo, as in bē, 'bee,' O.E. bēo; frē, 'free; O.E. frēo. (c) Kentish e (from y), lengthened in M.E. open syllables, as in ēvel, 'evil,' O. Kt. efel, W.S., etc.', yfel. (d) O.E. ē, from original e lengthened before -ld, etc., during the O.E. period, as in M.E. schēld, 'shield,' O.E. scēld, earlier scĕld; M.E. fēld 'field'; O.E. fēld, earlier fĕld. (e) Anglo-French ē as in chēfe, chiẹfe, appēren, appiēren.

We may conveniently deal first with the development of *M.E. tense ē.* The earliest sixteenth-century authorities show that before the middle of the century this sound had already been raised to the *high-front-tense* (ī). The words which appear in the pages of these writers as having un-mistakably (ī) are: *he, we, me, she, bee, bier, peer, cheese, chief, field, ease, lief, sheep, trees, queen, friend, feet, sheet, meet, geese, deed, weary, greet, ween, green, to wet* (Levins' *Manipulus*).

These all agree with the Present-day Standard English, except *friend*—at present (frɛnd), which is from a M.E. shortened form—though Scotch has (frīnd)—and to *wet.* Our (wɛt) is a M.E. shortening of the O.E. wǣtan, M.E. (wē̆ten), and apparently preserves the Saxon form, whereas sixteenth-century (wīt), like Mod. Sc. 'weet,' goes back to an Old Anglian wētan, which preserved its tense vowel in M.E. and underwent no shortening—at any rate not until quite recently. Whenever we find evidence of this raising to (ī) in sixteenth century, we must assume a form with tense (ē) in M.E. Most words of this class were spelled already in the sixteenth century with *ee*, in distinction to those with M.E. (ẹ̄), written *ea*. The sound thus developed undergoes no further change beyond the fact that in words like ' *bier* ' a vowel glide has developed after the (ī) before the *r*, which was subsequently lost in pronunciation, while (ī) has become (i) in Standard English : (biə), etc.

This raising of (ē) to (ī) could not have taken place until the old ī of O. and M.E. had been diphthongized, otherwise the new (ī) would have shared its fate.

The Treatment of M.E. Slack (ẹ̄).—After the raising of (ō), (ẹ̄) was gradually made tense, and thus a new (ē) arose. The raising of this sixteenth-century (e) to (ī) did not, apparently, take place in the received pronunciation before the eighteenth century, but it must have occurred among some speakers as early as the first quarter of the seventeenth century, since Gill complains of a foppish pronunciation of *meat* as (mīt) instead of (mēt), and (līv), *leave*, instead of (lēv). This is not merely a case of an old-fashioned speaker objecting to a new pronunciation which was already well established, since the change did not become widespread till much later. It is impossible to say whether this seventeenth-century raising of the new (ē) had its origin in a provincial or a class dialect, but in any case it is a good example of the fact that what is deemed, at one period, an affected pronunciation often represents a genuine tendency of language, which later on becomes universal.

It is interesting to note that the Irish brogue retains the seventeenth and eighteenth century pronunciations of M.E. (ẹ̄), as (ē); (hēt), heat, (sē), sea, (trēt), treat, (bēt) beat,

(konsēl), conceal, (dēl), deal, etc., are all regular seventeenth
and eighteenth century pronunciations, which are still
heard in Ireland.

Standard English retains (ē) as (*ei*) in a few words : *great*,
break—where, perhaps, the *r* may have prevented raising—
and *steak*, which must, perhaps, be regarded as a provincial
survival.   Curiously enough, (brīk) is quite a common pronunciation in Ireland to-day, and this form and (grīt) are
both recorded for the eighteenth century.   The vowel in
head, dead, bread, red, etc., which in M.E. was (ɛ̄), is the
result of an Early Modern shortening.   The unshortened
forms are heard in Sc. (hīd, dīd), etc., where the normal
eighteenth-century raising has taken place.   The shortening
of the vowel in these words which is common in Sc. must
be quite recent.

M.E. ī and oi.—The former sound has invariably become
the diphthong (*ai*) in Present-day English.   That the
process must have begun in the first quarter of the sixteenth
century is certain, as we have already indicated, from the
fact that Palsgrave (1530) distinctly identifies the pronunciation of M.E. (ē) with that of French *ī*, which latter,
he says, is pronounced 'almost as we sound *e* with vs.'   It is
curious that, although Palsgrave implies a difference between
French and English *ī*, he does not definitely suggest that
the latter is a diphthong, and neither Smith, Bullokar, nor
Gill hint at all clearly at diphthongal pronunciation.   On
the other hand, in the *Hymn to the Virgin ī* is transliterated *ei* in *ei = I—abeiding*, abiding, *Kreist*, Christ ; and
Salesbury writes *vein* for vine, *ddein*, thine, *deitses* (daitʃɛz)
for the provincial pronunciation of 'ditch,' etc.   Hart also
writes *ei—reid bei*, ' ride by,' which leaves no doubt that

21

these writers recognised the diphthongal character of the sound. In the next century the first element is identified by Wilkins as the sound in *but*, which, as we shall see, had in his day already a pronunciation not far removed from the present sound, probably that of rather a higher back vowel. Holder states that the sound is a diphthong composed of a, i, or e, i.   Cooper gives the same account of the sound as Wilkins, and Miege says the best way of describing the sound is by the two vowels a and i.

An important point is that both Cooper and Jones identify the sound of *ī* in *wine, guide*, with that of *oi* in *joint, broil*, etc.   In this connection we may note that Pope rhymes *join* with *line*.   (*Cf.* p. 67 above.)

The meaning of all this is that M.E. *ī* from early in the sixteenth century underwent a process of diphthongization, and by the last half of the seventeenth century had reached the stage (ai) or (əi), in which stage it was identical with the contemporary pronunciation of the old French diphthong *oi* (in joy, join, etc.).   This accounts for Pope's rhyme above.   Henceforth the *normal* development of both classes of words would, of course, have been the same, and Present-day English shows the last stage in that development in the diphthong (*ai*) in (w*ai*f, l*ai*n, f*ai*n, t*ai*m), etc., wife, *line*, *fine*, time, etc. In the other class of words, however, those with old *oi*, the old diphthong has been artificially reintroduced through the influence of the spelling; hence *line* and *join* no longer rhyme in Standard English.   In Vulgar and Dialectal English, however, the old *oi* has pursued its normal course of development, and has become (*ai*), just as old *ī* has.   Hence we get the 'vulgar' (b*ai*l, dž*ai*n, *ai*l), etc., which comic writers express

by the spellings *bile, jine, ile,* for *boil, join, oil,* etc.   Here
again the Irish brogue preserves the eighteenth-century
sound, and has (ai) or (əi) in both classes of words, which
is the explanation of the popular belief, in this country, that
an Irishman calls himself what the humorous writers spell
as ' *Oirishman,*' and that he pronounces (*woif, foiv, ʃoin*) for
wife, five, shine, etc.   The eighteenth-century pronunciation of this diphthong is approximately preserved also in
Oxfordshire and Berkshire.

M.E. ō.—The symbol *o* represented two distinct long
vowels in M.E. : (*a*) The old *tense* ō, as in *gōd,* ' good ';
blōd, ' blood '; *sōna,* ' soon,' etc. ; (*b*) a *slack* vowel with an
o-quality, and which had two origins : (1) the rounding of
O.E. *ā,* as in *stōn,* ' stone,' O.E. *stān ; old,* O.E. *āld ;* and
(2) the lengthening of O.E. *ŏ* in open syllables, as in *þrōte,*
' throat,' O.E. *þrŏtu ; ōpen,* O.E. *ŏpen,* etc.   The slack
sound was often written *oa* in M.E., but not with perfect
regularity, and the tense was frequently written *oo* to
express length, but this symbol is very often written for
the long slack also, as in *stoon,* etc.

Development of M.E. tense ō.—This sound, originally
probably the mid-back-tense-round, as in Modern French
beau, was gradually over-rounded, passing through the
stage of the Modern Swedish ō in *sol,* ' sun,' which, to
unaccustomed ears, has almost the acoustic effect of (ū),
and then raised until it became a fully-formed (ū).

The sixteenth-century writers on the subject leave no
doubt that this stage was reached by the middle of that
century.   It is frankly described by the best authorities
as an (ū)- sound.   This sound, when once developed,
either (1) remains until the present time, as in *spoon, root,*

fool, shoe, loose, etc. (=spūn, rūt, fūl, ʃū, lūs); or (2) it
has undergone (in Standard English) a recent (early nine-
teenth-century [?]) shortening, in which case it also becomes
slack, as in *good, book, wood, foot,* etc. (gud, buk, wud,
fut); or (3) it underwent shortening to (ŭ) already in the
sixteenth century. The fate of this sixteenth-century
shortening we shall discuss under the treatment of sixteenth-century and M.E. (ŭ).

[NOTE.—*Smith* (1568) says that the Scots pronounce (ȳ) in
cook, good, blood, hood, flood, book, took, evidently referring
to the same sound as is still heard in Sc. as the representative of O.E. tense *ō*.]

M.E. slack ō.—This sound, probably the mid-back-slack-
round, was preserved in early Mod. Eng. This is confirmed by the identification of it with Welsh *ō,* with the
Italian 'open' *o,* and as the long sound of short English *o.*
Smith (1568) gives the pairs *smock—smoke, hop—hope, sop
—soap, not—note, rob—robe,* etc., as showing the short and
long of the same vowel. *Florio* (1611) identifies the sound
of Italian 'open' *o* with that in English *bone, dog, God,
rod, stone, tone,* etc.

Gill (1621) recognises only one *o*-sound—short, as in *coll,*
long, as in *coal.* Up to this point, after the raising and
over-rounding of the old tense *ō* to (ū), no tense *ō* existed
in English, only (ō). In 1653, however, *Wallis* recognises
two long *o*-sounds, one identical with French *au* (ō), the
other long a variety of that in *folly, cost,* etc. The former
of these sounds is, of course, the tense *ō,* and has developed
out of the long slack of the former generation. It is mentioned by *Wallis* as occurring in *one, none, whole, coal, boat;*
and *Wilkins* also mentions an *ō,* obviously the same sound,

which has no corresponding short sound in English, which is found in *boat, foale, vote, mote, pole, rode*. *Wallis's one, none* (ōn, nōn) belong, of course, to a different type of pronunciation from that used to-day in these words. *Wallis's* other long *o*-sound is a new slack *o*, developed from an earlier (*a*u), which will be discussed later.

The new middle seventeenth-century long tense *o* just described, derived from the earlier long slack, was preserved in English until it was diphthongized to its present various diphthongal forms in the nineteenth century.

As regards M.E. *ŏ* little need be said, as it has changed but little, beyond being lowered, perhaps, during the eighteenth century, from a *mid* to a *low*-back-slack-round.

M.E. ŭ.—This was, in all probability, a tense vowel, and remained unchanged down to the end of the sixteenth century. During the sixteenth century the number of words containing this sound was increased by the addition of several with a shortened form of the new (ū) from M.E. tense (ō). Among words with original *ŭ* which are mentioned by the sixteenth-century writers as still retaining this sound are *buck, gut, lust, suffer, thunder*, all of which are transliterated with *w* by Salesbury (*bwck, gwt*, etc.); *but, luck, mud, full, pull*, etc., and among those with the new (ū) from (ō) for which a shortened pronunciation is established are : *good, flood, look, blood, book*.

During the seventeenth century short *u* was gradually unrounded in all those words in which it occurred. This is made clear by the statements of the authorities, some of whom are at a loss to describe the new sound. *Wallis* says short *u* has an ' obscure sound ' which resembles that of the final syllable of French *serviteur ;* Wilkins describes it as 'a simple letter, a pert, sonorous guttural, being framed by a free emission of breath from the throat.' Holder gives a very definite account of what we should now call a high-back-unrounded vowel, saying that that *u* is an (u) sound ' in which the lip does not concur, as in *cut*, *full* ' (kat, fal). This can only mean unrounded (u). This is the ancestor of our present sound, which has, however, been lowered from a high to a mid-back. It should be noted that in Present-day Standard the old (u) is still kept, as a rule, after lip consonants (*put*, *pull*, *bull*, *full*, etc.), though now pronounced slack, having probably been restored, if, indeed, it actually ever was unrounded, before the tongue position was lowered. This is not universally the case, however, as is seen from *but*, *mud*, *punt*, etc., which have the unrounded sound.

The seventeenth-century authorities are not always in agreement with Present-day polite usage as regards the distribution of the unrounded vowel, especially in words where it represents the shortened sixteenth-century (ū) from tense (ō). The following pronunciations are all recorded in the seventeenth century : from (bazəm), ' bosom,' (fat), ' foot,' (gad), ' good,' (had), ' hood,' (sat), ' soot,' (stad), ' stood,' (tak), ' took,' (wad), ' wood,' (wal), ' wool,' all of which would be regarded as vulgar provincialisms by educated society to-day. They may, of course, still be heard in the dialects. The Standard pronunciation of to-day, in the above words, namely (fut), etc., is, of course, a later shortening, as already pointed out, of a seventeenth-century type with (ū) or perhaps with (u), since the shortened types are also recorded in late seventeenth century, and side by side with (fat), which, by the way, is designated *barbare* by Cooper, we get also (fut) and (fūt).

On the other hand, (ŭ) is recorded by Cooper in *blood*, *flood*, *brother*, where we now have (a). In any case, it would appear that fashion has decided which type of an old (M.E.) tense $\bar{o}$-word shall be considered as correct at the present day. Thus in 'spoon' (spūn) we have six-teenth-century (ū) preserved; in 'book' (bᴜk) we have a seventeenth or eighteenth century shortening of this (ū); and in blood (blad), (maðə), 'mother,' (braðə), 'brother,' we have representatives of a sixteenth-century shortening of the new (ū), which, as we have seen, underwent un-rounding in the following century.

There is no reason, except fashion, why (blad) should be polite, but (fat) vulgar, nor why, on the other hand, (blᴜd) or (blud) should have vanished from educated speech.

The seventeenth-century unrounding was not carried out equally in all dialects. Thus, in Lancashire sixteenth-century ŭ was partially unrounded and lowered, and the characteristic tense sound which results is used in all cases to represent M.E. and sixteenth-century ŭ—that is, equally in *cut*, *pull*, *foot*, the full unrounded vowel of the Standard dialect being unknown, and also the fully rounded high-back-slack. Those sixteenth-century (ū)s which were not shortened during that century remain unchanged, as in (kūk, būk), etc.

In other forms of English, again, such as some of the Yorkshire dialects, sixteenth-century (ŭ) undergoes no unrounding at all, but remains everywhere as (ᴕ̈), with loss of tenseness—*e.g.*, *full*, *cut*, *nut*, etc. (*cf.* Wright, *Windhill Dialect*, § 111).

In Scotch dialects sixteenth-century (ŭ) has been unrounded, and has become the mid-back-tense, as in
Standard English.   In the Standard English as spoken in
Scotland the slack sound of short (u) is unknown, and the
archaic short tense sound is preserved, *full* and *fool* both
having the same sound, namely high-back-tense-round,
short.

In the genuine Sc. vernacular O.E. tense ō underwent a
totally different development already in the M.E. period
from that which it followed in Southern English.

M.E. ū.—Just before M.E. tense ō was raised to (ū),
the original ū underwent the beginnings of a process of
diphthongization.   From Palsgrave's remarks it would
appear that already in his day there was a very slight
degree of diphthongization, sufficient to distinguish the
sound from the newly-developed (ū), but not enough to confuse it with the older (au) in (graunt), 'grant,' (faul), 'fall'
(see below, pp. 333-336).   The process of diphthongization
probably consisted of, first, a sudden decrease of stress
during the utterance of (ū), thus giving (úu) or (ūu); then
the dissimilation of the two elements, possibly by partially
unrounding and lowering the first element to (ō), giving
(ŏu); then the complete unrounding of the first element to
(ắu); then shortening and slacking to (au), which is approximately the present pronunciation in the Standard
dialect.   Various vulgarisms and provincial forms of this
diphthong exist, such as (æu, eu).   In some dialects
monophthonging, apparently from the (au) stage, has
taken place—*e.g.*, *Windhill Dialect* hās, etc., from (haus).
On the other hand, the *Dialect of Addlington* (Lancs) has
(brēn, hēs, ɛ, ēnd), etc., = ' brown,' ' house,' ' how,' ' hound,'

where the monophthongization has apparently taken place from the (ɛu) stage. (*Cf.* Hargreaves, *Addlington Dialect*, § 12.) There is no reason to suppose that (ɛu, æu) are intermediate stages on the way to (au); they are, rather, special further developments of that sound.

M.E. ȳ written u.—The sound ȳ—that is, the high-front-tense-round—survived throughout the M.E. period. Its origins are: (1) O.E. ȳ (in the Southern or Saxon dialects); (2) Anglo-French ȳ (written *u*). There seems no doubt that the (ȳ) sound remained in English pronunciation down to the middle of the seventeenth century, since writers as late as *Wallis* (1653) identify the ' long *u*' in *muse, tune, lute, dure* (endure), *mute, view, lieu*, with French *u*, that is, of course (ȳ), and Wallis states that some also pronounce *eu* or *iu*. This would imply that there were two pronunciations, a simple (ȳ) and a diphthongized (iy). *Price* also (1688) suggests a diphthongal pronunciation in *muse, refuse*, etc., ' as if it were composed of *iw*.' On the other hand, Wilkins (1688) says that Englishmen cannot pronounce French, or, as he calls it, ' whistling *u*,' since to them, as ' to all nations among whom it is not used, it is of so laborious and difficult pronunciation that I shall not proceed further to any explication of it.' Wilkins transliterates ' communion' as (komiūnion). Apparently, then, by this time there were two old-fashioned types of pronunciation of this sound— (iȳ and ȳ), and the newer pronunciations (iū and ū). These sounds represented, not only M.E. ȳ, but also M.E. *eu*, as in (diȳ), 'dew,' M.E. *deu*; ([k]niȳ), 'knew,' M.E. *kneu*; (bliȳ), ' blue,' M.E. *bleu*, etc. It seems probable

that the (ȳ) lost its front quality in the third quarter of
the seventeenth century, so that the two types were (bliu),
corresponding to earlier (bliȳ), and blū), corresponding to
earlier (blȳ). At the present day, in the Standard language, we have on the one hand (blū), ' blue,' (þrū),
' threw,' (rūl), ' rule,' etc., and on the other (tjūzd*i*),
' tuesday,' (mjūz), ' muse,' (fjū), ' few,' (stjūpid), also
(stj*u*pi*d*), ' stupid,' (djūk), ' duke,' etc., corresponding to
sixteenth-century (iȳ) and (ȳ) respectively. In dialectal
speech different types often exist from those used in the
Standard, and (dūk) from (dȳk), (stūpid) from (stȳpid),
(tūzd*i*) from (tȳzdei), (nū), ' new,' from (nȳ), are quite
common. Again, provincial (rí̄ul), ' rule,' (blí̄ū), and
(bljū), ' blue,' (frí̄ut), ' fruit,' etc., also exist.

Cure is now variously (kjūə, kj*u*ə, kjɔə, and kjɔ̄), or, in
those dialects where the *r* is preserved, (kjūr) or (kjuər).
Wallis indicates the pronunciation (kȳr), and Cooper,
already, (kiuər). The only word which preserves O.E.
(Saxon) *ȳ* in the Standard dialect is *bruise* (brūz), where
the *ui* is actually a Southern M.E. spelling for *ȳ*.

The dialects of Devonshire and Somerset seem still to
preserve a sound approximating to the M.E. and sixteenth-
century (ȳ) to the present day.

The Middle English Diphthongs.

M.E. ai and ei.—These diphthongs were often confused
in Late M.E., to judge by the spelling. The Welsh
authorities of the sixteenth century make no distinction.
The *Hymn to the Virgin* writes *ai, ae, ay* in *away, awae,
kae, agaynst,* and *ei* only in *ddey, ddei. Salesbury* transliterates both sounds by ai, ay—*vain* = ' vein ' and ' vain ';

nayl = 'nail.'   Salesbury uses *ei* for the new diphthong
from old (ī).

On the other hand, Palsgrave (1530) distinguishes
between (ɛi) in *obey, grey,* in which '*e* shall have his distinct sound,' and (*ai*) in *rayne,* ' rain,' *payn,* ' pain,' *fayne,*
'fain,' etc., in which '*a* is sounded distinctly, and *i* shortly
and confusedly.'   *Smith* (1568) says the distinction between the two is very slight, but admits (ɛi) in *feint,
deinte, peint, fein* (verb).   He says that certain affected
women, who wish to appear to speak ' more urbanely,'
pronounce (ei) or (ɛi) not only in words where it is written,
but also in words with *ai,* as in *dai, wai, mai, tail, fail, pain,
claim, plai, arai,* etc.   Of these, *wai,* ' way,' should, from
the etymological point of view, have (ɛi).   *Smith* says the
first element is short among ' urbane ' speakers, but that
country folks pronounce it long, ' with an odious kind of
sound, fat and greasy to excess,' saying *daai, paai,* etc.

These remarks surely mean that the distinction between
ai and *ei* no longer existed, except, perhaps, artificially,
through the influence of the spelling.   Apparently *Smith*
himself pronounced (*ai*) with the first element very short
and slightly fronted ; old-fashioned people and country-
folk said (*ai*) with a full back vowel in the first element,
and affected persons and ' silly women,' or ' mopseys,' as
they were called, (æi) or even (ɛi), thus anticipating the
fashionable pronunciation of a later day.   There can be
no doubt that the pronunciation of the affected persons
was gaining the day, for Hart, in 1569, recognises no diphthong at all, but gives *pre, we, se,* etc., for ' pray,' ' way,'
' say.'   *Gill* (1629) strongly condemns ' mopseys' in general,
and Hart in particular, and disapproves of (mēdz) for

(ma͞ids), ' maids,' and (plɛ̄) for (plai). *Butler* (1623) records with disapproval the pronunciation (ɛ̄) in *may, nay, play, pray, say, stay, fray, slay, pay, bailey, travail. Wallis* and *Wilkins* both describe a diphthong that must be intended for (æi). *Price* (1668) admits a diphthong (æi) in a good many words with *ai* and *ey*, but a single vowel (ɛ̄) apparently in many others. *Cooper* (1685) admits a diphthong in a few words—*brain, eight, frail*—otherwise *ai, ay* for him has the sound of contemporary *a*, that is, (æ) or (ɛ), and he gives the following words as pairs containing the same vowel, long and short respectively : *sail—sell, saint—sent, tail—tell, taint—tent*, which must imply (ɛ̄) in (sɛ̄l), ' sail,' etc.

The result of these somewhat contradictory accounts seems to be that M.E. *ei, ai* were early (in the sixteenth century) levelled under one sound in the best speech, probably (ai). The diphthongal character was lost in some dialects, retained in others, though whether these were class dialects, or associated with a geographical area, we cannot say. The Standard language tended more and more to front and raise the first element in those cases where diphthongal pronunciation remained, and by the end of the seventeenth century the monophthongal pronunciation (ǣ), or among the younger generation (ɛ̄), was fully established, so that the sound was levelled under that of M.E. *ā*, and henceforth shared the same development, being gradually tensened to (ē), which was subsequently diphthongized again to (ei) or (ɛi) in the nineteenth century.

Many dialects retain to the present day the M.E. vowel (ai) recorded as that of country folks in the seventeenth century, in words like (tail, pail), ' tail,' ' pail,' etc.

Early Modern English au.—This sound existed in the sixteenth century in words of several classes. They were mostly inherited from M.E., and to this there is only one possible exception. The (*au*) diphthongs, which are certainly of M.E. origin, occurred in the following conditions:

1. M.E. *au* or *aw* from O.E. *-ag-:* M.E. *sāwe,* ' saw,' O.E. *sagu;* M.E. *drawen,* 'draw,' O.E. *dragan;* from O.E. *-aw-:* M.E. *clawe,* 'claw,' O.E. *clawu;* O.E. *-ah-:* M.E. *laughen,* O.E. *hlahhan.*

2. M.E. *au* from Anglo-Fr. *au: cause,* ' cause.'

3. In the combination original *an* followed by another consonant in words of Anglo-Fr. or Fr. origin : *daunger,* ' danger '; *aungel,* ' angel '; *haunt, jaundice,* etc.

(*au*) further occurred in stressed syllables where *a* was followed by *l* in words both of English and French origin : *all,* sixteenth-century (*aul*), *fall,* sixteenth-century (*faul*), *call,* sixteenth - century (*kaul*). According to Sweet (*H.E.S.,* 784), this diphthong was developed in the Early Modern period.

The history of this (*au*) from the sixteenth century onwards is clear. The diphthong persisted throughout the century, but towards the end, the pronunciation (ɔ)— *i.e.,* low-back-tense-round — or something very like it, appears to be already established. The process of change must have been : the first element was rounded through the influence of the (*u*), giving (ɔu), then the second element was absorbed, and the sound was monophthongized to (ɔ) and tensened to (ɔ), its present form. From the seventeenth century onwards (ɔ) is the only representative of the old (*au*).

Sixteenth-century examples are (baul, haul, waul, faul,

kɑul, hɑu, lɑuful, strɑu, mɑu, tʃɑuns, grɑunt, dʒɑundis, lɑuns), etc. = *ball, hall, wall, fall, call, haw, lawful, straw, maw, chance, grant, jaundice, lance*. The (ɔu) stage is occasionally recorded in the seventeenth century, but, presumably, did not last long. In that century most of these words are recorded with (ɔ), but occasionally, apparently, with (ɔu), written *ou* by Cooper and *oou* by Gill, which probably represents the intermediate stage.

Of the words mentioned above with (au) before *n*, however, only *jaundice* exists with (ɔ) in the Standard English of the present day, and many speakers, including the present writer, pronounce (dzāndis) here with (ā), as in all the other words in the list with a nasal.

In several other words of this group we have doublets in the polite pronunciation of to-day—*e.g.*, (hɔnʃ) and (hānʃ), 'haunch'; (lɔnʃ) and (lānʃ), as well as (lænʃ), 'launch'; (vɔnt) and (vānt), 'vaunt'; (lɔndri) and (lāndri), 'laundry'; (hɔnt) and (hānt), 'haunt'; also in the name *Saunders* or *Sanders*, which is pronounced according to the taste or traditions of its owner (sɔndəz) or (sāndəz). *Dance* is pronounced both (dāns) and (dæns), (dɔns) having disappeared; *lance* = (lāns) or (læns), but there is no (lɔns), and the name *Launcelot* is never (lɔnsilot), only (lānsilot) or (lænsilot).

The first point to be clear about is that the pronunciation (ɔ) in any of these words represents an older (au). But (au) or its descendant (ɔ) were not the only forms in use in the seventeenth century. Side by side with these we find also doublets with (æ) which are sometimes given by the same authorities as alternatives to the (ɔ) pronunciation. Thus we find (dænt, flænt, hænt, dʒænt, tænt) = daunt, flaunt, haunt, jaunt, taunt. These would appear

to be the ancestors of the modern forms with (ā). They
gave rise to two types—one which retained (æ), another in
which it was lengthened to (ǣ). The short forms remain,
and correspond to the present-day (dæns, lænʃ), etc. ;
the long forms develop (ā) in the late eighteenth century,
and are therefore the direct ancestors of (lānʃ, lāndri), etc.

The existence of the types (lænʃ, lɔnʃ) side by side in
the seventeenth century shows that by the side of (launʃ),
etc., which gave rise to the latter, forms such as (lanʃ), the
ancestor of the former, must have existed, although not
recorded, in the sixteenth century. This proves that in
M.E. the Anglo-French combination -an- before a consonant was not universally diphthongized to (aun), but
that a type -(an)- also existed. This probability is also
suggested by the fluctuation of M.E. spelling, which writes
both *haunten* and *hanten*. Non-diphthongized forms also
existed of the -al- combinations. Present-day (kāf),
' calf,' (kām), ' calm,' (kwām), ' qualm,' (sām), ' psalm,'
(hāf), ' half,' etc., are from eighteenth-century (kǣf),
seventeenth-century (kæf), sixteenth-century (kalf and
kaf), and so on with the others. The pronunciation
(kwɔm), which is sometimes heard, of course represents a
doublet (kwaulm). Scotch (hɔf), etc., is the representative
of sixteenth-century (haulf).

Present-day English has (lāftə, drāft) by the side of
(tɔt, fɔt), ' laughter, draught, taught, aught.' Here,
again, we have the survivals of two distinct types : (lāftə),
etc., comes from eighteenth-century (lǣftər), from (læftər),
from lafter). This may well be a M.E. treatment of (h),
in which case there would be no diphthonging. Those
speakers, on the other hand, who said (lahter) developed

the form (lauͅ[h]ter), which is, indeed, recorded for the sixteenth century, together with its descendant (lɔ[h]ter) later on. This is the form apparently represented by our traditional spelling. This type still survives in Scotch. (tɔt) is the normal development of M.E. *tāhte*, and in this word it would seem that no doublet with (f) survives.

M.E. ou.—The vowel in *thought, brought, daughter*, etc., which represents M.E. *o*, with a glide vowel developed before *h*, as in the case of M.E. *-ah-*, has apparently passed through an (ōu) stage, at which point it must have been levelled with the earlier (*au*), or the series may have been (*ou*) with slack *o*, (ō) with long slack *o* after absorption of *u*, and the levelling of such a long vowel with (ɔ) is a natural tendency.

The Consonants in the Modern Period.

On the whole, but little change has taken place in the pronunciation of the consonants since the sixteenth century. There are, however, a few points which deserve notice.

The symbols *-gh-* medially or finally were pronounced, according to the nature of the preceding vowel, as a front or back open voiceless consonant (h). That this had in some dialects a lip modification, when back, is evident from the fact that in a large number of words in Standard English it has become pure (f). In words where it represented a *Front* open consonant, and in a few where it was *Back*, (h) remained, apparently with a very slight consonantal friction, well into the seventeenth century, in the pronunciation of some speakers. It seems probable that in most words with back (h) two types of pronunciation existed in the sixteenth century—(lafter) and (lɑhter), (boft) and (boht), 'laughter,' 'bought,' etc.   At any rate, both of these types are proved to have existed in the above words and in many others, while the evidence of the Modern dialects, taken together with the Standard language, would greatly extend the list.   Of course, no (u) glide was developed in the (f) types, and there are consequently no examples of the combination (-ɔf-) in these words, unless, indeed, it exists in some of the popular dialects, in which case it is the result of a blending of two types—the vowel of one and the consonant of the other.

Initial kn-, gn-.—The combination *-kn-* retained the initial stop, at any rate until the seventeenth century. From the testimony of the authorities it seems probable that *n* was unvoiced in this position, and the (*k*) lost. Cooper says that *knave* is pronounced like *hnave*, which seems to imply a voiceless *n*.   In the late seventeenth and early eighteenth centuries the authorities are at variance as to the pronunciation of *gn-*, Jones making it ordinary (voiced) *n*, while Lediard describes voiceless *n*.   Possibly *gn-* and *kn-* had both been levelled under the latter sound, in which case we might conclude that in the early eighteenth century the voiceless pronunciation still existed, while the new voiced *n* was coming in.

Initial wr-.—The *w* was still heard down to the beginning of the eighteenth century.   It still remains in this position in certain Scotch dialects, as (v)—*e.g.*, *vrīt,* 'write,' in Aberdeenshire.

Loss of r.—This is, perhaps, one of the most considerable changes that has taken place in recent English, especially the Standard dialect.   *r* is lost medially before

22

consonants, and finally unless the next word in the breath-group begins with a vowel. With the loss of *r* certain modifications have occurred in the preceding vowels: (1) Development of vowel murmur, as in (faiə, biəd); (2) the levelling of several distinct vowels under (ā), as in (bād, wād, lān, wām, hād), or under (ɔ), as in (hɔd, mɔ, pjɔ).

CHAPTER XV

THE STUDY OF PRESENT-DAY ENGLISH

ALTHOUGH it has been found convenient, as a matter of systematic arrangement, to reserve this subject until the end of the present work, it is nevertheless strongly to be recommended that, in teaching, the study of actual living English should serve as the starting-point of, and as the preparation for, the historical study of our language.

The reason for this must have become apparent from the general tenor of this book. The first preparation for a competent study of the history of a language is some training in phonetics, and for this the native spoken language must serve as a basis. The first lessons in accurate observation and analysis of speech sounds must be learned, as has been repeatedly pointed out, from one's own speech, and that of one's associates.

From the study of the sounds of his own language, the student will naturally proceed to examine the structure, the accidence, and syntax of the spoken form of English. The methods of such an investigation have been exemplified in Mr. Sweet's *Primer of Spoken English*, 1900, and this admirable work may serve as a model to the teacher who conducts a class in the subject, though it must naturally be borne in mind that just as Mr. Sweet has described his *own* pronunciation, so the student must learn to observe and describe his own, noting the points of agreement and of difference between his own speech habits and those of his associates, and between that set forth in the *Primer*.

When at least some knowledge of the facts of contemporary English has been gained, the next step is to inquire how they arose; and to answer this question involves an inquiry into the earlier forms of our language. For this, one trained to observe the facts of actually existing speech has the best kind of preparation. He has been brought face to face with the *realities* of language in its spoken form; he has learnt to recognise that linguistic study is primarily concerned with what is uttered and heard; he has acquired to some extent the power of understanding what is meant by sound change; he has found from observation that various factors are at work in modifying the speech of the individual; he knows something of analogy; he has seen that speech habits vary from individual to individual, and from community to community. Thus, from a systematic and intelligent study of the spoken language, the beginner has been made familiar with many of the facts and general principles which it is essential to know and understand in order to grasp the vital points of linguistic development.

The Relation of Written and Spoken English.

The first ' vulgar error ' which it is necessary to dispel is the belief that good speakers, in ordinary conversation, merely reproduce the language of books, and that the Spoken is based upon the Literary language.

The language of conversation has an independent life,

quite apart from the written forms of speech. Literature, among a highly-educated community, especially one whose ideas and experiences are drawn more from books than from life, undoubtedly influences the Spoken language, but it is not the main source of this. The source of Spoken English is, mainly and primarily, direct tradition of utterance, passed on from one generation to another. The sources of the language of literature are twofold: first, literary tradition, and secondly, though equally important, the spoken language of the period. The term *Spoken English* has been used in the present case to cover all the various forms of the language spoken throughout the country ; the term *Written Language*, to cover at once the language of literature proper, and the humbler attempts of ordinary speakers to record their ideas in writing instead of in speech sounds—to use, that is, symbols of a different order to represent what is already a group of symbols.

It will be convenient, for purposes of contrast, to select one type of *Written English* on one hand, and of Spoken English on the other. For the former we take what we may call the *Literary English* proper : that form of the written language which is regulated by tradition, which is deliberate, self-conscious, and artistic. For the latter we take what may be called *Standard Spoken English*, which we have often referred to by this name in earlier chapters of this book.

There is what the present writer believes to be an unfortunate habit among some authorities on linguistic subjects, of bracketing Literary and Standard Spoken English together, under the single name *Literary English*, thereby confusing two distinct phenomena, and suggesting the very fallacy which it is so important to avoid, namely, that this form of the spoken language is derived from, or a reproduction of, the language of literature. The idea that those speakers of English who do not speak what is technically known as a *Dialect*, in the special sense of the term, are reproducing, or attempting to reproduce, in their speech the language of books is fundamentally erroneous. This would be possible, though not desirable, as regards style and vocabulary ; it is impossible in the domain of pronunciation. To speak of the *sounds* of Literary English is an absurdity, since what is written has no sounds until it is uttered, and then it naturally is pronounced according to the speech habits of the particular reader. When Dr. Wright, in the *English Dialect Gr.*, speaks of the pronunciation of 'Literary English,' he means, of course, *Standard Spoken English*. What we have called *Standard English*, but what may also be called *Polite English*, or, with certain qualifications, simply *Good English*, is as much a reality as the dialect of West Somerset or of Windhill ; it has had a normal and natural growth from a particular form of fifteenth-century English, and although it has, in the course of time, incorporated fresh elements from the outside, and discarded others that were once part and parcel of it, its history can be traced, as we have attempted to show in the former chapter, with considerable certainty for more than 300 years. Standard English, it is true, is no longer a regional dialect ; it is emphatically a class dialect, which is fast absorbing other forms of Spoken English. Present-day Standard English, as we have already seen, springs originally from the same source as the literary dialect—that is, from the London dialect of the fifteenth century ; and just as this, in its written form, at a much earlier date, gained universal currency in writings, so the former is now gradually but surely gaining ground among all classes and in all areas. What the printing press did long ago for the written form, modern means of locomotion are doing to-day for the spoken. We shall return later to the important question of 'good' and 'bad' in speech ; in the meantime, it may be pointed out that the Standard dialect of English is to some extent more artificial than other forms of Spoken English, in that it is more subject to fashion, and, it may perhaps be admitted, more shaped, in any given age, by a deliberate selective and eliminating process. What, then, is the relation of this form of Spoken English to the language of Literature ?

Both, as has been said, are sprung originally from the same source ; they have developed differently by virtue of the different conditions under which they severally exist. One great and obvious external difference between Written and Spoken English is that, whereas the spelling of the former is fixed, and no longer expresses the variations of sound which exist in different areas, and arise in different ages, the spoken form is for ever undergoing changes in pronunciation, with the passage of time and the spread of this dialect among all sections of the population. The spelling of Literary English, then, no longer expresses, even approximately, the facts of actual utterance, as they exist in Standard Spoken English, in its different varieties.

But the differences between Written and Spoken English are deeper than those produced merely by a pronunciation which has far outstripped its symbolical expression, and include also differences of style, of idiom, of choice of words, and grammatical forms.

The language of literature, in all these respects, is always slightly more archaic than the uttered speech of the same period ; certain words and expressions are avoided in writing a serious prose, because they are felt to be too familiar — too closely associated with the commonplaces and vulgarities of everyday existence; others, on the other hand, find no place in the Spoken language, because they seem to savour of pomposity or bookishness.

But literary style changes from age to age. To a certain extent each generation has its own style. Matthew Arnold appears to fail in perfect critical insight when he points to a noble passage from Dryden's Preface to his translation of the *Æneid*, and remarks that it is ' such a prose as we would all gladly use if we only knew how.' This is neither adequate as an appreciation of Dryden, nor is it strictly true. Only in very special circumstances, and as an exercise in imitation, would a writer of the present day ' gladly use' the prose of the seventeenth century. Herein, indeed, lies the heart of the whole matter. The literary language is kept living and flexible only by a close relation with the colloquial speech of the age. A purely literary tradition, however splendid, will not suffice for the style of a later period. A literary tradition alone, deprived of the living spirit which informs the great works that created the tradition, is a lifeless thing. The breath of life comes into literary form from the living spoken language, as it comes into literature itself from touch with life. Thus, while great prose owes much to tradition, it owes still more to the racy speech of the age in which it is produced. The best prose is never entirely remote in form from the best corresponding conversational style of the period. A robust, intense style glows with emotion, and pulsates with passion; a calm and restrained prose must yet be animated with an undercurrent of strenuous thought or genuine feeling. If these be lacking, the most accomplished reproduction of an old literary model is stiff and uninteresting.

The impression made by fine prose of any age, and not infrequently also by verse, of the less artificial and elaborate kind, is that the author writes very much as he would *speak*, if he were conveying the same ideas by word of mouth. This is felt strongly in reading Chaucer's *Canterbury Tales*, in those passages where the felicitousness and competence of expression reaches its highest point; it is felt in reading Latimer's Sermons; in nearly all of Dryden's critical prose; in the Letters of Horace Walpole and of Gray; in Swift, in Goldsmith, and in Sheridan.

It is this quality of vitality, which springs from a mastery of the best spoken form of English of his age, that compels our admiration in the prose of Dryden; but what we should 'gladly use' is not his precise form, which is no longer a living vehicle of thought and feeling, but a prose which should combine the elements of literary tradition on the one hand, with those of contemporary colloquial speech on the other, in that just proportion, and with that subtle blending, which is the secret of great writers in all ages. No writer can express himself adequately in a language which is not his own; the thoughts and emotions of one age cannot be conveyed in a style which is outworn; and this has come about when the relation between the language of literature and that of everyday life is severed.

It would probably be a fruitful investigation to trace the connection between the prose style of the seventeenth and eighteenth centuries and that of the closest repro-duction of the conversational style of the corresponding period which we possess—that is, the language of the Comic Drama.

The Spoken Language.

One of the most striking features of living, uttered speech is its adaptability. Standard English is not fixed and rigid in form; in the same period, and in the mouth of the same speaker, it is not invariable under all condi-tions, and in every kind of company. The actual sounds employed, the speed of utterance, the intonation, the sentence structure, the choice of vocabulary, are all variable according to the requirements of the moment. The speaker adapts his speech, both in public oration, and in private conversation, to suit his audience. This modi-fication of the language in its different elements may be deliberate, but for the most part is unconscious and instinctive.

In public speaking, the manner of the discourse of an accomplished and practised orator is determined to a great extent by the size of the audience; but also by the speaker's estimate of their mental calibre, no less than by his own. Upon this power of 'getting into touch' with his hearers, on the part of the speaker, the success and effectiveness of an academic lecture, a political harangue, or an after-dinner speech will largely depend. There is room for an investigation into the variations of style, vocabulary, idiom, and syntax of the same speaker, according to the size, intellectual quality, and general temper of his audience.

Public oratory is that form of the Spoken language which comes nearest to the language of literature in style. But if this form of uttered language is liable to modification in the manner indicated, the private speech of ordinary conversation is no less sensitive to the modifying influences of social atmosphere. There is room for a vast amount of variability in the colloquial speech of the same individual, according to the company in which he is placed. Phraseology, vocabulary, even pronunciation, tend, each and all, to adapt themselves to the personality and attainments of the person addressed. The manner of speech may be perfectly natural, or it may become stilted, pompous, flippant, archaic, or slangy, accordingly as the real or fancied personality of the hearer excites reverence, trepidation, confidence, affection, or contempt in the mind of the speaker. The disparity which provokes such departure from the normal colloquial style, may be of the most varied kind : it may consist in difference of rank, of official status, age, intellectual or moral worth, or in worldly success, all of which affect different minds in different ways.

In some cases convention, as it were, strikes the keynote, by prescribing by what title certain personages shall be addressed, but the rest is left to the instinct or intuition of the speaker. Thus, by a convention which will probably never change, the Deity, in both private and public devotions, is invariably addressed in the second person singular; and in this solitary case the pronoun of that person is preserved, which is otherwise completely obsolete in Standard English, except among members of the Society of Friends.

There can be no doubt that the best speaker, whether in private or public, is he, the form of whose discourse instinctively shapes itself to the requirements of the moment, without any apparent effort or deliberation.

For there is a limit beyond which adaptiveness cannot go, without awakening resentment or uneasiness in the hearers, or, what is perhaps worse, without imperilling the vividness and sense of reality in the expression; and this limit is reached very soon after the modification of form, or choice of verbiage becomes self-conscious and deliberate. If a speaker reacts too much to his environment—to borrow a phrase from the vocabulary of Biology—if he is either overawed by a sense of the superiority of those to whom he speaks, or too deeply conscious of the reverse quality, all naturalness of speech is at an end. For in one case a speaker will speak too carefully and pedantically: he will mince in his pronunciation, and, worst of all, perhaps tend to obsequiousness; in the other, a sense of self-importance may bloat his diction to pomposity, and convey the feeling that he is trying hard to be worthy of himself. Or, again, by a too familiar and undignified discourse, he may make his hearers feel that by an infinite condescension he is coming down from an immeasurable height to their level, and perhaps sinking below it. In both cases the speaker may fall back upon set phrases devoid of character. Thus the right and proper adaptation of spoken language cannot be carried out on any precon-

ceived principle, but must spring from a sympathetic and
humane insight into the personality of those to whom we
speak, a nice appreciation of the psychological conditions
of the moment.   If a speaker would sway his audience to
his own mood, or instil his own opinions into their minds,
if he would ' carry them with him,' as the phrase runs, he
must first lay his finger upon the pulse of their temper
and of their prejudices.   The speaker himself must barely
perceive the process of adaptation, the hearers not at all ;
they are merely conscious that the form in which the ideas
are clothed is entirely suitable and convincing.

Lifeless Forms of English.

A living form of speech is one which expresses real ideas
and feelings and genuine convictions in a form suited to
the audience and the occasion, springing from the mind of
the speaker in the process of his thought, and revealing
something at least of his personality.   In order to arrest
attention and compel interest, an utterance, whether it
be a public oration or familiar discourse, must contain
something more than the obvious truisms of a pro-
position in Euclid ; the style in which the thoughts are
clothed must be personal to the speaker, and not the mere
repetition of set phrases.   The essentials of *living* utterance are, then, reality of conviction, and individuality of
form and phrase.   Both of these qualities are very often
found to a remarkable degree in quite uncultivated, and
even in ' illiterate,' speakers.   From these realities of
speech life, we now turn aside for a short space, to consider
a dreary linguistic waste of crystallized phrases, lifeless
forms devoid of movement or feeling, peopled only with

the ghosts of ideas, and the spectral shadows of human desires.

There are many types of unreal, lifeless English; they range from the terrible phrases of 'Commercial English,' such as 'Your esteemed favour of even date to hand,' through those unconvincing fossils of language which help to fill space in the daily paper—'*The greatest consternation prevailed* when the news of the disaster reached the city,' or the curious jargon known as 'Committee English'—'Your committee beg to report that while fully recognising the importance of the subject of ——, they consider that, under the circumstances, it is undesirable to take any further steps in the matter for the present'—up to the language of public legal documents and of high officialdom. All these lifeless forms of English have at least this in common: they consist largely of cut-and-dried phrases pieced together. In these phrases, whether they be uttered or written, there lurks no human emotion, no intensity of thought; they reveal nothing of the state of mind of him who uses them; they kindle no hope or enthusiasm in the hearer. The cheap verbiage of the penny-a-liner is generally the cloak of his incapacity to express anything; the stereotyped phrases of the fluent committee debater, or of the official generally, are devices for politely shelving inconvenient questions, or are intended to guard the speaker from identifying himself, or his office, too intimately and irrevocably, with any particular line of thought or action. The characteristic effect of a diction of set expressions artfully tagged together, whether this be the result of incompetence, as in the case of a bad writer, or of design, as in that of a wary and

experienced official, is that it is singularly lacking in interest
or power of convincing those to whom it is addressed.
Thus the historian of the Police Court does not quicken
our pulses by a single beat by his account of ' a young lady
of prepossessing appearance, fashionably attired,' etc. If a
body of starving men petition Parliament to relieve their
necessities, it neither appeases their hunger, nor calms
their anxiety, to be told that their circumstances ' will
receive the careful consideration of the Government.'

Clothed in the language of conventional set phrase, the
noblest thoughts and loftiest aspirations are robbed of
their grandeur and become commonplace ; events of the
greatest solemnity and moment, or the actions of heroes,
shrink to the insignificance of a meeting of directors ;
while what is trite or vulgar, in feeling, or in ideas, simply
vanishes altogether amid the meaningless verbiage.

Distressing as the habit is of using a series of stereotyped expressions, even in formal deliverances on public
bodies, or in the written forms in journalism, it must be
recognised that it is very much worse to do so in private
intercourse, either in conversation or in correspondence.
It is felt that to speak ' Committee English ' in private is
an offence which can only arise, either, from ill-breeding,
or from ignorance of the proper forms of polite Spoken
English. ' Proverbial expressions and trite sayings,' says
Lord Chesterfield, ' are the flowers of the rhetoric of a
vulgar man.' Whatever be the cause which induces a
speaker to mask his real feelings and views in this lifeless
form of language, the result is fatal to a satisfactory
understanding. The sense of sincerity, ease, and reality
vanishes, and an uncomfortable atmosphere of uncertainty,

if not of absolute distrust, is created. There can be no doubt that for those who have not habitually heard good, racy, expressive Polite English spoken from childhood, this is a most necessary side of English study from a purely practical point of view. Unfortunately, it is almost universally supposed to be enough to acquire a fairly good knowledge of the *written* language, and the differences between good *Written* and good *Spoken* English are completely ignored, not only in primary schools, but also in the curriculum for the training of teachers.

The art of *speaking* English so as to be 'familiar, but by no means vulgar,' is apparently supposed to be the common heritage of the primary teacher. This is, however, as far as possible from being the case. It is perfectly true that the only way of learning to speak any dialect readily and fluently, whether it be good English or good French, is to hear it and use it so frequently that it becomes instinctive. At the same time, much help in the direction of observation can be given, and should be given systematically. Now, many persons in this country, who are otherwise highly educated, fail signally in possessing a command of easy, natural, Polite Spoken English. The reason for this is that they have not grown up in circles where this kind of English is current, neither have they had their attention directed to its characteristics. The result is they have the choice between the English of books or of set phrases on the one hand, or on the other, a form more or less 'incorrect' or 'provincial,' perhaps, but nevertheless a living form, which they have been carefully taught to avoid.

The fact is that the native form of Spoken English is

eliminated by training, but no colloquial form is put in its place.

The importance of the study of Spoken English has been constantly emphasized in the foregoing pages as a necessary preparation for the historical study of the language, and as a starting-point of phonetic training. From this point of view, the student's own natural speech forms the proper basis of study, and so long as that inquiry is confined to the above-mentioned limits, no question of 'Right' or 'Wrong' arises—merely that of what actually occurs in the speech of a given individual or group of individuals. But from the practical, as contrasted with the purely historical and scientific, standpoint the power of writing and speaking 'correct' English cannot be disregarded in any complete scheme of education, and it is now suggested that it is quite as necessary to *speak* well as to *write* well. In the study of *Spoken English*, from the practical point of view, three main sides of the subject must be dealt with : Pronunciation, Vocabulary, and the choice of Idiom.

Standards of Good or Bad Spoken English.

It has been made abundantly clear in the course of the present volume that there is no *absolute* standard of 'correctness' in language beyond that established by the habitual usage of a given community. Such a standard, as has been said, holds good for that community at a given moment. But as speech habit changes, so ideas of what is 'right' and 'wrong' have also to be readjusted. From this point of view, which is the purely scientific one, there is no question of degrees of worthiness between

23

different dialects ; they are each and all regarded merely
as varying phases of linguistic development—the facts of
each and all equally deserve attention. We now pass to
examine a little more closely a different view of language,
one which definitely holds that of the numerous forms of
English, *one* is pre-eminently *Good English*, the best and
most polite among the dialects.

It has been said in an earlier chapter (*cf.* pp. 22-25)
that it is possible to over-estimate the degree of uniformity
with which Standard English is spoken throughout the
country, and it should be remembered that a form of
language which is disseminated over so wide a geographical area and among such divers classes must inevitably undergo a certain degree of differentiation. The
checks which exist upon the tendency to differentiate
Standard English, and the forces which make possible so
large a degree of uniformity as undoubtedly exists, have
already been discussed (*cf.* pp. 99-105). It is perhaps not
strange that the very phrase Standard English should
arouse antagonism in minds which, possibly through no
fault of the individual, are prejudiced by being in-
sufficiently informed.

It is perhaps said, ' You admit a considerable amount
of differentiation in your so-called Standard English,
and yet you adhere to the conception of a Standard.
How is this logical?' The reply to this objection is,
that the distinctions between the different forms of
Standard English are very slight, almost imperceptible,
indeed, to any but the most alert and practised observer,
and that they shrink to a negligible quantity compared
with the differences between out-and-out ' Vulgarism ' on

the one hand, or provincial—that is, regional—dialects on the other.

In Standard English, as with all other forms of speech, a certain degree of divergence is possible, without such divergence being felt as constituting a different dialect. Of a dozen speakers of Standard English, each may possess slight differences of utterance, or phraseology, and yet none feel that the speech of any of the others, even where it differs from his own, verges towards Vulgarism or 'Dialect' in the special sense.

The most noteworthy criterion of *Good English*, or Standard English, is pronunciation. In this respect there are two main points to be observed—the actual sounds employed and the proper distribution of those sounds ; that is, the use of them in the right words. The fact that a certain group of sounds, and those sounds only (subject to the slight divergences already mentioned), and, further, a certain distribution of those sounds, is accepted in the polite usage is the result of convention. The fundamental reason of that convention is that certain pronunciations are associated by long habit with a cultivated mind, liberal education, refined taste, and good breeding generally ; other pronunciations are associated with the reverse qualities of mind and manners. The former mode of pronunciation is held to be an indication of the possession of the politer education. If it be asked where this superior form of English is heard, it may be answered, that *on the whole*, it is the speech in vogue at the Court, in the Church, at the Bar, at the older Universities, and at the great Public Schools. The English of the stage is also a form of Standard English, but it differs from the English of good

23—2

society, partly in being more archaic, partly also in being marred by certain artificialities and affectations of pronunciation. That a standard form of English has been in existence, sedulously cultivated, and jealously (if often foolishly) treasured, for the last 350 years at least, no one who has studied the authorities upon English Pronunciation, from the middle of the sixteenth century downwards, quoted in the preceding chapter, can have any doubt whatever.

At the present time it will not be denied that to inculcate the speaking of correct English is the chief solicitude of a very large number of persons engaged in Primary and Secondary Education in this country. Those whose business it is to teach, who are to become public speakers, or who wish to enter upon public life, or affairs of any kind, undoubtedly find it convenient to get rid of whatever native 'vulgarisms' or dialectal peculiarities their speech contains, and to attempt to approximate their Spoken English to that standard form which is no longer confined to a single province, or to a particular social class.

In the face of these facts it cannot be thought presumptuous to insist upon the existence of a recognised standard of English speech, to endeavour to arrive at some clear ideas as to its characteristics, and to indicate a reasonable way of regarding it.

In such an inquiry the main things to be avoided are, on the one hand, tolerating too great slackness and slovenliness, which is the fallacy of those who incline to reject the whole conception of a standard of speech, and on the other the pedantic insistence upon precious and artificial forms of language ; the setting up, in fact, of a false standard of perfection, which is the prevailing sin of those who are over-anxious to speak ' correctly.'

It has been said, that owing to social circumstances, a certain type of English speech is regarded as an evidence of cultivation and refinement, and this in itself would constitute a strong claim for this form of English to be considered as worthy of attention ; but it might further be urged that Standard English has an *absolute* superiority over any other dialect in the high degree of acoustic distinctness which it possesses, compared with the provincial or vulgar forms of English. This quality makes it eminently suitable for public speaking.

To what Extent Standard English is Artificial.

In a perfectly natural, unconventional, and popular form of speech, such as we may find in many of the remote provincial dialects of this country, the speakers do not consider the question of ' correctness ' or the reverse. They speak the dialect as it was transmitted to them, without inquiring whether one of two variants which may exist within the dialect, in certain cases, is ' better ' than the other.

In fact, ordinary dialect speakers have no standard of speech, or none, at least, determined by any canons of taste, or what is called ' *good form.*' Such is the position of all primitive languages, of all such as are not the vehicles of culture, or of such, as by the force of social conditions, have become, as it were, backwaters of the great stream of national speech. This subordinate position of the provincial dialects is the inevitable result of the rise of one immensely predominant form of language, as that of the official classes, and of the most cultivated portion of the community.   When one dialect obtains the dignity of becoming the channel of all that is worthiest in the national literature and the national civilization, the other less favoured dialects shrink into obscurity and insignificance. The latter preserve, however, this advantage, considered as types of linguistic development, that the primitive conditions under which language exists, and changes, are far more faithfully represented in them than in the cultivated dialect.   For it is a characteristic, and necessarily so, of a standard dialect, that the question of what is ' *Right* ' or ' *Wrong*,' ' *Correct* ' or ' *Incorrect*,' ' *Good Form* ' or ' *Bad Form*,' ' *Polite* ' or ' *Vulgar*,' should be raised.

From the moment that such conceptions as these are introduced, a certain element of artificiality arises in that form of language which is affected by them. This element of artificiality, however, lies, as a rule, not in the actual forms or phrases themselves, nor in the mode of their development, but simply in the fact that a more or less deliberate choice is exercised by the speakers in eliminating, or adopting for use this or that particular pronunciation, word, phrase, or construction.   It is important to realize that the most fastidious speaker does not create new forms himself, nor deliberately carry out a sound change.   Unless he is deliberately artificial, the individual merely exercises a power of selection from among speech elements, sounds, and the rest, which exist already, and which have arisen by a perfectly natural and normal process of development.   Thus even in the most highly cultivated form of Standard Dialects, whether it be English or any other language, speakers cannot consciously alter the course of

the natural trend of development; this goes on unperceived, here, as in the most barbarous and primitive form
of speech. But in the Standard Language, at any given
period, certain modes of speech may be definitely avoided,
while others are habitually used.

The standard of what is Polite or the reverse varies
from age to age, and in former chapters of this book
examples of this fluctuation have been given. One factor,
which determines the rejection of what was formerly held
to be the best usage, is undoubtedly the spread of Standard
English among various social classes, with the result that
a particular pronunciation, word or phrase, loses distinction, and acquires so common a currency, that with it an
association of vulgarity or lack of refinement is formed.
There is in this respect an analogy between fashion in
speech and other fashions or habits. They may start
high up in the social scale, and be gradually imitated and
adopted as signs of superiority by the lower grades of
society. By the time, however, that the fashion has
become firmly fixed among such classes as do not usually
enjoy a reputation for refinement and distinction, it has
been already discarded by those divisions of society whence
it originally proceeded. In the curious turns of fashion in
speech, not only is that given up which an earlier generation considered good, but what they held as vulgar is often
adopted by their successors.

The differences in pronunciation which exist at a given
time, between the various sections of English people who
speak what we may call a variety of Standard English,
consist for the most part, not of differences in the actual
sounds used, but in the distribution of the sounds. It is,

of course, merely a question of degree, but we must admit
that such a pronunciation as that of the Cockney (raiuwai)
'railway,' with the triphthong (aiu), which is absolutely
unknown in the best Standard English, in any word,
reveals a wider dialectal difference from the received form
(rɛilwɛi), than that of such a pronunciation as (dæns)
instead of the (in the South) more usual (dāns), or (kɔ̄fi),
'coffee,' as compared with (kɔfi). Again, the Cockney
sound in the unstressed syllable of 'father' (mid-flat-
tense, instead of slack), or in that 'boots' (high-back-out-
tense-round, instead of the full-back), are sounds which the
speakers of the best English never by any chance employ
—which, indeed, they would probably have considerable
difficulty in reproducing. Such differences as these constitute, as it appears, not a mere Variety, but a different
Dialect. On the other hand, such pronunciations as (kɔf,
ɔltə, hjūmərəs, pjuə, or pjūə, kɔ̄təsi) as compared with
(kɔ̄f, ɔ̄ltə, jūmərəs, pjɔ̄, kʌ̄təsi) do not constitute more
than varieties, or alternative pronunciations, both of which
are, at the present time, perhaps almost equally widespread
among speakers of good Standard English. The existence
of such alternatives seems to show a period of transition
as regards the standard of pronunciation in these particular
words. Probably fifty years hence fashion will have
decided definitely in favour of one or other of the above
types. The present writer inclines to believe that there is
a slight majority of speakers of Standard English at the
present time in favour of the latter group of pronunciations given above, and that in time those in the former
group will disappear, as possible standard forms. There
are cases where the distribution of particular sounds among

a given set of words is so definitely fixed by the received usage that a deviation from such a system of distribution would be quite enough to constitute a wide difference of dialect.   Thus there is not the faintest doubt that (spūn, bŭk, blad, klāk, dābi, vātjū, *or* vʌ̄tʃū, lʌ̄n, rɔ̄þ, əmaŋ) are the received forms of these words among the best speakers, and that such pronunciations as (spŭn, būk [or bak], blŭd, klʌ̄k, dʌ̄bi, vātju, lān, rāþ, əmɔŋ) are at the present time 'vulgarisms,' or provincial forms.

Thus the history of a standard form of language comprises these two aspects—natural development or gradual shifting of the speech habit, and the fluctuations of fashion which determine the particular action of the selective process.

[NOTE.—Since the above was written, Professor Rippmann's *Sounds of Spoken English* (Dent, 1906) has appeared.   Students will find this book useful, and the remarks on the distribution of vowel sounds in English are particularly interesting.]

Criteria of 'Good' Pronunciation.

The most usual way of dealing with this question is to lay down certain definite rules as to how English 'ought' to be pronounced. This is the worst possible method, because it implies the existence of an *absolute* standard of *Right* and *Wrong* in language.

The only test of what the conventional standard of any age really is, is simply the custom of good speakers. 'A man of fashion,' says Lord Chesterfield—and we may give the remark a wider application—'a man of fashion takes great care to speak very correctly and grammatically, and to pronounce properly—that is, according to the usage of the best companies.' That is the right definition of speaking ' correctly,' and it can hardly be improved upon. Any system of pronunciation which is not based upon one actually in use, is merely theoretical, and therefore worthless. It is impossible to say *a priori* how a doubtful word may or may not be pronounced. All that a teacher of pronunciation is justified in saying is, ' This word is pronounced in such and such a way by good speakers.' But if he has not heard good speakers pronounce the word ; if he himself is not naturally one (that is, from the time he learned to speak) ; or if, being a ' good speaker,' he has yet no personal experience of how the word in question actually is pronounced, then he simply does not know, and cannot teach the pronunciation of it. To go beyond such experience, and to say that the word ' *ought* ' to be pronounced thus or thus, is to court disaster. These theoretical pronunciations, so far from being 'refined' or showing culture, are merely laughable. For if a speaker has not *heard* a word pronounced, wnat means can he possibly have for knowing what the sound of it ' *ought* ' to be ? There are, indeed, two ways by which he might arrive at a conclusion. The first, and the worst, and yet that usually employed by those who theorize about pronunciation, is the spelling ; the other is the early history of the word in question, and of other words originally containing the same sound. To start with, let us say at once that neither of these tests will enable us to determine how the word ' *ought* ' to have developed, since neither the schoolmaster nor the elocutionist can prescribe the path along which language shall change, any more than they can 'bind the Unicorn, or draw out Leviathan with an hook.' Now as to how far either of the above methods can help us to arrive at what the pronunciation of a word *is*, which is the true object of our inquiry. The most unreliable of all guides to the pronunciation of an English word is its spelling, and nothing is more ludicrous than a theoretical pronunciation based solely upon it. On the other hand, a knowledge of the history of English sounds would certainly enable us to say, 'The pronunciation may be so and so.' It could not do more than suggest the *possibilities;* only a knowledge of the actual usage of the time could decide between the variously differentiated forms which our historical method would enable us to infer. For instance, a speaker (let us say a German philologist) who had never heard the word 'good' pronounced might know that O.E. *gōd* is capable of producing three types in Modern English (gūd, g*u*d, gad), but he could not possibly say which is actually in use among 'good speakers' until he had gained the living experience.

As a matter of fact, any scholar so well versed in the history of English as to be able to reconstruct the possible forms of a word, would also know that, in Lord Chesterfield's phrase, only the 'usage of the best companies' could decide between them.

In the case of words which are very rarely used, or which are revivals of obsolete forms, the tradition has naturally died out; there *is* no modern form, and the speaker who uses such words has his choice between the historical pronunciation (that which the word would probably have obtained if it had survived), or of a spelling pronunciation pure and simple. A curious example of a word which is really obsolete, because the institution which it denotes has passed away, is ' chivalry.' This word only survives in historical or romantic diction, and the old tradition has been lost. It is now very commonly pronounced (ʃivəlri), as if it were a word of recent importation from French, whereas it came into English through Norman-French ; and there is no doubt that in that tongue, and in Middle English, it was pronounced (tʃivalrī), which would become (tʃivəlri) in Modern English. This pronunciation is indicated in Campbell's lines :

> ' Wave, Munich, all thy banners wave,
> And charge with all thy chivalry,'

where the alliteration is obviously (tʃādž wið ɔl ðai tʃivəlri).

The sport of falconry has practically died out in England, and both it, and the bird from which it takes its name, are known to most people only from books. The result is that the old pronunciation, without the l, has been lost, and the present pronunciation is due to the spelling. I have observed, however, that those few persons who have personal knowledge of the bird, and of the sport, invariably pronounce (fɔkən, fɔkənri), or at any rate the oldest generation do, instead of the now received (fɔlkən). The general question of spelling-pronunciations which have .become fixed and received will be discussed later on.

But if such artificial pronunciations are practically inevitable in the case of rare and obsolete words, they are inadmissible and ridiculous for words which are in common use, and which the speakers must have heard hundreds of times.

The chief cause of these absurdities occurring among

educated speakers is a mistaken striving after refinement
Public speakers, especially those whose traditions are purely
academic rather than of a wider social world, are not infrequently guilty of extraordinary lapses from decorum and
propriety in the matter of pronunciation.

It may seem incredible that men of learning, who convey
the general impression that they expect to be taken seriously,
should corrupt the English tongue to the extent of pronouncing (pɔignənt, læmb, litəratjɔə, raitias, fɔhɛd, grīnwitʃ,
sauðĀn), all of which pronunciations the present writer has
heard in the course of the last few years, instead of the
' proper pronunciation '—in the sense of Lord Chesterfield
—(pɔinənt, læm, litərətʃə, raitʃəs, fɔrid, grinidž, saðən).
The speakers who perpetrated these forms *pour rire* must
have known quite well what the ordinary pronunciation
was ; they must have been aware that their forms were
deliberately falsified on the spur of the moment, from some
vague idea of importing greater dignity (as they supposed)
to their discourse.   In these cases the speakers must
have been anxious to deserve the praise, often ignorantly
bestowed by the injudicious, that they ' pronounced every
letter distinctly.'   On the same principle, apparently, an
eminent actor delights provincial audiences with the fervid
expression of his (lov) ' love.'

If we consider that we write many ' letters ' in English
spelling which represent no sound that has been heard in
English speech for 500 years, or sometimes longer, it is
easy to see that the practice, if consistently carried out,
would result in an altogether unintelligible jargon, one
which would, in most cases, resemble nothing that had ever
existed in English, during the whole course of its history

It is a great fallacy to imagine that 'Good English' is to be obtained by distorting natural and usual pronunciation to suit some arbitrary standard of 'refinement' set up by an individual. Besides the monstrosities cited above, this effort at 'refinement' not infrequently leads to the production of strange and, in their context, quite un-English sounds, such as (εi, $\bar{e}$) instead of (ai) in 'light,' 'rhyme,' 'prime,' 'desire,' and so on, which has not even the specious justification of 'giving every letter its full sound.'

The first pitfall to avoid, then, is a *bogus 'refinement'* of utterance.

The next error, closely allied to it, but often springing from a different motive, is *over-carefulness*. It may be laid down as a general principle that just as 'refined' speech such as we have been considering is always absurd, so 'careful' speech is always vulgar. The best English never conveys the impression of carefully-studied utterance on the part of the speaker; there is never any suspicion of mincing, as if to avoid some irretrievable vulgarism. This kind of pedantic and unreal pronunciation has nothing to be said in its favour. It may proceed from any one of the following causes : (1) Ignorance of the habitual pronunciation of good speakers. (2) A foolish desire to improve upon the received pronunciation, either by giving greater fulness, or, perhaps, even by introducing some sound which has either long disappeared, or has never existed at all ; this motive is that wish for 'refinement' or 'correctness' already discussed. (3) In addressing a large audience public speakers feel a need for great precision, distinctness, and volume. To attain these ends they are sometimes unfortunately led into an exaggerated modification of their pronunciation, beyond the limits of the natural. We have already noted that there is a necessary and legitimate adaptation of speech under these circumstances, but a good speaker does not deviate so far from his natural modes of utterance as to produce something strange and manifestly artificial. It is surely absurd to maintain that the English of the present day is unfitted, in its natural form, for public oratory, and that it needs to be distorted for this purpose into something altogether different. (4) Many speakers have a curious sentimentality with regard to English. They are so solicitous of its purity and integrity, that practically no existing form of natural Spoken English comes up to their ideal of what the language ought to be. The ideal of this school is based entirely upon the present-day spelling. They may be quite ignorant of how that spelling came about, they may know nothing of the history of English pronunciation, but they show a remarkable tenderness for the letters, which they have come to think really *are* the word. This point of view is responsible for more eccentricities and affectations in pronunciation than any of the others, excepting, perhaps, that which aims at a personal distinction of utterance, as a kind of protest against the prevailing vulgarity. Both the speaker who wishes to speak better than anyone else, and the sentimentalist who lovingly clings to the ' letters,' are open to the grave reproach that they generally carry their vagaries into the colloquial speech of everyday life; and that while they are often fully conversant with polite usage, they yet deliberately set it at nought.

Assuming that a speaker had a thorough knowledge of

the history of English pronunciation, it would, of course, be possible for him to select for his own usage the sound system in vogue in any century that he preferred. In this case he would at least be employing forms that had once had a real existence. Probably few would commend such a practice in speech, any more than they would welcome the return on the part of isolated individuals to the wigs of Charles the Second's day, or the ruffs of the age of the first James. But the sentimental speaker of English is not as a rule familiar with any earlier phase of his language, but simply concocts a fancy dialect on the most unreliable of all bases—that of spelling, a guide which, as we have seen, is certain to lead the theorist into endless error.

The only safe course as regards pronunciation is frankly to recognise the fact that language changes, that standards of excellence shift, that the individual cannot delay the process, and that he is consulted as to which direction development will take.

The only good reason for deviating from the received standard of English speech is ignorance of it. The best substitute for such a form of English is a genuine provincial dialect, or an honest ' vulgarism.' For lack of knowledge may be informed, and, if necessary, a new dialect can be acquired.

The Teaching of Polite Pronunciation.

If it is desired to instruct those who do not possess it, in polite English pronunciation, there are three Perfect Points which demand attention, if success is to be attained. They are : The attitude of the teacher towards the actual dialect of the pupil; the setting up of true standards of speech ; the method of imparting the new pronunciation. It is not too harsh a criticism on most of those who undertake this task, whether it be in schools, in training colleges, or among private pupils, in this country, to say that in the great majority of cases, the three points just mentioned do not meet with satisfactory or adequate treatment at their hands.

The instruction is given either by a regular elocutionist, or by any ordinary master or mistress, just as occasion serves. In the former case, the instruction, so far as it goes, is more or less systematic ; in the latter it is purely haphazard, and takes the form of the occasional correction of isolated ' mistakes ' as they occur in reading. The professed teacher of elocution, it is true, is primarily concerned with showing how poetry or prose should be read, in such a way as to ' interpret the author's meaning ' ; incidentally he also ' corrects ' pronunciation. We may take the three points in order, and endeavour to state fairly the necessary shortcomings both of professional elocutionist and ordinary master or mistress.

The Attitude of the Teacher towards the Dialect of the Pupil.

The possession of a certain dialect as a native form of speech implies, as we know, the possession of a certain speech basis. The nature of this determines the natural tendencies and habits of pronunciation. If it is proposed to acquire a new and different pronunciation, a new speech basis must first be gradually formed. The first step in this process is for the speaker to know thoroughly, and

24

understand, the facts of his own speech habits. Thence he
can proceed to learn different habits.

Now, what is the practice of the inexperienced and untrained teacher of pronunciation ? He brushes aside, as
of no interest, no value, and as having no justification, the
speech habits of a lifetime ; he throws contempt or ridicule
upon the pupil's accent. His one idea is to ignore and
forget the natural pronunciation of those whose speech he
is to 'improve.' He asserts that it is 'wrong,' but he
gives no reason for the statement; he abuses and dis-
parages that which the pupil has learnt, from his mother,
perhaps, and which he has heard and used himself so long
as he can remember. He is quite ignorant of the ways of
that ever-varying mystery, human speech ; yet he takes
upon himself to abuse and condemn a form of it which
may have had a historical existence and development as
'regular' as Standard English itself, and which is, perhaps,
a far purer dialect. He could not inform his class *why* his
own speech ought to serve as a model, nor why it differs
from theirs, nor, indeed, with any degree of accuracy, *how*
it differs from theirs ; yet he presumes to reiterate his own
pronunciation of this or that word, and to assert that it
is 'Right.' During the whole course of his instruction
he never explains the meaning of the terms 'Right' and
'Wrong,' which he uses so often, beyond, perhaps, conveying
the idea that the 'wrong' pronunciations of the students are
bad attempts on their part to pronounce as he does himself.

Now, as most people with self-respect are keenly sensitive
on the question of their language, such a method as that
described (as it is believed without exaggeration), merely
wounds without enlightening.

The Standards which are set up.

It is almost inevitable that a professional elocutionist, from his training, should seek his models of pronunciation and delivery, not in the best *colloquial* forms of English, but in the artificial declamatory utterance usual on the stage, or in high-flown public oratory. The standards, therefore, which he submits for the imitation of his pupils, and which he himself strives to illustrate in private converse, no less than in public recitation, are generally apt to be artificial to the last degree. There is a danger that, considered as types of public speaking, these standards will be archaic and pedantic ; while as forms of colloquial speech they will be as far removed from the familiar pronunciation of good society as any dialect or out-and-out vulgarism could be. In this form of English we generally find all the distressing symptoms discussed above—overcarefulness, bogus refinement, impossible pronunciations, based, not on the fact of what *is*, but on a theory of what ' *ought* ' to be. Undesirable as this kind of pronunciation is, even in public speaking, it is intolerable in private conversation ; and he who practises it can hardly hope to escape the reproach of being a coxcomb and a pedant ; he will certainly not pass for a well-spoken, well-bred person. We may grant that a competent teacher of elocution *as such*, even one who teaches on the above lines, has the power of imparting an intelligible and an expressive, if, perhaps, rather too ' theatrical ' a delivery ; but we can but feel that his method, even if considered as a training in public speaking only, is an inversion of the natural process. Before a man can speak well in public, he must first learn to speak well in private. The latter mode of speech must, above all things, be natural, and must not be based primarily upon models derived from public oratory, neither in pronunciation, nor in choice of diction.   Good colloquial English, in a word, is not a modification of the English of the platform.   On the other hand, it might with greater propriety be held that the best public speaking is a modified and adapted form of the best colloquial speech—of that which follows 'the usage of the best companies.'   The teacher of elocution, by training and tradition, belongs to that sentimental order of persons, already referred to, who are jealous guardians of what they conceive to be the purity of English pronunciation, and strenuous opponents of new-fangled looseness and easy carelessness in utterance.   He bewails the corrupt state into which the English language has fallen ; he regards every pronunciation which differs from his own highly-wrought system as wrong and vulgar.   So far from attempting to follow the best usage of his age in pronunciation, he denounces all natural pronunciation as slovenly, and wishes rather to lead contemporary speech into other paths, and to insist upon a pronunciation partly of his own making, partly delivered to him by tradition from those who taught him his craft.   It will, perhaps, be apparent, from what has been already said concerning artificial pronunciations, that those who attempt to preserve an old pronunciation, rather than adopt that in common use, are in reality, too often the worst innovators, since they ' restore,' from insufficient knowledge, a pronunciation which has never existed, and which is entirely new.   It is difficult to understand why it should be held that a new and natural development in language is a matter for regret. Modern English has slowly reached its present form by slow development, and has passed through numerous phases on its way thither from parent Aryan. By a series of minute but unceasing changes which have gone on during a period which a moderate estimate counts at 10,000 years, that far-off mother-tongue has passed here into Greek, there into Russian, there again into English, and into innumerable other forms of speech. Change may be slower in Modern English to-day than it was thousands of years ago in Central Europe, but none the less is the drama of transformation being enacted here as there. If it were not so, if it had not always been so, there could be no comparative philology, no possibility of 'wrong' speech, or 'faulty' delivery, and, consequently, no Art of Elocution; for Aryan speech would be undifferentiated, all individuals would speak alike—'all the earth would be of one speech and one language.'

Whether this would have been an advantage or not we need not consider, for the fact is that language is always changing, and always will change. This being the case, the only reasonable attitude is that which observes and notes the changes as they occur, and accepts them with a good grace. Those who teach a younger generation must be prepared to find tendencies in the speech of their pupils which are absent from, or less fully developed in, their own. Careful observation over a wide field is necessary to enable us to distinguish these new tendencies, which are natural, and which are foreshadowings of future development, from other deviations from what we take to be Standard English, which are dialectal or personal peculiarities.

Methods of Teaching a New Pronunciation

We have already insisted so frequently, in the earlier chapters of this book, upon the importance of phonetics in the practical and historical study of language that it is unnecessary to return at any length to the question. It is enough to say that to learn a new pronunciation of the native language involves the same kind of difficulties as to learn any other new pronunciation. In approaching this practical side of linguistic study, mere imitation is inadequate and unsatisfactory, and systematic phonetic method is necessary. Since the proper pronunciation of a language includes two problems, the mastery of the right sounds, and the use of them in the right words, it will be found desirable, not only to make a phonetic analysis of the sounds of Standard English, which should be compared with that first made of the learner's own sounds, but also to use texts in phonetic transcription which show the distribution of the sounds. The use of a simple phonetic alphabet should be practised, and the student should make transcripts of prose and verse in his own native pronunciation, and also take down his teacher's pronunciation from dictation. It is, perhaps, necessary to warn those who have not experience in this kind of work that the passages must be written down according to the natural pronunciation of the words in breath-groups, and not as consisting of isolated words. Thus, if Shenstone's lines were dictated—

> ' So sweetly she bade me adieu,
> I thought that she bade me return,'

they should be read and taken down thus ·

and not

> ('Sou swītli ʃi bæd mi ədjū,
> ai þɔ̄t ðət ʃi bæd mi rītān),

> ('Sou swītli ʃī bæd mī ədjū,
> ai þɔ̄t ðæt ʃī bæd mī rītān).

In this way the student learns, not only a natural instead of a pedantic and forced pronunciation of the sentence, but he also realizes how the sounds of words vary according to the degree of stress and the character of neighbouring sounds in any given context.

It should be remembered that very important elements in Polite English are proper stress, intonation, rate of utterance, and the accomplished use of the voice. Mr. Sweet in his *New English Grammar* has shown what vital elements stress and intonation are in English syntax. What is known as ' over-emphasis ' is a vulgarism which must at all costs be eliminated. It consists in placing certain parts of the sentence in too strong a relief, by a disproportionate contrast between strong and weak stress, and also in allowing strong stress to recur too frequently in the breath-group. The result is a noisy clatter which suggests a series of jerks, instead of a quiet, even flow of speech, with occasional salient syllables strongly stressed, as good sense, good ·syntax, and good taste demand.

Intonation is the most difficult element in pronunciation to describe or to acquire. Vulgar speakers often affect the frequent use of compound tones to express persuasiveness, self-confidence, or good-natured cunning and sagacity. Good speakers avoid this means for the expression of these emotions, or use it very sparingly. The exaggerated use of the compound tones suggests impertinent familiarity. The Scotch peculiarity of finishing a sentence with a rising tone suggests querulousness, or cavilling, to English ears.   One of the most characteristic features in a dialect is the *precise degree* of rise or fall, which it would demand to express with exactness a musical notation.   Foreigners often produce a very curious effect by raising or lowering the pitch too much or too little as the case may be.

As regards the management of the speaking voice, nothing can make a poor voice into a good one; but an element in the best manner of speech is undoubtedly good resonance.   In men a full chest note is usual among the best speakers, and a throttled, choky, wheezy utterance is not impressive.   It is not given to everyone to possess a fine voice, but training and practice can give control and resonance even to a voice which is naturally weak and thin.   Among certain classes of academic speakers a peculiar shrill, squeaky falsetto is in vogue, which we must pity as a misfortune in those who are naturally so afflicted, but which some will consider an absurd affectation in those who adopt it, being able to speak otherwise.   This is probably another instance of that sham refinement too often deliberately acquired by the misguided.   Among women shrill falsetto is rarely heard, except from those who have no pretentions to culture or manners.   It is strange that some men, who represent the most fastidious and precious class in the world, should apparently have come to regard a squeaky voice as the sign of an enlightened mind and an exquisite taste.   This manner of speech conveys the impression of querulous and impotent weakness, a quality in itself devoid of dignity and charm.

The Influence of Spelling on English Pronunciation.

The number of words in English, of which the ' spelling pronunciation ' has become current, in place of the traditional sound, is relatively small. An imposing list of these is given by Professor Koeppel, in his interesting little book, *Spelling Pronunciations : Bemerkungen über den Einfluss des Schriftbildes auf den Laut im Englischen ;* Strassburg, 1901. (*Quellen und Forschungen*, Bd. lxxxix.) The principles which underlie this curious phenomenon are, in most cases, either the loss of the tradition of pronunciation of an obsolete word, which has been revived from literary sources as a semi-colloquial word ; or, in the case of common, genuine colloquial words, the victory of a pedantic effort at refinement and correctness. In the case of proper names, the cause is often sheer ignorance of the traditional pronunciation, on the part of those who are strangers to a person or a place. With the arrival of the Railway in remote districts, porters, from London perhaps, din into the ears of travellers the name of the station, which they know chiefly from printed sources. The rising generation of natives very soon adopt the new pronunciation, and the mere tourist does so the more readily that he himself has no knowledge of the local, and therefore true, pronunciation. A few examples must suffice, as Professor Koeppel has dealt so copiously with the subject.

The name of St. Alphege is a good example of a literary revival, which, however, is not treated in his book. This saint's day, as is recorded in the Prayer-Book Calendar, is April 19. A certain number of churches in England are dedicated to him, and he is (I believe) universally known

at the present day as (sənt ælfɛdž). The O.E. form of
the name is *Ælfhēah,* which in Mod. English could only
normally become either (ɛlvi) or (ælvi). The present
actual pronunciation is apparently from a M.E. spelling
Alpheȝȝe (alfɛjɛ), which later on, when the memory of the
stout old Archbishop had faded from men's minds, and his
name from their lips was spelt *Alphegge* or *Alphege,* and
pronounced (alfɛdž).

The pronunciation of ' forward ' as (fɔ̄wəd) instead of
the normal (fɔrəd) can only be the result of the same
tendency which still makes some people say (fɔhɛd) instead
of (fɔrid) or (fɔrɛd).   But while the latter is still the sign
either of a prig, or of one who is unacquainted with the
speech of ' the best companies,' the former is the accepted
and ' correct ' form, except in the Navy.   (fɔrəd) survives,
of course, in provincial dialects, and in very colloquial
speech among all classes.

The Fifeshire place-name *Kilconquahar,* which the
present writer has heard old Fife people call (kɛnjahər) or
(kɛnjūhər), is now apparently always called (kilkɔŋkər).
The present writer can also remember the old-fashioned
pronunciation of the Sussex villages *Ardingly* and *Helingly*
as (ādiŋlai), or among the lower orders themselves
(ærdiŋlai), and (hīliŋlai).   These have now given .place to
(ādiŋli) and (hīliŋli).   Sussex people still talk of (wɔdəst,
midəst) for *Wadhurst, Midhurst,* and this is the pronunciation of the local gentry ; but (wɔdhāst, midhāst)
are fast coming in through porters and trippers.

(sairinsɛstə), *Cirencester,* is more common now than
either (sisitə) or (sisistə) even, or perhaps especially, among
those who know the place quite well.

The village in which these words are written is locally
known as (ɔlskət) or (ælskət) ; but the inhabitant of this
village, when he takes his ticket at Oxford Station, less
than twenty miles away, is usually corrected by the
booking-clerk, who insists on (ælvɛskɔt).

Lord Derby's Lancashire seat *Knowsley* is almost universally called (nouzli), yet this pronunciation cannot
conceivably have developed from M.E. *Knouesli*, or
Knou(l)wesli, O.E. *Kenulfes lēah*. The true descendant
of the old forms is heard in the now ' vulgar' (nauzli),
which, I am told, still persists among the aged in the
district.

In fact, English Place-names are now so generally
corrupted in their pronunciation through the influence
of spelling, that in many cases it is impossible to understand the connection between the old forms and the
current pronunciation.   It becomes, therefore, of the
utmost importance to ascertain the true pronunciation
among old people in the district itself, and to pay but
small attention, until this is done, either to the spelling, or
to the conventional pronunciation, if we wish to trace the
history of the name.   In the case of other English words,
whose modern forms do not square with the older forms,
as regards normal sound change, the possibility of a
corrupt modern pronunciation, based upon the spelling,
must be borne in mind.   We should rather assume this,
than an ' exception' to the known tendencies of change in
the language.

We occasionally hear peculiarly flagrant breaches of
polite usage, such as (iz nɔt it) for (iznt it) or (æm nɒt ai),
for the now rather old-fashioned, but still commendable,

(εint *ai*) or the more usual and familiar (ānt *ai*), or, in
Ireland (æmnt *ai*).   These forms, which can only be
based upon an uneasy and nervous stumbling after 'correctness,' are perfectly indefensible, for no one ever uttered
them naturally and spontaneously.   They are struck out
by the individual, in a painful gasp of false refinement.
There is little chance of such abortive creations getting
a secure foothold in traditional English, unless linguistic
education becomes altogether divorced from life, and until
the native language is taught as though it were a dead
language, with which the schoolmaster had but an imperfect acquaintance.

This imperfect treatment of a great subject must now
draw to a close.   The mere thought of human speech,
passed on from lip to lip through unnumbered ages,
changing along a definite path among each race as it
flashes through them, unconsciously shaped to the needs
of every mind, which it mirrors, and yet, in spite of all,
preserving an identity which the ear of science can recognise, is one which must kindle a strange sense of wonder
and reverence.   The most commonplace form of language
which we can think of has an ancestry more ancient than
any custom or myth which survives.   The humblest form
of English, whether spoken in a remote Devonshire
hamlet or in a Northern pit village, is an echo of a tongue
that once sounded in far-distant countries, among alien
and savage men, and in ages possibly, when the present
configuration of the globe was not yet determined.

Language, so familiar, and yet so mysterious, lies all
about us.   The human mind and the human vocal organs,

the one more complex, the others defter, than in the remote past, but still essentially the same now as then, are an ever-present field for the observation of the student. The root of all science may lie in an awakened and alert curiosity concerning the obvious and the commonplace.

This little book could find no more fitting conclusion than the words of Ælfric, in the Preface of his *Lives of the Saints:*

> ' Ne secge we nan þing niwes on þissere gesetnysse,
> forþan þe hit stod gefyrn awriten
> . . . þeah þe þa læwedan men þæt nyston.'

' We say nothing new in this work, for it all stood written long ago, albeit laymen did not know it.'

SUBJECT INDEX

Ablaut, nature of, 163; in Aryan, 182; name due to Grimm, 183; accent and, 184, 185; grades, 185, 186, 187; quantitative, 184; qualitative, 184, 188; diphthongal combinations in, 189; examples of, 190-194.

Accent, Aryan, 184; Parent Germanic, 199.

Alphabet, International, 50.

Analogy, 'exceptions' due to, 115, 213; process of, 129; memory and, 129; 'false,' 132; mistakes due to, 132, 133; results in new formations, 134, 135; prevention of differentiation by, 136; normal sound change and, 137; continual process of, 138-140.

Anglo-French, 288, 289.

Anglo-Frisian Unity, views of Siebs and Bremer, 195; Morsbach and Wyld, 196.

Archaisms, revival of, 127.

Arnold, Matthew, appreciation of Dryden, 344.

Aryan, Mother-tongue, 8, 9, 170, 171; reconstructed forms, value of, 144; relative homogeneity of, 103; wealthy vowel system of, 161; divisions of, 169, 373; race, 172, 173; its cradle, 171, 172; relative primitiveness of chief divisions, 173, 174; mutual relations of these, 175-181; consonants, 181; vowels, 182; ablaut, 182-194; accent, 184; Modern English and, 373.

Association groups, 130-131; levelling of exceptions due to, 133; isolation from, 135, 136.

Avesta, the, dialect of, 169.

Barbour's 'Bruce,' rhymes in, 262.

Björkman, remarks on Scandinavian loan-words in O.E., 249; on close resemblance between English and Norse, 282.

Bopp, Franz, 8; views on sound change, 82.

Brugmann asserts inadmissibility of 'exceptions,' 114; principles of method used in reconstruction, stated by, 163; works of, 166; views of Aryan affinities, 179, 180; on reduced vowels, 186, 187; principles of philological method formulated by, 215.

Bülbring on pronunciation of O.E. c3, 225.

Caxton, Literary English and, 294; London dialect and, 295, 296, 297.

Chaucer, persistence of Norman-French accent in, 123; Literary dialect and, 251; rhymes of, 259; O.E. *ǎ*, *ǣ* in, 265; French influence on language of, 289; London dialect and, 296, 297; *Canterbury Tales*, expression in, 345.

Chesterfield, Lord, his definition of correct speech, 361, 362; condemns trite phrases, 351.

Cognates, examples of, 142; tests of identity of origin, 142.

Comparison, reconstruction based on, 142, 150; words suitable for, 143; conditions necessary for, 142; limitations within one language, 145, 147; importance of early forms for, 145, 146, 147; light thrown by widening range of, 147-149, 155-163; limitations, within one speech-family of, 151-155.

Consonants, classification of, 32-35; natural series of, 35, 36; long and double, 48.

Conversation, Language of, independent life of, 340, 341; adaptation to environment, 347, 348; limits of adaptation, 348, 349.

'Correctness' in language, standard of, 353; fluctuation of standard of, 359; Lord Chesterfield's definition of, 361, 362.

Corruptions, 12; common use of the term, 19.

Darmsteter, views on sound change, 84.

'Dialect' and 'language' compared, 91.

Dialects, mixture of, 22; tests of relative superiority of,

22, 23 ; importance of study of, 25, 26, 205 ; rise of, 95, 96 ; class, 99 ; artificial, literary, 212 ; decay of English, 104 ; scientific view of equality among, 353, 354 ; absence of standard in, 357 ; subordinate position of, 357, 358 ; linguistic development in, 358 standard, artificiality in, 358, 359.

Dryden, French influence in, 289 ; appreciation by Matthew Arnold, 344 ; prose of, 344, 345.

Ellis interprets authorities on pronunciation, 67, 68, 301, 309.

English, development of vocabulary of, 209 ; modified inflexional system of, 208 ; Norman words in, 124 ; Scandinavian words in, 124 ; Indian words in, 124 ; lifeless forms of, 349-353.

English, Correct, practical advantages of its study and use, 352, 353.

English dialects, decay of, 104.

English, Good, reality of existence of, 342.

English, History of, what it involves, 205 ; methods of study, 205, 206.

English, Literary, ' sounds ' of, inaccurate use of term, 341, 342 ; sources of, 251, 342, 343 ; rise of, 294-297 ; Chaucer and, 251 ; Wycliff and, 251 ; Gower and, 251 ; Caxton and, 294 ; Standard English and, 251, 295, 340-346.

English, Middle, apparently exceptional spellings in, 210, 211 ; relation to Modern English, 250 ; authorities on, 252, 253 ; chronological divisions, 253 ; dialects, 253, 254 ; texts, 254, 255 ; orthography, 255-259 ; pronunciation, how established, 259, 260 ; sound changes in, 260-265 ; treatment of O.E. diphthongs, 265, 266 ; rise of new diphthongs in, 266, 267 ; vowel-lengthening, 268, 269 ; vowel-shortening, 270-273 ; doublets in, 273 ; treatment of O.E. consonants, 273-280 ; O.E. ċ, and ċġ, difficulties concerning. in, 275-277 ; summary of dialectal differences in, 280 ; French element in, 287-289 ; inflexions, 289-293 ; Scandinavian element, 281-284 ; tests of Scandinavian origin, 285-287.

English, Modern, development of M.E. vowels in, 309-330 : *ă*, statements of authorities concerning, 309-316 ; *ā*, summary of development of, 316, 317 ; *e*, 317, 318 ; *ē* 'tense,' 319, 320 ; *ī*, *oi*, 321-323 ; *ē* ' slack,' 320, 321 ; *ō* 'tense,' 323-327 ; *ō* tense, Scotch pronunciation of, 324 ; *ō* 'slack,' development of, 324, 325 ; *ŏ*, 325 ; *ŭ*, 325-327 ; *ŭ* in Scotch dialects, 328 ; *ū*, 328 ; *ȳ*, 329, 330 ; treatment of M.E. diphthongs, 330-336 : *ai*, *ei*, development of, 330-332 ; *au*, 333-336 ; *ou*, 336 ; consonants, development of, in, 336-338 ; slow development of, 373 : Aryan and, 373.

English, Old, problems presented by MSS., 210 ; significance of ' exceptional' spellings, 210 ; stages of development, 216 ; dialects, 216 217 ; sources of knowledge of, 217 ; texts, 217-220 ; monographs on, 220-222 ; pronunciation, 222, 223 ; values of vowel symbols, 223-224 ; pronunciation of consonants, 224-225 ; symbols, 224, 225 ; *c*, *g*, *ġ*, *ċġ* in, 225 ; authorities on pronunciation of, 225-226 ; books for beginners on, 226 ; W. Germanic vowel changes affecting, 227-231 ; *an, on* in, 229 ; Fracture or ' Brechung,' 229-231 ; nasals, loss of, 232, 233 ; i-mutation, 233, 234 ; lengthening of vowels, 235 ; dialectal divergences, 235-238 ; Celtic loan-words, 238-239 ; Latin loan-words, 239-248 ; Scandinavian loan-words, 248-249 ; native words adapted to Christian uses, 247, 248.

English Place-Names, 378, 379.

English, Polite, 342 ; rate of utterance in, 375.

English, Spoken, historical study and, 205, 339 ; first steps in study of, 339, 340 ; source of, 341 ; use of term, 341 ; importance of study of, 206, 353 ; standards of Good or Bad, 353-357.

English of the Stage, 355, 356.

English, Standard, existence of, 23 ; historical position of, 24 ; varying standard of, 24, 25, 318, 359 ; uniformity in, 22-25, 101, 102, 354 ; spread of, 104, 105 ; source of, 251, 295, 342, 343 ; provincial speech and, 297, 298 ; changes in, 299 ; Literary English

25

and, 251, 295, 340-346; existence and growth of, 342, 356; nature of, 342; artificiality of, 343, 357-364; adaptability of, 346-349 ; checks upon differentiation in, 354 ; pronunciation, chief criterion of, 355 ; where heard, 355; possible divergences in, 355, 359, 360 ; importance of, for teacher, etc., 356 ; 'absolute' superiority of, 24, 357 ; influence of fashion on, 327, 359.

Environment, Influence of, 63 ; normally unperceived, 63; gradually lessens, 64.

Esperanto, 105 ; its probable future, 105-109.

Exceptions, explanations of apparent, 114-115, 212-214, 379.

Foreign words, translations of, 122 ; conditions for incorporation of, 122, 123.

Germanic, 8, 168, 196 ; divisions of, 195 ; authorities, 196; sources of knowledge of, 197 ; characteristics of, 197 ; consonant shifting, 198-201 ; 'free' accent, 199 ; treatment of Aryan vowels, 202-203 ; West, characteristics, 203.

Glides, 44 ; p, t, k, in English and French, 44.

Gower, and the literary dialect, 251 ; distinguishes between tense and slack ē, 257.

Grammar, comparative and historical, 9.

Grassmann's Law, 174.

Greek, faithfully preserves primitive vowel system, 160, 174 ; Grassmann's Law, 174.

Grimm's Law, 197, 198.

Hirt, views on sound change, 85, 87, 179 ; on reduced vowels, 186, 187, 191.

Historical linguistic study, 1-3 ; aim, 6 ; methods of, 4-10, 211-215 ; necessary equipment for, 10-11 ; proper basis of, 61, 206, 339.

Imitation, limitations of, 56, 374 ; dangers of faulty, 58, 59 ; native tongue learnt by, 54 ; sound change and faulty theories concerning, 84 ; changes due to faulty, 125.

i-mutation, 10, 150, 233, 234.

Intonaton, 47 ; in Polite English, 375, 376.

-jan suffix in Gothic and Old Saxon, 148.
Kluge on pronunciation of O.E. c3, 225, 226; Scandinavian
    words in O.E., 249.
Language, continual change in, 14, 373.
Language, Life of, psychological aspect, 11, 13; physio-
    logical, 11, 13.
Language, Literary, danger of exclusive study of, 11, 13;
    position with regard to spoken language, 12, 340,
    341 ; comparatively archaic, 344 ; sources of, 341.
Language, Spoken, limitations, 5 ; changes in, 14 ; writing
    and, 5, 62 ; unconscious process of, 61, 62, 63; im-
    portance of study of, 10, 11, 13, 206 ; advantage of
    training in facts of, 340; independent life of, 340,
    341 ; influence of literature on, 341 ; adaptability
    of, 346
Language, Standard, two aspects of history of, 361.
Language transmission, changes involved in, 65.
Language, Written, use of term, 341.
Latin, corruptions in, 12; the primitive vowels and diph-
    thongs in, 174 ; the primitive consonants in, 174.
Leskien asserts inadmissibility of 'exceptions,' 114, 117;
    position of, in linguistic science, 166; modifies ' Über-
    gangstheorie,' 177-179.
Linguistic contact, through literature, 125, 126 ; introduc-
    tion of foreign elements, 122-124.
Loan-words, development indicated by, 121, 122 ; points
    of interest concerning, 209 ; popular fallacies con-
    cerning, 209 ; test of source of, 210; importance of
    form, 245 ; Scandinavian, 248, 249, 281-285 ; Latin,
    239-248 ; Celtic, 238-239; tests for Scandinavian
    origin of, 285-287.
London Dialect, Standard English and, 294-298, 342, 343.
Max Müller, original home of the Aryans, views on, 171.
Memory Pictures, 57-59; gradual alteration of, 72; sub-
    conscious, 70, 71.
'Mistake,' significance of term, 19, 20.
Napier, Professor, his discovery of Orm's new symbol, 258.
Obsolete Forms, possible pronunciations of, 363, 364.
Orm, value of his orthography, 256 ; establishes M.E

quantities, 260, 268, 269, 270, 271, 272; his new symbol for back-stop (g), 258.

Osthoff defines 'correctness' in language, 21; views on sound change, 83; asserts inadmissibility of 'exceptions,' 114; position in science of language, 166.

Passy, views on sound change, 84, 90.

Paston Letters, Oxford dialect and, 296.

Paul, remarks on relation of individual speaker to community, 103; asserts inadmissibility of 'exceptions,' 114; position of, in science of language, 166; 'Wellentheorie,' views on, 177.

Philology, comparative, meaning of, 8; task of, 141; advance of science of, 142; method of, 143, 144.

Phonetic Analysis, pronunciation and, 374.

Phonetic Laws, meaning of term, 112; nature of, 117; exceptions to, inadmissible, 114.

Phonetic practice, 60; exercises, 35, 36, 38, 39, 40, 41.

Phonetic symbols, 50, 51; tables of, 52, 53; explanation of, 54; usefulness of, 374.

Phonetic training, ingenious objections to, 16, 17; importance of, 15, 374; what it involves, 17, 18, 27, 59, 60; why advantageous, 18, 19; proper basis for, 27, 60, 61, 339; historical linguistic study and, 339.

Phonological investigation, nature and importance of, 113.

Place-names, English, 378, 379.

Pogatscher, views on use of Latin by Britons, 242, 243.

Pronunciation, spelling and, 14, 15, 116, 212; sixteenth-century, authorities on, 302-304; seventeenth-century, authorities on, 304, 305; eighteenth-century, authorities on, 306; interpretation of authorities on, 307, 308; influence of fashion on, 327, 359; varieties within Standard Dialect of, 359, 360; varieties indicating difference of dialect, 361; English spelling and, 363, 377-380; vulgarity of 'overcarefulness' in, 366, 367; difficulties involved in unfamiliar, 374.

Pronunciation, Correct, decided by experience, 362, 363.

Pronunciation 'Good,' criteria of, 361-368.

Pronunciation, Polite, teaching of, 368-376 ; present methods of teaching, criticism of, 369-371.
Pronunciations, Spelling, 377-379 ; absurdity of, 364-366 ; causes of, 365, 377, 378, 380.
Prose, natural language of good, 345.
Public Speaking, 346, 347, 348.
Quantity, 47, 48.
Reconstruction, possibility of, 142 ; test of accurate, 151 ; principles of, 163, 164 ; necessity of, 206 ; varying methods of, 207 ; Modern period, problem of, 300.
Reconstructed Forms, value of, 144.
'Right' and 'Wrong' in Language, definition of, 21, 129 ; analogy and, 132, 139 ; scientific and practical views of, 353 ; constant change in, 353 ; Standard Dialects and, 358 ; no 'absolute' standard of, 361 ; ignorant use of terms, 370.
Rig-Veda, hymns of, 169.
Salesbury, William, 301.
Sanscrit, a, an in Lithuanian and, 156, 157 ; sounds in Greek and Latin corresponding to a in, 156-159 ; palatalization in, 159, 160 ; vowel system less primitive than Greek, 160, 174 ; consonants relatively primitive in, 174.
Scherer, views on sound change, 82 ; position of, in science of language, 166.
Schleicher, views on sound change, 82 ; his 'Stammbaum' theory, 175, 178, 180.
Schmidt, Johann, original home of Aryans, views on, 171 ; attacks 'Stammbaum' theory, 176 ; 'Wellentheorie,' 176, 177, 178, 179.
Schrader accepts Schmidt's 'Wellentheorie,' 177.
Scotch, sixteenth-century ŭ in dialects of, 328 ; O.E. ō tense in, 328.
Scots, distinguished history of, 208.
Seek, 'beseech' and, 145, 146, 147 ; 'sought' and, 147-150.
Shakespeare, reconstruction of his pronunciation, 207.
Sievers, use of term 'bedingt,' 81 ; asserts inadmissibility of 'exceptions.' 114; position of, in science of language,

166 ; on pronunciation of O.E. c3, 225 ; on -*n*- verbs in O.E., 284.

Skeat, on French element in English, 287, 288.

Sound change, fact of, 14, 15 ; evidence of, in written records, 67 ; in cognate forms, 68 ; inaccuracy of term, 69 ; process of, 70, 71, 72, 73 ; cause of, 73, 81 ; isolative, 73, 74 ; combinative, 75-77, 214 ; transitoriness of tendencies, 76-78, 373 ; theories in explanation of, 82-85 ; caused by foreign contact, 85-87 ; occupation as factor in, 88 ; inadequacy of theories to explain it, 89 ; spread of, 110, 111 ; unconscious nature of, 113 ; importance of study of, 113 ; laws of, 111, 112 ; analogy and, 137.

Sound changes, Old English, 226, 232, 233 ; West Germanic affecting Old English, 227-232 ; Middle English, 260-265 ; Modern English, 309, etc. (see English, Modern).

Sound Laws, meaning of term, 77 ; admit of no exceptions, 114, 117.

Speech of a Town, how far homogeneous, 99.

Speech basis, 70 ; factors involved in, 81 ; influence of race on, 86 ; influenced by physical type, 87 ; change in, 87 ; by occupation, 88 ; foreign sounds modified by native, 120, 121.

Speech communities, meaning of term, 92-93 ; possibilities and limitations of change in, 93, 94 ; relative homogeneity within, 94, 109 ; contact between, 119-121 ; modes of isolation of, 97, 98.

Speech, 'correct,' popular view of, 21 ; scientific conception of, 21, 129.

Speech family, Aryan, existence of, 8 ; Aryan, divisions of, 169 ; conception of, 166-168.

Speech habits, formation of, 58, 59.

Speech, Individual, various influences on, 100-102 ; divergence originates from, 103, 104.

Speech, Living, essentials of, 349.

Speech sounds, classification of, 28-31 ; processes involved in utterance of, 56, 57, 58.

Spelling, English, fixed, 15 ; pronunciation and, 14, 15,

116, 212; Middle English, 116, 255-259; English pronunciation and, 363, 377-380.

Spelling Pronunciations, absurdity of, 364, 365, 366; in English, 377-380; causes of, 365, 377, 378, 380.

'Stammbaum' theory, Schleicher and the, 175; Johann Schmidt, attack on, 176, 177; Leskien, views on, 177, 178.

Standard, constant shifting of, 353, 359.

Stereotyped Phrases, 350, 351; effect of use of, 351; Lord Chesterfield's opinion of, 351.

Streitberg on lengthening of original short vowels, 186.

Stress, 45; degrees of, 46; distribution of, 46; importance of, 106; preservation of, 123; Ablaut and, 184; doublets due to, 215; in Polite English, 375.

Sweet, improves Organic Method, 28; use of terms 'narrow' and 'wide,' 39, 40; discovers 'shifted' vowels, 42; his phonetic symbols, 50, 51; remarks on 'exceptional' forms, 132; on pronunciation of O.E. cȝ, 225; remarks on -aṇ and -oṇ forms in Old English, 229; his divisions of Middle English, 253; on Scandinavian verbs with -n- suffix, 284; discusses problems of Modern English pronunciation, 309; on development of au, 333; spoken English, indicates method of study of, 339; on importance of stress and intonation in English, 375.

Syllable, limits of, 50; division, 48, 49.

Texts, O.E., 217-220; M.E., 254, 255.

Tunþus-tōþ-dent, etc., methods of comparison and reconstruction illustrated by, 151-163.

Verner's Law, 198, 199, 200.

Voice, management of, in speech, 376.

Vowels, consonants and, 31; analysis of, 37; tongue activities for, 37; muscular activities for, 39; lip activity for, 40, 41; description of, 41, 42; positions, 42; difficulty of 'low-front,' 38; 'shifted,' 42; intermediate varieties of, 43.

'Vulgarism,' 19.

Wechsler, views on sound change, 85, 87.

'Wellen' or 'Übergangstheorie,' Johann Schmidt and the, 176, 177 ; Schrader, views on, 177 ; Paul, views on, 177 ; Leskien, modification of, 177-179.

Whitney, views on sound change, 82.

Wright, views on the use of Latin in Britain, 242, 243.

Wycliff, Literary dialect and, 251 ; Oxford type and, 296, 297.

WORD INDEX

Sanskrit.

abhi-jnú, 193
aditas, 192
ajami, 157
ajñasam, 194
ajras, 157, 191
anti, 156
asti, 157
ašva, 157
avi-, 157
bandhus, 156, 162
bhrá-tar, 201
ca, 157
catvâras, 160
dadarša, 157
dadáti, 192
dádhāmi, 192, 201
dadhmas, 192
damas, 156
dant-, 155, 161
dēváttas, 192
dhūmas, 68
ditiš, 192
gōštha, 193
hitás, 192
jambha, 156

janas, 156
jắnu, 193
jñātás, 194
kákša, 160
kakúd, 160
katara, 157
madhu, 157
mati-, 162
nasấ, 191
păd-, 142
panca, 160
pāni, 74
pári-jman, 191
parīnas, 194
pátati, 157
pati, 157, 198
pitár, 200
prnāti, 194
pūrnás, 194
saptá, 199
šatám, 112, 162
sthitás, 193
stighnutē, 201
stri, 192
svašrū, 200
tam, 156
ukṣan, 204

Greek.

ἀγρός, 157, 191
ἄγω, 157, 191
ἀ-κούω, 202
ἄκτωρ, 191
ἀντὶ, 156
ἀ-σκηθής, 199
βαίτη (Thracian), 201
γένος, 156
γέρανος, 201
γι-γνώ-σκω, 194
γνύξ, 193
γόνυ, 193
γομφίος, 156
γόμφος, 156
γωνία, 193
δαμάω, 201
δέδορκε, 157
δίδομεν, 192
δίδωμι, 186, 192
δί-φρ-ος, 190
δόμος, 156
δοτός, 186
δώσω, 192
ἔδω, 203

393

ἕζομαι, 190, 203
ἑκατόν, 112, 162
ἑκυρᾶ, 200
εἰμί, 157
ἕνος, 157
ἐπί-βδ-αι, 190
ἑπτά, 199
ἔργον, 203
ἐστί, 157
ἔφυγον, 182
ἦχε, 191
θατός, 187
θετός, 186
θυμός, 68
ἵ-σταμεν, 193
ἱστᾶμι, 186
ἵστημι, 193
καρδία, 199
κυριακά, 240
λέγω, 182
ληδεῖν, 192
λόγος, 182
λύκος, 290
μέθυ, 157
μέσσος, 203
νῆ-μα, 202
ὀδμή, 191
ὀ-δόντ-, 155, 161
ὀδωδή, 191
οἴνη, 202
ὄις, 157, 202
ὄπ-ωπ-α, 191
ὄσσε, 191
οὖς, 202
ὄψομαι, 191
πατέρα, 182, 291
πατήρ, 182, 190, 200
πέζα, 190

πείθω, 202
πενθερός, 156, 162, 163, 203
πέντε, 160
πέσσαρες, 160
πέτε-ται, 157
πλῆ-ρες, 194
ποδός, 190
πόσις, 157, 198
πότερος, 157
πούς, 142
πρόχνυ, 193
πρωί, 194
πῶς (Doric), 190
ῥητήρ, ῥήτωρ, 183, 184
στατός, 186, 193
στείχω, 201
στήσω, 193
σφάλλω, 198
τε, 157
τιθεμεν, 192
τίθημι, 186, 192, 201, 202
τόν, 156
φαμέν, 193
φᾱμί (Doric), 182
φέρω, 190
φεύγω, 182
φημί, 193
φορᾱ, 190
φρᾱ-τηρ, 190
φρᾱ-τωρ, 190, 201, 202
φρά-τρ-α, 190
φώγω, 192
φωνή, 182
φώρ, 190
ὤψ, 191

Latin.

actor, 191
ager, 157
ago, 157, 191
ambāges, 191
ante, 156
appodix, 190
auctor, 190
auris, 202
cacūmen, 160
Cæsar, 241
capistrum, 244
eāseus, 241
centum, 112, 162, 163
colonia, 244
coquere, 158
coquīna, 76, 244
cordis, 199
coxa, 160
cuculla, 244
cucurbita, 242
Dānuvius, 201
dāre, 182
datio, 192
datus, 182, 192
dēdi, 192
dent-, 155, 161, 163
domare, 201
domus, 156
dōnare, 192
dōnum, 182, 192
edo, 203
equus, 157
est, 157
exāmen, 191
facio, 192
fœnuculum, 244

fāma, 193
fāri, 193
fēci, 192
fēmella, 134
fero, 190
fīcus, 241
fīdo, 202
fors, 190
fortūna, 190
frāter, 202
fūmus, 68
fūr, 190
genus, 156
hominem, 291
hospitis, 198
hostis, 202
lassus, 192
marmor, 244
medius, 203
memini, 182
ment-, 162
mentum, 199
mercātum, 248
moneo, 182
moneta, 241
morātum, 244
mūtare (> moi-
   tare), 202
nāpus, 241
nāres, 191
nāsus, 191
nēre, 202
nīdus, 190, 203
nōsco, 194
nox, 157
oculus, 191
odor, 191
offendix, 162, 163,
   203

oleum, 234
ovis, 157, 202
pater, 190
patria, 122
patris, 190
pedem, 190
pedes, 203
pēs, 142, 190,
   290
petit, 157
piscis, 113
plēnus, 194
præpositus, 244
psalmus, 244
que, 157
quinque, 160
rego, 239
regula, 79
rēx, 239
ruta, 244
sāgire, 202
satus, 192
sedēre, 190, 203
sēdimus, 190
sēmen, 192
senex, 157
sēvi, 192
sodālis, 190
stāmen, 193
stāre, 193
statim, 193
status, 193
strāta via, 241
tabula, 242
tego, tēxi, 182
uncia, 245
ūnus > oinos,
   202
veho, vēxi, 186

Gallo-Roman.
Moguntiacum.
   158
Vosegus, 158

Old French.
femelle, 134

French.
beau, 53
bête, 48
bon, 30
but, 41, 51
content, 54
dé, 53
dur, 41
enfant, 76
été, 39, 40
fin, 30
fini, 31
français, 35
génie, 123
jamais, 35
lune, 38
rendre, 35
si, 53
un, 30
vu, 41, 51

Old Irish.
āg, 191
brocc, 239
cethir, 160
drui, 239
rī, rīg, 239

Irish.
donn, 239
iasc, 113

Welsh.

dwn, 239
Llandudno, 35

Gothic.

ains, 202
akrs, 157, 191
andbundnan, 154
anþar, 152, 153
augō, 228
auhsa, 204
ausō, 202
awistr, 193, 202
bairan, 190
bandi, 154
bar, 190
batists, 150
batiza, 284
baur, 190
beidan, 202
bērum, 190
bindan, 154, 203
brōþar, 190, 201, 202
broþrahans, 190
bug-jan, 148
dags, 227
dauns, 68
dōmjan, 10
drōbjan, 148
fadar, 200
-faþs, 198
fōdjan, 148
fōtus, 142, 190
fruma, 194
fulljan, 148
fulls, 194
gabinda, 154

gadēþs, 192, 201, 202
gaf, 182
gaits, 228
gamōtjan, 148
gamunds, 162
gasinþa, 154
gasinþja, 152
gastim (dat.), 290
gasts, 202
gatamjan, 201
gēbum, 182
giban, 182
haims, 228
hairtō, 199
handus, 154, 183
hansa, 152
haubiþ, 228
hausjan, 202, 236
-hinþan, 154, 183
huggrjan, 148
hund, 112, 153, 162
hunsl, 247
hunþs, 154
juggs, 153
kaisar, 241
kann, 194
kaus, 182
kinnus, 76
kiusan, 182
kniu, 193
knussjan, 193
kuni, 77, 234
kunnaida, 194
kunþs, 153
kusum, 182
lats, 192
lētan, 192

maidjan, 202
mana-sēþs, 192
midjis, 203
munþs, 152, 153, 199
namnjan, 148
nēþla, 202
paida, 201
reiki, 239
reiks, 239
sandjan, 154
sat, 190
satjan, 148
sētum, 190
sibun, 199
sinþs, 152, 154, 232
skaþjan, 199
sōkjan, 147, 202
staþs, 193
steigan, 201
stōls, 193
tunþus, 151, 153, 161, 163
þāhta, 228, 231
þagkjan, 231
þana, 156
unkja, 245
warjan, 148
-windan, 154
-winnan, 154
wulfs, 290

Old Norse.

bleikr, 286
fōtr, 142
geva, 279
heimsōcn, 283
hvītna, 284

læte, 261
lāt, 261
mjūkr, 287
skamt, 285
sōma, 282
sveinn, 283
tannr, 153
veikr, 286

Old West Scandinavian.

blikna, 284
bustla, 284
dogg, 286
egg, 286
hoggua, 286
tryggr, 286

Old Swedish.

batna, 284

Swedish.

babbla, 284
dagg, 286
dangla (dial.), 284
en, 167
fem, 167
fyra, 167
höra, 167
hörde, 167
komma, 167
moder, 167
tre, 167
twå, 167

Danish.

dag, 167
sang, 167
skygge, 286

synge, 167
sunget, 167

Old English.

Abbod, 247
æcer, 191, 227
æg, 286
ælfhēah, 378
ælmesse, 247
ær, 262
āld, 45, 236, 260, 323
ān-buend, 247
ān-setl, 247
ār, 269
ā-wæcnian, 284
bacan, 192
bæcere, 192
bær, 190, 213
bæron, 190, 214
bānd, 273
barda, 281
beald, bāld, 45, 236
bēċ, 133
beġinnan, 278
beō, 319
beran, 190, 213, 259, 319
beter, 284
betst, 150
bīdan, 202
bindan, 154, 203
blāc, 286
blōd, 323
bōc, 192
boren, 190, 214
bræc, 213
bræþan, brēþan, 6

bræþ, brēþ, 3
breogo, 79
brēost, 272
bringan, 231
brocc, 239
brōhte, 231, 274
brōþor, 134, 201, 202
bryċġ, 238, 258
brȳsan, 264
byċġan, 148
byrġean, 237
cæfester, 244
cāld, 75, 236
cāmb, 156, 235
cāsere, 241
cēāc, 257
ċeaf, cafu, 277
ċeald, 231, 236
ċēāpmenn, 270
ċeaster, ċæster, 244
cēlan, 136
ċele, 236, 269
cēlnesse, 136
cēpte, 270
ċester, 257
ċiele, 75, 236
ċīese, 241
ċietel, ċetel, 277
ċild, 7, 235
ċildru, 7
ċin(n), 76, 77
ċiriċe, 240
clǣnlīce, 271
clawu, 333
clēne, 236
cleopode, 79
cnāwan, 194, 274

398 **WORD INDEX**

cnear, 249, 281
cnēo, 193
cōl, 136
coren, 269
costnian, 284
cran, 201
cugele, 244
cūþ, 153
cræft, 287
cwēn, 259, 319
cwĕne, 259
cwicu, cweocu,
  c(w)ucu, 79
cȳ, 133
cyčene, 76, 244
cynn, 77, 233 n.,
  234
ċyrċe, 237, 238,
  277
cyrfet, 242
dǣd, 192, 201,
  202, 236, 263
dæg,183,227,265
dægas, 80
dægum, 80
dagas, 265
dagian, 265, 284
deáþ, 265
dēa(w), 286
dēd, 236,-263
dēman, 7, 10, 135
deōfol, 271
discipul, 247
dōgor, 183
dohter, 266
dōm, 7, 10
domne, 247
dragan, 267, 274,
  333

drēam, 262
drēfan, 148
drȳ, 239
dunn, 239
dūst, 68, 234
dȳstiġ, 234
Eādward, 270
ēage, 228
ēāgena, 289
eahta, 231
eald, āld, 45, 236
earm, 231
ēāðġete, 269
efel, 259, 319
efete, 267
ele, 234
eofor, 79
eolh, 231
eorþe, 231
etan, 203, 269
fæder, 134, 190,
  200, 264, 269
fæsten, 284
fæstenian, 284
fæt, 78, 280
fatu, 78
featu, 78
fēdan, 148, 149
fēld, 319
feohtan, 231
feōnd, 272
fēt, 203, 234
fetor, 79
fīc-bēam, 241
fīndan, 235
finugl, 244
fiscas, 133
flēmde, 271
fō, fēhþ, 234

fōda, 149, 263
forġeofan, 80
forfōr, 263
forloren, 269
forma, 194
forþ, 259
fōt, 142, 232, 234
fox, 234
frēo, 319
frēond, 272
freoðu-, 79
friðu, 79
from, 194
full, 149, 234
fulluht, 248
fulwian, 247
fulwiht, 248
furðor, 150
fylcian, 249
fyllan, 148, 149,
  234
fȳlþ, 234, 271
fyrst, 150
fyxen, 234, 280
gāstlīc, 137
gāt, 228
ġeār, 279
ġefan, 278, 279
ġelaþung, 248
ġelīce, 138
gelt, 237
genōġe, 267
ġenōh, 258, 266
gēs, 8, 234
ġesīþ, 152
ġeslæġen, 234
ġest, 278
ġetan, 278
ġetrīewe, 286

ġiċċan, 277
ġicel, 277
ġiefan, 54, 80, 258, 278, 279
ġielpan, 278
ġiest, 278
-ġietan, 278
ġif, 277
ġim-stān, 277
god, 234
gōd, 363
godspellere, 248
gold, 204, 234
gōs, 8, 152, 232, 233, 234
gōshafoc, 271
gyden, 234
gylden, 234
gylt, 237
hæfde, 259
hǣþ, 263, 319
hafoc, 267
hām, 213, 228, 260
hāmsocn, 283
hand, 154, 260
handġeweorc, 277
hē, 319
hēafod, 228
hēawan, 286
hēh, 266
heolstor, 79
heorot, 79
heorte, 199
hēr, 135, 319
hēran, 236, 257, 259
here, 233
hīeran, hȳran, 236

hie, hira, heom, 287
hlāford, 259
hlahhan, 333
hnitu, 79
hopu, 269
hōs, 152
hryċġ, 238
hund, 153
hūs, 257
hūsl, 247
hūsl-þegn, 248
hūþ, 154
hwæl, 275
hwǣte, 275
hwǣr, 135
hȳd, 287
hynġr(i)an, 148
hȳran, 257, 280
lǣtan, 192
lāmb, 260
land, 228
leornung, 292
līc, 138
Lin(d)cylene, 244
lond, 228
lȳtle, 270
mæsse, 247
mǣþ, 227
mann, 228
māra, 262
market, 248
martyr, 247
mearm-stān, 244
medu, 157
meolc, 79
meriġ, 237
mētan, 148, 149
mete, 319

mētte, 270
midd, 203
mōdor, 134
mōna, 76, 229
mōnaþ, 271
monn, 228, 233
moraþ, 244
ġemōt, 149
mūþ, 152, 199
mynet, 241
myriġ, 237
nǣdl, 202
nǣp, 241
nama, 149, 228, 270, 291
nemnan, 148, 149
nest, 190, 203
nigun, 79
niman, 229, 287
nimanne, 80
to niomanne, 80
noma, 228
nōmon, 229
open, 323
ōra, 249, 281
ōþer, 152, 153
oxa, 204
pād, 201
pæll, 247
pāpa, 247
plōges, 267
plōh, 266
prāfost, 244
racu, 214
rāran, 262
reahte, 214
reċċean, 214
reġn, 265
regol, 79

reogol, 79
rīċe, 239
rūde, 244
sācerd, 247
sǣd, sēd, 236
sǣlan, 234
sæt, 186
sǣton, 190
sagu, 333
sāl, 234
sār, 260
sċ(e)amu, 213
sċēap, sċēp, 133
sċearn, 247
sċēawan, 286
sċēld, 236, 319
sċīeld, sċyld, 236
sċieran, 247
se, seo, þæt, 293
sealm, 244
sēċan, 147
sēc(e)an, 145, 146, 149
sēcst, sēcþ, 276
sēd, 319
sēman, 282
sendan, 154
senn, 237
seofon, 79
settan, 148
sicol, 79
sinu, 79
sīþ, 152, 154, 232
sittan, 190, 203
slēpte, 270
snetor, 237
snytor, 237
sōft, 152
sōfte, 232, 270

sōhte, 147, 149, 270
sōna, 323
sōt, 186, 190
sp(r)æc, 213
sprecol, 79
stān, 323
stānas, 289
stīgan, 201
strǣt, 241
sunu, 257
sunum (dat.), 290
swān, 283
Swegen, 283
sweger, 200
sweord, swurd, 237
sweotol, 79
swēte, 269
sword, 237
synn, 237
tæfl, 242
temian, 201
tēþ, 8
tōh, 274
tōþ, 8, 151, 153, 161, 163, 232
trēowe, 286
þæc, 234
þeċċean, 234
þenċan, 228
þēof, 265
þēon, 232
þōhte, 228, 231
þrǣll, 285
þrotu, 323
þūhte, 232
þynċean, 232
ūs, 232

ūtmest, 270
wæcen, 284
wæġn, 265
wǣpn, 227
wǣtan, 319
wæter, 264, 269
wāk, 286
wāld, 237, 266
weald, 236, 266
weġ, 258, 265
weodu, wudu, 78, 79
weorþ, wurþ, 237
werian, 148
wēron, 262
wētan, 319
wīflīc, 138
windan, 154
winnan, 154
wiodu, 78
wiorþeþ, 231
wīsdōm, 270
wiurþiþ, 231
worþ, 237
wudu, 78, 79, 289
wulf, 290
wyrċan, 257
Wyrtġeorn, 244
yfel, 287
ynċe, 245, 246
yndse, 245
yntse, 245, 246

Middle English.

appēren, 319
appīeren, 319
ansuér, 262
auentūre, 263
aungel, 267, 333

babblen, 284
bē, 319
bēren, 259, 319
besēchen, 145
besēken, 145
bleu, 329
bliknen, 284
blōk, 286
blūd, 263
bond, 273
brēst, 272
brigge, 258
brofte, 274
brugge, 258
burien, 237
bustlen, 284
caf, 277
cause, 333
chappmenn, 270
chaunce, 123 n.
chaunge, 123 n.
chēfe, 319
chēke, 257
chele, 269
chester, 257
chetel, 277
chiefe, 319
chīld, 272
childre, 7
children, 7
chilldre, 272
chirche, 277
chōld, 266
chosenn, 269
clawe, 333
clennlike, 271
conclūd, 263
costnen, 285
court, 257

dai, 265, 266
dāme, 213, 261, 270
daunger, 333
daungerous, 267
dawen, 265
dawes, 265
dawnen, 284
day, 265
dayes, 265
deffles, 271
dei, 266
depthe, 270
deu, 286, 329
douhter, 266
drawen, 267, 274, 333
drēme, 262
dyath, 265
Edward, 270
ēȝene, 289
ei, 286
ere, 262
etenn, 269
eðgēte, 269
euel, 259
eute, 267
ēvel, 259, 319
fāder, 134, 264, 270, 271
faderr, 269
fāme, 261
fāðer, 317
fēld, 268, 319
fēnd, 272
field, 268
fillthe, 271
findenn, 268
flemmde, 27

fless, flessch, 259
forfūre, 263
for-ȝete(n),
  yete(n), 277
fortōne, 263
frē, 319
frēnd, 272
frendschipe, 272
fūde, 263
gǣfen, 278
gastli, 137
gastlich(e), 137
gate, 287
ȝelle(n), yelle(n), 277
ȝelpe(n), yelpe(n), 277
gentil, 123 n.
ȝēre, yēre, 277
ȝif, 277
ȝim, 277
ȝiuen, 258
god, 258, 323
goshauk, 271
gosling, 270
gōst, 137
gūd, 263
guod, 258
haggen, 286
hallghenn, 271
halwen, 271
hāme, 262
hand, 268
handfull, 235, 272
hanten, 335
hauk, 267
haunt, 333
haunten, 335
heeth, 260

26

hefde, 259
heih, 266
hem, 287
hēren, 259, 280
hēþ, 319
hieren, 257
hir, 287
hit, 275
hōm, 213, 260
hōnd, 260, 268
hope, 269
hound, 268
hous, 257
huiren, 257, 280
hund, 268
huswīf, 271
hwīten, 284
icche(n), 277
icching, 277
i-cume, 277
if, 277
ikyl, 277
ille, 287
inogh, 58
inōuh, 266
inōwe, 267
itt, 275
jaundice, 333
joie, 123 n.
jointe, 123 n.
juge, 123 n.
jugement, 258
keppte, 270
kingene, 292
kingue, 258
kneu, 329
lāmb, 260
lambre, 272
lammbre, 260

lānd, 273
lātes, 261
lauerd, 259
laughen, 333
legges, 275
licóur ⎱ 123
lícour ⎰
līf, 259
little, 270
lōmb, 260, 272
lōnd, 273
long, 273
manér, 262
manéir, 262
mar, 262
meōc, 287
mēte, 319
mette, 270
monthe, 271
mōre, 261
nǎme, 260, 270
neir, 262
ōld, 260, 323
ōpen, 323
ōre, 269
plesand, 293
plōuh, 266
plōwes, 267
quāle, 275
queen, 259
quēn, 319
quēne, 259
quēt, 275
rair, 262
rǎðer, 75, 317
rein, 266
rūde, 263
sāwe, 333
sayand, 293

scatteren, 283
schāme, 213
schēld, 319
schip, 259
sēchen, 145, 146
sēken, 145, 147
sēkst, 276
sēkþ, 276
seldcēne, 257
sēmelich, 282
sēmen, 282
sēmli, 282
serrfenn, 256
serruen, 256
shatteren, 283
skill, 287
skinn, 287
sleppte, 270
soffte, 270
sohhte, 270
sone, 257
sōne, 263
sōr, 260
ssip, 259
stōn, 291, 323
stōnes, 289
stoon, 260
strang, 268
strōng, 268, 273
swēte, 269
syngand, 293
tāhte, 336
takenn, 287
þe, þeo, þet, 293
thinken, 259
þrōte, 323
þyef, 265
til, 287
uader, 280

uorþ, 259
utmōst, 270
vertúe ⎱ 123
vértue ⎰
vorlōre(n), 269
wæld, 266
wain, 265
war, 262
wāt, 261
wăter, 264, 271
weȝ, 258
wei, 265
were, 262
wigt, 285
wimman, 271
wissdōm, 270
wode, 289
wōk, 286
wurchen, 257
ylde, 277
ym-stōn, 277
zēchen, 280

English.

ale, 230
all, 267, 312, 333
Alphege, 377
alter [ōltə], 360
Alvescot [ōlskət, etc.], 379
among [əmaŋ, etc.], 361
Ardingley, 378
ass, 229
Atterbury, 293
aught, 335
aunt, 267
ball, 334
band, 273

bat, 38
bath, 317
batten, 284
bawl, 267
to bear, 214
bee, 60
begin, 278, 279
beseech, 145, 147, 276
beseek (dial.), 145
bet, 38, 39, 43
better, 284, 318
bird, 38, 53
bishopric, 239
bit, 38, 40, 43
bite, 49
bitterly, 131
bleak, 286
blood, 307, 325, 327, 361
blue, 329, 330
boil, 323
bold, 237
bond, 273
book, 133, 324, 325, 327, 361
book-case, 48
boot, 38, 42, 53
boots, 360
bought, 337
boys, 130
brandy pawnee, 74
bread, 321
break, 321
breath, 6, 318
breathe, 6, 318
bridge, 238
broft (dial.), 274

broil, 322
broken, 213
brother, 130, 134, 327
brought, 336
bruise, 264, 330
buck, 325
buik (Sc.), 53
bull, 326
bury, 237
bush, 41
but, 53, 314, 322, 325, 326
butcher, 41
Cabul, 74
calf, 335
call, 333, 334
calm, 335
came, 131
can, 313
cane, 314
car, 35
cast, 313
cat, 53, 130
Cawnpore, 74
chance, 334
charmed, 131
cheese, 241
child, 7, 235, 272
children, 7, 131, 235, 272
chill, 75, 136, 236
chin, 76, 77
chivalry, 364
chu.ch, 237
Cirencester, 378
Clark, 318
clerk, 74, 317, 318, 361

cletch (dial.), 277
clutch (dial.), 277
coffee, 360
cold, 75, 136, 237
contradict, 127
cool, 136
to cool, 136
coolness, 136
cough [kɔf, etc.] 360
courtesy [kɔtəsi, etc.], 360
cows, 133
cure, 330
cut, 327
dag (dial.), 285
daggle (dial.), 284
dame, 213, 270
dams, 133
dance, 334, 360
dangle, 284
daughter, 336
daunt, 334
dead, 321
deed, 236, 263
deem, 7, 135, 137
Derby, 317, 318, 361
desire, 366
dew, 286, 329
disaster, 127
ditch, 276
dog, 130
-dom, 135
doom, 7, 135, 137
draught, 325
draw, 274
druid, 239
duke, 330

dust, 68
eat, 269
eave (dial.), 278
egg, 286
enow, 267
envelope, 123
face, 259, 317
falcon, 364
falconry, 364
fall, 333, 334
far, 317
father, 38, 39, 42, 53, 54, 74, 130, 134, 269, 360
feet, 137
female, 134
few, 330
field, 268
fiend, 272
find, 268
fine, 322
fish, 113, 133
fishes, 134
flaunt, 334
fleck (dial.), 276
flick (dial.), 276
flesh, 133, 272
fling, 131, 132
flitch, 276
flock, 133
flood, 325
flung, 131, 132
food, 133
fool, 324, 328
foot, 137, 324, 327
forehead [fɔrid, etc.], 365, 378
forlorn, 135

forsworn, 136
forward, 378
friend, 272, 318, 319
frighten, 284
full, 325, 326, 327, 328
gall, 312
gave, 131
geese, 8
get, 278
ghastly, 137
ghostly, 137
gif (dial.), 278
gift, 278
gilpie (dial.), 278
give, 278, 279
gladden, 284
good, 31, 35, 324 325
goose, 8
grant, 334
great, 321
Greenwich [grinidž, etc.], 365
ground, 73
guest, 258, 278
guide, 322
gut, 325
hale, 311
hall, 334
hand, 272
handiwork, 277
hang, 273
hardly, 131
hat, 311
haw, 334
haunch, 267, 334
haunt, 267, 334

have, 46
head, 53, 321
hear, 167, 236
heard, 167, 318
heart, 317, 318
hearth, 317, 318
heath, 263
(h)eave (dial.), 278
Helingly, 378
herd, 133
here, there, everywhere, 131, 134
here, 131, 135
hew, 286
hit (Sc.), 275
horse, hoarse, 16
hot, 53, 54
hound, 268
house, 73
housen (dial.), 292
houses, 131
humorous, [jū-mərəs, etc.], 360
humour, 127
hundred, 112
icicle, 277
ill, 131
inch, 245
itch, 277
jaundice, 267, 334
jaunt, 334
jest, 275
join, 322, 323
joint, 322
joy, 275
judge, 275
ken, 314
kernel, colonel, 16

kettle, 277
Kilconquahar, 378
kin, 77
king, 35, 134
kirk (Sc.), 277
knave, 337
knew, 329
Knowsley, 379
lamb, 235, 272, 365
lambs, 133
lance, 334
land, 273
laughter, 335, 337
Launcelot, 334
launch, 334
laundry, 267, 334
lawful, 334
learn [lȧn, etc.], 318, 361
leave, 320
light, 366
-like, 138
Lincoln, 244
line, 322
literature [litərə-tʃə, etc.], 365
loch (Sc.), 32, 35
long, 229, 273
look, 325
loose, 324
lorn, 136
lose, 135, 136
love, 365
luck, 325
lust, 325
man, 132
manlike, 138
manly, 138

maw, 334
meat, 320
men, 132, 318
merry, 237
mice, 131
midge (dial.), 276
Midhurst, 378
mirth, 237
moon, 76
mother, 130, 134, 327
mud, 325, 326
muse, 330
name, 260, 270, 317
nim (dial.), 287
nonce, for the, 293
nut, 327
of, 214, 215
off, 214, 215
oil, 323
old, 45, 237
pail, 332
Parma — Palmer, 16
pass, 313
past, 314
phonograph, 127
placed, 131
pleasure, 35
plough, 266
poignant [poi-nənt, etc.], 365
priest, 272
prime, 366
primrosen (dial.), 292
psalm, 335
pull, 325, 326, 327

punt, 326
pure [pjō, etc.], 360
put, 53, 326, (Sc.) 53
quality, 308
qualm, 335
quantity, 308
queen (Sc.), 134
railway, 360
rang, 131
rather, 74, 317
red, 321
redden, 284
rhyme, 366
ridge, 238, 276
righteous [raitʃəs, etc.], 365
ring, 131
root, 323
Rudge, 238
rule, 330
rung, 131
saint, St., 215
Sanders, 334
sang, 131, 167, 273
salt, 267
Saunders, 334
saw, 53, 60
scag (dial.), 286
scant, 285
scug (dial.), 286
sea, 31
sedge, 276
see, 38, 39, 53
seech (dial.), 145
seed, 236
seek, 145, 147, 276

seemly, 282
seg (dial.), 276
sent, 131
servant, 318
set, 318
shame, 213
sheep, 133
shemale (pop.), 134
shield, 236
ship, 35
shoe, 324
sing, 29, 33, 35, 131, 167
sit, 39
small, 312
sought, 147
southern [saðən, etc.], 365
spoken, 213
spoon [spūn, etc.], 323, 327, 361
star, 317
steak, 321
stick, 132
straw, 334
street, 241
strong, 229, 273
stuck, 132
stupid, 330
suffer, 325
sung, 131, 167
tail, 332
tane and the tither, the (Sc.), 294
taught, 335
taunt, 334
teeth,

telegraph, 127
telephone, 127
the, 112
their, they, them, 287
there, 135
think, 29, 32
this, 29
thoft (dial.), 274
thought, 336
threw, 330
thunder, 325
til (dial.), 287
time, 322
told, 131
tooth, 8, 151, 161
t'other, the (obs.), 294
tough, 274
trees, 130
trig (dial.), 286
true, 286
Tuesday, 330
until, 287
vase, 74
vat, 280
vaunt, 334
virtue [vᴀ̄tjū, etc.], 361
vixen, 280
Wadhurst, 378
wall, 334
wane, 314
was, 314
water, 269
weak, 286
weald, 266
weet (Sc.), 319
well, 131

went, 131
wet, 319
where, 135
wife, 322
wifelike, 138
wifely, 138
wight (dial.), 285
wine, 322
winefat, 280
wold, 237, 266
womanly, 138
wood, 324
wrath [rōþ, etc.], 361
write, 337
wrote, 131
yclept, 277
yeave (dial. obs.), 278
yeavey (dial. obs.), 278

Old Saxon.

ahto, 231
akkar, 227
bindan, 203
crano, 201
ertha, 231
etan, 203
fallan, 198
fūliþa, 234
gast, 202
jung, 153
māno, 229
middi, 203
rīki, 239
sibun, 199
sittian, 203
sōkian, 147

strāta, 241
thīhan, 232
werk, 203

Old Frisian.

jung, 153

Dutch.

dag, 167
drie, 167
een, 167
hoorde, 167
hooren, 167
komme(n), 167
moeder, 167
twee, 167
vier, 167
vijf, 167
zingen, 167
zong, 167
ge-zongen, 167

Old High German.

acchar, 227
ahto, 231
andar, 152
arm, 231
bintan, 154
bītan, 202
chāsi, 241
chirihha, 240
cheisar, 241
chund, 153
churbizz, 242
dāhta, 228
denken, dâchta, 231
dīhan, 232
dunst, 234

erda, 229
ewist, 193
fallan, 198
fehtan, 231
fuoz, 142
gans, 152, 232
gast, 202
geiz, 228
gisindo, 152
gitriuwi, 286
hansa, 152
hant, 154
heim, 228
heri-hunda, 154
houbit, 228
houwan, 286
hunt, 153
jung, 153
kalt, 231
kocchōn, 158
kunst, 194
mād, 227
Maginza, 158
māno, 229
metu, 157
mund, 152
mūs, 112
nādala, 202
nāmum, 229
nasa, 191
nest, 203
ouga, 228
rīhhi, 239
samfto, 152, 232
sind, 152, 232
sizzen, 203
strāzza, 241
suohhan, 147
tac, 227

tāt, 202
tou, 286
tuomian, 10
uns, 232
vinnan, 154
vintan, 154
vruo, 194
wāfan, 227
Wascono walt,158
werc, 203
zabal, 242
zand, 151, 153, 161, 163, 232

Middle High German.

elch, 231

German.

alt, 45
blume, 53
drei, 167
ei, 286
ein, 167
fünf, 167
genie [ʃɛníˆ], 123

hat, 53
hören, hörte, 167
käse, 241
kommen, 167
lohn, 53
maus, 112
mutter, 167
reich, 239
sang, 167
schauen, 286
singen, 167
sorge, 35
stock, 53
ge-sungen, 167
tag, 167
träue, 286
vaterland, 122
vier, 167
zwei, 167

Lithuanian.

avimis, 290
avis, 157, 158
bendras, 156,162, 163, 203
dantis, 155, 161

esmi, 157
ěsti, 157
keturi, 160
medùs, 157
naktis, 157, 158
-patis, 157
pílnas, 194
pirmas, 194
sěnas, 157
szimtas, 112, 162, 163
žinóti, 194

Old Slavonic.

dȳ-mŭ, 68
nosti, 158
ovitsa, 158
sedeti, 190

Russian.

[ɫoʃad], 35
otíchestvo, 122

Finnish.

kulta, 204

LIST OF AUTHORITIES
REFERRED TO

[This list does not include the monographs, etc., enumerated in the lists in Chapters XII. and XIV.]

BECHTEL   Hauptprobleme der indogerm. Lautlehre seit Schleicher, 1892.

BELL, MELVILLE : Visible Speech.

BJÖRKMAN : Scandinavian Loan-Words in Middle English, Part I., Halle, 1900.

BOPP, F. : Vergleichende Grammatik (3rd ed.); Vocalismus, 1836.

BRATE, E. : Nordische lehnwörter im Ormulum, Beitr. X. (1884), 1-80.

BREMER, O. : Ethnographie der germ. Stamme,[2] 1900.

BRUGMANN : Griechische Grammatik,[3] 1900 ; Grundriss der Vergleichenden Grammatik der Indogermanischen Sprachen (2nd ed.), Bd. I. (Lautlehre), 1897 : Kurze Vergleichende Grammatik der Indogermanischen Sprachen, Bd. I. (Lautlehre), 1902 ; Zum heutigen Stand der Sprachwissenschaft, 1885 ; Zur Frage nach den Verwandtschaftsverhältnissen der Idg. Spr. (in Techmer's Zeitschrift für allgemeine Sprachwissenschaft I.).

BÜLBRING, K. D. : Altenglisches Elementarbuch. I. Lautlehre, Heidelberg, 1902.

DARMSTETER : La Vie des Mots, 1887.

DIBELIUS : John Capgrave und die englische Schriftsprache, Anglia XXIII., p. 152, etc.

DIETER : Laut- und Formenlehre d. altgermanischen Dialekte, vol. i., 1898.

410   LIST OF AUTHORITIES REFERRED TO

ELLIS, A. J.: Early English Pronunciation, Parts I.-IV., 1869-1874.

GREENOUGH AND KITTREDGE: Words and their Ways in English Speech, 1902.

GRIMM: Deutsche Grammatik, vols. i.-iv., 1822-1837.

HARGREAVES: The Addlington Dialect. Heidelberg, 1904.

HIRT: d. Idg. Ablaut, 1900; Griechische Grammatik, 1902; Verwandtschaftsverhältnisse der Indogermanen, in Indogermanische Forschungen IV., pp. 36-45; Urheimat der Indogerm., in Indog. Forsch. I.

JESPERSEN: Lehrbuch der Phonetik, 1904.

KOEPPEL: Spelling Pronunciations: Bemerkungen über den Einfluss des Schriftbildes auf den Laut im Englischen. Strassbourg, 1901. (Quellen u. Forschungen, Bd. 89).

KALUZA, M.: Historische Grammatik der Englischen Sprache, vol. i. Berlin, 1900. Vol. ii., 1901.

KLUGE, FR.: Geschichte der Englischen Sprache, in *Paul's* Grundriss; Vorgeschichte der germanischen Sprachen, in *Paul's* Grundriss.[2]

KRETSCHMER: Einleitung in die Gesch. d. griech. Sprache, 1896.

LESKIEN: Deklination im Slavisch und Deutsch, 1876.

LOTH: Angelsachsen und Romanen, in Englische Studien XIX; Les Mots Latins dans les Langues Brittoniques, 1892.

MACGILLIVRAY, H. S.: The Influence of Christianity on the Vocabulary of Old English. Part I. Halle, 1902.

MORRIS: Historical Outlines of English Accidençe, edited by *Bradley.*

MORRIS AND SKEAT: Specimens of Early English.

MORSBACH, L.: Anglia Beiblatt VII; Mittelenglische Grammatik, 1 Theil. Halle, 1896; Über den Ursprung der neuenglischen Schriftsprache, Heilbronn, 1888.

NAPIER, A.: Notes on the Orthography of the Ormulum, Academy, 1890; and in History of the Holy Rood-tree, E. E. T. S., 1894, p. 71.

NOREEN, A.: Urgermanische Lautlehre, 1894.

OSTERMANN: Lautlehre Ancren Riwle, Bonner Beiträge, 1905.

OSTHOFF: Das physiologische und das psychologische Moment in der sprachlichen Formenbildung, 1879; Schriftsprache und Volksmundart, Berlin, 1883.

OSTHOFF AND BRUGMANN: Morphologische Untersuchungen, Vol. I., 1878.

PASSY, PAUL: Changements Phonétiques du Langage. Paris, 1891.

PAUL: Principien der Sprachgeschichte.

POGATSCHER: Zur Lautlehre der griech., lat. und roman. lehnwörter im altenglischen (Q. F. 64). Strassburg, 1888.

RIPPMANN, W.: The Sounds of Spoken English. London, 1906.

SCHERER: Geschichte d. deutschen Sprache, 1868.

SCHLEICHER: Compendium,[2] 1866; Deutsche Sprache,[2] 1869.

SCHMIDT, JOHANN: Verwandtschaftsverhältnisse der Idg. Sprachen, 1872.

SCHRADER: Urheimat der Indogermanen, in Reallexikon der Indogerm. Altertumskunde 1901; Sprachvergleichung und Urgeschichte, 1890.

SIEBS: Zur Geschichte der engl.-friesisch. Sprache, 1889.

SIEVERS, E.: Angelsächsische Grammatik,[3] Halle, 1898; Phonetik, 4th ed.

SKEAT: Concise Etymological Dictionary of the English Language, 1901; Principles of English Etymology.

SMITH, GREGORY: Specimens of Middle Scots.

STREITBERG, W., Indogerm, Forschungen, iii. 305, etc.; Urgermanische Grammatik.

STRONG, LOGEMANN AND WHEELER: History of Language, 1891.

SWEET, HENRY: Cura Pastoralis, Introduction; History of English Sounds, Oxford, 1888; History of Language, 1900; New English Grammar, Part I., Oxford, 1892; Primer of Phonetics (2nd ed.), Oxford, 1902; Primer of Historical English Grammar; Primer of

Spoken English (3rd ed.), Oxford, 1900; Shorter English Historical Grammar; Words, Logic, and Grammar, Trans. Phil. Soc., 1875-76.

TAYLOR, ISAAC: The Origin of the Aryans, 1890.

TEN BRINK: Chaucers Sprache und Verskunst, Leipzig, 1899.

WECHSSLER: Gibt es Lautgesetze? 1900.

WHITNEY: Language and its Study, 1875; Life and Growth of Language, 1886.

WRIGHT, JOSEPH: English Dialect Grammar, 1905; Grammar of the Dialect of Windhill, E.D.S., 1892.

WYLD: History of O.E. ġ in the Middle and Modern English Dialects, Otia Merseiana, vol. ii. ; Engl. Studien, XXVIII., p. 393, etc. ; Otia Merseiana, IV., p. 75, etc.

THE END